LINKING EMOTIONAL INTELLIGENCE AND PERFORMANCE AT WORK

*Current Research Evidence
with Individuals and Groups*

LINKING EMOTIONAL INTELLIGENCE AND PERFORMANCE AT WORK

Current Research Evidence with Individuals and Groups

Edited by

Vanessa Urch Druskat
Whittemore School of Business and Economics,
University of New Hampshire

Fabio Sala
Millennium Pharmaceuticals, Inc.

Gerald Mount
Seidman School of Business
Grand Valley State University

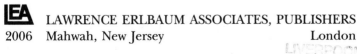 LAWRENCE ERLBAUM ASSOCIATES, PUBLISHERS
2006   Mahwah, New Jersey   London

Lawrence Erlbaum Associates, Inc., Publishers
10 Industrial Avenue
Mahwah, New Jersey 07430

Cover design by Kathryn Houghtaling Lacey

Library of Congress Cataloging-in-Publication Data

Linking emotional intelligence and performance at work : current research evidence with individuals and groups / edited by Fabio Sala, Vanessa Urch Druskat, Gerald Mount.
    p. cm.
Includes bibliographical references and index.
ISBN 0-8058-5073-2 (alk. paper)
ISBN 0-8058-5074-0 (pbk. : alk. paper)
  1. Psychology, Industrial.   2. Emotional intelligence.   3. Organizational behavior.
I. Sala, Fabio. II. Urch Druskat, Vanessa. III. Mount, Gerald.

HF5548.8.L536   2005
158.7—dc22
                                          2004056287
                                               CIP

Books published by Lawrence Erlbaum Associates are printed on acid-free paper, and their bindings are chosen for strength and durability.

Printed in the United States of America
10 9 8 7 6 5 4 3 2 1

Contents

Foreword

In all likelihood, readers of this book bring a variety of interests and disciplinary backgrounds to it. Scholars in the fields of Education, Psychology, Organizational Behavior, and related social sciences, will find a collection of the latest research on Emotional Intelligence (EI) by the most renowned scholars in this new field of study. Practitioners—including HR specialists, Executive Coaches, Organizational Development Consultants, leaders, and managers—will find compelling evidence for the link between Emotional Intelligence and Performance, as well as suggestions for how to help individuals and organizations develop the personal and social competencies that are so critical in today's workplace.

About eight years ago, I was invited to be a founding member of the Consortium for Research on Emotional Intelligence (CREIO). At that point in my own work, I was deeply interested in why some individuals readily develop growth-enhancing relationships with colleagues and mentors, and why others do not. As an organizational psychologist I knew that the answer had to be a complex one, and that no one individual or group-level factor would suffice. Then I read Dan Goleman's 1995 book and began to use the EI framework in my work to gain more insight into the multiple factors that shape these important alliances.

My journey with the concept of Emotional Intelligence has been much like that of other scholars who want to understand human behavior in work settings. First, I wrestled with the definition of the concept, and just when I thought I could accept the one offered in Dan's work, I read about several other definitions that differed in terms of whether abilities, skills, behaviors, or competencies were the attributes of interest (e.g., Bar-On, 1997; Bar-On & Parker, 2000; Salovey & Mayer, 1990; Salovey et al., 2000). I also noticed that much of the Emotional Competence framework that the Consortium was developing as a result of very fruitful partnerships among researchers and practitioners overlapped considerably with Leadership Competencies, Interpersonal Skills, and other constructs that had been a part of my teaching and research vocabulary for 20 years.

When I presented my own work, incorporating the lens of Emotional Intelligence, I was frequently asked, "Is this anything new?" Over the years I have gotten better at addressing this query by noting that the concept may overlap with others that we have readily used in our research and teaching over the years. However, the development of the construct, its specific components, and the measurement tools now available, make it possible to better address a concern that leaders, executives, HR practitioners, and scholars share: When it comes to job-related performance and success, we know that technical skills and analytic intelligence are not enough. How do we adequately explain and assess this other domain?

Emotional Intelligence offers a very useful frame. Although several definitions of emotional competence currently exist, there is tremendous overlap among them. This is quite common in the early stages of development of a new construct. Researchers have made significant progress in defining the construct, measuring it, and providing tests of reliability and validity. As a result of their diligent and competent work, we now have the tools to empirically demonstrate that emotional competence affects both relationships *and* performance at work. The studies reported here illustrate to readers the various ways in which emotional competence (or the lack thereof) affects individual and organizational performance, as well as various approaches to enabling organizations to develop this critical capability.

This volume is a "must have" resource for anyone who wants to be brought up to date on the substantial progress that has been made in the last decade in defining and measuring the important linkages between emotional competence and performance. The authors represent a range of disciplinary perspectives on the subject, which in the end are quite complementary rather than contradictory. Varied research methods have been employed to measure the construct, and to assess its impact on performance in a number of settings ranging from corporations to the Armed Forces to educational settings, both in the US and in other parts of the world. Those authors who are particularly interested in how these personal and social competencies can be enhanced through training and other interventions offer a number of alternatives worthy of consideration.

Vanessa Druskat, Fabio Sala, and Gerald Mount have done important service to this domain of study by putting this volume together. This work pro-

vides compelling evidence to support our efforts to foster emotional competence in educational, business, and government contexts. Researchers and
practitioners will find insights and tools that will undoubtedly enhance their
work and ultimately contribute to addressing many of the persistent social,
political, and economic problems that we face. I am grateful to be part of this
community of practice.

—Kathy E. Kram, PhD
Boston University
October, 2004

Preface

The concept of *emotional intelligence* (EI) has such intuitive appeal and face validity that in a short period of time it has captured the attention of social scientists and organizational practitioners around the world. The key questions that many want answered are whether there is validity to the idea of a form of intelligence rooted in emotion and whether EI really supports positive life outcomes such as work success. The purpose of this book is to help answer these questions. Its chapters are written by a group of the foremost scholars and practitioners studying emotional intelligence in the workplace. It presents their cutting-edge thinking and research on EI. The authors' perspectives differ on a number of dimensions including their definitions and models of EI. However, together their chapters provide a strong case for a link between EI and effective work performance. Together, they also provide detailed information about the various paths and routes through which EI can affect the performance of individuals and groups. All the authors agree that their promising findings call attention to the need for further research on EI.

We have two objectives for this book. Our primary objective is to share leading-edge research on the link between EI and workplace performance. Research is a painstakingly slow process, especially when researchers are in the early stages of determining how to define and measure a construct. Thus, we aimed to compile and make available these often pre-published, leading-edge ideas for researchers and organizational practitioners wanting to learn about the current status of knowledge on EI and workplace outcomes.

Our second objective for this book is to emphasize the value of examining EI from multiple vantage points and perspectives. We therefore invited the contribution of authors with differing perspectives on EI. Sometimes their perspectives differ slightly and sometimes greatly from one another. Their research methods and research populations also differ. What unifies these authors is their interest in developing a better understanding of how EI can influence work performance and in determining whether research supports that it does influence work performance.

A unique feature of this book is that it integrates the work of social scientists and organizational practitioners. Their mutual interests in EI provide a unique opportunity for basic and applied research and practice to learn from one another in order to continually refine and advance knowledge on EI. Moreover, both groups have called for (a) rigorous research to determine the reliability and validity of EI for predicting real-life outcomes like work success and life satisfaction and (b) information about how EI can best be developed at all stages of the life span. These similar interests undoubtedly provide the perfect opportunity for science and practice to work together.

The primary audience for this book is researchers, teachers, and students of psychology, management, and organizational behavior. However, because of its clear practical application to the workplace, we hope it will also be of interest to organizational consultants and human resource practitioners. We believe this volume will be readable and useful for a multidisciplinary audience consisting of both experts and newcomers to EI. Toward that end, we worked with our authors to write in a clear and accessible style and to address the implications of their ideas and findings for practicing managers.

This is the second volume in the series *Advances in Emotional Intelligence: Research and Practice*, sponsored by the Consortium for Research on Emotional Intelligence in Organizations [www.eiconsortium.org], co-chaired by Cary Cherniss of Rutgers University and Daniel Goleman. The first volume, *The Emotionally Intelligent Workplace*, was co-edited by Cary Cherniss and Daniel Goleman and was published by Jossey-Bass in 2001.

ACKNOWLEDGMENTS

We have a great number of people to thank for their contributions to this book. First, we want to thank the members of the Consortium for Research on Emotional Intelligence in Organizations and particularly the editors of their book series, *Advances in Emotional Intelligence: Research and Practice*: Cary Cherniss of Rutgers University, Richard E. Boyatzis of Case Western Reserve University, and Maurice Elias of Rutgers University. We thank them for their confidence in and support for us as editors of volume 2 of that series. We also thank them for introducing us to one another. It has been an enjoyable and synergistic collaboration. Our easy working relationship might stem from our similar academic backgrounds. The late David C. McClelland was the PhD thesis adviser for Vanessa and Fabio. Jerry could also be considered an academic great-grandson to McClelland, because his thesis adviser, Ram Tenkasi, worked with Richard Boyatzis, who was himself a student of Mc-Clelland's. Dave McClelland valued collaborations between scientists and practitioners and worked hard to ensure that his research was used to make a difference in the world. We hope this book continues his legacy.

We also acknowledge the hard work and trust of the authors of the chapters in this volume. They are a stellar group of scholars and were each invited to contribute because of the quality of their past research on emotion and emotional intelligence. They graciously accepted and we learned tremendously from each of them. We've discovered that editing a book is like managing a number of gourmet chefs so that they get their intricate meals finished and served at the same time (i.e., on deadline). We appreciate the patience of those of you who served your chapters earlier (i.e., more on time) than the rest of us.

We also express our appreciation to Anne Duffy, our editor at Lawrence Erlbaum Associates, Inc., and her editorial assistant, Kristin Duch, for their support. We also thank Anne and LEA for recognizing the value in this book.

Vanessa thanks her friend and mentor Richard E. Boyatzis, who introduced her to EI, for always believing that she had a contribution to make; Sigal Barsade, for brainstorming with her at the beginning of this process and for introducing her to a number of the chapter authors; Steven B. Wolff, for his partnership and never-ending drive for quality; and finally Paul, Ethan, and Deanna Lee Druskat, for their love and support.

Fabio thanks the worldwide network of ECI researchers for their immense contribution to the growing body of research with the ECI. He also expresses his gratitude to Heidemarie Nel, Matthew Lloyd, and Levent Sevinc, whose research provided the basis for his current chapter. Finally, he thanks his colleagues at the Hay Group for teaching him how to positively affect practical workplace problems and issues, and his clients for what they have taught him about the value of emotional intelligence in the workplace. Most important, he thanks his wife, Kathryn, for her love and partnership.

Jerry thanks Mike Johnson and Gregg Rich for the vision to sponsor this politically sensitive research, Jim Burruss for being a role model of EI, and finally, his wife Mary Lynne, for her love and patience, and his daughter Ingrid, for her support and critical assistance.

—Vanessa Urch Druskat
Fabio Sala
Gerald Mount

About the Authors

Neal Ashkanasy is professor of management in the UQ Business School, The University of Queensland, Brisbane, Australia. He came into academic life after an 18-year career in professional engineering and management and has since worked in the departments of psychology, commerce, engineering, and management. He has a PhD (1989) in social and organizational psychology from the University of Queensland and has research interests in leadership, organizational culture, and business ethics. In recent years, however, his research has focused on the role of emotions in organizational life. He has published his work in journals such as *Academy of Management Review, Academy of Management Executive, Accounting, Organizations and Society, Journal of Management, Journal of Organizational Behavior, Journal of Personality and Social Psychology*, and *Organizational Behavior and Human Decision Processes*. He is co-editor of three books: *The Handbook of Organizational Culture and Climate* (Sage); *Emotions in the Workplace; Theory, Research, and Practice* (Quorum); and *Managing Emotions in the Workplace* (ME Sharpe). In addition, he administers two e-mail discussion lists: *Orgcult*, the Organizational Culture Caucus list; and *Emonet*, the Emotions in the Workplace list. He has organized three International Conferences on Emotions in Organizational Life and is now planning the fourth conference to be held in England in July 2004. Professor Ashkanasy is also on the editorial boards of *Academy of Management Journal, Journal of Organizational Behavior, Applied Psychology: An International Review*, and *Journal of Management*. Finally, he was the 2001–2002 chair of the managerial and organizational cognition division of the Academy of Management.

Reuven Bar-On holds an adjunct associate professorship at the University of Texas Medical Branch in Galveston, where he directs research in emotional and social intelligence. He is a member of the Consortium for Research on Emotional Intelligence in Organizations at Rutgers University and is also associated with the Collaborative to Advance Social and Emotional Learning at the University of Illinois. Dr. Bar-On is an internationally acknowledged expert and pioneer in emotional intelligence and has been involved in defining, measuring, and applying various aspects of this concept since 1980. He coined the term EQ (emotional quotient) in 1985 to describe his approach to assessing emotionally and socially intelligent behavior. He created the Emotional Quotient Inventory (EQ-i), which is the first test of emotionally intelligent behavior to be published by a psychological test publisher (Multi-Health Systems, 1996) and reviewed by the *Buros Mental Measurement Yearbook* (1999). Together with James Parker, he also coauthored the first commercially available test designed to assess emotionally intelligent behavior in children and adolescents (the EQ-i:YV, published by Multi-Health Systems in 2000). Also with Dr. Parker, he co-edited the *Handbook of Emotional Intelligence* (published by Jossey-Bass in 2000). Based on a workbook he coauthored with Richard Handley (*Optimizing People*), both authors developed an Internet-based training program designed to improve emotional and social competencies related to emotional intelligence. With Dr. Handley, he also developed the EQ-360 Assessment and EQ Interview, two additional instruments designed to assess emotionally intelligent behavior published by Multi-Health Systems. Dr. Bar-On has been involved in numerous research projects related to emotional intelligence in the past 2 decades. Together with Dr. Marian Ruderman, he was recently involved in an extensive research project conducted at the Center for Creative Leadership that confirms the ability of emotional intelligence to identify and predict successful corporate leaders. And together with Suzanne Fund, he recently completed a 3-year study in the Israeli Defense Forces that demonstrates the impact of emotional intelligence on general performance as well as its ability to predict command leadership. More recently, he has been asked by Human Resources Development Canada to be involved in a 20-year longitudinal study of 20,000 Canadian youth designed to determine the interrelation between emotional intelligence and biomedical, cognitive, developmental, social and educational factors.

Richard E. Boyatzis is professor of organizational behavior and past chair of the Department of Organizational Behavior at the Weatherhead School of Management at Case Western Reserve University. In addition, from 1994 to 1999 he was responsible for executive education and served as associate dean for executive education programs at the Weatherhead School.

Prior to joining the faculty at CWRU, he was president and CEO of McBer & Co. from 1976 to 1987, having been with McBer from 1969. From 1983 to 1985 he was chief operating officer of Yankelovich, Skelly & White, while on its board of directors and the board of the Reliance Consulting Group. From 1985 to 1986 he was on the board of the Hay Group when they were owned by Saatchi & Saatchi. He has been consultant to many Fortune 500 companies, government agencies, and companies in Europe on various topics including executive and management development, organization structure, culture change, research & development (R&D) productivity, economic development, selection, promotion, performance appraisal, and career planning.

Professor Boyatzis is the author of numerous articles on human motivation, self-directed behavior change, leadership, value trends, managerial competencies, power, alcohol, and aggression and a research book titled, *The Competent Manager: A Model for Effective Performance.* He is also author of *Transforming Qualitative Information: Thematic Analysis and Code Development* and coauthor of *Innovations in Professional Education: Steps on a Journey From Teaching to Learning* with S. S. Cowen and D. A. Kolb. His latest book, with Daniel Goleman and Annie McKee, *Primal Leadership: Realizing the Power of Emotional Intelligence,* is a national best-seller and is being published in 26 languages besides English. Professor Boyatzis has a PhD and an MA in social psychology from Harvard University and a BS in aeronautics and astronautics from MIT.

Dottie D. Brienza has 20 years experience in Organization Development, Human Resources Management and Sales at Johnson & Johnson, Novartis Pharmaceutical, and Honeywell. She has also worked in the private, non-profit sector. She completed her graduate studies in OD at American University in Washington, DC. And her areas of passion include change management and organization design, culture, leadership development and emotional intelligence.

Dr. Kathleen Cavallo is an Organizational Psychologist and a founding partner of Corporate Consulting Group, a consulting firm specializing in leadership education and enhancement. She is a Visiting Faculty member at the Graduate School of Applied and Professional Psychology at Rutgers University, where she is also the Director of the Career and Performance Counseling Group.

Dr. Joseph Ciarrochi is a university academic and is conducting cutting-edge research on how emotional intelligence promotes effectiveness and well-being. He has published numerous articles in high-profile journals on emotional intelligence and recently published an edited book on the role of emotional intelligence in everyday life. Currently, he is working on interventions that are designed to increase emotional intelligence in organizations such as the police force.

Stéphane Côté is assistant professor of organizational behavior at the Rotman School of Management at the University of Toronto. He received his PhD in organizational psychology from the University of Michigan. His current research interests include the influence of affective experiences and emotional intelligence on work performance, the effects of emotion regulation on strain at work, and the prediction of affective experiences at work from personality and context. He has published in the *Journal of Applied Psychology*, the *Journal of Personality and Social Psychology*, and the *Academy of Management Review*, and has presented his research at meetings of the Academy of Management. He teaches courses on Leadership and Organizational Behaviour at the Ralman School of Management.

Ronald R. Crain is the Director, Human Resources, Defense Finance and Accounting Service (DFAS), part of the Department of Defense and is responsible for the Agency's entire HR organization consisting of a staff of 300 HR professionals and support personnel with an annual budget of over $40 million. DFAS employs 15,000 DoD civilian and military personnel at 5 major centers and 20 operating locations in the United States and Europe. Mr. Crain's organization also provides personnel servicing for an additional 10,000 civilian employees throughout DoD. Each business day, DFAS distributes in excess of $1 billion in payments in various forms or another, i.e., paychecks, vouchers, settlements, etc. In little over 2 years, Mr. Crain has led a complete restructuring of HR installing strategic HR partners within business units, moving to a shared service center operation, fostering a strategic learning and development approach, and forging new ground in adoption of "HR to the desktop." Mr. Crain's HR organization has won awards for its work, and he has spoken at the Excellence in Government conference, various military schools, IMA National Student Conference, and other programs.

Mr. Crain is an Army veteran. He holds an MS degree in Organizational Management and a BS degree in Business Administration. He is a certified Senior Professional in Human Resources from the Society for HR Management.

Vanessa Urch Druskat is associate professor of organizational behavior at the Whittemore School of Business and Economics at the University of New Hampshire. Previously, she was associate professor in the Department of Organizational Behavior at the Weatherhead School of Management at Case Western Reserve University in Cleveland. Her research and publications focus on group structures and processes that increase group effectiveness. She has written articles on the team competencies required of empowered teams; the organizational inputs that support team competence; effective formal and informal leadership in work teams; and group emotional competence, which have appeared in publications such as *Academy of Management Journal, Human Relations, Journal of Applied Psychology, Leadership Quarterly, Small Group Research,* and *Harvard Business Review.* She is an incoming associate editor for the journal *Small Group Research.* Currently, she is writing a coauthored book (with Steven B. Wolff) on emotionally competent teams.

Vanessa has received two awards from the Center of Creative Leadership for her research on leadership. At Case Western she received a Glennan Fellows Award for Outstanding Teaching and Scholarship in 1998 and the John S. Diekhoff Award for Distinguished Graduate-Level Teaching in 2001. She has an undergraduate degree in psychology from Indiana University, a master's degree in organizational psychology from Teacher's College at Columbia University, and a PhD in social and organizational psychology from Boston University.

Hillary Anger Elfenbein graduated from Harvard University with degrees in physics and Sanskrit language and literature before working as a management consultant with the Monitor Group in Cambridge, MA. She returned to Harvard for a PhD from the joint Organizational Program specializing in psychology and management, during which time she also completed a master's degree in statistics and the core curriculum of the master's in business administration. After two years as a senior researcher at the Harvard Business School, Dr. Elfenbein joined the faculty at the University of California, Berkeley's Haas School of Business, in the organizational behavior and industrial relations group. Her current research focuses on how emotion serves as a tool for communication in the workplace and on cross-cultural differences in the communication of emotion. Dr. Elfenbein's work has appeared in *Current Directions in Psychological Science, Emotion, Journal of Applied Psychology, Journal of Cross-Cultural Psychology, Journal of Personality and Social Psychology, Psychological Bulletin,* and *Psychological Science.*

Suzanne Fund received her doctorate in organizational psychology from New York University. For many years, Dr. Fund has researched the ability to manage emotions and deal with stress as key factors affecting performance in the workplace. She has focused on the empirical examination and application of a variety of psychometric tools designed to measure these constructs for recruitment and selection purposes in organizational settings. Drawing on her professional background and expertise in this area, Dr. Fund pioneered the application of emotional intelligence in the Israel Defense Forces (IDF). With the assistance of Reuven Bar-On, she recently completed one of the largest and longest predictive studies to date demonstrating the connection between emotional intelligence and performance. The findings of this 3-year study, on over 5,000 new recruits in the IDF, represent a monumental contribution to what Reuven Bar-On and Richard Handley refer to as "the EQ profiling of occupational performance."

Claire Godsell is a doctoral candidate in Clinical Psychology at the University of Wollongong, Australia. She has a keen interest in positive psychology and is involved in organizational training in emotional intelligence in the police services. She is presently conducting research on the relationship between emotional intelligence, workplace effectiveness and well-being.

Marilyn K. Gowing is vice president for public sector consulting and services with the Washington office of AON Consulting. Prior to joining AON, Dr. Gowing was a member of the Senior Executive Service for the U.S. Office of Personnel Management, where she directed the Personnel Resources and Development Center. In 1999, she received the Presidential Meritorious Rank Award for reengineering government processes, building strategic partnerships of federal, state, and local government, and directing the use of advanced technology including Internet administration of organizational culture surveys. Dr. Gowing has also received awards from the Internal Revenue Service, the U.S. Department of Housing and Urban Development, the American Society of Association Executives, the U.S. Office of Personnel Management, and the National Partnership for Reinventing Government, among others. Dr. Gowing was named The Distinguished Psychologist in Management for the Year 2000 by the Society of Psychologists in Management and was elected to serve on the board of directors. In 2001, both the American Psychological Association and the Society of Industrial and Organizational Psychology named Dr. Gowing to Fellow status. She is a past board member of the Society of Industrial and Organizational Psychology, past president of the Personnel Testing Council of Metropolitan Washington, past secretary of the IPMA Assessment Council, and president-elect of the Society of Psychologists in Management. Her publications include two books, *Taxonomies of Human Performance* (with Edwin A. Fleishman) and *The New Organizational Reality: Downsizing, Restructuring and Revitalization* (with John Kraft and James Campbell Quick); several book chapters; and many professional journal articles. At the invitation of Dave Ulrich and Mark Huselid, she served as guest editor for a special issue of *Human Resources Management Journal* on the public sector. Dr. Gowing is a graduate of the College of William and Mary and a distinguished alumna of George Washington University, where she received her PhD in industrial and organizational psychology.

Richard Handley is a pioneer in bringing emotional intelligence to the workplace and uniquely applying it in the area of human capital profiling for recruitment, selection, and training. His pioneering work in applying this concept in the U.S. Armed Forces was praised in a 1998 U.S. Congressional Report, representing the first time that emotional intelligence was mentioned in a congressional report and marking an important milestone in its application in the workplace. Building on this unique background and expertise, Dr. Handley has become a leading business strategist in leveraged, high-performance human capital solutions in the corporate world; he has been providing this innovative type of consultation to several Fortune 500 companies over the years. Drawing on a workbook that he wrote in collaboration with Reuven Bar-On (*Optimizing People*), Dr. Handley co-developed the first Internet-delivered training program designed to enhance emotionally intelligent behavior. Together with Dr. Bar-On, he co-authored the EQ-360 Assessment and the EQ Interview as well. He is also the coauthor of the Behavioral Health Survey, another instrument designed to assess human effectiveness and its impact on performance in the workplace. Dr. Handley has presented at numerous national and international business conferences on the subject of emotional intelligence and the power of applying it to optimize individual and organizational performance. His work has been featured in *Fast Company Magazine, Inc. Magazine, Harvard Business Update, Training Magazine, H.R. Magazine, Controller Magazine, Selling Power, The Dallas Morning News, MSN, ABC,* and *Fox News.*

Karen A. Jehn received her PhD from Northwestern's Kellogg Graduate School of Management and is now professor of social and organizational psychology at Leiden University in the Netherlands. Previously, she was a professor at the Wharton School of the University of Pennsylvania, where she also was an affiliated professor of psychology and an associate director of the Solomon Asch Center for the Study of Ethnopolitical Conflict. Professor "Etty" Jehn has researched conflict in the United States and internationally, focusing on the constructive aspects of group conflict, in addition to the destructive aspects. Most recently she has been interested in two new topic areas related to group, organizational, and national conflict: diversity and deviance. Professor Jehn has authored numerous scholarly publications in these areas, including articles in *Academy of Management Journal, Administrative Science Quarterly, Journal of Personality and Social Psychology, International Journal of Conflict Management, Journal of Business Ethics, Business Ethics Quarterly,* and *Group Decision and Negotiation.* She has served on the boards of *Administrative Science Quarterly, Academy of Management Review,* and *Journal of Organizational Behavior.* She has been an associate editor of *International Journal of Conflict Management* and has recently finished a review piece of her and others' work on conflict for *Research in Organization Behavior.*

Professor Jehn has worked in the People's Republic of China, Russia, and Korea as a representative of the U.S. State Department in discussions of economics and management of international joint ventures. She has served as the faculty coordinator of the George Harvey Program on Redefining Diversity supported by Pitney Bowes and the SEI Center of the Wharton School, the research director of the Alfred P. Sloan Foundation's Diversity Research Network, and the chair of the Conflict Management Division of the Academy of Management.

Peter Jordan is a lecturer in the School of Management at Griffith University, Australia. He gained his PhD in management at the University of Queensland. His current research interests include emotional intelligence, emotions in organizations, team performance, and leadership. He has published in a range of international journals, including *Academy of Management Review, Human Resource Management Review,* and *Advances in Developing Human Resources.*

Elizabeth Stubbs Koman is a co-founder and Director of the Organizational Improvement Division of the Stubman Group, a consulting organization specializing in employing a systems approach to maximizing human performance and organizational effectiveness. Liz is a native of Diamond Bar, California and graduated Cum Laude from California State Polytechnic University, Pomona where she earned BA degrees in psychology and sociology, and minored in quantitative research. She earned her MA degree in psychology with emphasis on evaluation and organizational behavior from Claremont Graduate University. Liz's PhD is in organizational behavior from Case Western Reserve University in Cleveland, Ohio. Her doctoral work examined the relationship between leadership competencies, team norms, and team performance. Her research focuses on team performance, leadership, emotional intelligence, human performance, and organizational effectiveness.

Paulo N. Lopes received his BA in Economics and PhD in psychology from Yale University. He worked for 13 years in business and journalism. As a lecturer in psychology at the University of Surrey, in England, he teaches courses on social psychology, emotion, and conflict. He also teaches courses on emotional intelligence for MBA and executive audiences. He has held appointments as Adjunct Professor of Organizational Behavior at INSEAD, in France, and as Visiting Assistant Professor at the School of Economics and Management of *Universidade Católica Portuguesa,* in Portugal. His publications include more than 10 journal articles and book chapters on emotional abilities and interpersonal interaction. His research yielded some of the earliest evidence for the predictive validity of ability measures of emotional inteillgence. Additionally, Paulo has co-produced and co-directed an award-winning documentary film portaying a case study of resilience in a traditional fishuig community.

Tracey Messer is a doctoral candidate in Organizational Behavior at the Weatherhead School of Management, Case Western Reserve University. Tracey has a long-standing interest in team performance and group dynamics. Her interest extends to research exploring the norms that foster group emotional intelligence and research examining the development of social capital in family enterprises. Tracey is a graduate of Goucher College (BA) and Case Western Reserve University (MBA).

A. Alexandra Michel received her PhD from The Wharton School of Business, University of Pennsylvania, and is now assistant professor in the Management and Organization Group of the Marshall School at the University of Southern California. Professor Michel also has degrees in economics and psychology from the University of Western Ontario. Her research shows how emotions can function either as the attributes of an individual or as a social process and investigates how these distinct ways of functioning result in differential task and moral performance for individuals and groups. She previously worked as an investment banker for Goldman Sachs, New York, and held positions at other international organizations, including Dresdner Bank, Germany. The author of scholarly articles in management and psychology, she also has presented numerous invited papers at management, psychology, and anthropology conferences. Informed by her research on extraordinary task and moral performance, her consulting has assisted organizations in such areas as executive selection, appraisal, and coaching; group effectiveness; and organizational change. She has conducted several large-scale organizational change projects in investment banking and other international professional service organizations.

Gerald Mount is visiting professor of strategy and organizational behavior at the Seidman School of Business, Grand Valley State University. He specializes in helping executives and organizations implement their strategies by building leadership capabilities, developing emotional intelligence competencies, and creating the framework of management practices needed to stimulate a high performance climate. He has more than 20 years of experience as a business executive in addition to 12 years as a management consultant. Prior to consulting, he developed a solid foundation of business experience as vice president of technical and international services for the marine transportation subsidiary company of a Fortune 100 international petroleum corporation. Initially trained as a merchant marine officer, he developed leadership capabilities during 12 years at sea on oceangoing tank ships. He holds an unlimited shipmaster's license.

Professor Mount's consulting activities have primarily been focused on the role of emotional intelligence in the development of leadership capabilities and helping leaders modify their managerial styles to achieve successful implementation of desired business strategies. He has been a consultant to clients in health care delivery and management, logistics management, and the international petroleum and chemical industry.

Jerry has been a frequent presenter at national and international conferences on competencies and their role in creating organizational capabilities. He has a PhD in organization development from Benedictine University, an MBA from the Kellogg School of Management at Northwestern University, and a BS from Maine Maritime Academy, where he was the recipient of the United States Steamship Lines Award for Outstanding Leadership.

Brian S. O'Leary is director of the Assessment and Training Assistance Services Group in the Center for Talent Services at the U.S. Office of Personnel Management. This unit conducts basic, applied, and innovative research to support numerous initiatives to ensure the quality and effectiveness of the government workforce. The unit is staffed with psychologists that carry out reimbursable work for federal, state, and local government agencies. This has included competency-based human resource practices for recruitment, selection, performance management, training, organizational assessment, and outcome measures. Brian has a PhD in industrial and organizational psychology from the University of Maryland and a BA from Penn State.

Fabio Sala is an Associate Director of Learning and Development at Millennium Pharmaceuticals, Inc. where he is responsible for leadership and organizational development initiatives. Prior to joining Millennium, Fabio was a consultant at the Hay Group's, McClelland Center for Research and Innovation. He received his PhD in social psychology from Boston University under David C. McClelland. Fabio's client work at the McClelland Center was with leading global organizations such as IBM, Pfizer, AeroMexico, Caterpillar, Toyota, HealthNet, and UNDP. Prior to joining the Hay Group, Fabio was an adjunct lecturer at the University of Massachusetts where he taught Organizational Behavior, Research Methods, Statistics, and Social Psychology courses. He also was a lecturer at Boston University and Johns Hopkins University. His research at the McClelland Center served to identify the characteristics of outstanding performers, evaluate the effectiveness of development interventions, and evaluate the impact of assessment and intervention on workplace performance. Fabio's research has been published in *Harvard Business Review*, the *Journal of Consulting Psychology: Practice and Research*, the *Journal of Psychology and Health*, and *Nonprofit Management & Leadership*.

Peter Salovey completed his undergraduate education at Stanford University and his PhD in clinical psychology at Yale University in 1986. He now serves as the Chris Argyris Professor of Psychology, professor of management and of Epidemiology and Public Health, and dean of Yale College. Professor Salovey is also the director of the Department of Psychology's Health, Emotion, and Behavior (HEB) Laboratory and Deputy Director of the Yale Center for Interdisciplinary Research on AIDS (CIRA).

The program of research conducted in Professor Salovey's laboratory concerns two general issues: (a) the psychological significance and function of human moods and emotions and (b) the application of social psychological principles to motivating health protective behaviors. His recent work on emotion has focused on the ways in which feelings facilitate adaptive cognitive and behavioral functioning; with John D. Mayer, he developed the broad framework called emotional intelligence that organizes this work and an ability-based measure of emotional intelligence known as the Mayer–Salovey–Caruso Emotional Intelligence Test (MSCEIT). The goal of much of his recent health behavior research is to investigate the role of the framing and psychological tailoring of messages in developing maximally persuasive educational and public health communication interventions promoting prevention and early detection behaviors relevant to cancer and HIV/AIDS.

Professor Salovey has published over 200 articles in the scientific literature. He is the coauthor with V. J. D'Andrea of *Peer Counseling* (1983) and *Peer Counseling: Skills, Ethics, and Perspectives* (1996), and he edited *Reasoning, Inference, and Judgment in Clinical Psychology* (1988) with Dennis C. Turk. Some of his more recent books include *The Psychology of Jealousy and Envy* (1991), *The Remembered Self: Emotions and Memory in Personality* (1993, with Jefferson A. Singer), *Psychology* (1993, with Zick Rubin and Letitia Anne Peplau), *Emotional Development and Emotional Intelligence: Educational Implications* (1997, with David Sluyter), *At Play in the Fields of Consciousness* (1999, with Jefferson A. Singer), *The Wisdom in Feeling: Psychological Processes in Emotional Intelligence* (2002, with Lisa Feldman Barrett), and *The Emotionally Intelligent Manager* (2004, with David Caruso). Professor Salovey edits the Guilford Press series on Emotions and Social Behavior.

Professor Salovey is a recipient of the National Science Foundation's Presidential Young Investigator Award. His research has been funded by the National Cancer Institute, the American Cancer Society, the National Institute of Mental Health, the National Center for Health Statistics, the Andrew W. Mellon Foundation, and the Ethel F. Donaghue Foundation.

In Yale College, about 4,000 undergraduates have enrolled in his Introduction to Psychology course since 1986. A videotape version of his course, *The Intelligent Emotions,* is available through the Association of Yale Alumni's Great Teachers Series. He received the William Clyde DeVane Medal for

Distinguished Scholarship and Teaching in Yale College in 2000 and the Lex Hixon Prize for Teaching in the Social Sciences at Yale in 2002.

Steven B. Wolff is a partner in Innovative Systems Associates, an organization that consults to businesses from the perspective of complex living systems, an approach that helps organizations adapt in an increasingly complex world. He received his MBA from Babson College and his DBA, concentrating in organizational behavior with a minor in adult learning and development, from Boston University. He also holds a master's in electrical engineering from Northeastern University and a bachelor of engineering from Stevens Institute of Technology. He has had over 15 years of experience in the high-tech industry as an engineer and manager. Steve has conducted research in the areas of managing performance in self-managed teams, team effectiveness, team leadership, peer feedback, organizational learning, and partnerships between business and public schools. He has coauthored two books titled *OB in Action: Cases and Exercises.* His article "Building the Emotional Intelligence of Groups" appeared in the March 2001 issue of *Harvard Business Review.* Steve can be reached at steve@ sbwolff.com.

Introduction: Emotional Intelligence and Work Performance

It is a common belief that workers should leave their emotions at the door when they walk into work. In the last two decades, however, research has revealed that this practice may not be possible or desirable. Reports about the unavoidable influence of emotion on behavior and decision making have emerged from a variety of academic disciplines including psychology (e.g., Lewis & Haviland-Jones, 2000), organizational behavior (e.g., Ashforth & Humphrey, 1995; Martin, Knopoff, & Beckman, 1998), sociology (e.g., Ollilainen, 2000), anthropology (e.g., Levy, 1984) and neuroscience (e.g., Damasio, 1994). These scholars have argued that emotion provides a unique source of information about the environment and that it unavoidably informs thoughts and actions. Research by Antonio Damasio, Head of the Department of Neurology at the University of Iowa College of Medicine, shows that emotion is an adaptive response and part of the process of normal reasoning and decision making; his research suggests that emotion information helps the brain make decisions and establish priorities and is critical to learning and memory (Damasio, 1994, 1999).

The suggestion that individuals differ in their ability to perceive, understand, and use emotion as a source of information was first proposed by psychologists Peter Salovey and Jack Mayer (1990). They labeled this ability *emotional intelligence* (EI) and formally defined it as involving (a) the ability to perceive, appraise, and express emotion accurately; (b) the ability to access and generate feelings when they facilitate cognition; (c) the ability to understand affect-laden information and make use of emotional knowledge; and (d) the ability to regulate emotions to promote emotional and intellectual growth and well-being (Mayer & Salovey, 1997; for a more thorough definition and discussion of this theory see chap. 3 in this volume).

As a result of Salovey and Mayer's initial proposal, a number of scholars, many of whom were already doing similar work, were attracted to the idea, and soon other viable conceptualizations of EI emerged. As happens in science, variations on the theory stem from the interests and backgrounds of the theorists. For example, Salovey and Mayer's theory (see chap. 3) is rooted in their vision of EI as a type of intelligence. Bar-On's theory (see chap. 1) is influenced by his interest in personality, life success, and personal well-being. This is seen in his inclusion of factors of "happiness" and "self-actualization" in theory of EI. The foundation of Ciarrochi's theory of EI (see chap. 2) is his interest in emotional well-being and, as a clinical psychologist, his interests in rational–emotive and cognitive behavioral therapies. Goleman and Boyatzis's theory (see chaps. 4 and 6) grows out of their interests in the competencies that support superior work performance. Both Goleman and Boyatzis studied under David McClelland, whose work in the 1970s started the workplace competency movement.

In a similar vein, scholars with interests in small groups have also begun to theorize and study EI and its role in groups. They join a long line of group researchers who have argued that emotions influence group dynamics and group effectiveness (see Bales, 1950, 1953; Barsade & Gibson, 1998; Homans, 1950; Janis, 1982). Again, their specific ideas about EI in groups stem from their unique interests and backgrounds. Jordan and Ashkanasy (see chap. 7) conceptualize and study EI in groups as the impact of emotional self-awareness on group member interactions and performance. Elfenbein's interests in emotion recognition (see chap. 8) led her to conceptualize and study EI in groups in terms of how well members understand each other's expressions of emotion (verbal and non-verbal). Michel and Jehn's (see chap. 9) interests in the social context led them to question whether thinking about emotion causes a group member to focus excessively on his or her self rather than on the social situation where the more relevant social information exists. Michel and Jehn, therefore, conceptualize and favor a less self-focused form of EI that they label "direct involvement" in the situation. Finally, Wolff, Druskat, and colleagues are interested in group-level processes and norms. They believe that groups are greater than the sum of their parts (i.e., more than just a sum of individuals) and therefore that a group of members who score high on EI will not ensure that the group or its members operate in an emotionally intelligent fashion. These authors argue that emotionally intelligent groups develop and operate under a set of norms that encourage awareness and management of emotion at multiple levels in the group.

The different conceptualizations of EI presented in this volume comple-ment rather than contradict one another. For example, a basic assumption of all of the authors in this book is that individuals or groups who attend to emotion in the self, in others, and in the social situation and who can man-age their own emotion appropriately have an advantage in life and at work. Another shared assumption is that there is valuable information to be learned from this interesting area of research and practice.

The Controversy Surrounding EI

Despite acceptance that emotion is a source of information that influences behavior, important questions about the concept of emotional intelligence abound. Some of these questions stem from the fact that, as discussed previ-ously, there exist a number of definitions and measurements for the con-struct (see also the *Handbook of Emotional Intelligence,* edited by Bar-On and Parker, 2000). Other concerns stem from the media's interest and the hype surrounding Goleman's best-selling books on the topic (see Goleman, 1995, 1998; Goleman, Boyatzis, & McKee, 2001), including the publication of Goleman's 1995 book in over 33 foreign editions. Academics and practi-tioners whose interests have been peaked by the potential for EI to teach us something new about human competence want concrete evidence that emotional intelligence is not just hype but is something "real" that can be reliably and validly assessed and that its assessment does predict aspects of work and life success. Academics also understandably want to be assured that it is not an old concept dressed up with a new and intriguing label.

In the last decade, scholars and practitioners alike have worked hard to answer these questions. They have conducted research using a wide range of methodologies to explore its measurement (Bar-On, 1997; Mayer, Salo-vey, Caruso, & Sitarenios, 2003; Sala, 2002), its manifestation in work-related competencies (Goleman, 1998, 2001), its application to everyday life (Ciarocchi, Forgas, & Mayer, 2001), its relation to effective leadership (Ashkanasy, Hartel, & Zerbe, 2000; Goleman, Boyatzis & McKee, 2002), its influence on team effectiveness (Druskat & Wolff, 2001; Elfenbein, & Am-bady, 2002; Jordan, Ashkanasy, Härtel, & Hooper, 2002), and its validity as a form of intelligence (Lopes, Salovey, & Straus, 2003; Mayer, Salovey, & Caruso, 1999). After a decade of studying EI, these scientists, everyone of whom have numerous research studies in process, are the first to say that a clear and definitive understanding of a concept like EI takes decades of re-search and that the study of EI is still in its infancy. As seen by their pres-ence in this book, these researchers are also best able to share their research and offer their informed insights into the current state of knowledge on the relationship between EI and important life and work outcomes.

Origins of this Book

Linking Emotional Intelligence and Performance at Work is the second in a series titled *Advances in Emotional Intelligence: Research and Practice*, which is sponsored by the Consortium for Research on Emotional Intelligence (www. eiconsortium.org). The mission of the consortium is to aid the advancement of research and practice related to emotional intelligence in organizations. The consortium was founded in the spring of 1996 with the support of the Fetzer Institute. Members of the consortium are individuals who come from academia, government, the corporate sector, and private consulting who are actively engaged in research on emotional intelligence in organizations. Drs. Daniel Goleman and Cary Cherniss currently serve as co-chairs.

The first volume in this book series was *The Emotionally Intelligent Workplace*, edited by Cary Cherniss and Daniel Goleman (2001). Future volumes will focus on issues of measurement and development and will explore facets of EI in different settings including schools, the family, and colleges and universities.

CHAPTER SUMMARIES

This book is divided into three parts. Part 1 (chaps. 1–6) focuses on research and theory examining the relationship between EI and individual performance effectiveness. Part 2 (chaps. 7–10) focuses on the relationship between EI and group effectiveness. Part 3 (chaps. 11–12) focuses on the future agenda for practitioners and researchers interested in EI. Next, we present a summary of each chapter in the book.

Chapter 1: The Impact of Emotional Intelligence on Performance, by Reuven Bar-On, Richard Handley, and Suzanne Fund, presents the results of two major studies examining emotional intelligence and occupational performance in the U.S. Air Force (USAF) and the Israeli Defense Forces (IDF). In both studies, emotional intelligence was measured using the self-report Bar-On Emotional Quotient Inventory (EQ-i). The USAF study examined Air Force recruiters; the overall sample pool included 1,171 Air Force recruiters or 70% of all recruiters. This sample was broken into subsamples of 114 high-performing recruiters and 114 low-performing recruiters. High performers were defined as those who met or exceeded 100% of their annual recruitment quotas. Low performers met less than 80% of their quotas. Results showed that high performers had significantly higher EI scores than the low performers. The model predicted 28% of the variance in performance. The study discredited myths regarding recruitment in the Air Force as it determined that the following were not related to job success: geographic area, gender, ethnicity, education, age, or hours worked. In fact, the most successful recruiters were found to work the fewest hours.

The IDF study examined four questions aimed at understanding the relation between EI and various measures of performance. The first question was whether EI would predict the performance of recruits serving in combat units or "combatants" in the IDF up to 15 months after taking the EI survey. Commanders rated each combatant on the following dimensions: (a) performs professionally, (b) cooperates with others, (c) fits in socially, (d) performs under pressure, (e) can be counted on, and (f) should remain in the unit. Specific EI competencies predicting combatant performance included self-regard, impulse control, emotional self-awareness, and reality testing. The model predicted 30% of the variance in performance in combatant soldiers.

The second question was whether EI would predict the difference between soldiers selected into an elite, highly stressful, and dangerous flying unit and recruits going into noncombatant roles in the IDF. Results showed that the members of the elite combat units had significantly higher EI scores than the low performers. Analysis showed that the specific EI competencies predicting selection into the elite unit included assertiveness, impulse control, stress tolerance, and flexibility. The model predicted 26% of the variance in the ability to serve in a dangerous elite combat unit.

The third question was whether EI would predict the difference between combatants whose peers nominated them as suitable to be officers and as having leadership potential. The analysis compared the 25% with the highest number of nominations with the 25% with the lowest number of nominations. Results showed that the members with leadership potential had significantly higher EI scores than those without leadership potential Analysis showed that the specific EI competencies predicting leadership potential included empathy, reality testing, stress tolerance, self-regard, and flexibility. The model predicted 15% of the variance in peer assessed leadership potential.

The fourth and final question examined whether EI would predict the difference between IDF recruits who requested and were accepted into "officer training" with those who either did not express the desire to be an officer or did not meet the minimum requirements. Results showed that the members with leadership potential had significantly higher EI scores than those without leadership potential. The specific EI competencies predicting officer selection were interpersonal relationships, stress tolerance, independence, reality testing, empathy, problem solving, self-regard, emotional self-awareness, and happiness. The model predicted 24% of the variance in being accepted into the officer training program.

Results of the studies reveal a clear relation between self-reported EI and occupational performance in the USAF and IDF. The authors argue that using EI measures to test job applicants could reduce the number of costly mismatches in organizations. For example, before the authors conducted this study with the USAF, the organization was losing $3 million per year for an average 100 mismatches a year. After 1 year of using a preemployment screening device for hiring recruiters, the USAF cut financial loses by approximately 92%, or $2,760,000.

Chapter 2: Mindfulness-Based Emotional Intelligence: Research and Training, by Joseph Ciarrochi and Claire Godsell, presents a new (although technically old) way of conceptualizing emotional intelligence. Mindfulness-based emotional intelligence grows out of research in clinical psychology on destructive responses to emotional stress and on the clinical interventions that have been used successfully to manage these destructive responses. Mindfulness-based EI is composed of two sets of abilities: The ability to use emotions as information and the ability to act effectively in the context of emotions and emotionally charged thoughts. Like other theories of EI, it contains externally focused dimensions and internally focused dimensions. It differs from previous theories of EI in that the EI behaviors within these dimensions represent constructive responses to common emotional stressors. For the most part, these behaviors focus on accepting and mindfully addressing emotional stressors that are shown through research to harm well-being, goal achievement, and work performance.

The theory is rooted in clinical research suggesting that two challenges stimulate and intensify emotional stress in modern life. The first challenge is that physiologically, our bodies treat psychological stress (e.g., nervousness, or fear when one has to speak in front of a large audience) the same way they treat physical threats (e.g., nervousness or fear when a lion is running after you). Specifically, the sympathetic nervous system becomes activated and hormones such as epinephrine, norepinephrine, and cortisol that are useful for fight-or-flight responses are released into the bloodstream. This creates a tendency to overreact to psychological stress and treat it as if it were a real physical threat. The second challenge grows out of a psychological process called "fusion" through which symbols, language, and ideas create the same level of emotional stress as the events they symbolize. For example, ideas or thoughts of failure can create the same level of stress (if not more) than actual failure.

The theory of mindfulness-based EI produces a model of EI that includes seven dimensions of behavior that define healthy responses to emotional stress because they emphasize being mindful of emotion and recognizing that one can experience unpleasant or stressful emotion and still move toward a valued goal. The seven dimensions are broken into the two categories of externally focused EI (including expressing emotion, identifying others' emotions, and managing others' emotions) and internally focused EI (including effective emotional orientation, using emotion as information, undermining "fusion," and undermining "self-concept fusion").

The authors present a list of measures used to study the effects of the behaviors in the model and discuss research with those measures showing how the EI behaviors improve individual well-being and performance (and that the lack of EI behaviors harms well-being and performance). For example, the dimension of "effective emotional orientation" includes behaviors such as (a) accepting the inevitability of a certain amount of unpleasant affect and negative self-evaluation and (b) understanding that private experiences (e.g., nervousness, fear) do not have to stop one from pursing a valued direction. The studies reviewed reveal that these behaviors predict task performance and long-term mental health. As another example, the dimension of "undermining fusion" includes behaviors such as recognizing that emotionally charged thoughts about life (e.g., thoughts of failure) are not equivalent to life. The studies reviewed reveal that fusion and focusing on negative possibilities have a negative impact on problem solving and cognitive tasks. Finally, the chapter discusses interesting training interventions that have been used successfully to build the EI behaviors in the model.

Chapter 3: An Ability Model of Emotional Intelligence: Implications for Assessment and Training, by Paulo N. Lopes, Stéphane Côté, and Peter Salovey, focuses on the ability theory of emotional intelligence developed by Salovey and Mayer in the early 1990s. This theory proposes that emotional intelligence encompasses four interrelated abilities: perceiving and expressing emotions, using emotions to facilitate thinking, understanding emotions, and managing emotions in self and others. Each of these abilities encompasses a set of lower order skills (e.g., managing emotions in self and others includes skills such as reframing negative events and empathic listening). The authors argue that this model of EI differs from other models by focusing on a narrower definition of the EI ability, one that can be differentiated from personality traits, motivational factors, and related skills (e.g., social skills). The authors recognize that when it comes to assessment and training, it is important to consider the roles of personality, motivation, and related skills. However, their unique focus has been on defining and measuring EI as an ability and a form of intelligence that is distinct from related concepts. They view emotional skills, abilities, and intelligence as forms of expertise that develop through learning and experience and are likely influenced by genetic factors.

As such, the research discussed in this chapter uses the Mayer–Salovey–Caruso Emotional Intelligence Test (MSCEIT), which assesses people's performance on the four dimensions of emotional intelligence through tasks such as decoding the emotional information conveyed by facial expressions and demonstrating understanding of blends of emotions and emotional dynamics. The MSCEIT is distinct from other measures of EI because it is not a self-report measure and therefore is a more objective measure of EI abilities.

The authors discuss the results of studies that have examined the influence of EI on task performance, leadership ability, and interpersonal competence. What makes this research powerful is that most of the researchers have controlled for the effects of variables such as personality, experience, and cognitive ability (IQ). Thus, one can be more confident that the positive impact of EI stands over and above the effects of other individual factors that may affect performance. The studies reviewed suggest that EI is associated with various measures of interpersonal competence including prosocial behavior, self-reports of the quality of interpersonal relationships, favorable ratings by peers on interpersonal sensitivity and reciprocal friendship and liking, and more positive and fewer negative interpersonal events. The authors also suggest that the "managing emotions" ability may have a stronger link to social interactions and interpersonal relationships than the other branches of emotional intelligence measured in the MSCEIT. With regard to work performance, the studies reviewed suggest that EI is associated with better outcomes in work groups, leadership qualities such as the ability to propose compelling goals and ideas, better performance in group decision-making activities, higher supervisor ratings of job performance, higher performance rankings from managers, and higher percentage increase in merit pay.

Finally, the chapter discusses ideas for training interventions that can be used to develop the EI abilities in their model. The authors call for more research evaluating the effectiveness of emotional skills training for adults.

Chapter 4: Core Competencies in Coaching Others to Overcome Dysfunctional Behavior, by Richard E. Boyatzis, presents two studies examining the competencies that differentiate successful peer coach/counselors working with alcoholism and substance abuse problems from less than successful peer coach/counselors. The study was conducted in the U.S. Navy. A competency is defined as a characteristic of an individual that is causally related to criterion-referenced effective performance in a job or situation. The author's purpose for reviewing these studies is to determine the roles of emotional intelligence competencies and cognitive competencies in explaining the success of coach/counselors. In this study, emotional intelligence is defined using Goleman's theory of emotional intelligence competencies.

In the first study, the authors identified a pool of 45 counselors with an average number of clients per coach/counselor of 49 and obtained nominations to identify a subsample that were considered "outstanding" coach/counselors. A second subsample of coach/counselors was nominated to serve as a comparison sample. The 26 coach/counselors selected into these samples were interviewed for 3 hrs using the critical event interview format. The interviews were content analyzed and produced a list of eight competencies that significantly differentiated the sample of outstanding performing coach/counselors from the comparison sample of average performing coach/counselors. The eight competencies included optimism about people's ability to change (in the self-management cluster of EI competencies), initiative (again, in the self-management cluster of EI), pattern recognition (a cognitive competency), client awareness (in the self-awareness cluster of EI), accurate self-assessment (in the self-awareness cluster of EI), ego maturity (in the self-management cluster of EI), empathy (in the social awareness cluster of EI), and emotional self-awareness (in the self-awareness cluster of EI competencies).

Results suggested that of the eight competencies originally identified, four of the EI competencies and the one cognitive competency could be considered valid differentiators of superior versus average coaching/counseling performance. These were empathy, initiative, client awareness, emotional self-awareness, and pattern recognition. In an extension of the study, a regression analysis was conducted and the EI competencies of empathy and emotional self-awareness distinguished effective counseling and predicted client work performance. The other three competencies, pattern recognition, initiative, and client awareness, contributed to overall effectiveness but did not add unique variance to the analysis.

This study is unique because few studies have attempted to identify coach/counselor behaviors that predict behavior change—most studies use satisfaction with coaches or counselors or perceptions of progress as indicators of coach or counselor effectiveness.

Chapter 5: The Role of Emotional Intelligence in Developing International Business Capability: EI Provides Traction, by Gerald Mount, presents an inductive, in-depth field study of the role of emotional intelligence competencies in five work roles in a major international petroleum corporation with extensive international operations. The five work roles include corporate strategist, international business developer, international negotiator, international business services manager, and international asset construction project manager with a total population of 387. The author chose to study these specific roles because together they represent the process of international business from strategic idea conceptualization to operational performance and revenue realization. In this study, emotional intelligence is defined using Goleman's theory of EI competencies.

Data were collected from three sources. The first source included 108 critical incident interviews that lasted between 2 and 3 hrs each. These interviews were conducted with criterion samples of "superior performing" employees in each of the five roles and "average performing" employees in each of the roles. Interviews were audiorecorded, transcribed verbatim, and coded by multiple coders using the Hay/McBer Competency Dictionary as a codebook and a few additional inductive competencies identified by the author.

A second source of data included 20 4-hr focus group sessions (four for each work role) conducted by the author with the senior employees within each of the five roles. Members of the focus groups identified the individual competencies they believed to be necessary by role incumbents to maximize the role's contribution to corporate goals.

The third source of data included the administration of the Hay/McBer Competency Rating Questionnaire (CRQ, which assess 24 generic competencies) to the full population of employees within each the five work roles being studied (65% response rate). In this questionnaire, role incumbents rated on a 1 to 5 Likert scale the relevance of each competency to superior performance in their work role.

Interview data revealed 10 core competencies that differentiated superior from average performers across the five work roles. Seven of these fall under the category of emotional intelligence competencies. They include, in order of relevance to performance, achievement orientation, impact and influence, self-confidence, teamwork and cooperation, organizational awareness, empathy, and international flexibility. Three of the relevant competencies fall under the category of cognitive intelligence. In order of relevance they include analytical thinking, conceptual thinking, and information seeking.

The survey data revealed competencies perceived to be critical but not identified in interview analyses. The most consistent of these included self-control and customer service orientation, both of which are emotional intelligence competencies.

In-depth analyses led the author to develop a theory of the interaction between IQ and EI in these five roles. Specifically, the author proposes that EI competencies create an environment that enables the cognitive intelligence competencies and technical skills and knowledge to be used effectively (traction), resulting in an organizational capability to achieve international business successes. Quotes and examples are provided to support this idea.

The results are particularly noteworthy because of the population studied. The capital-intensive, asset-based, international petroleum industry does not traditionally place value on employee skills that are not technical or financial.

Chapter 6: The International Business Case: Emotional Intelligence Competencies and Important Business Outcomes, by Fabio Sala, focuses on the emotional competence theory of emotional intelligence developed by Goleman and Boyatzis in the late 1990s. This theory proposes that emotional intelligence is manifested in a set of 18 workplace competencies. A competency is defined as a characteristic of an individual that is causally related to criterion-referenced effective performance in a job or situation. The 18 competencies in the competency theory of EI are organized into four clusters: self-awareness (including emotional self-awareness, accurate self-assessment, and self-confidence), self-management (including emotional self-control, transparency, conscientiousness, adaptability, achievement, initiative, and optimism), social awareness (including empathy, organizational awareness, and service orientation), and relationship management (developing others, inspirational leadership, influence, change catalyst, conflict management, and teamwork and collaboration). This model of EI differs from other models by focusing on the emotional intelligence competencies that lead to or cause effective or superior performance.

The chapter presents the results of three field studies examining emotional intelligence competencies and work performance in (a) South African insurance call center employees, (b) sales agents at Bass Brewers in the United Kingdom, and (c) business school graduates from Istanbul University in Turkey, 11 years after their graduation. Two aspects of these studies that stand out as unique include their international locations and the compelling performance data used in each study. In all three studies, emotional intelligence was measured using the Emotional Competence Inventory (ECI) developed by Boyatzis, Goleman, and the Hay Group. The ECI is a multirater survey that includes a 360 assessment in which the individual rates him- or herself and is rated by others on the frequency with which he or she demonstrates the behaviors in the EI competency model.

The study with South African insurance call center agents examined the relation between agents' ECI ratings (as completed by the agents' team leaders) in three call center environments and a composite of four objective performance measures of call center performance (e.g., amount of transactions processed within a period of time and percentage of successful sales transactions). In all three call center environments, performance was associated with the following EI competencies: self-confidence, trustworthiness, conscientiousness, initiative, influence, change catalyst, and conflict management.

The study with sales agents from Bass Brewers in the United Kingdom examined the relation between a composite of competency ratings on the ECI (including the ECI rated by self and manager) and six performance measures (e.g., annual performance ratings, customer service audits, number of new accounts, etc.) and a composite of all six performance measures. Performance data were assessed 6 months after the ECI was completed. This permits an argument for the predictive validity of the ECI. The composite ratings for the ECI self-rating and manager rating were found to be significantly associated with overall performance. More specifically, the ECI self-ratings were significantly related to number of new distribution points, number of new accounts, and career progression. The ECI manager ratings were significantly related to number of new accounts.

The study with Turkish business school graduates examined the relation between graduates' ECI ratings (as rated by self and as rated by another person) and aspects of career success and life satisfaction (e.g., salary, satisfaction with job, satisfaction with life, satisfaction with interpersonal relationships, etc.). Salary level was significantly associated with self-ratings and other ratings of self-awareness, self-management, social awareness, and social skills. Ratings of job satisfaction and life and interpersonal satisfaction were related to self-ECI ratings and other-ECI ratings with similar patterns as those described previously.

The author ends with a discussion of the limitations of these studies and with the suggestion that employers select employees who have EI competencies and work to develop EI competencies in other employees.

Chapter 7: Emotional Intelligence, Emotional Self-Awareness, and Team Effectiveness, by Peter J. Jordan and Neal M. Ashkanasy, examines the influence of individual emotional intelligence and individual emotional self-awareness on team effectiveness. Team effectiveness is defined and measured as team goal focus and team process effectiveness. Emotional intelligence is defined using Salovey and Mayer's theory of emotional intelligence. EI is measured through the use of the Workgroup Emotional Intelligence Profile (WEIP), developed and previously published by the authors and their colleagues (Jordan et al., 2002). The WEIP involves both self-assessment and peer (i.e., team member) assessment on survey items measuring the application of emotional intelligence in the team context. For example, one item asks, "When I'm angry with a member of my team, I can overcome that emotion quickly." The item is worded similarly in the peer-assessment version.

A strong emphasis in this chapter is on the hypothesized relation between team member emotional self-awareness and team effectiveness. The authors argue, as have previous theorists, that self-awareness is the cornerstone of emotional intelligence. They also argue that self-awareness is fundamental in team settings because it enables team members to resolve discrepancies between personal goals and team goals. Their review of the literature suggests that self-awareness is best measured not through self-reports or peer reports but through a comparative analysis of self-reports and peer reports. Thus, self-awareness in this study is measured through difference scores between self-reports and peer reports using the WEIP. Furthermore, the authors hypothesize that this link would be highest among members of the sample whose self-awareness scores were deemed accurate. In other words, if one's measurement of self-awareness is accurate (based on a comparative analysis), than self-awareness will be linked to team effectiveness.

The study was conducted with 140 students in a business communication course in an Australian university. Study participants worked together in self-managing teams for 10 weeks. Team effectiveness (defined as team goal focus and team process effectiveness) was measured through coding weekly team meeting reports. Results showed a significant relation between peer (team member) ratings of work group emotional intelligence and group effectiveness. As hypothesized, results using the sample of participants deemed accurate self-assessors showed significant relations between emotional self-awareness and team process effectiveness, emotional self-awareness and team goal focus, and emotional self-awareness and overall team effectiveness.

Study results suggest that organizations should spend time building team member emotional self-awareness because (a) it has the strongest link to team effectiveness and (b) it is the cornerstone of emotional intelligence and therefore is a good first step in developing abilities that may take longer to develop.

Chapter 8: Team Emotional Intelligence: What It Can Mean and How It can Affect Performance, by Hilary Anger Elfenbein, discusses two complimentary ways that the influence of emotional intelligence can be studied in the team context: first by examining the EI of the individual members in a team, and second by examining how much EI team members display in their interactions with each other. The first way examines EI as an individual resource that team members bring to a team. The second way examines EI as patterns of interaction in the team. The author proceeds to review research that she and her colleagues have conducted that supports the relevance of both forms of EI to team performance.

The author reviews two studies that support the relation between team member EI and team performance. In the first study, team member EI was measured as the ability to recognize emotion in others and was tested using the Diagnostic Analysis of Nonverbal Accuracy (DANVA), which tested for accuracy of identifying emotion in photographs. The study found that teams with higher average ability for emotion recognition also scored higher on tests of team psychological safety, collaborative decision making, and team learning and lower on levels of team conflict. A second study found that average team member scores on emotion recognition were associated with higher self-reported performance and had greater retention of team members over a challenging year period. Results showed there was a benefit for teams whose members overall had a high minimum score on the DANVA, that is, teams that had no members with low emotion recognition ability. There was not a benefit for teams whose members had a high maximum DANVA score. Teams with members who had high levels of variability in their emotion recognition scores suffered negative consequences. In these teams, members reported lower levels of psychological safety, lower levels of retention of members (i.e., higher turnover), lower self-reported performance, and lower performance as rated by their management. In sum, these two studies reveal that teams with members scoring high in EI, measured as emotion recognition, and teams with members that have similar levels of EI perform the highest.

For evidence examining the relation between team EI and team performance when EI is measured as patterns of behavior or norms, the author reviews a study conducted with her colleagues that measured how well each member on a team could understand his or her other team members' expressions of emotions. Teams with members who could accurately understand the emotional expressions of other team members were found to be higher performing teams. In fact, the measure predicted 40% of the variance in team member performance. Interestingly, greater accuracy in understanding team members' positive emotions predicted better team performance, whereas greater accuracy with negative emotions actually predicted worse team performance. It appeared that understanding negative emotions did not necessarily mean that teams knew how to translate this sensitivity into productive use.

The chapter concludes with a discussion of the implications of the study findings for research and practice.

In chapter 9: About the "I" in the EI Construct: A More Social Approach to Intelligence and Its Performance Implications, by A. Alexandra Michel and Karen A. Jehn, the authors present theory and research suggesting that emotional intelligence is not a fully social approach to social intelligence (defined as effective adaptation to the social context) and, thus, falls short of fully predicting individual and team effectiveness. Specifically, the authors argue that when emotion is activated (i.e., emotion is experienced), the self-concept including its cognitive and motivational processes is also activated. As such, the person experiences the social context in relation to self-relevant information, which disconnects the person from unique and dynamic aspects of the social context. Thus, "thinking about emotion" unintentionally impedes social intelligence by diverting or drawing attention away from the social context and situation-specific information. The authors argue that because emotional intelligence is self-focused, it can unwittingly decrease rather than increase social intelligence. Social intelligence, as defined by the authors, requires one to step out of oneself and become completely involved in the situation.

The authors came to their conclusions through their 2-year ethnographic study of two comparable Wall Street investment banks, which they refer to as "People Bank" and "Organization Bank." During this research, the authors came to recognize two distinct approaches to the work with clients. Employees at People Bank relied on their own cognitive, motivational, and emotional resources and the regulation of those resources to be effective. Employees at Organization Bank relied less on regulating their own resources and more on using resources available in the social situation. Rich examples of how these differences played out in the two banks are provided. For example, the authors describe a situation in which both banks were competing for the same client. The researchers were privy to the preparations for the client meetings. The People Bank team anticipated client needs, showed up with a 90-page report, and presented themselves as fully competent at the meeting. The Organization Bank team showed up with a 12-page spreadsheet, weren't sure how their resources would apply, and chose to focus on the situation in the meeting for guidance. Thus, during the meeting they worked with the client to determine client needs. This example is used to illustrate the point that activation of the person's self with its abstract concepts (cognition, motivation, and emotion) gets in the way of sensitivity to the situation and thereby impedes social intelligence. The authors refer to engagement with concrete aspects of the situation as "direct involvement" and compare it to their term *identity-induced involvement*, which is used to describe engagement when the "self" is involved. The term *direct* indicates that the involvement is not mediated by constant reference to the self-concept. The authors argue that direct involvement expands the cognitive resources the individual uses from a primary reliance on mental resources to a flexible use of both mental and social resources including task structures, other people, and objects.

The authors' theory is supported by continuous data collection over the 2 years they spent at the banks. For example, when they interviewed employees of the two banks, they found two very different answers to questions about individual employee skills and attributes. At People Bank, employees could quickly and easily elaborate on their personal attributes and on the attributes they ideally wished to possess. In Organization Bank, employees had great difficulty answering questions about themselves and their attributes—they would answer with responses such as, "You know, that really depends on the situation." The researchers subsequently measured self-schemas in members of each bank and through the use of multiple methods found the Organization Bank members, compared with the People Bank members, to be aschematic with regard to the "self." That is, Organization Bank members rarely reflected on and rarely activated the abstract attributes that constitute the self-concept. In text analysis, they also less frequently used the term *I*. Also, the frequency with which People Bank members used the term *I* was consistent across all situations, whereas the frequency with which Organization Bank members used the term *I* varied across situations. Along with more often thinking about themselves and their attributes, the People Bank employees were found to more often think about emotions and regulating emotions because they were aware of their need to control their anxiety and anger so that these emotions would not interfere with their performance.

The greater effectiveness of Organization Bank and the authors' in-depth analyses led them to present an alternative model for social intelligence that combines current conceptions of EI with the authors' conception of direct involvement in the situation. The model proposes that social intelligence involves two forms of involvement: (a) identity-induced involvement (or EI as defined by Salovey and Mayer, 1990) and self-regulation through one's own mental resources, and (b) direct involvement, which involves self-regulation through situationally available resources, that is, by getting directly involved in the concrete situation. It is further proposed that the direct involvement model differs from and complements Salovey and Mayer's model in which the integration between cognitive and emotional processes is located within the individual and requires an individual aptitude. The direct involvement model proposes that managing emotions effectively involves connecting the mind with extramental resources available in the situation.

The implications for this model of social intelligence are discussed. These include the proposition that the unit of analysis for research and intervention should be the situation and situated activity, instead of the individual.

Chapter 10: The Link Between Group Emotional Competence and Group Effectiveness, by Steven B. Wolff, Vanessa Urch Druskat, Elizabeth Stubbs Koman, and Tracey Eira Messer, follows the journey of these researchers as they develop a theory of group-level emotional competence, test their theory, refine their measures, and refine their theory. The authors argue that because work groups exist to enable social interaction, debate, and innovation, groups are hotbeds for emotion. However, because groups are greater than the sum of their parts, individual team member EI cannot by itself manage emotion in teams. Thus, the authors developed a "group emotional competence theory," which proposes that when the group as a whole is aware of emotion and effectively manages that emotion, it has a positive influence on team social capital and team effectiveness.

Group emotional competence theory is rooted in three premises. The first premise is that behavior in groups is not random; it is structured through norms defined as standards or informal rules adopted by group members to ensure predictability in member behavior. The second premise is that activities and interactions in groups occur at three levels: individual (team member) level, group level, and cross-boundary level (because all work groups exist within larger systems). The third premise is that emotional competence in groups involves awareness and management of emotion at these three levels of group dynamics.

Following these three premises, it is proposed that in every group an emotional structure emerges and influences group norms about emotion. Emotionally competent groups are proposed to develop an emotional structure that consists of six categories of norms that involve (a) emotional awareness and (b) management of emotion at the individual, group, and cross-boundary levels. The theory further proposes that building these norms leads to three constructive emergent states within a group: group trust or safety, group efficacy, and group networks. These emergent states, which together are referred to as "group social capital" (i.e., value added by the structure and quality of social relationships), are proposed to lead to effective task processes in groups such as cooperation and effective boundary management, which lead to group effectiveness.

The group emotional competence theory of group effectiveness makes three contributions to current knowledge. First, it proposes a manifestation of EI at the group level. Second, it is the first theory to propose that an emotional structure in groups is at the root of constructive group interaction and, thus, group effectiveness. Third, it defines an effective emotional structure as consisting of nine team norms that nest within the six categories discussed previously. These team norms are interpersonal understanding, confronting members who break norms, caring behavior, team self-evaluation, creating resources for working with emotion, creating an optimistic environment, proactive problem solving, organizational understanding, and building external relationships.

The latter part of the chapter presents two studies conducted with six of the nine norms. Both studies support the theory. Study 1 was conducted with MBAs who worked together in teams of eight for a full year. Results showed that norms of interpersonal understanding, team self-evaluation, proactive problem solving, organizational understanding, and building external relationships were significantly correlated with team performance measures at intervals of 1 month and 6 months after norm measurement. Study 2 took a more sophisticated look at the model. It was conducted in six organizations. In this study it was predicted and found that the relation between the same six norms and team performance would be mediated by the social capital variables of trust/safety, efficacy, and networks.

The authors continue discussing their research journey by describing a new group emotional competence questionnaire that was developed and validated by a graduate student at Rutgers University. This questionnaire measures the nine norms that define the effective emotional structure. The authors describe current research being conducted with this survey, and they discuss the implications of their theory and their findings for research and practice.

Chapter 11: A Practitioner's Research Agenda: Exploring Real-World Applications and Issues, by Marilyn K. Gowing and her colleagues, discusses the authors' guidance on what steps need to be taken to bring emotional intelligence into organizations based on the authors' experiences dealing with the introduction and application of emotional intelligence characteristics in the management practices of large complex organizations. Although the authors focus primarily on application (i.e., how you do it), they also identify the underlying research concerns surrounding these application issues. True to the mission of the Consortium for Research of Emotional Intelligence in Organizations (CREIO), which is to aid in the advancement of research and practice related to emotional intelligence in organizations, the chapter discusses a number of research partnerships undertaken by CREIO members. These include the development of the U.S. Government Office of Personnel Management's (OPM) Senior Executive Service Competency Model, Johnson and Johnson's (JNJ) Leadership Competency Model, the Defense Finance and Accounting Service's (DFAS) EI Professional Certification Program, and OPM's EI Index for Emotionally Intelligent Organizations. Results of an extensive literature review to identify the competencies that differentiated effective leaders were incorporated into a survey administered to a random sample of 20,000 federal government employees (response 50%) yielding a Leadership Effectiveness Framework of 22 managerial competencies that were later stratified by level of supervisory responsibility. These characteristics were then clustered into five categories: leading change, leading people, results driven, building coalitions/communication, and business acumen. The authors discuss the application of these clusters to the practices of selection, development, and evaluation of nearly 7,000 members of the government's Senior Executive Services. The authors also describe the results of a crosswalk process to map the OPM competency clusters to Goleman's model of emotional intelligence competencies and the implications of discontinuities across competency frameworks with explanations for the important differences and nuances in operational definitions.

The authors describe the process employed by Johnson and Johnson Corporation (JNJ) to integrate EI competencies into their existing framework of leadership behaviors using a Delphi technique with five to six experts to identify gaps between the different behavioral groups for further investigation by multirater surveys across an international population of 1,030 raters. Using the outcomes from these studies, JNJ modified its framework of leadership behaviors to include the distinguishing emotional intelligence competencies found to be missing from the model. This enhanced model has been integrated into the management practices of performance review and succession planning/development.

The authors suggest that practitioners wishing to incorporate EI behaviors in their organizations need to determine the alignment between existing behavior frameworks and the EI behaviors and, if such alignment exists, explore how the EI behaviors relate to effective individual and organizational performance outcomes. The authors' rich discussion of the process of validating EI as a component of actual performance reinforces the argument for establishing a foundation if organizations are to be successful in introducing EI training in their leadership development programs. Examples are provided of both public and private sector approaches for EI development programs. Finally, the authors call for practitioners/researchers to institute pre and post individual and team EI performance measures to determine effectiveness of EI training, especially if post measures are structured for 6-month to 1-year intervals to assess actual impact on the job in organizational settings.

This chapter addresses the concerns of many practitioners interested in introducing EI behaviors in organizations with existing leadership behavioral models and especially how to overcome the organizational inertia associated with status quo frameworks irrespective of their contribution to performance.

In chapter 12: Epilogue: The Agenda for Future Research, by Peter Salovey, one of the pioneers of emotional intelligence, the author discusses the evolution of EI to its present state and some of the issues emerging as appropriate for future consideration.

He notes that great strides have been made in the single decade since the utility and importance of emotional intelligence were popularized in Goleman's best-selling book. The chapters in the present volume suggest that the idea of an emotional intelligence has been useful to the field of organizational behavior and that outcomes relevant to business success are predicted by skills and competencies not traditionally thought to be job related, in the technical sense, or measured by conventional tests of intelligence.

Perhaps in light of these research achievements and the popular appeal of the emotional intelligence construct, it is timely to pause and reflect on research that still needs to be carried out. Salovey's comments are by no means meant as criticism of the significant scholarship represented in the chapters. Rather, as with any research enterprise, he suggests that new findings raise new questions.

One of his points is to note that what is called emotional intelligence varies considerably from investigator to investigator (let alone from practitioner to practitioner). He believes that emotional intelligence should be clearly distinguished from related constructs such as more cognitively oriented intelligences, personality traits, social skills, and the collection of "good attributes" that only tangentially involve emotion (e.g., zeal, persistence, and appreciating diversity).

He also makes the point that critics' claim of a scientific construct of the positive qualities of humans not measured by traditional tests of intelligence is untenable and argues that to call something emotional intelligence it should have something to do with emotions and with intelligence. Whether these constructions are best viewed as a "true" intelligence or as sets of competencies, collections of skills, or behavior styles is an interesting but less critical issue.

In this chapter he discusses the problems associated with measures purporting to assess emotional intelligence generally based on either self-report, performance on ability tests, or the ratings of others in one's social or workplace environment (360 assessments) without intercorrelations among the measures. This leads to the critical question empirically: Is there anything new here? The multiple correlations between some measures of emotional intelligence and standard measures of personality are alarmingly high such that it is difficult to defend against the charge that emotional intelligence is "nothing but old wine in new bottles," especially if the measures are substantially overlapped with preexisting constructs.

Salovey closes by advising the need for better studies of the efficacy of interventions designed to enhance the competencies involved in emotional intelligence to convince the skeptics, especially if it includes hard-headed, cost-effectiveness modeling.

Certainly, a harder headed approach to emotional intelligence will serve scientists and practitioners alike quite well. We need to be able to figure out those ingredients of emotional intelligence that are truly novel, that are associated with important outcomes in the workplace, and that are teachable while being critical of overly broad conceptualizations and overly optimistic claims. Salovey suggests we should also feel some collective pride: The contributors to this book have all, in various ways, advanced an important understanding—that when it comes to job-related success, technical skills and analytic intelligence are not enough, and we can begin to specify what else is needed. Although such a view may not be revolutionary, it motivates important directions for future research and professional practice.

REFERENCES

Ashforth, B., & Humphrey, R. E. (1995). Emotions in the workplace: A reappraisal. *Human Relations, 48*, 97–125.

Ashkanasy, N. M., Hartel, C. E. J., & Zerbe, W. J. (2000). Emotions in the workplace: Research, theory, and practice. In N. M. Ashkanasy, C. E. J. Hartel, & W. J. Zerbe (Eds.), *Emotions in the workplace* pp. 3–18). Westport, CT: Quorum.

Bales, R. F. (1950). *Interaction process analysis: A method for the study of small groups.* Chicago: University of Chicago Press.

Bales, R. F. (1953). The equilibrium problem in small groups. In T. Parsons, R. F. Bales, & E. A. Shils (Eds.), *Working papers in the theory of action* (pp. 111–161). New York: Free Press.

Bar-On, R. (1997). *The Emotional Quotient Inventory (EQ-I): Technical manual.* Toronto: Multi-Health Systems.

Bar-On, R., & Parker, J. D. A. (2000). *Handbook of emotional intelligence.* San Francisco: Jossey-Bass.

Barsade, S. G., & Gibson, D. E. (1998). Group emotion: A view from top and bottom. In D. Gruenfeld (Ed.), *Composition* (pp. 81–102). Stamford, CT: JAI.

Ciarrochi, J., Chan, A. Y. C., & Caputi, P. (2000). A critical evaluation of the emotional intelligence construct. *Personality and Individual Differences, 28,* 539–561.

Ciarrochi, J., Forgas, J., & Mayer, J. D. (2001). *Emotional intelligence and everyday life: A scientific inquiry.* Philadelphia, PA: Psychological Press.

Cherniss, C., & Goleman, D. (Eds.). (2001). *The emotionally intelligent workplace: How to select for, measure, and improve emotional intelligence in individuals, groups, and organizations.* San Francisco: Jossey-Bass.

Damasio, A. (1994). *Descartes' error: Emotion, reason and the human brain.* New York: Avon.

Damasio, A. (1999). *The feeling of what happens.* New York: Harcourt Brace.

Druskat, V. U., & Wolff, S. B. (2001). Group emotional intelligence and its influence on group effectiveness. In C. Cherniss & D. Goleman (Eds.), *The emotionally intelligent workplace* (pp. 132–156). San Francisco: Jossey-Bass.

Elfenbein, H. A., & Ambady, N. (2002). On the universality and cultural specificity of emotion recognition: A meta-analysis. *Psychological Bulletin, 128,* 203–235.

Goleman, D. (1995). *Emotional intelligence.* New York: Bantam Books.

Goleman, D. (1998). *Working with emotional intelligence.* New York: Bantam Books.

Goleman, D. (2001). Emotional intelligence: Issues in paradigm building. In C. Cherniss & D. Goleman (Eds.), *The emotionally intelligent workplace* (pp. 13–26). San Francisco: Jossey-Bass.

Goleman, D., Boyatzis, R., & McKee, A. (2002). *Primal leadership.* Boston: Harvard Business School Press.

Homans, G. (1950). *The human group.* New York: Harcourt Brace Jovanovich.

Janis, I. L. (1982). *Groupthink.* Boston: Houghton Mifflin.

Jordan, P. J., Ashkanasy, N. M., Härtel, C. E. J., & Hooper, G. S. (2002). Workgroup emotional intelligence: Scale development and relationship to team process effectiveness and goal focus. *Human Resource Management Review, 12,* 195–214.

Lewis, M., & Haviland-Jones, J. M. (2000). *Handbook of emotions* (2nd ed.). New York: Guilford.

Levy, R. I. (1984). Emotion, knowing, and culture. In R. A. Sweder & R. A. LeVine (Eds.), *Culture theory: Essays on mind, self, and emotion* (pp. 214–237). Cambridge, UK: Cambridge University Press.

Lopes, P. N., Salovey, P., & Straus, R. (2003). Emotional intelligence, personality, and the perceived quality of social relationships. *Personality & Individual Differences, 35,* 641–658.

Martin, J., Knopoff, K., & Beckman, C. (1998). An alternative to bureaucratic impersonality and emotional labor: Bounded emotionality at The Body Shop. *Administrative Science Quarterly, 43,* 429–469.

Mayer, J. D., & Salovey, P. (1997). What is emotional intelligence? In P. Salovey & D. J. Sluyter (Eds.), *Emotional development and emotional intelligence: Educational implications* (pp. 3–31). New York: Basic Books.

Mayer, J. D., Salovey, P., & Caruso, D. (1999). Emotional intelligence meets traditional standards for an intelligence. *Intelligence, 27,* 267–298.

Mayer, J. D., Salovey, P., Caruso, D., & Sitarenios, G. (2003). Measuring emotional intelligence with the MSCEIT V2.0. *Emotion, 3,* 97–105.

Ollilainen, M. (2000). Gendering emotions, gendering teams: Construction of emotions in self-managing teamwork. In N. M. Ashkanasy, C. E. J. Hartel, & W. J. Zerbe (Eds.), *Emotions in the workplace* (pp. 3–18). Westport, CT: Quorum.

Sala, F. (2002). *Emotional Competence Inventory (ECI): Technical manual.* Boston: Hay/McBer Group.

Salovey, P., Bedell, B. T., et al. (2000). Current directions in emotional intelligence research. In M. Lewis & J. M. Haviland-Jones (Eds.), *Handbook of emotions* (2nd ed., pp. 504–522). New York: Guilford.

Salovey, P., & Mayer, J. D. (1990). Emotional intelligence. *Imagination, Cognition, and Personality, 9*(3), 185–211.

Part I

EMOTIONAL INTELLIGENCE
AND INDIVIDUAL PERFORMANCE
EFFECTIVENESS

Chapter 1

The Impact of Emotional Intelligence on Performance

Reuven Bar-On
University of Texas Medical Branch

Richard Handley
United States Air Force

Suzanne Fund
Israeli Defense Forces

Much has been said about the impact of emotional intelligence (EI) on human performance since the 1995 publication of a best-seller by the same name (Goleman, 1995). However, a great deal of what has been said is, unfortunately, based on supposition rather than scientific research. It is the purpose of this chapter to empirically demonstrate that EI does indeed impact performance.

Rather than beginning with an in-depth and lengthy review of the EI literature from Charles Darwin (Darwin, 1872/1965) to the present, exhaustively comparing what we want to do with what others have and have not done, we will suffice to explain only what we have found, how we found it, and how it may be applied to improve individual and organizational performance. In an effort "to tell it like it is," our chapter presents the empirical evidence that we have regarding the impact of emotional intelligence on performance. Findings are presented that might help explain why some people function better than others, assume positions of leadership, and even volunteer for highly stressful and potentially dangerous tasks at times, whereas others are unable to emotionally and socially deal with daily demands in a more intelligent and effective manner.

Two major studies provide the foundation for our discussion. One study was conducted in the U.S. Air Force (USAF) and the other in the Israeli Defense Forces (IDF). To the best of our knowledge, the former is the first study that has directly examined the impact of emotional intelligence on occupational performance (Handley, 1997), and the latter is the most extensive validity study conducted to date based on over 5,000 participants during a 3-year period. Both the USAF and IDF were interested in examining the impact of EI on performance and to see if it could be applied in recruiting the right people for the job and reducing mismatches. The USAF was interested in seeing if EI assessment could help predict performance in military recruiters. More specifically, they wanted to improve their recruitment of successful recruiters and decrease the high cost of mismatches. Essentially, they were asking: Do people with higher EQs make more effective recruiters, and how can we use this information to recruit them if so? In addition to examining the extent to which EI assessment could improve their ability to evaluate new recruits in general, the IDF also expressed a specific interest in examining if this type of assessment could help identify leadership potential as well as predict performance and attrition among recruits who serve in combat units that demand performance in stressful and potentially dangerous situations.

The Bar-On model of emotional and social intelligence provides the theoretical foundation of the present chapter, and the Emotional Quotient Inventory (EQ-i) was used in both studies to assess and examine various aspects of this construct. Performance ratings were based on individual productivity in the USAF study and on peer nomination, criterion group membership, and commander evaluations in the IDF study. The conceptual model and psychometric measure of EI, the databases, as well as the method of rating performance used in both studies are explained. The EI models that were found to significantly predict performance are described in depth. The implications of these models are discussed, and possibilities are explored for applying them in recruiting, hiring, training, and promoting "the right people with the right stuff."

THEORETICAL FRAMEWORK

Although the term *emotional intelligence* was coined in 1966 by Leuner, the general concept was first defined by Thorndike in 1920 and the construct itself was initially studied by Darwin as early as 1837 (Darwin, 1872/1965). From Darwin to the present, most descriptions of this construct have included one or more of the following key components: (a) the ability to understand and express oneself; (b) the ability to understand others and relate with them; (c) the ability to manage and control emotions; (d) the ability to manage change, adapt, and solve problems of a personal and interpersonal nature; and (e) the ability to generate positive mood and to be self-motivated. The *Encyclopedia of Applied Psychology* (in press) describes three major conceptual models of emotional intelligence, which are the Salovey–Mayer model, the Goleman model, and the Bar-On model. The

Bar-On model of "emotional and social intelligence" provides the theoretical framework for the present chapter. Bar-On's definition of this construct states that emotional and social intelligence is a cross-section of interrelated emotional and social competencies that determine how effectively we understand and express ourselves, understand others and relate with them, and cope with daily demands and pressures (Bar-On, 2000). The emotional and social competencies described in this conceptualization of the construct include the five key components described previously, and each of these components comprises a number of closely related emotional and social competencies, all of which are measured by the EQ-i as defined in the appendix. After more than two decades of empirically developing this model, the senior coauthor of this chapter is now convinced that self-motivation is a facilitator of emotionally and socially intelligent behavior rather than an actual component of the construct itself (Bar-On, 2000).

METHOD

EI Assessment in the USAF and IDF Studies

The Bar-On Emotional Quotient Inventory was used to measure various aspects of emotional intelligence in both of the studies that are presented in this chapter. According to the *Encyclopedia of Applied Psychology* (in press), the three most popular measures of emotional intelligence are the Mayer–Salovey–Caruso Emotional Intelligence Test (MSCEIT; Mayer, Salovey, & Caruso, 2002), the Emotional Competence Inventory (ECI; Boyatzis, Goleman, & Hay Group, 2001), and the Bar-On Emotional Quotient Inventory (EQ-i; Bar-On, 1997a). The EQ-i is a self-report measure of emotionally and socially intelligent behavior, which provides an estimate of one's underlying emotional and social intelligence. The EQ-i was the first EI measure to be published by a psychological test publisher and the first such measure to be reviewed in the *Buros Mental Measurement Yearbook* (Plake & Impara, 1999). More than one million assessments have been administered worldwide during the first 5 years since its publication in 1997, making it the most widely used EI measure. A detailed description of the psychometric properties of this measure and how it was developed is found in the instrument's technical manual (Bar-On, 1997b), in the *Buros Mental Measurement Yearbook* (Plake & Impara, 1999); and in a recent publication by the senior coauthor (Bar-On, 2004). In brief, the EQ-i comprises 133 items and uses a 5-point response scale with a textual response format ranging from *very seldom or not true of me* (1) to *very often true of me or true of me* (5). A list of the inventory's items is found in the *EQ-i Technical Manual* (Bar-On,

1997b). The individual's responses render a total EQ score and the following five composite scale scores comprising 15 subscale scores:

- Intrapersonal (comprising Self-Regard, Emotional Self-Awareness, As-
  sertiveness, Independence, and Self-Actualization)
- Interpersonal (comprising Empathy, Social Responsibility, and Inter-
  personal Relationship)
- Stress Management (comprising Stress Tolerance and Impulse Con-
  trol)
- Adaptability (comprising Reality-Testing, Flexibility, and Problem-
  Solving)
- General Mood (comprising Optimism and Happiness)

A brief description of the emotional and social intelligence competencies
measured by the 15 subscales is found in the Appendix. The EQ-i was developed over a period of 17 years and normed (standardized) on 3,831 adults
in North America. It has been translated into more than 30 languages, and
data have been collected in numerous settings around the world. Raw
scores are computer-tabulated and automatically converted into standard
scores based on a mean of 100 and standard deviations of 15. The EQ-i has a
built-in correction factor that automatically adjusts the scale scores based
on scores obtained from the Positive Impression and Negative Impression
scales (two of the instrument's validity indexes); this is an important
psychometric feature for self-report measures in that it reduces the potentially distorting effects of response bias, thereby increasing the accuracy of
the results obtained. The correlation between the EQ-i self-assessment of
emotionally intelligent behavior and ratings of this behavior made by
friends and family members is .69 based on a North American sample of
185 (Bar-On & Handley, 2003). It is also important to point out that brain-
damaged individuals suffering from anosognosia (the lack of self-awareness) obtained scores on the Emotional Self-Awareness subscale, and on
other closely related subscales like Assertiveness, that were significantly
lower than a control group (Bar-On, Tranel, Denburg, & Bechara, 2003).
These findings suggest that this particular self-report measure is capable of
fairly accurately assessing emotional intelligence even in respondents
whose emotional intelligence is below average. The EQ-i is acknowledged
as a valid and reliable measure of emotionally and socially intelligent behavior based on independent review (Plake & Impara, 1999). Moreover, the
EQ-i is significantly correlated with other measures that assess various aspects of this construct—for example, with the Mayer–Salovey–Caruso Emotional Intelligence Test, the Trait Meta Mood Scale, the Emotional Intelligence Questionnaire, and the 20-item Toronto Alexithymia Scale (Bar-On,

2000) and more recently with the Emotional Intelligence Scale (Kohan & Mazmanian, 2003). This suggests that the EQ-i indeed measures various aspects of emotional intelligence.

**Participants, Performance Ratings, and Data Collection
in the USAF Study**

After we received permission from the U.S. Air Force, 1,171 recruiters agreed to participate in this study to determine the impact of EI on occupational performance. This rather large number of volunteers represented approximately 70% of all Air Force recruiters at the time this study was conducted in 1996. The participants were from every state in the United States, and the vast majority of them were White (75%) males (91%) with an average age of 33. To assess their EI, they were all administered the EQ-i, and these scores were then compared with their performance as recruiters. The USAF defined high performance among recruiters as meeting or exceeding 100% of their annual recruitment quotas, whereas low performance was defined as meeting less than 80%. Using this operational definition of performance, we divided the USAF database into a group of 477 high performers and 114 low performers. The results presented in this chapter are based on comparing the EI of 114 low performers with that of a randomly selected group of 114 recruiters among the 477 high performers. Recruiters were assigned to geographical regions in a way that gave each of them a comparable number of potential recruits so that they had a relatively equal chance to meet annual quotas, which were determined by population density, military propensity, and past recruitment success in a particular region.

**Participants, Performance Ratings, and Data Collection
in the IDF Study**

The database used in the IDF study comprised the following three samples, which included a total of 5,412 recruits:

- Combatants ($n = 2,428$)
- Noncombatants ($n = 2,514$)
- Officer trainees ($n = 470$)

The age of the combatants ranged from 18 to 19 when they completed the EQ-i, during the first 2 weeks of basic training in one of eight different combat units; a few of these recruits were later involved in noncombatant roles, and some of them completed active service as officers. The noncombatants completed the EQ-i at the age of 17 to 18 in the Office of Mobilization before induction into active service; although some of these recruits ended up in combat units, very few of them were trained to be officers during their tour of duty. The officer trainees were between the age of 19 and 20 when they completed the EQ-i during officer training.

Four different analyses were performed on these three samples in the IDF database to examine the impact of EI on performance.

In the first analysis, 335 recruits who obtained the same performance ratings by their commanders over a period of 6 to 12 months were identified among the sample of combatants ($n = 2,428$); the first time their performance was rated was approximately 3 months after they completed the EQ-i, and the second time was approximately 6 to 12 months later. This consistency in performance ratings between raters based on the same factors over a number of months represents a very robust assessment of performance. The performance of each soldier was rated on a 7-point scale indicating how well the commander thought the soldier (a) performs professionally, (b) cooperates with others, (c) fits in socially, (d) performs under pressure, (e) can be counted on, and (f) should remain in the unit. An overall performance score was created for each soldier by summing the ratings obtained in each of these six areas. Based on quartiles, the soldiers were divided into high and low performers each time they were rated. The EI of the top 25% ($n = 63$) was then compared with the EI of the bottom 25% ($n = 67$). In addition to examining the impact of EI on performance, this approach allowed us to observe the predictive validity of EI assessment over a period of approximately 1 year.

In the second analysis that was carried out on this database, 240 soldiers from an elite fighting unit were selected from the sample of combatants ($n = 2,428$), and their EI was compared with that of a randomly selected group of 240 recruits from the sample of 2,514 noncombatants.[1] This comparison represents an additional approach to examining the relationship of EI to different levels of performance. Whereas one group of soldiers were required to perform a wide variety of noncombatant functions for the most part, the other group found themselves in units that demanded performance in highly stressful, dangerous, and life-threatening situations at times. We thought that this represented a measure of performance in very challenging conditions.

In the third analysis, we selected a group of 1,096 recruits from the sample of 2,514 noncombatants who were identified by their peers, during basic training, as being suitable for command leadership. Their peers were asked: "Choose those people in your unit who are most suitable to be offi-

---

[1]As was previously mentioned, the sample of noncombatants included some recruits who ended up in combat units or in officer training. In retrospect, however, these numbers were nearly negligible and would probably not have significantly altered the results.

cers, those who you think have leadership potential." A total score for "leadership potential" was created by calculating the number of times they were nominated by their peers for possessing this particular attribute. The scores were then divided into upper and lower quartiles to identify recruits with high and low leadership potential (i.e., those who received the highest peer nominations vs. those who received the lowest). The EI of the bottom 25% ($n = 268$) was compared with that of the upper 25% ($n = 268$), who were thought to possess higher leadership potential. We hoped that this comparison would shed light on the relationship of EI to different levels of performance as well. Whereas one group of recruits were expected to perform in a wide variety of occupations the best they could, those perceived to be suitable for command leadership may have been thought to perform better than the rest and perhaps on a higher and more responsible level.

In the fourth analysis carried out, 470 officer trainees were compared with a randomly selected group of 470 recruits from the sample of 2,513 noncombatants.[2] This was thought to represent a very robust approach to identifying leadership potential, because a group of recruits who were actually enrolled in officer training were compared with a group of recruits who did not meet the minimum requirements for officer training, did not pass the personal screening required, or did not express a desire to be officers.

RESULTS

The Ability of EI Models to Predict Occupational Performance in Recruiters

Our first analysis of the USAF data consisted of simply comparing the total EQ scores between the high- and low-performing recruiters (i.e., those who were able to meet or exceed 100% of their annual recruitment quotas and those who were unable to meet more than 80% of their quotas as was previously described). A t test for independent groups revealed that the average total EQ score for the high performers was 102 in comparison to 95 for the low performers ($t = 3.36$, $p = .001$) representing a significant difference between them. These initial results suggested that successful recruiters are more emotionally intelligent than less successful ones, and vice versa.

Discriminant function analysis was then applied to the data, using the ability to meet annual recruitment quotas as the dependent variable (performance) and the 15 EQ-i subscales as the independent variables (EI). The results of a stepwise forward analysis determined that the EI model that

---

[2]See comments in the previous footnote.

TABLE 1.1
The EI Model That Best Predicts Performance
in USAF Recruiters ($n = 228$)

EI Predictors	Low Performers	High Performers	Lambda	F Value	p Level
Assertiveness	93	105	.831	33.34	<.000
Interpersonal Relationship	97	98	.789	20.62	<.000
Happiness	92	99	.761	12.20	.001
Empathy	99	100	.754	10.20	.002
Stress Tolerance	95	100	.754	10.10	.002
Social Responsibility	103	103	.753	10.00	.002
Problem-Solving	94	103	.736	4.78	.030

Note. Only those predictors with $p \leq .05$ are presented.

best predicts performance in recruiters comprises the emotional and social competencies listed in Table 1.1.

The higher the lambda and F value in Table 1.1, the stronger the predictive value of the EI competency in the model; based on the model that emerged, this would mean that the most important EI competency needed by recruiters appears to be assertiveness, which makes sense when we think about what recruiters do. This model rendered a canonical R of .53, suggesting that at least 28% of the variance in the performance of recruiters can be accounted for by emotional intelligence. And the ability of this model to identify high and low performance in recruiters is 72% accurate (based on the classification matrix, which is generated by discriminant function analysis). This means that nearly 7 of 10 individuals can be correctly identified as having the potential for being a high- or low-performing recruiter when this model is used. And when this model was used to select recruiters in the USAF, the results were astonishing, as described in the discussion.

The Ability of EI Models to Predict Performance in Recruits Serving in Combat Units

To expand the examination of the relationship between emotional intelligence and performance, we observed 335 combat soldiers whose performance was rated in six major areas on two separate occasions over a period of 6 to 12 months as was previously described. This also provided a very robust approach for examining the ability of EI assessment to predict performance over a year. The total EQ score for the high performers proved to be significantly higher than for the low performers (107 vs. 96; $t = 5.18$, $p < .000$). When we used performance as the dependent variable and the 15 EQ-i

TABLE 1.2
The EI Model That Best Predicts Performance in
IDF Recruits Serving in Combat Units (n = 335)

EI Predictors	Low Performers	High Performers	Lambda	F Value	p Level
Self-Regard	93	105	.731	6.48	.012
Impulse Control	98	108	.721	4.68	.032
Emotional Self-Awareness	102	102	.720	4.47	.037
Reality-Testing	98	107	.720	4.50	.036

Note. Only those predictors with $p \le .05$ are presented.

subscale scores as the independent variables, discriminant function analysis revealed a four-factor EI model, which is presented in Table 1.2.

This model rendered a canonical R of .55, indicating that 30% of the variance in performance in combat solders can be accounted for by emotional intelligence. The classification matrix indicated that this EI model is expected to correctly identify 78% of the high and low performers (8 of 10 recruits) serving in combat units.

The Ability of EI Models to Identify Individuals Who Serve in Elite Combat Units

An additional question asked in the IDF study was the degree to which we could identify recruits who would serve in units that demand performance in highly stressful conditions and potentially dangerous situations. We thought that this was a way of further expanding our examination of the relationship between emotional intelligence and performance. We initially compared the total EQ score between 240 volunteers who were accepted to serve in an elite combat unit with a randomly selected group of 240 noncombatants who did not volunteer or were not accepted for this type of service. A t test for independent groups revealed that the total EQ score for the elite combat soldiers was dramatically higher than for the noncombatants: 111 versus 98, respectively (t = 11.75, p < .000). The difference in total EQ scores between the two groups is close to 1 SD. The second comparison we made of the EQ-i scores between these two groups was carried out with discriminant function analysis using membership in the elite combat unit as the dependent variable and the 15 EQ-i subscale scores as the independent variables. Based on the population sample studied, the EI model that best identifies elite combatants comprises the four emotional and social competencies that are listed in Table 1.3.

This model rendered a canonical R of .51 explaining 26% of the variance, meaning that the ability to serve in an elite combat unit is at least 26%

TABLE 1.3
The EI Model That Best Identifies Elite
Combatants in the IDF ($n = 480$)

EI Predictors	Noncombatants	Elite Combatants	Lambda	F Value	p Level
Assertiveness	98	110	.755	9.04	.003
Impulse Control	100	110	.754	7.94	.005
Stress Tolerance	98	111	.749	4.76	.030
Flexibility	98	110	.749	5.06	.025

Note. Only those predictors with $p \leq .05$ are presented.

EQ based on the sample studied. According to the classification matrix, moreover, the ability of this model to correctly identify these particular recruits is 72% accurate, meaning that recruiters will be able to correctly identify 7 of 10 recruits as "having the stuff" to serve in elite combat units that make very challenging demands on individual performance.

The Ability of EI Models to Identify and Predict Leadership Potential in New Recruits

To examine the feasibility of using EI assessment to help identify leadership potential, we compared the total EQ score for those IDF recruits who were considered by their peers to possess high levels of leadership potential with those who were considered to possess low levels of leadership potential (i.e., based on the upper and lower 25% of peer nominations, as was previously explained). The average total EQ score for recruits with high leadership potential proved to be 106 in comparison with 98 for the those with lower leadership potential ($t = 6.74$, $p < .000$). We then used the level of perceived leadership potential as the dependent variable and the 15 EQ-i subscale scores as the independent variables in a discriminant function analysis of the data. This analysis determined that the EI model that best identifies leadership potential comprises the emotional and social competencies listed in Table 1.4.

This model rendered a canonical R of .39, revealing that 15% of the variance in (peer-assessed) leadership potential can be accounted for by emotional intelligence. Based on the classification matrix, the ability of this model to identify leadership potential is 65% accurate for the population sample studied, meaning that we can expect to correctly predict leadership potential in approximately 7 of 10 recruits if this model were used in the selection process.

In addition to identifying leadership potential based on peer nomination, an even more robust and real-world approach was applied to see if we

TABLE 1.4
The EI Model That Best Identifies Leadership
Potential in IDF Recruits (n = 536)

EI Predictors	Low Leadership Potential	High Leadership Potential	Lambda	F Value	p Level
Empathy	98	105	.866	12.76	<.000
Reality-Testing	100	103	.861	9.09	.003
Stress Tolerance	98	106	.858	7.74	.006
Self-Regard	99	105	.858	7.41	.007
Flexibility	97	104	.855	5.41	.021

Note. Only those predictors with $p \le .05$ are presented.

could distinguish between those IDF recruits who requested and were actually accepted to officer training and those who did not express a desire to be officers or who were unable to meet the minimum requirements. The total EQ scores for 470 officer trainees were compared with those of a randomly selected group of 470 recruits who did not serve as officers as was previously mentioned. The mean score for the officer trainees was significantly higher than that of the enlisted men: 108 versus 100, respectively (t = 9.60, $p < .000$). In a more sophisticated examination of the EI differences between the two groups, we applied discriminant function analysis using acceptance to officer training as the dependent variable and the 15 EQ-i subscale scores as the independent variables. The results of the analysis revealed that the EI model that best identifies "leadership material" comprises the emotional and social competencies listed in Table 1.5.

This model rendered a canonical R of .49, showing that 24% of the variance in leadership potential is accounted for by emotional intelligence.

TABLE 1.5
The EI Model That Best Predicts Officer
Trainees in the IDF (n = 940)

EI Predictors	Enlisted Men	Officers	Lambda	F Value	p Level
Interpersonal Relationship	101	103	.798	47.36	<.000
Stress Tolerance	100	109	.795	44.47	<.000
Independence	99	109	.791	39.66	<.000
Reality-Testing	100	105	.774	17.87	<.000
Empathy	100	107	.772	16.29	<.000
Problem-Solving	99	108	.771	14.46	<.000
Self-Regard	100	104	.769	12.84	<.000
Emotional Self-awareness	100	105	.769	12.08	.001
Happiness	100	104	.766	8.83	.003

Note. Only those predictors with $p \le .05$ are presented.

Based on the classification matrix, the ability of this model to predict leadership potential is 69% accurate. For the sample studied, this means that we could expect to correctly identify approximately 7 of 10 potentially successful candidates for officer training if this model were applied as part of the procedure used in selecting officer candidates.

DISCUSSION AND CONCLUDING COMMENTS

What Do the Findings Tell Us About the Impact of EI on Performance?

The results from the USAF and IDF studies clearly indicate a significant relationship between emotional intelligence and occupational performance.

We have shown that high performers have significantly higher EQs than low performers and vice versa. This was demonstrated in military recruiters (102 vs. 94, $p < .000$) as well as in combat soldiers (107 vs. 96, $p < .000$). This infers that high performers are more emotionally intelligent than low performers based on the population samples that were studied.

The results also demonstrate that emotional intelligence is able to predict performance in the workplace. This was demonstrated in recruiters (canonical $R = .49$) and in combat soldiers (canonical $R = .51$). In the latter example, moreover, the EQ-i was able to predict performance approximately 1 year after it was administered, which tells us something very important about the predictive validity of the specific instrument used as well as the potential for EI assessment in general. The findings clearly indicate that individuals who are more emotionally intelligent are expected to perform better in the workplace.

Results were presented in this chapter that demonstrate the ability of emotional intelligence to identify occupational potential as well. More specifically, the results indicate that leadership potential, assessed by peer nomination and especially by criterion group membership, can be identified by EI assessment. Based on the population samples studied, emotional intelligence can explain approximately 20% of leadership potential as was shown.

When compared with Wagner's extensive meta-analysis revealing that cognitive intelligence accounts for about 6% of occupational performance (Wagner, 1997), the findings presented in this chapter suggest that EQ accounts for approximately four times more variance than IQ when explaining performance. However, this finding can be confirmed only after more research is conducted that will focus on a wider variety of occupational performance in more diverse population samples.

The EI models that emerged from the studies presented are expected to correctly predict performance in approximately 7 of 10 individuals. It is logical to assume that the use of such models could reduce the number of costly mismatches in organizations.

As the organization's headhunters, recruiters perform an important task. Without them, the organization would cease to grow and inevitably cease to exist. And when we take a close look at the EI model that best predicts their performance that emerged from the USAF study, the factorial components of this model make sense. To recruit employees into their organization, recruiters have to strongly identify with the organization, adopt its values, and believe in it (Social Responsibility). Only then can they try to convince others that it is a good place to be associated with, which has to be done in a very assertive and convincing manner (Assertiveness). They have to be able to make contact and relate with the person they are trying to recruit (Interpersonal Relationship), which depends on their ability to understand the person's concerns, needs, and feelings (Empathy). Additionally, they need to be well motivated and positive (Happiness) as well as to work well under pressure (Stress Tolerance) to effectively deal with and solve problems (Problem-Solving).

Whereas the recruiters are the headhunters, the leaders are the brains of the organization, and without this key executive function, the organization would become immobilized and eventually cease to exist. The EI model that best predicts effective leadership is a complex combination of competencies as can be seen from the results that emerged in the IDF study. Based on this model, leaders need, first and foremost, to be aware of their emotions (Emotional Self-Awareness) and accurately understand themselves (Self-Regard); they also need to be adept in understanding others (Empathy) to relate well with them (Interpersonal Relationship). And to get the work done, leaders also need to be self-reliant and decisive (Independence) in making realistic (Reality-Testing) and effective solutions to problems as they arise (Problem-Solving). And that which facilitates this process is apparently the ability to work well under pressure (Stress Tolerance) and maintain a positive approach (Happiness).

In addition to relating specifically to the EI profile of combat soldiers per se, the model that was generated in the IDF study could convey something important about a special breed of employees who are required to perform highly demanding and stressful tasks. It could be that the model that surfaced provides a rough prototype of an elite "all-weather" employee who would be an asset to any organization when there is a need to carry out an extremely difficult and highly stressful task. The person that the organization may want to deploy in such circumstances might resemble, at least to some extent, the profile that emerged here. As such, this organizational "top-gun" (or "corporate commando") would have to be highly flexible and able to quickly adapt to the situation at hand (Flexibility), be highly motivated and positive (Happiness) to carry out the task, and simply do what must be done with a great deal of confidence and assertiveness (Assertiveness); such an employee would have to be adept at managing and controlling his or her emotions (Stress Tolerance and Impulse Control) to get the job done. However, such a job description will emerge only after EQ profiles are developed for police officers, firefighters, and other individuals who work under very challenging conditions and extremely stressful situations; additionally, these profiles would have to be compared with those for individuals who have proven to be highly successful in conducting negotiations, arbitration, and conflict resolution.

How Can the Findings Be Used?

The findings presented here have already provided a roadmap for the USAF for decreasing the high cost of mismatches in their recruitment procedure. Before 1996, it was costing the Air Force approximately $3 million for an average 100 mismatches a year (representing 25% of all recruiters hired within the first year). After 1 year of combining preemployment EI screening with interviewing and comparing EQ-i scores with the EI model for successful recruiters, the USAF increased its ability to predict successful recruiters by nearly threefold, dramatically reduced first-year attrition due to mismatches, and cut financial loses by approximately 92%. When the actual success of those whose EQ-i scores matched the EI model was examined, EI assessment proved to be a powerful predictor for meeting annual recruitment quotas. Of 262 individuals whose EQ-i scores matched the EI model the closest, 95% of them proved to be successful recruiters (i.e., they exceeded 100% of their annual quota). Overall, this model correctly classified 81% of all successful and unsuccessful recruiters, which was more than anticipated based on the initial findings previously described. Finally, the study discredited several myths regarding recruitment in the Air Force. For example, it was found that the geographic area that the recruiter was assigned to was not predictive of success, nor was gender, ethnicity, education, age, or hours worked. It is interesting to note that the more successful recruiters were those who worked the fewest hours (i.e., they simply accomplished more in less time). By selecting more effective recruiters, the USAF was also decreasing the number of costly mismatches among recruits, making EI screening even more financially advantageous (i.e., more effective recruiters are able to make more professional decisions regarding the people they recruit). Based on these results, the U.S. General Accounting Office submitted a Congressional Report praising the USAF's use of EI screening, and as a result of this report, the U.S. Senate Committee on Armed Services called on the Secretary of Defense to implement this selection procedure throughout the U.S. Armed Forces (United States General Accounting Office, 1998).

One of the primary messages that we want to convey in this chapter is that it is possible to scientifically develop EI models within organizations that can be used to accurately predict performance in various occupations. These models can be and are reliably employed to recruit, hire, and promote potentially effective employees. The factorial components of such models provide valuable content in training programs tailored to the specific needs of individual organizations. And when selection, training, and succession planning are based on these EI models, organizational as well as individual effectiveness improves. Over the past couple of years, EI models have been applied by a growing number of organizations worldwide.

Are We Entering the Era of the EQ?

We are well into the era of the EQ, as the senior coauthor predicted in 1985 when he coined the term EQ (Bar-On, 1985) and again in 1996 when he proposed the idea of EI assessment (Bar-On, 1996). Despite some degree of misunderstanding and misuse of what was originally meant by this term,[3] psychometrically valid instruments, like the EQ-i, are currently available and provide EQ scores that are widely used in assessment, consultation, and research.

We are already in an advanced phase of the era of the EQ, which the first two coauthors have been referring to as the "EQ profiling" phase, in which we are presently laying the empirical foundations for identifying occupational potential and predicting performance based on statistically generated models. We hope that these efforts will have an important impact on improving human effectiveness and organizational productivity.

---

[3]The term EQ has become one of the most popular buzzwords since it first appeared on the cover of *Time Magazine* in 1995 (Gibbs, 1995).

APPENDIX
The EQ-i Scales and What They Assess

EQ-i Scales	The EI Competencies Assessed by Each Scale
Intrapersonal	Self-awareness and self-expression:
Self-Regard	To accurately perceive, understand, and accept oneself.
Emotional Self-Awareness	To be aware of and understand one's emotions.
Assertiveness	To effectively and constructively express one's emotions and oneself.
Independence	To be self-reliant and free of emotional dependency on others.
Self-Actualization	To strive to achieve personal goals and actualize one's potential.
Interpersonal	Social awareness and interpersonal relationship:
Empathy	To be aware of and understand how others feel.
Social Responsibility	To identify with one's social group and cooperate with others.
Interpersonal Relationship	To establish mutually satisfying relationships and relate well with others.
Stress Management	Emotional management and regulation:
Stress Tolerance	To effectively and constructively manage emotions.
Impulse Control	To effectively and constructively control emotions.
Adaptability	Change management:
Reality-Testing	To objectively validate one's feelings and thinking with external reality.
Flexibility	To adapt and adjust one's feelings and thinking to new situations.
Problem-Solving	To effectively solve problems of a personal and interpersonal nature.
General Mood	Self-motivation:
Optimism	To be positive and look at the brighter side of life.
Happiness	To feel content with oneself, others, and life in general.

ACKNOWLEDGMENTS

We would like to thank Gill Sitarenios at Multi-Health Systems in Toronto for sharing with us the USAF database as well as his initial analyses of the data. We are also very appreciative for the cooperation of both the U.S. Armed Forces and the Israeli Defense Forces in agreeing to conduct these pioneering studies, which have shed light on emotional intelligence and its impact on performance.

REFERENCES

Bar-On, R. (1985). *The development of an operational concept of psychological well-being.* Unpublished doctoral dissertation, Rhodes University, South Africa.

Bar-On, R. (1996, August). *The era of the EQ: Defining and assessing emotional intelligence.* Poster session presented at the 104th Annual Convention of the American Psychological Association, Toronto, ON.

Bar-On, R. (1997a). *The Bar-On Emotional Quotient Inventory (EQ-i): A test of emotional intelligence.* Toronto, Canada: Multi-Health Systems.

Bar-On, R. (1997b). *The Bar-On Emotional Quotient Inventory (EQ-i): Technical manual.* Toronto, Canada: Multi-Health Systems.

Bar-On, R. (2000). Emotional and social intelligence: Insights from the Emotional Quotient Inventory (EQ-i). In R. Bar-On & J. D. A. Parker (Eds.), *Handbook of emotional intelligence* (pp. 363–388). San Francisco: Jossey-Bass.

Bar-On, R. (2004). The Bar-On Emotional Quotient Inventory (EQ-i): Rationale, description, and summary of psychometric properties. In G. Geher (Ed.), *Measuring emotional intelligence: Common ground and controversy* (pp. 111–142). Hauppauge, NY: Nova Science Publishers.

Bar-On, R., & Handley, R. (2003). *The Bar-On EQ-360: Technical manual.* Toronto, ON: Multi-Health Systems.

Bar-On, R., Tranel, D., Denburg, N. L., & Bechara, A. (2003). Exploring the neurological substrate of emotional and social intelligence. *Brain, 126,* 1790–1800.

Boyatzis, R. E., Goleman, D., & Hay Group (2001). *The Emotional Competence Inventory (ECI).* Boston: Hay Group.

Darwin, C. (1965). *The expression of the emotions in man and animals.* Chicago: University of Chicago Press. (Original work published 1872)

Encyclopedia of Applied Psychology. (in press). New York: Academic Press.

Gibbs, N. (1995, October). The EQ factor. *Time Magazine, 146,* 60–68.

Goleman, D. (1995). *Emotional intelligence.* New York: Bantam Books.

Handley. R. (1997, April). AFRS rates emotional intelligence. *Air Force Recruiter News.*

Kohan, A., & Mazmanian, D. (2003, June). *Emotional intelligence: Construct validity in an organizational context.* Poster session presented at the Annual Canadian Psychological Association Conference, Hamilton, ON.

Leuner, B. (1966). Emotional intelligence and emancipation. *Praxis der Kinderpsychologie und Kinderpsychiatrie, 15,* 196–203.

Mayer, J. D., Salovey, P., & Caruso, D. R. (2002). *Mayer–Salovey–Caruso Emotional Intelligence Test (MSCEIT).* Toronto, ON: Multi-Health Systems.

Plake, B. S., & Impara, J. C. (Eds.). (1999). *The Bar-On Emotional Quotient Inventory (EQ-i). Supplement to the thirteenth mental measurement yearbook.* Lincoln, NE: Buros Institute for Mental Measurement.

Thorndike, E. L. (1920). Intelligence and its uses. *Harper's Magazine, 140,* 227–235.

Unites States General Accounting Office. (1998). *Military recruiting: The Department of Defense could improve its recruiter selection and incentive systems.* A United States Congressional Report submitted to the Committee on Armed Services in the United States Senate on the 30th of January, 1998 (GAO/NSIAD–98–58).

Wagner, R. K. (1997). Intelligence, training, and employment. *American Psychologist, 52*(10), 1059–1069.

Chapter 2

Mindfulness-Based Emotional Intelligence: Research and Training

Joseph Ciarrochi and Claire Godsell
Department of Psychology,
University of Wollongong

We have made great strides in gaining control over our physical world, but how much progress have we made in controlling ourselves? We have far more material comfort than our great grandfathers (Csikszentmihalyi, 1999), yet we are no happier (Myers, 1992) and we still experience surprisingly high amounts of stress, anger, anxiety, and depression (Ciarrochi, Scott, Deane, & Heaven, 2003). Humans are the only animals who kill themselves (Hayes, Strosahl, & Wilson, 1999). We build weapons of mass destruction. We abuse and murder each other. Can there be any doubt that humans are a bit crazy?

Humans also allow their emotional struggles to undermine their effectiveness. When distressed, people often resort to insults, bullying, incessant complaining, indecisiveness, procrastination, and unnecessary conflict. We pay for our emotional stress with sickness, sleepless nights, and burnout. It saps our creativity, makes us hostile, and destroys our ability to get along with others. It can even hurt our ability to think and reason clearly

DEFINING EMOTIONAL INTELLIGENCE

Previous theorizing about emotional intelligence focuses on how individuals differ in their handling of emotional problems (Ciarrochi, Caputi, & Mayer, 2003; Ciarrochi, Dean, & Anderson, 2002; Ciarrochi, Forgas, & Mayer, 2001; Mayer, Salovey, Caruso, & Sitarenios, 2001). We start from a very different point, that is, by examining how people commonly handle emotional problems and by exploring why they often handle emotional problems so poorly. We then examine techniques that can be used to help people improve how they handle emotional problems.

Our EI model will look somewhat different from those previously proposed and those discussed in the other chapters of this volume. Our goal is not so much to propose a better model of EI but rather to propose a different model that is based on a theory about the causes of universal human suffering and ineffectiveness. The EI intervention that stems from this model focuses on acceptance and mindfulness (paying attention on purpose to the present moment, nonjudgmentally).

There has been some controversy about whether what is labeled "emotional intelligence" actually refers to a type of intelligence (Davies, Stankov, & Roberts, 1998; Mayer, 2001). Researchers point out rightly that EI measures are fundamentally different from IQ measures. We acknowledge these differences but argue that EI measures don't need to be similar to IQ measures. Many aspects of EI are probably unrelated to IQ, which is consistent with the common intuition that smart people can be emotionally stupid (Goleman, 1995).

We argue that the use of the term *intelligence* is justified because EI has pragmatic value and can be defined in a rigorous way. Pragmatically, the label *emotional intelligence* has been powerful in getting people to recognize the adaptive value of emotions and to understand that cognitive intelligence is not the only factor that is important to effective performance. Goleman's (1995) bestseller and other popular work (Goleman, 1998) have brought the concept into the boardrooms and bedrooms and motivated people to improve their emotional functioning.

We also believe that the term *emotional intelligence* can be defined in a scientifically rigorous way, even if the measures used to assess EI differ from cognitive intelligence tests. We argue that emotional intelligence has two parts, namely (a) the ability to use emotions as information and (b) the ability to act effectively in the context of emotions and emotionally charged thoughts. Effective actions are those that maximize the likelihood of moving toward a valued goal. Common workplace goals include innovation, collaboration, working well with others, motivating others, managing conflict, asserting rights, communicating feedback, and using feedback for self-improvement.

We now discuss the theory that underlies our mindfulness-based approach to emotional intelligence training. We then discuss the EI interventions that directly follow from this theory.

THE THEORY UNDERLYING MBEIT

All humans suffer. We argue that some forms of suffering are unnecessary. All humans have the same vulnerability to suffering, which can be captured in the acronym Primitive FEAR.

Primitive Responses to Modern Threats

Our physiology has evolved to deal rapidly with physical threats such as fighting a rival for food or fleeing from a lion (Sapolsky, 1999). However, modern threats are often psychological and social in nature. We worry about money, deadlines, and other people's opinions. Modern threats also tend to occur in the distant future. We must fight or flee immediately when we confront a lion. In contrast, we often must commit ourselves to long-term goals to prepare for such modern threats as potential job loss. Finally, modern threats often involve many small hassles rather than one large threat (DeLongis, Coyne, Dakof, Folkman, & Lazarus, 1982).

When we are faced with a psychological or social threat, our body often mobilizes to deal with a physical threat. The sympathetic nervous system becomes activated, and hormones such as epinephrine, norepinephrine, and cortisol are released into the bloodstream. There is increased respiration, blood pressure, heartbeat, and muscle tension. Under prolonged stress, there is a massive shutdown of those bodily activities that are directed toward growth, reproduction, and resistance to existing infection, in favor of mechanisms that promote readiness for immediate high-energy action (Gray, 1987; Sapolsky, 1999).

These dramatic changes in physiology are often unnecessary in dealing with social and psychological threats. Our bodies are essentially exaggerating the significance of the threat. For example, we may be faced with a crucial deadline. If we don't meet the deadline, we will not get a bonus. We get extremely anxious about not getting the bonus. Suddenly, we are responding with an extremity of emotion that would make sense if we were in a war zone. But it does not make sense in the work environment, where our lives are not at risk. We incorrectly respond as if it would be catastrophic if we did not meet the deadline. Most often, all that would happen is that we would have a bit less money and our pride might be hurt. However, it is likely that we would survive.

In responding to psychological threats as if they are physical, we also waste a lot of energy. Constantly preparing ourselves for physical threats has a number of costs, including exhaustion and vulnerability to illness (Salovey, 2001; Sapolsky, 1999; Smith, 1992). There is another downside to our primitive physiological system. Negative affective states narrow our thought–action repertoire (Fredrickson, 2002; Geller, 1960; Wilson & Murrel, 2003). When anxious or angry, we tend to consider fewer alternatives to a problem and think of fewer ways of behaving. Such narrowing makes sense in a primitive, physically threatening world. For example, if a rabbit were to see a lion on the savannah, it would not be advantageous for the rabbit to continue foraging or to notice the flowers and other features of the landscape. The evolutionary advantage would go to rabbits who immediately suppressed less critical behaviors (narrowing) and rapidly moved to a hiding place (Wilson & Murrel, 2003).

However, narrowing does not make as much sense in a modern world, where the threats are often not physical. For example, let's say you have to make an important decision and you are quite anxious about it. The anxiety narrows your attention and makes it likely that you will consider fewer decision alternatives. As a consequence, you are more likely to make a poor decision unless you take action to deliberately expand your decision alternatives.

The Dangers of Language: Fusion, Evaluation, Avoidance, and Reason Giving (FEAR)

Language helps us to survive. It allows us to quickly communicate dangers to others (Don't go by the river; I saw a lion there). Thus, we can avoid dangers without having to learn about them ourselves. It also allows us to communicate where to locate resources (The fruit is over there).

Language also has a dark side. It helps us to inflict unnecessary suffering on ourselves. The problems of language and how we use it can captured in the acronym FEAR: fusion, evaluation, avoidance/attacking of symbols, and reason giving. The FEAR framework is presented in more detail by its creators, namely, Hayes, Wilson, and colleagues (Hayes, Barnes-Holmes, & Roche, 2001; Hayes et al., 1999; Wilson & Murrel, 2003).

Fusion. Fusion involves symbols becoming functionally equivalent, to some extent, with the events they symbolize (Hayes et al., 1999). To illustrate fusion, consider the following example involving two police officers. Smith initially has no strong emotions linked to the word *John.* Then, he is assigned a partner named John, who maliciously accuses him of corruption. The royal commission starts an investigation, and Officer Smith feels humiliated. He develops a hatred and aversion to John. Fusion suggests that he will also develop an aversion to the word *John.* Just mentioning the word *John* in the right context will bring forth humiliation and anger. Smith may seek to avoid thinking about John just as he would avoid being around the actual John. Importantly, the word *John* can now be used to transform formally neutral stimuli. For example, let's say someone says, "Sam is just like John." Now, Smith may develop a strong aversion to Sam, even though he has never had any direct experience with him. Such is the power of language and fusion.

Language is useful for all kinds of things (e.g., quickly communicating dangers), but it also allows us to bring psychological and emotional reactions to previous painful events into the present. That is, verbal reports of past pain can themselves produce pain.

Evaluation. For millions of years, one of the major goals of a human being has been to avoid getting attacked or eaten. We thus evolved an "evaluating mind" that is constantly checking to see if there are any warning signs, threats, or problems in the environment. For example, if we see an apple on the ground we might evaluate "good" but then see a lion next the apple and evaluate "bad."

Our evaluating or critical mind searches for problems and threats and has been essential for human survival. Unfortunately, today, our mind also gets turned against us. Language allows us to create an abstracted concept of "I." Our mind can then be turned on this "I," just as it would be turned on the external world. It critically evaluates "I." It compares "I" to others, and can find "I" to be bad or inadequate.

Language also allows us to create labels such as "our life." Once this label exists, our critical mind can then evaluate our life as worthless and unbearable, which make suicide possible. Language also allows us to create ideals ("I would like to be special"). We can then compare the ideal to present reality and find the present to be unacceptable. Finally, we also create labels for our internal states such as anxiety and stress. Again, once the label exists, we can evaluate these states and declare them to be bad. We may then try to avoid the internal states just as we avoid genuinely threatening external events.

Avoidance and Attacking of Our Symbols. It is adaptive to avoid or attack threats in the outside world. We must either flee from the lion or kill it. Humans create an internal, private world of symbols and learn to avoid or attack aspects of it. Avoidance and attacking of symbols serve a similar function, namely, to defend us against aversive feelings.

Avoidance of private experience makes us feel better in the short run. However, often such avoidance harms our ability to achieve our goals in the long run (Hayes et al., 1999; Norem, 2002). For example, we may be terrified of getting cancer and therefore avoid thoughts of cancer and of cancer screenings. Avoiding these thoughts may help us feel better immediately, but we also increase our risk of being harmed by cancer. Another problem with deliberate avoidance is that it often has a paradoxical rebound effect. The very thing we were trying to avoid often comes back with more strength. The more you try to avoid it, the more it dominates your life (Hayes et al., 1999; Wegner, 1994).

Attacking our symbolic world can also be a problem. For example, let's say you are driving your car and somebody cuts you off in traffic and performs an obscene gesture. Let's also say you were not and are not in any real physical danger. You might still get angry because this person seems to be attacking you, at least symbolically. If this was a physical attack and your life was in danger, it would make sense for you to attack back. However, we often respond to the symbolic attack as if it was a real attack. We react to the other driver with anger and by yelling insults of our own. We react as if our self-worth was being physically assaulted and we must defend it.

Another way we respond to an insult is by disparaging the insulter. We think: "That bastard has problems. He is nothing. Everybody hates him." By saying this, we are symbolically attacking back and weakening the enemy. We feel better and safer. Of course our verbal attacks have not actually changed anything in reality. They have only changed the way we think about our symbolic world.

Attacking our symbolic world is not always harmful. For example, we can disparage a bad driver until we feel better. However, many times the attacking comes out in the form of unhelpful behavior. For example, we may feel the need to act aggressively toward a coworker because she is saying disparaging things about us. We feel we are under attack, and we respond by attacking back. Unfortunately, attacking back is often not the most effective response.

In sum, we very reasonably avoid and attack real threats. However, we also learn to avoid and attack symbols of those threats.

Reason Giving/Rule Creation. People learn to put forth reasons as valid and sensible causes of behavior (Hayes et al., 1999). You might ask someone, "Why didn't you give the speech?" He might respond with something like, "I was too anxious." This seems perfectly reasonable. If, in contrast, he responded with, "I have no idea," we would be likely to find this explanation unacceptable and insist that he give us a reason. Thus, the social community reinforces reason giving.

Unfortunately, people begin to believe their own reasons and stories (Hayes et al., 1999), even when they are harmful if followed. People tell themselves, "I am worthless," and behave accordingly. They might tell themselves, "I must have other people's approval," and waste a great deal of energy trying to get approval from every significant other. Or they might think, "I can't take a risk, because I am too anxious." They act as if they really can't take a risk, although experience will quickly show them that they can take risks and be anxious. Language allows us to easily formulate rules that then may decrease our sensitivity to learning from experience (Hayes, Brownstein, Zettle, Rosenfarb, & Korn, 1986).

Linking Primitive With FEAR

Our primitive system responds to social and psychological threats as if we are in physical danger. As we have argued, such a response is often excessive and has detrimental effects on our thinking and behavior. FEAR helps to create and maintain this emotional response.

For example, let's say you believe you might fail to meet a deadline and respond with anxiety. You are so anxious that you feel like you are being hunted like an animal. If you continue to honestly confront the possibility of failing to meet the deadline, and if there are no dire consequences for such failure, then your anxiety will naturally diminish. However, FEAR helps keep the anxiety response potent. Here is one way this can happen.

- Fusion: Thoughts of failure take on the aversive properties of actually failing.
- Evaluation of thoughts: "Failure is awful (and thoughts of failure are awful)."
- Avoidance of failure thoughts: "I can't work on this anymore. I'll just tell my colleagues that I'm horrible at this kind of work and ask to be given another assignment or taken off the project."
- Reasons giving/rule creation. "I can't continue with this work because I'm far too anxious and I'd be risking failure and embarrassment if I failed."

In the previous example, we responded to the failure to meet a deadline as if it was a real physical danger. Then, via fusion, we reacted to our own thoughts as if they were a physical threat that had to be avoided. We generate a rule, which suggests that our fear stops us from taking a risk. The end result is that our work life becomes "smaller" as we increase the number of things we avoid.

THE DIMENSIONS TARGETED IN MINDFULNESS-BASED EMOTIONAL INTELLIGENCE TRAINING

We now turn our attention to the implications of this theory for defining the dimensions of emotional intelligence (see Table 2.1). Each dimension of EI is meant to undermine some aspect of FEAR. (For a book-length treatment of how FEAR might be undermined, see Hayes et al., 1999.) Additional work can be found under the heading of acceptance and commitment therapy (Hayes, Strosahl, & Wilson, 2002; Wilson & Murrel, 2003).

The following subsections are broken down into (a) a description of the EI dimension and its link to the previous theory, (b) the proposed link between the dimension and workplace effectiveness, (c) a discussion of intervention techniques to develop this dimension of EI, (d) a brief discussion of individual difference measures used to study behaviors within this dimension, and (e) research evidence showing the relationship between the dimension and individual performance and well-being. Table 2.2 summa-

TABLE 2.1
Dimensions of Mindfulness-Based Emotional
Intelligence and Their Definitions

Dimension	Definition
External focus	
Managing others' emotions	Skills related to increasing enthusiasm and pride, managing other people's anger, aggressive behavior, anxiety, and stress; reducing emotional conflict; communicating in a way that arouses minimal unhelpful emotions in others
Identifying others' emotions	Accurate identification of others' emotions from facial expressions, tone of voice, etc.
Expressing emotions	Accurate sending of emotional signals to others
Internal focus	
Undermining self-concept fusion (i.e., undermining the power of unhelpful self-concepts to act as barriers to effective action)	• Recognizing that self-evaluations are not descriptions of our essence • Escaping the perceived need to defend self-esteem • Recognizing that emotionally charged evaluations of the self do not have to stop us from pursuing our goals • Making contact with the "observer self"; finding the safe place from which to accept all negative emotions, self-doubts, and other unpleasant inner experiences
Undermining fusion (i.e., undermining the power of unhelpful thoughts and emotions to act as barriers to effective action)	• Seeing that emotionally charged thoughts about life are not equivalent to life • Looking *at* emotionally charged verbal content rather than *through* it • Being able to be mindful of moment to moment experience (either internal or external)
Using emotion as information	• Identifying emotions • Understanding the appraisals that activate different emotions • Understanding the consequences of emotions on cognition, health, etc. • Understanding how emotions progress over time • Distinguishing between more helpful and less helpful emotions and emotionally charged thoughts
Effective emotional orientation	• Letting go of unhelpful emotion control strategies • Willingness to have emotionally charged private experiences (thoughts, images, emotions) when doing so fosters effective action • Accepting the inevitability of a certain amount of unpleasant affect and negative self-evaluation • Understand that private experiences do not have to stop one from pursuing a valued direction (and therefore one doesn't have to get rid of them)

TABLE 2.2
Summary of EI-Relevant Findings

Measures	Key findings
Undermining self-concept fusion	
1. Self Esteem/Acceptance Inventory (SEI; Rosenberg, 1965)	Fusion with negative self-concept (low self-acceptance and variable self-acceptance) • Associated with poor performance (Sommer & Baumeister, 2002; Tang & Reynolds, 1993; Campbell & Fairey, 1986)
2. Narcissistic Personality Inventory (NPI; Raskin & Terry, 1988)	• Related to the tendency to procrastinate to the detriment of performance (Beswick et al., 1988) • Associated with decreased effort and persistence following performance failure (Tafarodi & Vu, 1997) • Correlates with proneness to overgeneralize negative implications of poor performance to other aspects of self-identity (Kernis et al., 1989)
3. Fusion with unhelpful rules about self-concepts (CBS-III; Thorpe, Walter, Kingery, & Nay, 2001); Dysfunctional Attitudes Scale (Weissman, 1980) • Self worth depends on approval • Self worth depends on power/success	• Negatively associated with adaptive perfectionism, which facilitates optimal performance (Ashby & Rice, 2003) • Positively correlated with adaptive coping behaviours (Green, 1996) • Significantly predicts academic performance (Metofe, 2002) • Positively related to academic achievement and persistence in task performance (Leondari et al., 1998) • Linked to goal-related affect characterized by greater tenseness and less interest (Kernis et al., 2000) • Related to a tendency to experience elevated levels of anger and hostility (Kernis et al., 1989)
	Fusion with positive self-concept (narcissism)
4. Self-regard scales of EI measures e.g., (Bar-On, 1997)	• Associated with poor self-regulation, which in turn impedes performance (Wansink, 2000) • Correlates with a tendency to respond reactively to performance evaluations via significant changes in anxiety, anger, and self-esteem (Rhodewalt & Morf, 1998) • Related to social ineffectiveness, in the extreme manifesting as "narcissistic rage" (Fiske, 2004) • Predicts propensity to respond to threatening feedback with anger and interpersonal aggression (Rhodewalt, 2001) • Associated with displays of extreme affective reactions to positive and negative information about self (Rhodewalt & Morf, 1998) • Correlates with tendencies to attribute performance success to ability, and to respond to performance failures with extreme anger and reactivity (Rhodewalt & Morf, 1998) Fusion with unhelpful rules about the self: This variable is associated with anxiety and depression (Brown, Hammen, Craske, & Wickens, 1995; Ciarrochi & West, 2003)

(Continued)

TABLE 2.2
(Continued)

Measures	Key findings
Undermining fusion	
1. Mindfulness Attention Awareness Scale (MAAS; Brown & Ryan, 2003)	• Both dispositional and state mindfulness predict self-regulated behavior and positive emotional states (Brown & Ryan, 2003)
2. Rumination (Nolen-Hoeksema, 1987; Roger & Najarian, 1989)	• Ruminators commit significantly more preservative errors on cognitive tasks relative to nonruminators and they demonstrate greater cognitive inflexibility (Davis & Nolen-Hoeksema, 2000)
	• Rumination impairs concentration and facilitates interfering thoughts on performance measures of reading, comprehension, and proofreading (Lyubomirsky & Fazilet, 2003)
	• Rumination interferes with the ability to effectively problem-solve (Lyubomirsky & Nolen-Hoeksema, 1995)
	• Correlation between rumination and low mastery (Nolen-Hoeksema et al., 1999)
	• Self-focused rumination maintains or increases depressed mood (Nolen-Hoeksema & Morrow, 1993)
Using emotion as information	
1. Toronto Alexithymia Scale (Bagby, Parker, & Taylor, 1994) • Difficulty identifying emotions • Difficulty describing emotions	• Alexithymia predicts persistent physical symptoms at 2-year follow-up (Bach & Bach, 1995)
	• High levels of somatization correlate with poor coping and low satisfaction in the workplace (Pomaki & Anagnostopoulou, 2003)
	• Alexithymia subscales, difficulty identifying and describing emotions, are related to a variety of negative indexes of well-being even after controlling for other measures of EI (Ciarrochi et al., in press)
2. Trait meta-mood scale (TMMS; Salovey et al., 1995) • Emotional clarity	• Alexithymia is strongly associated with hypertension (Todarello et al., 1995; Salminen & Saarijarvi, 1999)
	• Alexithymia is linked with gastrointestinal and bowel problems (Porcelli et al., 1995; Weiner, 1992; and also chronic pain (Cox et al., 1994)
3. Emotional Identification subscales EI measures. (Mayer et al., 2002); Bar-on EQI (Bar-On, 1997; Schutte, et al., 1998)	• Elevated incidence of alexithymia appears in clinical samples comprised of individuals with anxiety disorders (Zeitlin & McNally, 1993; Parker et al., 1993), eating disorders (Jimmerson et al., 1994) and substance abuse disorders (Taylor, 2001)
	• Alexithymia is linked with early mortality (Kauhanen et al., 1996)
	• Difficulty identifying feelings is strongly associated with reporting of physical symptoms (De Gucht & Heiser, 2003)

Effective emotional orientation

1. Acceptance & Action Questionnaire (AAQ; Bond & Bunce, in press; Hayes et al., 2003)

- AAQ predicts long-term mental health and work performance over and above job control, negative affectivity, and locus of control at 1 year follow-up (Bond & Bunce, in press)
- Emotional avoidance (high AAQ score) corresponds with elevated anxiety levels during task performance, particularly when emotional suppression instructions are given (Feldner et al., 2003)
- Acceptance-based performance enhancement intervention improves performance and reduces frequency of suppression of unwanted thoughts and feelings (Little & Simpson, 2001)

2. Social Problem Solving Inventory (SPSI; Frauenknecht & Black, 1995)
   - Effective Problem Orientation

- High levels of negative problem orientation in a college sample correlate with greater performance errors in a concept formation and hypothesis task. Lower levels of negative orientation correspond with improved performance over trials (Shewchuk et al., 2000)
- Effective problem orientation is associated with adaptive problem-engagement coping strategies (D'Zurilla & Chang, 1995)
- Self-appraised effective problem solving ability (i.e., confidence, approach, and personal control) predicts adaptive study habits and GPA (Elliott et al., 1990)

3. White Bear Suppression Inventory (WBSI; Wegner & Zanakos, 1994).

- Thought suppression is related to elevated levels of interpersonal discomfort and tension during engagement in social interaction (Bouman, 2003)
- Imagery suppression interferes with performance on visuo-motor tasks (Beilock et al., 2001)
- Avoidance of negative affect is correlated with a perceived lack of control (Forsyth et al., 2003)

4. Repressive Coping Scale (Weinberger et al., 1979)

- Thought suppression is associated with poor task performance (Harvey & Bryant, 1999)
- Emotional suppression impairs incidental memory for information presented while suppression is taking place (Richards & Gross, 1999)
- Thought suppression corresponds with a subsequent increase in the suppressed thought (Wenzlaff & Wegner, 2000)
- Emotional suppression (e.g., withdrawal., acting out) predicts physical and psychological stress symptoms that accumulate over increasing years of work service (Wastell, 2002)

rizes the research evidence showing the links between each dimension and individual performance and well-being and the measures used in that research.

We discuss a variety of private experiences (e.g., thoughts, images, feelings, and sensations). Sometimes we do not explicitly use the word *emotion* in the discussion. However, any of the private experiences we discuss are assumed to be emotionally charged and therefore the appropriate subject matter of a chapter on emotional intelligence.

Dimension 1: Effective Emotional Orientation (EEO)

Effective emotional orientation involves letting go of unhelpful emotion control strategies and being willing to have emotionally charged private experiences (e.g., anxiety), when doing so fosters effective action (Hayes et al., 1999). People quite reasonably avoid things in the world that are aversive. Cognitive fusion means that the thoughts about things are also aversive. People naturally evaluate their aversive thoughts as bad and seek to avoid them. As discussed, avoidance often does not work and indeed can make matters worse. As described by Hayes and his colleagues (1999), the rule of private experience is, If you're not willing to have it (e.g., anxiety), you usually have it anyway. Indeed, you may have it even worse than before (Wegner, 1994). This differs from the rule of public experience. If you not willing to have something unpleasant in the public world (say an ugly sofa), you can usually get rid of it.

Poor emotional orientation is likely to undermine effectiveness at work. For example, let's say a coworker insults you or "stabs you in the back." You start to feel angry but you are worried that if you feel angry you will ruin your working relationship or do something you'll regret. So you try to avoid your feelings of anger (poor emotional orientation). The only catch is, the more you try to get rid of it, the more it hangs around (Hayes et al., 2001). Maybe you can suppress it for a while, but suppression just makes it worse in the long run. Eventually, you might explode and act aggressively toward the coworker instead of doing what is in your best interest (e.g., acting assertively).

Consider another example. You want to take a risk that might advance your career (e.g., give a presentation or introduce a workplace innovation). However, whenever you think about giving the presentation, you feel anxious. Then you become anxious about your anxiety. You worry that if you feel anxious, you won't be able to deliver a good presentation. So you try to get rid of your anxiety (poor orientation). You tell yourself, "Just relax, to stay calm, you must not feel anxious." Unfortunately, these attempts to control anxiety often result in increases in anxiety (Barlow, 1988; Hayes et al., 2001). Your control strategies bring about the very state you were trying to avoid.

Improving Emotional Orientation.   Language and reasoning are the stuff that entrap us. They disconnect us from our experiences and from discovering what works (see FEAR, described previously). Thus, all the intervention techniques discussed in this chapter attempt to minimize the use of language and reasoning. Instead, they tend to involve metaphors and exercises that attempt to put people in touch with their own experiences (Hayes et al., 1999). The exercises also tend to shift people into the present moment and away from excessive reasoning about the future or past. The techniques used in Mindfulness-Based Emotional Intelligence Training (MBEIT) are largely taken from Hayes et al. (1999) and to a lesser extent from Linehan (1993), Segal, Williams, and Teasdale (2002), and Kabat-Zin (1990).

An early step in improving emotional orientation is to show people the paradoxical nature of control strategies. An excellent example of this is an exercise involving a polygraph metaphor (Hayes et al., 1999). People are asked to imagine that they are hooked up to a polygraph that measures exactly how anxious they are feeling. They are told that all they have to do is not feel anxious for the next 3 min. To make sure they are sufficiently motivated, and to exaggerate the point, we then tell them we will point a gun at their head and say that if they feel anxious then we will pull the trigger. So all they have to do is not get anxious.

People very quickly see the problems of trying to control private experience. Another exercise involves telling people to not think about a white bear for 2 min. They are asked to raise their hand every time they think of the white bear. Usually, people will think about the white bear again and again.

One major problem with increasing the effectiveness of emotional orientation is that people believe their emotions must act as barriers to effective actions. Therefore, they believe they have to get rid of the emotions to be effective. They want to stop feeling anxious before they give the speech. They want to feel calm and cool before they approach the boss for the raise. Thus, a big component of our intervention research involves showing people that emotions don't have to subvert effective action. One can give a speech or act assertively when anxious. One can treat another with respect, even if one feels angry with that person. Perhaps the best way to illustrate this point is to encourage people to pursue their valued direction, even when they are having the aversive emotions (see the following passenger on the bus metaphor).

We have talked about negative emotions as perceived barriers to effective action. People also perceive the lack of a certain emotion to be a barrier. They believe that they need to feel good to be able to work. They may feel they need to feel confident and strong to be able to succeed. Thus, they use control strategies to increase the positive mood (e.g., they tell themselves, "I am great. I have unlimited energy."). As we have seen, such deliberate attempts to control emotions often don't work, at least not in the long run. Also, depending on positive emotions to take positive action means that when you are not feeling good, you stop moving in your valued direction. Finally, positive emotion is often the result of engaging in valued activities rather than the cause. Our interventions involve exercises that show people that they can accept the absence of positive affect and still commit to a valued direction.

Measuring Effective Emotional Orientation (EEO).   Three important points should be kept in mind in reading our discussion of EI-relevant measures. First, with few exceptions, these measures were not specifically designed to measure the EI dimensions we have described here. Thus, they at best imperfectly measure the proposed dimension. Second, we describe the EI dimensions as fairly unitary constructs, but in reality we believe it is more of a group or family of constructs. The "family" members are interrelated, yet sometimes statistically separable. For example, measures of thought suppression and experiential avoidance are expected to measure similar constructs (e.g., avoidance of private experience) yet have different emphases (e.g., thought vs. emotional avoidance). Finally, our discussion is not to be taken as an attempt to relabel old measures as EI. Rather, it focuses on these older measures and the decades of research associated with them to get a better understanding of what it means to be emotionally intelligent.

The first measure we discuss is the effective problem orientation scale, which assesses the tendency to respond to emotional problems with challenge rather than threat orientation and the tendency to face problems rather than avoid them (Frauenknecht & Black, 1995). People with poor problem orientation appear to put off solving problems for as long as they can, possibly to avoid the negative affect associated with those problems.

Effective problem orientation has been related to a number of objective indexes of cognitive performance. For instance, Elliot and his colleagues (1990) investigated the relation between problem orientation and academic performance in a sample of college students and found that self-appraised effective problem-solving ability, consisting of confidence, approach strategies, and sense of personal control, was a positive predictor of both adaptive study habits and grade point average scores.

In another study, researchers examined the relation between problem orientation and performance in a concept formation and hypothesis testing task (Shewchuk, Johnson, & Elliott, 2000). Participants completed the social problem-solving inventory (Frauenknecht & Black, 1995) as well as a cognitive task (Wetzel & Boll, 1987, cited in Shewchuk et al., 2000). In the latter task, participants were presented with cards depicting geometric shapes, lines, colors, and figures and were required to make hypotheses about the underlying principle by which the cards were arranged. They were also required to make dynamic evaluations and adjustments of their responses based on immediate feedback given by the examiner as to whether initial hypotheses were right or wrong. Results revealed that participants who had an ineffective problem orientation tended to make more performance errors. In contrast, those with an effective orientation tended to improve their performance on the task.

Other empirical research suggests that effective problem orientation is associated with adaptive problem-engagement coping strategies (D'Zurilla & Chang, 1995) that in turn are likely to contribute to promoting efficacy and high performance. Collectively, these findings suggest that effective emotional orientation has a positive effect on both performance motivation and performance outcomes.

Two other measures of effective orientation include the White Bear Suppression Inventory and the Repressive Coping Scale (Weinberger, Schwartz, & Davidson, 1979). They measure the tendency to avoid unpleasant private thoughts and experiences, respectively. Research indicates that both forms of avoidance can be ineffective. For instance, thought suppression is related to elevated levels of interpersonal discomfort and tension during engagement in social interaction (Bouman, 2003); is correlated with intrusions, anxiety, and impeded task performance (Harvey & Bryant, 1999; Turvey & Salovey, 1994); and has been shown to interfere with performance on visuomotor tasks (Beilock, Afremow, Rabe, & Carr, 2001).

Richards and Gross (1999) provided evidence that emotional suppression impairs incidental memory for information presented while suppression is taking place. Other research has looked at what happens when ambulance officers use emotion-suppressing defenses (e.g., withdrawal, acting out) in response to exposure to trauma. The findings indicate that suppressors experience more physical and psychological stress symptoms and that these symptoms accumulate over increasing years of service (Wastell, 2002).

Another well-documented downside to experiential avoidance is the tendency for suppressed thoughts and feelings to rebound with increased intensity. Research has shown that when subjects are asked to suppress a thought, they later show an increase in this suppressed thought compared with those not given suppression instructions (Wenzlaff & Wegner, 2000). Indeed, the suppression strategy may actually stimulate the suppressed mood in a kind of self-amplifying loop (Feldner, Zvolensky, Eifert, & Spira, 2003). Similar results have been found in the coping literature. Avoidant coping strategies predict negative outcomes for substance abuse, depression, and effects of child sexual abuse (for review, see Hayes et al., 1999).

The final orientation measure, the Acceptance and Action Questionnaire (AAQ; Bond & Bunce, in press; Hayes et al., 2003), measures the willingness to experience thoughts, feelings, and physiological sensations without having to control them or let them determine one's actions. Bond and Bunce recently conducted a longitudinal study examining the role of individual differences in acceptance in mental health, job satisfaction, and performance in a work domain (Bond & Bunce, in press). At a 1-year follow-up, the AAQ predicted mental health and an objective measure of workplace performance, even after the authors controlled for other common workplace variables (e.g., job control, negative affectivity). In another study, participants high in emotional avoidance (high on the AAQ) showed more anxiety in response to CO_2 (biological challenge), particularly when instructed to suppress their emotions (Feldner et al., 2003).

Dimension 2: Using Emotion as Information (UEI)

Emotions are messengers. They usually tell us something about the world and about our own desires. For example, anxiety results from the appraisal that something undesirable might happen. Anger results from the appraisal that someone has acted unfairly and this has resulted in something undesirable (Ortony, Clore, & Collins, 1988).

The FEAR framework suggests that we tend to evaluate our unpleasant private experiences as bad and avoid them. Unfortunately, avoiding the messenger (the emotion) does not change the message. If we don't know what the message is, we will find it difficult to act effectively. For example, if we do not know we are angry, then we may not realize that an injustice is being directed at us and we may not take effective action to correct this injustice. If we do not know that we are anxious about an upcoming meeting, then we may mistakenly think our anxious sensations are due to a physical sickness (Taylor, 2000). Or we may mistakenly blame our anxiety on some irrelevant event (our colleague's behavior) and seek to change this irrelevant event rather than focusing effectively on the source of the problem.

Once we are willing to experience both positive and negative emotions (effective emotion orientation), we are better able to discover and use the information they provide. We can become mindful of their transitoriness and perhaps even overcome the human bias to overestimate how long negative emotions will last (Gilbert, Pinel, Wilson, Blumberg, & Wheatley, 1998). We can also become mindful of how our negative emotions tend to narrow our thought–action repertoire (Geller, 1960; Wilson & Murrel, 2003) and perhaps take behavioral steps (i.e., structured problem solving) to overcome such narrowing.

Improving the Use of Emotional Information. The process of improving UEI is relatively straightforward. We teach people to discriminate between different emotions such as anxiety and anger. We build up their emotional vocabulary and teach them the appraisals that underlie each emotion. We teach them that the adversities or activating events in their lives are not the only determinants of their behavior. Rather, the activating events plus believed thoughts (e.g., the thought, "this is horrible") determine the reaction.

Almost all the techniques described in the orientation section and the following sections are expected to improve UEI. For example, people are expected to be better able to identify their emotions if they are not constantly seeking to escape them (effective orientation dimension) and if they are mindful of their emotions as they show up in the present moment (see next section).

Measuring Individual Differences in Using Emotion as Information. The measures discussed here focus on people's ability to identify their emotions, which we conceptualize as an early step in using emotions as information.

Alexithymia is a condition that involves difficulty identifying and describing emotions, minimizing emotional experience, and focusing attention externally rather than internally (Taylor, 2001). Therefore, it involves problems with the two dimensions of emotional intelligence we have discussed thus far, namely, using emotional information and effective emotional orientation. The Toronto Alexithymia Scale (TAS-20) is one of the most commonly used measures of alexithymia and has been shown to be related to a number of important life outcomes. For example, the alexithymia subscales—Difficulty Identifying and Describing Emotions—are related to a variety of negative indexes of well-being (e.g., depression), even after controlling for other measures of emotional intelligence (Ciarrochi et al., in press). Alexithymics are also at significantly higher risk than the general population for developing psychological disorders, including anxiety disorders (Parker, Taylor, Bagby, & Acklin, 1993; Zeitlin & McNally, 1993), eating disorders (Jimerson, Wolfe, Franko, Covino, & Sifneos, 1994), and substance abuse disorders (Taylor, 2001).

Other empirical evidence reveals that alexithymics are prone to experiencing somatic complaints (Taylor, 2001), a finding that likely reflects a propensity for psychological or emotional difficulties to manifest as physical symptoms. Medical conditions that have been linked with alexithymia include hypertension (Salminen & Saarijarvi, 1999; Todarello, Taylor, Parker, & Fanelli, 1995), gastrointestinal and bowel problems (Porcelli et al., 1996), and chronic pain (Cox et al., 1994). Additionally, alexithymia has also been linked with early mortality (Kauhanen et al., 1996).

Research indicates that the somatic complaints experienced by alexithymics may have a protracted negative effect on individual performance. High levels of somatization have been linked with poor coping and low satisfaction in the workplace (Pomaki & Anagnostopoulou, 2003). A longitudinal study found that alexithymia predicts persistent experience of physical symptoms at a 2-year follow-up (Bach & Bach, 1995). Some long-term negative consequences of persistent physical problems are likely to include more sick leave, decreased productivity, and diminished effectiveness within the workplace.

Emotional identification seems to be an aspect of just about every model and measure of EI including the Mayer–Salovey–Caruso emotional intelligence test (Mayer, Salovey, & Caruso, 2002), the Bar-On emotional quotient inventory (Bar-On, 1997), and the Schutte et al. emotional intelligence inventory (Schutte et al., 1998). Review of each of these measures is beyond the scope of this chapter.

Dimension 3: Undermining Fusion

When language processes dominate, "humans fuse with the psychological contents of verbal events. The distinction between thinking and the referent of thought is diminished. As a result, emotionally charged thoughts or feelings (particularly those with provocative or pejorative meanings) become connected to powerful and predictable behaviour patterns" (Hayes et al., 1999, p. 149). Thus, unhelpful thoughts and emotions can act as barriers to effective action.

People can spend decades on automatic pilot, being bullied by their unhelpful thoughts and feelings. For example, we feel anger, and then we see injustice everywhere and behave aggressively. We feel irritable, and then we treat our coworkers poorly. Sometimes this "mindless" behavior is useful, as in the case, for example, when a mom impulsively risks her life to save her baby from a fire. However, mindless reacting can be less useful if the action tendency associated with the emotion is inconsistent with our goals. Few people wake up in the morning saying, "Today, my goal is to irritate somebody at work." Yet that is often what happens, when anger and irritation becomes connected with aggressive behavior.

The key techniques in this section do not seek to get rid of or change private experiences. Rather, they involve changing our relationship to these experiences. They involve learning to be mindful of the experiences as they come and go and learning to look at the experiences, rather than through them. It is as if there is a sign that says "bad mountain" and then a mountain in front of it. Fusion means that people often don't distinguish the sign from the mountain. They see the mountain through the sign "bad mountain." The techniques here involve teaching people to see "bad mountain" separately from the mountain.

The goal is to become better at seeing thoughts and feelings for what they are—just thoughts and feelings—not what they say they are (i.e., facts, or dangers that most be avoided). For example, anxiety is just anxiety (a bundle of sensations and thoughts). It does not necessarily mean that you are about to get eaten, or that you have to run away. Anxiety seems dangerous, like you should avoid it. But anxiety is just a passing state.

Once we are able be mindful of our experiences as they occur, we are less likely to be bullied around by those experiences. For example, if we notice that we are feeling anxious about an important talk, we can consciously make the decision to give the talk despite the anxiety. If, however, we don't notice the anxiety and unconsciously avoid situations that evoke anxiety, then we may avoid the talk, even though it is important to us.

Techniques to Increase the Ability to Undermine Fusion.   One can use a number of metaphors to physicalize and objectify thoughts and feelings. This makes it easier to look at them rather than through them. Consider the passenger on the bus metaphor used by Hayes et al. (1999). Imagine that you are driving a bus toward your valued direction, and all your thoughts and feelings are passengers. Your valued direction involves taking some risk (e.g., asking for a promotion). While driving, many scary passengers show up (e.g., a feeling of anxiety, the thought, "I might fail"). You don't want to look at these passengers. You know you want to drive straight ahead, but the passengers keep coming up to the front of the bus, demanding that you turn left, turn left (e.g., don't go for the promotion). They are telling you not to take the risk. They are scary, and you want them to go away, so you make a deal. You agree that if they go to the back of the bus and hide from you, you will do what they say. So they hide in the back of the bus, and you don't take the risk. The only catch is that now you are driving where they want you to go, rather than where you want to go.

The important thing to recognize is this: These passengers can't really take control of the bus without your permission. All they can do is come to the front of the bus and look scary.

This metaphor can be used to deal with many kinds of performance problems. Consider speech anxiety. You want to give a speech to an important group of colleagues. A number of scary passengers show up when you think about the speech. Anxiety shows up, and the thought "they may think me a fool" shows up. You don't want to see these unpleasant passengers, so you make a deal with them. You won't give the speech, if they don't show up. Unfortunately, now you are failing to achieve your goals. All you get in return is that the anxiety and unpleasant thoughts hide in the back of the bus for a little while.

Another technique to undermine fusion is to teach mindfulness skills (Linehan, 1993). Mindfulness skills include "what" skills (observe things as they come and go, describe them, and participate fully in life) and "how" skills (nonjudgmental stance, mindfully focus on what you are doing, do what works). Essentially, mindfulness helps people to see thoughts and feelings as thoughts and feelings (not as literal truths) and to see their moment-to-moment experience as it is (not as it seems to be when seen through language or intense emotion).

Individual Differences in Fusion Tendency and in Believing Unhelpful Thoughts. There are several scales related to this dimension. The Mindfulness Attention Awareness Scale (MAAS) measures people's tendency to be mindful of moment-to-moment experiences (Brown & Ryan, 2003). Brown and Ryan (2003) demonstrated that both dispositional and state mindfulness predict self-regulated behavior and positive emotional states. These findings indirectly implicate the significance of mindfulness in optimizing performance, because the links between self-regulation, positive emotions, and positive performance are well documented (Lee, Sheldon, & Turban, 2003).

Individual differences in rumination appear to relate to the fusion dimension. Ruminators seem to be stuck in their thoughts, engaging in repetitive and passive thinking about a problem (Nolen-Hoeksema, 1987). Rumination often involves mindlessly bouncing from one negative thought to another in an attempt to escape unpleasant affect by controlling the uncontrollable (e.g., uncertainty; Dugas, Gagnon, Ladouceur, & Freeston, 1998). Rumination might also be seen as an ineffective emotional orientation, because it appears to involve attempts to escape from unpleasant private experiences. However, we include it here because it seems to involve a mindless absorption in the content of thought (fusion), rather than looking at thought, and a focus on the future or the past, while the present goes unnoticed.

Rumination has been associated with a range of emotional difficulties, including anger, depression, and stress (Nolen-Hoeksema, Larson, & Grayson, 1999; Rusting & Nolen-Hoeksema, 1998). Research suggests that there is also an association between rumination and performance. Rumination has been shown to negatively correlate with athletic performance (Scott, Stiles, Raines, & Koth, 2002). Nolen-Hoeksema and colleagues (1999) studied the effects of rumination on mastery and found that low mastery corresponds with high frequency of rumination.

Rumination has also been shown to negatively affect performance on cognitive tasks. A study comparing the performance of a group of ruminators and nonruminators on measures of cognitive flexibility and related cognitive processes revealed that ruminators committed significantly more preservative errors and demonstrated greater cognitive inflexibility than nonruminators (Davis & Nolen-Hoeksema, 2000). In another study, Nolen-Hoeksema and Morrow (1993) found that self-focused rumination maintains or increases depressed mood as well as adversely effects thinking and problem solving. Finally, research suggests that rumination impairs concentration on performance measures of reading, comprehension, and proofreading (Lyubomirsky, Kasri, & Zehm, 2003).

We have discussed both mindfulness and rumination as two imperfect indicators of low and high fusion, respectively. There are also scales that focus on attachment to (or fusion with) specific unhelpful thoughts. For example, measures of rigidity/intolerance of uncertainty appear to assess fusion with thoughts such as, "Uncertainty is horrible; I can't stand uncertainty" (Dugas, Freeston, & Ladouceur, 1997; Wulfert, Greenway, Farkas, & Hayes, 1994). Rigidity appears to be associated with poor mental health and reduced creativity (Dugas et al., 1998; Langer, 1989).

Dimension 4: Undermining Self-Concept Fusion

Humans develop a concept of self. The mind then proceeds to evaluate it. We readily evaluate this self as good, bad, kind, flawed, incomplete, special, or unethical. Cognitive fusion means we tend to treat these evaluations as literal properties of our self. For example, we can evaluate a cup as "bad," but this badness is not a property of the cup. Ceramic is a property of the cup. Similarly, badness or goodness cannot be a property of the self. It is merely a transient reaction. Everybody in the world can suddenly believe you are bad, and you would still be exactly the same person.

Problems arise when people come to identify with the concept of self. The concept of "me" becomes equal to me. People are then drawn into protecting the concept of self as if it is part of the self (Hayes et al., 1999). They seek to feed it or defend it against attack. People talk about "building self-esteem" or repairing "damage" done to it. The problem is that the "self" is only a concept. It is not out there in the world to be attacked or fixed.

Identification with unhelpful self-concepts can undermine effectiveness in several ways. First, it makes us insensitive to feedback that is inconsistent with the self-concept. If we believe we are "incredibly effective," then we can become insensitive to examples where we don't act effectively. We distort or reinterpret events and don't make room to deal directly and openly with criticism (Hayes et al., 1999). Second, if we believe that our global evaluations describe our essence, then we can never change or redeem ourselves. A person who believes he or she has a primary attribute called "ineffective" will find it difficult to become effective. Even if these people do behave in an effective fashion, they will often discount the behavior as an exception to the rule.

Finally, identification with self-concept can act as a barrier to taking the risks that help us to achieve our goals. We often make our self-concepts dependent on success or approval. If we fail or are rejected, then we feel like we lose value as a person. It is difficult to take risks when we feel our self-worth is at stake. People sometimes don't want to give a speech, because if it goes badly they believe they are inadequate. People don't risk introducing an innovation at work, because if the innovation fails, they believe they are ineffective.

Techniques for Undermining Fusion With
Unhelpful Self-Concepts

All the techniques used in the previous section (undermining fusion) apply here. The procedures in this section are designed to help people make experiential contact with the self as an observer. For example, the chessboard metaphor is designed to help people see that they are not equivalent to their self-evaluations (Hayes et al., 1999). Imagine that all of your private experiences are pieces on a chessboard. The pleasant thoughts and feelings are the white pieces and the unpleasant thoughts and feelings are the black pieces. Many people don't like the black pieces and want to get rid of them. So they get on one of the white pieces and ride off to war against the black pieces. The goal is to push the bad pieces off of the board. Unfortunately, in this metaphor, the pieces can never be pushed off the board (see preceding avoidance section). Sometimes the pleasant pieces show up, sometimes the unpleasant pieces show up, and you can't really get rid of any of them.

The participants are led to see that they are not the chess pieces (the private experiences that come and go). Rather they are the chessboard (the observer perspective). The chessboard can only do two things. It can hold the pieces and it can pick all the pieces up and move them to another place (the valued direction). No matter what content shows up—good or bad—this observer perspective is unchanging.

This metaphor helps people to make contact with a sense of self that is a safe and consistent perspective from which to observe and accept all changing inner experiences (Hayes et al., 1999). It also illustrates that the self-as-observer does not depend on success or other people's approval. Thus, people can take risks, have unpleasant self-evaluations show up (the black pieces), and recognize that the self-evaluations are passing reactions whereas the self-as-observer stays constant.

In addition to the chessboard metaphor, there are a substantial number of exercises that help people connect with this unchanging observer self. See Hayes et al. (1999) for more exercises. Once people learn that their self-worth is not under threat, they often feel freer to pursue their valued goals.

Measuring Conditional Self-Acceptance and Overidentification
With Unhelpful Self-Concepts

Fusion With Negative Self-Concepts.   No self-concept is by itself helpful or unhelpful. Everything depends on context. For example, a person could fuse with (believe), "I am great." This may help the person to take on a challenging leadership position in one context. Or, if the person clings to it even when she is performing poorly, she may become insensitive to critical feedback.

There do appear to be certain concepts that are generally unhelpful. Such concepts involve global, negative ratings of oneself. The Self Esteem Inventory (SEI; Rosenberg, 1965) provides an approximate measure of fusion with negative self-concepts. For example, the negative items on the SEI include, "I feel useless," "I am a failure," and "I am no good at all." Examples of positive items include "I am a person of worth, at least on equal basis with others," "I have a number of good qualities," and "I am able to do things as well as most people." We use the term *self-acceptance* instead of self-esteem to highlight that the SEI does not measure inflated positive self-concepts ("I am an extraordinary person").

Research has demonstrated a link between low self-acceptance and poor performance (Sommer & Baumeister, 2002; Tang & Reynolds, 1993). Beswick, Rothblum, and Mann (1988) linked low self-acceptance with a tendency to procrastinate to the detriment of performance (Beswick et al., 1988). Tafarodi and Vu (1997) found an association between low self-acceptance and decreased effort and persistence following performance failure (Tafarodi & Vu, 1997). Kernis, Brockner, and Frankel (1989) demonstrated that individuals with low self-acceptance are prone to overgeneralizing the negative implications of poor performance to other aspects of their identities (Kernis et al., 1989). Low self-acceptance has also been shown to be negatively associated with adaptive perfectionism (i.e., adaptive in that it facilitates optimal performance; Ashby & Rice, 2002). Other research has shown that high self-acceptance is related to a number of positive outcomes including adaptive coping behaviors (Green, 1996), academic achievement (Metofe, 2002), and persistence in task performance (Leondari, Syngollitou, & Kiosseoglou, 1998).

We have been discussing self-acceptance as if it is a constant thing. However, other research has looked at the instability of self-acceptance (Kernis, Grannemann, & Barclay, 1989; Kernis, Grannemann, & Mathis, 1991). If a person's self-concept is unstable, then this suggests that self-acceptance depends on external events or transitory internal states. Failure or rejection is likely to lower acceptance, whereas success and approval increase it. In contrast, we assume that people who unconditionally accept themselves will not tend to show fluctuating self-acceptance. Research suggests that people who experience unstable self-acceptance tend to also experience more anger and hostility, perhaps because they feel the need to defend their self-worth (Kernis, Grannemann, et al., 1989). Other research shows that unstable self-acceptance is associated with goal-related affect characterized by greater tenseness and less interest (Kernis, Paradise, Whitaker, Wheatman, & Goldman, 2000).

Self-report EI measures appear to either explicitly measure self-acceptance as an aspect of EI (e.g., Bar-on, 1997) or moderately relate to self-acceptance (Ciarrochi, Chan, & Bajgar, 2001). This is consistent with our notion that self-esteem/acceptance is a central aspect of effective emotional functioning. What is distinctive about MBEIT is its approach to self-esteem problems. MBEIT does not try to build self-esteem or get rid of negative self-concepts. Rather, it attempts to change our relationship to these self-concepts. We encourage people to become mindful of the coming and going of negative self-evaluations and to recognize that one can "inhale" these unpleasant evaluations and still move toward a valued goal.

Fusion With Positive Self-Concepts. It is not only fusion with negative self-concepts that can be problematic. Fusion with positive self-concepts might also be harmful. For example, narcissists identify with a highly positive self-concept ("I'm special"). They scan the social context for evidence that supports their elevated sense of self and tend to construct high self-esteem in the absence of objective evidence. They are prone to respond to threatening feedback with anger and interpersonal aggression (Rhodewalt, 2001), display extreme affective reactions to positive and negative information about themselves (Rhodewalt & Morf, 1998), and are prone to social ineffectiveness, which in extreme instances manifests as "narcissistic rage" (Fiske, 2004, p. 391). Narcissism has also been linked with poor self-regulation, which in turn is likely to impede performance (Wansink, 2000).

Fusion With Self-Defeating Rules About the Self. Two classes of unhelpful rules/beliefs appear to emerge across a number of different belief measures (Clark & Beck, 1991; Thorpe, Parker, & Barnes, 1992; Weissman, 2000). One belief type deals with interpersonal concerns ("I must have love or approval to be worthwhile"), and the other deals with power concerns ("I must have success or power to be worthwhile"). These rules are self-defeating. Once people fail to succeed or get approval, the rule tells them they are not worthwhile. Once one "is not worthwhile," it can seem impossible to change (in the same way that one can not change a plastic cup into a glass cup without destroying the plastic cup). These rules can lead to anxiety and depression (Ciarrochi & West, in press), as rejection and failure lead to feelings that one's self-worth is damaged.

Values and Emotional Intelligence

The interventions described in the last two sections are designed to undermine the ability of emotionally charged private experiences (e.g., self-evaluations) to act as barriers to valued action. Though we have not discussed it explicitly, work on values is central to all of these interventions. Once people know what they value, they are better able to withstand their emotional storms and maintain a fixed course (see Hayes et al., 1999, for one of the best discussions on the subject).

Externally Focused Emotional Intelligence

Given our space constraints, we will talk only briefly about externally focused EI or what also might be termed *social intelligence*. For a more complete coverage of this topic, see books on assertiveness (e.g., Jakubowski & Lange, 1978) and social skills training (e.g., Bolton, 1987).

A key aspect of our EI framework is the assumption that external EI depends on internal EI. This approach is quite different from other approaches that focus on the training of social skills (Bolton, 1987) but similar to other conceptions of EI (see Goleman, 1998). We do not believe that one can optimally teach external EI without first teaching internal EI. For example, if someone is poor at dealing with his own hostility (internal EI), then he is going to have trouble dealing effectively with others (external EI). If someone is seeing the world through anger-colored glasses (low internal EI), then she is going to have trouble accurately identifying how other people feel.

To further illustrate how the internal depends on the external, consider assertiveness skills training. It would be straightforward to teach people how to engage in assertive behavior. We might teach them the three-part assertion statement: "When you do *x* behaviour, I feel *y*, because it has *z* concrete effects on my life" (Jakubowski & Lange, 1978). However, people are unlikely to use this skill appropriately if they are low in internal EI. For example, let's say a person low in EI (a) believes that "people must approve of me at all times," (b) feels anxious when she uses assertive behavior, and (c) believes that anxiety stops one from asserting. We could teach this person the three-part assertion statement, but she would be unlikely to use it appropriately. She would first have to learn to recognize that she does not have to believe the thought that "people must approve of me" or "anxiety must stop me from acting." She could learn to look at these thoughts, rather than through them, and then act assertively.

Putting Our Approach Into Context

The EI theory proposed here is grounded firmly in what has been termed the "third wave" of cognitive–behavioral therapy (CBT; Hayes, in press; Kabat-Zinn, 1990; Linehan, 1993; Segal et al., 2002). The second wave of CBT focused on eliminating irrational thoughts or pathological schemas and replacing them with more functional ones (Beck, 1995; Meichenbaum, 1985). In contrast, third-wave CBT deemphasizes attempts to directly change the content of thought or emotion. Rather, it focuses on mindful acceptance of thoughts and feelings. The goal is to change one's relationship to such private experiences.

Approaches in second-wave CBT were largely driven by research on how clinical populations (e.g., depressed) differed from normal populations. As such, these approaches do not seem as relevant to EI researchers who are interested in improving the EI of "normal," often highly effective people. In contrast, third-wave CBT appears to be grounded in principles that apply to everyone. For example, it is based on techniques that have been used for centuries by Buddhists (as opposed to clinical groups), who developed the techniques to relieve humans from the universal causes of suffering. Third-wave CBT has also been grounded in theory of language that is meant to be applicable to everyone (Hayes et al., 2001).

What is the evidence supporting the principles underlying third-wave/acceptance-based approaches? Substantial evidence was reviewed earlier and will not be repeated here. There is increasing evidence that acceptance-based approaches are useful in the treatment of emotional problems, relapse prevention for drug addition, pain management, and marital and couples' problems (for a review, see Hayes et al., 1999). Although it is a relatively new area, there is now evidence that acceptance-based approaches can be used effectively in the workplace. Bond and Bunce (2000) found that an acceptance and commitment therapy (ACT) intervention reduced the occurrence of emotional difficulties and increased the tendency to innovate. In another study, Dahl and her colleagues examined the effects of a brief ACT intervention for the treatment of people who were at high risk of sick leave utilization (Dahl, Wilson, & Nilsson, in press). ACT significantly reduced utilization of sick leave, compared with a control group.

How does our approach to EI map to previous EI approaches? Our approach looks very different from the ability approach of Mayer and his colleagues (Mayer et al., 2001; Mayer, Salovey, Caruso, & Sitarenios, 2003), who started with the assumption that EI should share certain features with traditional IQ (e.g., EI should develop with time and should be measured with an ability test). Their EI test has proven to be quite useful in predicting such things as job performance, social problem behavior, and relationship quality. The test has also proven to be largely distinctive from self-report measures of EI and personality (Ciarrochi, Chan, & Caputi, 2000; Mayer et al., 2002).

Our approach has focused on self-report and therefore will tend to be reasonably distinct from that of Mayer and his colleagues. Thus, we do not see ourselves as competitors. Our focus on currently existing measures is not an attempt to relabel old measures as EI. Rather, it focuses on these older measures and the decades of research associated with them to get a better understanding of what it means to be emotionally intelligent.

The self-report measures we reviewed do overlap with self-report measures of EI. For example, identifying emotions and self-acceptance are prominent aspects of other self-report EI models (Bar-On, 1997; Salovey,

Mayer, Goldman, Turvey, & Palfai, 1995; Schutte et al., 1998). Our mindfulness-based EI training (MBEIT) differs from these previous approaches in that it is based on a specific theory of language (Hayes et al., 2001) and uses this theory to specify exactly how each EI dimension might be improved. For example, MBEIT does not seek to increase self-esteem. Rather, it helps people to defuse from negative and positive unhelpful self-concepts. That is, it encourages people to give up the whole self-esteeming game. MBEIT also does not encourage people to fix or repair negative emotional states. Indeed, effective emotion management is absent from our model, though it appears to be present in every other EI model. MBEIT conceptualizes emotion management strategies as often being the problem rather than the solution.

Why focus on self-report measures? The primitive FEAR framework is based on how people manage personally relevant private experiences. Self-reports seem to allow people to answer questions about personally relevant experiences. When asked the question, "To what extent do you have feelings that you can't quite identify?" people can look into the context of their lives and provide a reasonably accurate report (Taylor & Bagby, 2000). In contrast, ability EI measures appear to ask questions about stimuli to which participant are unfamiliar (e.g., unfamiliar faces and stories). We believe it is possible to be emotionally intelligent with regard to the processing of unfamiliar emotional information but not be emotionally intelligent when it comes to processing emotional information in the context of our everyday lives.

CONCLUSIONS

Over 150 years ago, Thoreau wrote, "The mass of men lead lives of quiet desperation" (Thoreau, 1908). This quote still rings true today. We have changed little. Is it not possible for the humans to improve?

We have described a theory of why humans seem to so often suffer and behave contrary to their own values. We have also described a series of EI interventions that stem directly from this theory. More research is needed to put these approaches to the test. To what extent can we help people (and ourselves) to escape some suffering and become more vital? Can MBEIT improve people's effectiveness in pursuing their valued direction? We believe the initial evidence concerning these questions is promising.

REFERENCES

Ashby, J. S., & Rice, K. G. (2002). Perfectionism, dysfunctional attitudes, and self-esteem: A structural equations analysis. *Journal of Counseling & Development, 80,* 197–203.

Bach, M., & Bach, D. (1995). Predictive value of alexithymia: A prospective study in somatizing patients. *Psychotherapy & Psychosomatics, 64,* 43–48.

Barlow, D. H. (1988). *Anxiety and its disorders.* New York: Guilford.

Bar-On, R. (1997). *Bar-On Emotional Quotient Inventory (EQ-i): Technical manual.* Toronto, ON: Multi-Health Systems.

Beck, J. S. (1995). *Cognitive therapy: Basics and beyond.* New York: Guilford.

Beilock, S., Afremow, J., Rabe, A., & Carr, T. (2001). "Don't miss!" The debilitating effects of suppressive imagery on golf putting performance. *Journal of Sport & Exercise Psychology, 23*(3), 200–221.

Beswick, G., Rothblum, E. D., & Mann, L. (1988). Psychological antecedents of student procrastination. *Australian Psychologist, 23,* 207–217.

Bolton, R. (1987). *People skills: How to assert yourself, listen to others, and resolve conflicts.* Brookvale, NSW: Simon & Schuster.

Bond, F. W., & Bunce, D. (2000). Mediators of change in emotion-focused and problem-focused worksite stress management interventions. *Journal of Occupational Health Psychology, 5,* 156–163.

Bond, F. W., & Bunce, D. (in press). The role of acceptance and job control in mental health, job satisfaction, and work performance. *Journal of Applied Psychology.*

Bouman, T. (2003). Intra- and interpersonal consequences of experimentally induced concealment. *Behaviour Research & Therapy, 41*(8), 959–968.

Brown, K. W., & Ryan, R. M. (2003). The benefits of being present: Mindfulness and its role in psychological well-being. *Journal of Personality & Social Psychology, 84,* 822–848.

Ciarrochi, J., Caputi, P., & Mayer, J. D. (2003). The distinctiveness and utility of a measure of trait emotional awareness. *Personality & Individual Differences, 34,* 1477–1490.

Ciarrochi, J., Chan, A. Y., & Bajgar, J. (2001). Measuring emotional intelligence in adolescents. *Personality & Individual Differences, 31,* 1105–1119.

Ciarrochi, J. V., Chan, A. Y. C., & Caputi, P. (2000). A critical evaluation of the emotional intelligence construct. *Personality & Individual Differences, 28*(3), 539–561.

Ciarrochi, J., Dean, F. P., & Anderson, S. (2002). Emotional intelligence moderates the relationship between stress and mental health. *Personality & Individual Differences, 32,* 197–209.

Ciarrochi, J., Forgas, J. P., & Mayer, J. D. (Eds.). (2001). *Emotional intelligence in everyday life: A scientific inquiry.* Philadelphia: Psychology Press/Taylor & Francis.

Ciarrochi, J., Scott, G., Deane, F. P., & Heaven, P. C. L. (2003). Relations between social and emotional competence and mental health: A construct validation study. *Personality & Individual Differences, 35,* 1947–1963.

Ciarrochi, J., & West, M. (in press). Relationships between dysfunctional beliefs and positive and negative indices of well-being: A critical evaluation of the Common Beliefs Survey–III. *Journal of Rational-Emotive & Cognitive Behavior Therapy.*

Clark, D. A., & Beck, A. T. (1991). Personality factors in dysphoria: A psychometric refinement of Beck's Sociotropy–Autonomy Scale. *Journal of Psychopathology & Behavioral Assessment, 13,* 369–388.

Cox, B. J., Kuch, K., Parker, J. D., Shulman, I. D., & Evans, R. J. (1994). Alexithymia in somatoform disorder patients with chronic pain. *Journal of Psychosomatic Research, 38,* 523–527.

Csikszentmihalyi, M. (1999). If we are so rich, why aren't we happy? *American Psychologist, 54,* 821–827.

Dahl, J., Wilson, K. G., & Nilsson, A. (in press). Acceptance and commitment therapy and the treatment of persons at risk of long-term disability resulting from stress and pain symptoms: A randomized clinical trial. *Behavior Therapy.*

Davies, M., Stankov, L., & Roberts, R. D. (1998). Emotional intelligence: In search of an elusive construct. *Journal of Personality & Social Psychology, 75,* 989–1015.

Davis, R., & Nolen-Hoeksema, S. (2000). Cognitive inflexibility among ruminators and nonruminators. *Cognitive Therapy & Research, 24*(6), 699–711.

DeLongis, A., Coyne, J. C., Dakof, G., Folkman, S., & Lazarus, R. S. (1982). Relationship of daily hassles, uplifts, and major life events to health status. *Health Psychology, 1,* 119–136.

Dugas, M. J., Freeston, M. H., & Ladouceur, R. (1997). Intolerance of uncertainty and problem orientation in worry. *Cognitive Therapy & Research, 21,* 593–606.

Dugas, M. J., Gagnon, F., Ladouceur, R., & Freeston, M. H. (1998). Generalized anxiety disorder: A preliminary test of a conceptual model. *Behaviour Research & Therapy, 36,* 215–226.

D'Zurilla, T., & Chang, E. C. (1995). The relations between social problem solving and coping. *Cognitive Therapy & Research, 19*(5), 547–562.

Elliot, T. R., Godshall, F., Shrout, J. R., & Witty, T. E. (1990). Problem-solving appraisal, self-reported study habits, and performance of academically at-risk college students, *Journal of Counseling Psychology, 37*(2), 203–207.

Feldner, M., Zvolensky, M., Eifert, G., & Spira, A. (2003). Emotional avoidance: An experimental test of individual differences and response suppression using biological challenge. *Behaviour Research & Therapy, 41,* 403–411.

Fiske, S. (2004). *Social beings: A core motives approach to social psychology.* New York: Wiley.

Frauenknecht, M., & Black, D. R. (1995). Social Problem-Solving Inventory for Adolescents (SPSI-A): Development and preliminary psychometric evaluation. *Journal of Personality Assessment, 64,* 522–539.

Fredrickson, B. L. (2002). Positive emotions. In C. R. Snyder & S. J. Lopez (Eds.), *Handbook of positive psychology* (pp. 120–134). London: Oxford University Press.

Geller, I. (1960). The acquisition and extinction of conditioned suppression as a function of the base-line reinforcer. *Journal of the experimental Analysis of Behavior, 3,* 235–340.

Gilbert, D. T., Pinel, E. C., Wilson, T. D., Blumberg, S. J., & Wheatley, T. P. (1998). Immune neglect: A source of durability bias in affective forecasting. *Journal of Personality & Social Psychology, 75,* 617–638.

Goleman, D. (1995). *Emotional intelligence.* New York: Bantam.

Goleman, D. (1998). *Working with emotional intelligence.* London: Bloomsbury.

Gray, J. A. (1987). *The psychology of fear and stress* (2nd ed.). New York: Cambridge University Press.

Green, J. A. W. (1996). *Self esteem associated with coping behaviors of adolescents in divorced/single parent families with implications for school counselors.* Kent, OH: Kent State University.

Harvey, A., & Bryant, R. (1999). The role of anxiety in attempted thought suppression following exposure to distressing or neutral stimuli. *Cognitive Therapy & Research, 23*(1), 39–52.

Hayes, S. C. (in press). ACT, RFT, and the third wave of behavior therapy. *Behavior Therapy.*

Hayes, S. C., Barnes-Holmes, D., & Roche, B. (Eds.). (2001). *Relational frame theory: A post-Skinnerian account of human language and cognition.* New York: Kluwer Academic/Plenum Publishers.

Hayes, S. C., Brownstein, A. J., Zettle, R. D., Rosenfarb, I., & Korn, Z. (1986). Rule-governed behavior and sensitivity to changing consequences of responding. *Journal of the Experimental Analysis of Behavior, 45,* 237–256.

Hayes, S. C., Strosahl, K. D., & Wilson, K. G. (1999). *Acceptance and commitment therapy: An experiential approach to behavior change.* New York: Guilford.

Hayes, S. C., Strosahl, K. D., & Wilson, K. G. (2002). Acceptance and commitment therapy: An experiential approach to behavior change. *Child & Family Behavior Therapy, 24,* 51–57.

Hayes, S. C., Strosahl, K. D., Wilson, K. G., Bissett, R. T., Pistorello, J., Toarmino, D., Polusny, M. A., Dykstra, T. A., Batten, S. V., Bergan, J., Stewart, S. H., Zvolensky, M. J., Eifert, G. H., Bond, F. W. P. F. J., Karekla, M., & McCurry, S. M. (in press). Measuring experiential avoidance: A preliminary test of a working model. *The Psychological Record.*

Jakubowski, P., & Lange, A. J. (1978). *The assertive option.* Champaign, IL: Research Press.

Jimerson, D. C., Wolfe, B. E., Franko, D. L., Covino, N. A., & Sifneos, P. E. (1994). Alexithymia ratings in bulimia nervosa: Clinical correlates. *Psychosomatic Medicine, 56,* 90–93.

Kabat-Zinn, J. (1990). *Full catastrophe living: Using the wisdom of your body and mind to face stress, pain, and illness.* New York: Dell.

Kauhanen, J., Kaplan, G. A., Cohen, R. D., Julkunen, J., & Salonen, J. T. (1996). Alexithymia and risk of death in middle-aged men. *Journal of Psychosomatic Research, 41,* 541–549.

Kernis, M. H., Brockner, J., & Frankel, B. S. (1989). Self-esteem and reactions to failure: The mediating role of overgeneralization. *Journal of Personality & Social Psychology, 57,* 707–714.

Kernis, M. H., Grannemann, B. D., & Barclay, L. C. (1989). Stability and level of self-esteem as predictors of anger arousal and hostility. *Journal of Personality & Social Psychology, 56,* 1013–1022.

Kernis, M. H., Grannemann, B. D., & Mathis, L. C. (1991). Stability of self-esteem as a moderator of the relation between level of self-esteem and depression. *Journal of Personality & Social Psychology, 61,* 80–84.

Kernis, M. H., Paradise, A. W., Whitaker, D. J., Wheatman, S. R., & Goldman, B. N. (2000). Master of one's psychological domain? Not likely if one's self-esteem is unstable. *Personality & Social Psychology Bulletin, 26,* 1297–1305.

Langer, E. J. (1989). *Mindfulness.* New York: De Capo Press.

Lee, F. K., Sheldon, K. M., & Turban, D. B. (2003). Personality and the goal-striving process: The influence of achievement goal patterns, goal level, and mental focus on performance and enjoyment. *Journal of Applied Psychology, 88,* 256–265.

Leondari, A., Syngollitou, E., & Kiosseoglou, G. (1998). Academic achievement, motivation and future selves. *Educational Studies, 24,* 153–163.

Linehan, M. M. (1993). *Cognitive-behavioral treatment of borderline personality disorder.* New York: Guilford.

Lyubomirsky, S., Kasri, F., & Zehm, K. (2003). Dysphoric rumination impairs concentration on academic tasks. *Cognitive Therapy & Research, 27*(3), 309–330.

Lyubomirsky, S., & Nolen-Hoeksema, S. (1995). Effects of self-focused rumination on negative thinking and interpersonal problem solving. *Journal of Personality and Social Psychology, 69*(1), 176–190.

Mayer, J. D. (2001). A field guide to emotional intelligence. In J. Ciarrochi & J. P. Forgas (Eds.), *Emotional intelligence in everyday life: A scientific inquiry* (pp. 3–24). Philadelphia: Psychology Press/Taylor & Francis.

Mayer, J. D., Salovey, P., & Caruso, D. (2002). *Mayer–Salovey–Caruso Emotional Intelligence Test (MSCEIT): User's manual.* North Tonawanda, NY: Multi-Health Systems.

Mayer, J. D., Salovey, P., Caruso, D. R., & Sitarenios, G. (2001). Emotional intelligence as a standard intelligence. *Emotion, 1,* 232–242.

Mayer, J. D., Salovey, P., Caruso, D. R., & Sitarenios, G. (2003). Measuring emotional intelligence with the MSCEIT V2.0. *Emotion, 3,* 97–105.

Meichenbaum, D. (1985). *Stress inoculation training.* New York: Pergamon.

Metofe, P. A. (2002). *Prediction of academic performance in historically Black colleges and universities (HBCU's).* Houston: Texas Southern University.

Nolen-Hoeksema, S. (1987). Sex differences in unipolar depression: Evidence and theory. *Psychological Bulletin, 101,* 259–282.

Nolen-Hoeksema, S., Larson, J., & Grayson, C. (1999). Explaining the gender difference in depressive symptoms. *Journal of Personality & Social Psychology, 77,* 1061–1072.

Nolen-Hoeksema, S., & Morrow, J. (1993). Effects of rumination and distraction on naturally occurring depressed mood. *Cognition & Emotion, 7*(6), 561–570.

Norem, J. K. (2002). Defensive self-deception and social adaptation among optimists. *Journal of Research in Personality, 36,* 549–555.

Ortony, A., Clore, G., & Collins, A. (1988). *The cognitive structure of emotion.* New York: Cambridge University Press.

Parker, J. D., Taylor, G. J., Bagby, R., & Acklin, M. W. (1993). Alexithymia in panic disorder and simple phobia: A comparative study. *American Journal of Psychiatry, 150,* 1105–1107.

Pomaki, G., & Anagnostopoulou, T. (2003). A test and extension of the demand/control/social support model: Prediction of wellness/health outcomes in Greek teachers. *Psychology & Health, 18,* 537–550.

Porcelli, P., Leoci, C., Guerra, V., Taylor, G. J., & Bagby, R. (1996). A longitudinal study of alexithymia and psychological distress in inflammatory bowel disease. *Journal of Psychomatic Research, 41,* 569–573.

Rhodewalt, F. (2001). The social mind of the narcissist: Cognitive and motivational aspects of interpersonal self-construction. In J. P. Forgas & K. D. Williams (Eds.), *The social mind: Cognitive and motivational aspects of interpersonal behavior* (pp. 117–198). Cambridge: Cambridge University Press.

Rhodewalt, F., & Morf, C. (1998). On self-aggrandizement and anger: A temporal analysis of narcissism and affective reactions to success and failure. *Journal of Personality & Social Psychology, 74*(3), 672–685.

Richards, J., & Gross, J. (1999). Composure at any cost? The cognitive consequences of emotion suppression. *Personality & Social Psychology Bulletin, 25*(8), 1033–1044.

Rosenberg, M. (1965). *Society and the adolescent self-image.* Princeton, NJ: Princeton University Press.

Rusting, C. L., & Nolen-Hoeksema, S. (1998). Regulating responses to anger: Effects of rumination and distraction on angry mood. *Journal of Personality & Social Psychology, 74,* 790–803.

Salminen, J., & Saarijarvi, S. (1999). Alexithymia: A facet of essential hypertension. *Hypertension, 33,* 1057–1061.

Salovey, P. (2001). Applied emotional intelligence: Regulating emotions to become healthy, wealthy, and wise. In J. Ciarrochi & J. P. Forgas (Eds.), *Emotional intelligence in everyday life: A scientific inquiry* (pp. 168–184). Philadelphia: Psychology Press/Taylor & Francis.

Salovey, P., Mayer, J. D., Goldman, S. L., Turvey, C., & Palfai, T. P. (1995). Emotional attention, clarity, and repair: Exploring emotional intelligence using the Trait Meta-Mood Scale. In J. W. Pennebaker (Ed.), *Emotion, disclosure, & health* (pp. 125–154). Washington, DC: American Psychological Association.

Sapolsky, R. M. (1999). The physiology and pathophysiology of unhappiness. In D. Kahneman, E. Diener, & N. Schwarz (Eds.), *Well-being: The foundation of hedonic psychology* (pp. 453–469). New York: Russell Sage Foundation.

Schutte, N. S., Malouff, J. M., Hall, L. E., Haggerty, D. J., Cooper, J. T., Golden, C. J., & Dornheim, L. (1998). Development and validation of a measure of emotional intelligence. *Personality & Individual Differences, 25,* 167–177.

Scott, V., Stiles, K., Raines, D., & Koth, A. (2002). Mood, rumination, and mood awareness in the athletic performance of collegiate tennis players. *North American Journal of Psychology, 4*(3), 457–468.

Segal, Z. V., Williams, J. M. G., & Teasdale, J. D. (2002). *Mindfulness-based cognitive therapy for depression: A new approach to preventing relapse.* New York: Guilford.

Shewchuk, R. M., Johnson, M. O., & Elliott, T. R. (2000). Self-appraised social problem solving abilities, emotional reactions and actual problem solving performance. *Behaviour Research & Therapy, 38,* 727–740.

Smith, T. W. (1992). Hostility and health: Current status of a psychosomatic hypothesis. *Health Psychology, 11,* 139–150.

Sommer, K. L., & Baumeister, R. F. (2002). Self-evaluation, persistence, and performance following implicit rejection: The role of trait self-esteem. *Personality & Social Psychology Bulletin, 28,* 926–938.

Tafarodi, R. W., & Vu, C. (1997). Two-dimensional self-esteem and reactions to success and failure. *Personality & Social Psychology Bulletin, 23,* 626–635.

Tang, T. L.-P., & Reynolds, D. B. (1993). Effects of self-esteem and perceived goal difficulty on goal setting, certainty, task performance, and attributions. *Human Resource Development Quarterly, 4,* 153–170.

Taylor, G. J. (2000). Recent developments in alexithymia theory and research. *Canadian Journal of Psychiatry, 45,* 134–142.

Taylor, G. J. (2001). Low emotional intelligence and mental illness. In J. Ciarrochi & J. P. Forgas (Eds.), *Emotional intelligence in everyday life: A scientific inquiry* (pp. 67–81). Philadelphia: Psychology Press/Taylor & Francis.

Taylor, G. J., & Bagby, R. (2000). An overview of the alexithymia construct. In R. Bar-On & J. D. A. Parker (Eds.), *The handbook of emotional intelligence: Theory, development, assessment, and application at home, school, and in the workplace* (pp. 40–67). San Francisco: Jossey-Bass.

Thoreau, H. D. (1908). *Walden.* London: J. M. Dent.

Thorpe, G. L., Parker, J. D., & Barnes, G. S. (1992). The Common Beliefs Survey III and its subscales: Discriminant validity in clinical and nonclinical subjects. *Journal of Rational-Emotive & Cognitive Behavior Therapy, 10,* 95–104.

Thorpe, G. L., Walter, M. I., Kingery, L. R., & Nay, W. T. (2002). The Common Beliefs Survey–III and the Situational Self-Statement and Affective State Inventory: Test-rest reliability, internal consistency, and further psychometric consideration. *Journal of Rational-Emotive & Cognitive Behavior Therapy, 19,* 89–103.

Todarello, O., Taylor, G. J., Parker, J. D., & Fanelli, M. (1995). Alexithymia in essential hypertensive and psychiatric outpatients: A comparative study. *Journal of Psychosomatic Research, 39,* 987–994.

Turvey, C., & Salovey, P. (1994). Measures of repression: Converging on the same construct? *Imagination, Cognition & Personality, 13*(4), 279–289.

Wansink, D. (2000). *The role of defensive self-enhancement in self-regulation failure by people with high self-esteem.* Buffalo, New York: State University of New York at Buffalo.

Wastell, C. (2002). Exposure to trauma: The long-term effects of suppressing emotional reactions. *Journal of Nervous & Mental Disease, 190*(12), 839–845.

Wegner, D. M. (1994). Ironic processes of mental control. *Psychological Review, 10,* 34–52.

Wegner, D. M., & Zanakos, S. (1994). Chronic thought suppression. *Journal of Personality, 62,* 615–640.

Weinberger, D. A., Schwartz, G. E., & Davidson, R. J. (1979). Low-anxious, high-anxious, and repressive coping styles: Psychometric patterns and behavioral and physiological responses to stress. *Journal of Abnormal Psychology, 88,* 369–380.

Weissman, A. (2000). Dysfunctional Attitude Scale (DAS). In K. Corcoran & J. Fischer (Eds.), *Measures for clinical practice; A sourcebook* (Vol. 2, pp. 187–190). New York: Free Press.

Wenzlaff, R. M., & Wegner, D. M. (2000). Though suppression. *Annual Review of Psychology, 51,* 59–91.

Wilson, K. G., & Murrel, A. R. (2003). Value-centered interventions: Setting a course for behavioral treatment. In S. C. Hayes, V. M. Follette, & M. Linehan (Eds.), *The new behavior therapies: Expanding the cognitive-behavioral tradition.* New York: Guilford Press.

Wulfert, E., Greenway, D. E., Farkas, P., & Hayes, S. C. (1994). Correlation between self-reported rigidity and rule-governed insensitivity to operant contingencies. *Journal of Applied Behavior Analysis, 27,* 659–671.

Zeitlin, S. B., & McNally, R. J. (1993). Alexithymia and anxiety sensitivity in panic disorder and obsessive-compulsive disorder. *American Journal of Psychiatry, 150,* 658–660.

Chapter 3

An Ability Model of Emotional Intelligence: Implications for Assessment and Training

Paulo N. Lopes
Yale University

Stéphane Côté
University of Toronto

Peter Salovey
Yale University

In this chapter, we discuss a theoretical model that views emotional intelligence as a set of interrelated abilities involved in perceiving, using, understanding, and managing emotions. These abilities rely on knowledge of emotional processes and information-processing skills. They are thought to develop through learning and experience and are amenable to training. In relation to broader conceptions of emotional intelligence encompassing personality traits and motivational factors, the model we adopt has two advantages. One is that it can stimulate more focused research aimed at understanding the information-processing skills and strategies that underlie emotional intelligence. Another advantage is that it paves the way for assessing emotional intelligence through performance tests that measure people's actual rather than self-perceived abilities. This helps to overcome the limitations of self-report measures, which assess self-perceived abilities. These tend to overlap with well-established measures of personality traits and are prone to self-enhancement and faking. Research based on performance measures has yielded substantially different findings from that based on self-report measures of emotional intelligence.

We review empirical evidence suggesting that emotional abilities, assessed through performance-based tests, are related to a number of outcomes likely to contribute to work performance. These outcomes include quality of interpersonal interactions, teamwork, stress tolerance, and leadership qualities. We also review findings from workplace studies suggesting that emotional abilities are related to job performance, assessed by peer and supervisor ratings as well as by objective criteria such as merit increases and company rank.

Then we discuss the implications of these findings for workplace assessment and training and outline possible strategies for training emotional abilities in the workplace. We try to address questions such as, To what extent can these abilities really be modified? To what extent are emotional abilities linked to personality traits that seem very difficult to change? What sort of results can companies expect from training programs designed to enhance emotional skills in the workplace? In addressing these questions, we broaden the discussion and synthesize findings from different lines of work.

The media and popular press have often conveyed overinflated expectations about emotional intelligence. Given the dearth of rigorous evaluations of training programs aimed at developing emotional abilities, we try to provide a balanced discussion of the potential and limitations of such programs. We hope this will help readers to make sound decisions about assessment and training. We argue that an important part of the benefits of emotional skills training is likely to be deferred over time. Learning to manage emotions and relationships with others is a lifelong process. As the years go by, we are always learning to adjust to new situations, fine-tuning emotional reactions, and honing social skills. Accordingly, we should not expect any training program to make adults more emotionally intelligent overnight. However, emotional skills training may help people to pay more attention to social and emotional dynamics as well as to learn from their everyday experiences and interactions with others. Training may give people the motivation and resources to learn and develop. If this happens, organizations may reap immediate benefits from a boost in workers' self-confidence and motivation and deferred benefits as people learn to manage their emotions and interact more effectively with others.

AN ABILITY MODEL OF EMOTIONAL INTELLIGENCE

Many investigators have argued that IQ or analytical intelligence does not encompass the full spectrum of abilities that contribute to adaptation and success in life (Cantor & Kihlstrom, 1987; Gardner, 1983; Sternberg, 1999a). IQ explains about 15% to 25% of individual differences in job performance or career success (Herrnstein & Murray, 1994; Schmidt & Hunter, 1998). Personality traits such as conscientiousness also contribute to these outcomes (Barrick & Mount, 1991; Tett, Jackson, & Rothstein, 1991). Nevertheless, IQ and broad personality traits together leave unexplained a large amount of variability associated with individual differences in job performance. It is most likely that emotional, social, creative, and practical abilities also influence work-related outcomes.

For most of Western history, emotions were viewed as disrupting clear thinking and decision making. "Rule thy feelings, lest thy feelings rule you," wrote Publilius Syrus in the first century B.C. Darwin (1965/1872) was one of the first scientists to recognize the adaptive value of emotions for communication and for guiding behavior, energizing reactions such as fighting or fleeing from danger. Yet it was only over the last 5 decades that psychologists began to systematically investigate the adaptive role of emotions (Leeper, 1948). This led to a functionalist perspective that views emotions as motivating adaptive behavior, communicating nonverbal information, and regulating social interaction.

A large body of research now suggests that emotions play an important role in guiding thinking and decision making (Loewenstein, Weber, Hsee, & Welch, 2001). For example, happy moods can facilitate divergent thinking and enhance creativity (Isen & Daubman, 1984; Isen, Daubman, & Nowicki, 1987). Conversely, sad moods or anxiety can focus attention on threats, enhance deductive reasoning and attention to detail, and contribute to a sober assessment of risks (Isen, 1987; Palfai & Salovey, 1993; Schwarz, 1990; Schwarz & Clore, 1996). Emotions can also have a profound influence on interpersonal and group dynamics (Barsade, 2002). As a result, emotional processes have received increasing attention in the study of organizational behavior (Barsade, Brief, & Spataro, 2003).

The quest for a broader understanding of intelligence, and increasing evidence that emotions play an adaptive role in guiding human behavior, thinking, and communication, led to the idea that emotional abilities represent a distinct form of intelligence. Salovey and Mayer proposed a theory of emotional intelligence that encompasses four interrelated abilities: perceiving and expressing emotions, using emotions to facilitate thinking, understanding emotions, and managing emotions in self and others (Mayer & Salovey, 1997; Salovey & Mayer, 1990; Salovey, Woolery, & Mayer, 2001). These abilities are expected to influence people's capacity to interact well with others, communicate effectively, handle conflict, manage stress, perform under pressure, and create a positive work environment. All these processes are likely to contribute to work performance.

Our research on emotional intelligence focuses on abilities that are closely linked to emotional processes. Others have written about emotional intelligence as a much broader concept, encompassing personality traits, motivational factors, and many different skills (e.g., Bar-On, 2000; Boyatzis, Goleman, & Rhee, 2000; Goleman, 1995, 1998). As a result, the term *emotional intelligence* is now used to mean different things. To avoid confusion, it is important to distinguish between these perspectives (see Mayer, Salovey, & Caruso, 2000). This is especially true because different perspectives have led to different approaches to the measurement of emotional intelligence and yielded substantially different research findings. In this chapter we focus on the narrower definition of emotional intelligence. We think this approach is particularly useful for research. It may enable us to reach a deeper understanding of emotional abilities and avoid redundancy with concepts that have already been studied extensively by other researchers. In drawing conclusions for assessment and training, however, we must look at the broader picture and consider findings from related lines of research.

Because different researchers often use the same terms to mean different things, it is important to clarify the terms used in this chapter. When we refer to emotional intelligence, emotional abilities, and emotional skills, we refer to capacities that involve emotional information processing and range from the more general (intelligence) to the more specific (skills; see Carroll, 1993). Thus, emotional intelligence encompasses four abilities (perceiving, using, understanding, and managing emotions), and each of these abilities encompasses lower order skills. For example, the ability to manage emotions in self and others encompasses skills involved in relaxation, reframing negative events in a more positive light, empathic listening, and so forth.

Common definitions of intelligence posit that intelligence represents a cohesive domain of ability. In this chapter, we use the term *emotional intelligence* because there is evidence that emotional abilities are interrelated and represent a distinct construct (Mayer, Salovey, Caruso, & Sitarenios, 2003), although further research is needed to evaluate to what extent they truly define a cohesive domain of ability. According to general intelligence theory, intelligence and abilities are largely innately determined, whereas the development of skills is influenced to a greater extent by people's interests, effort, and learning. In contrast, we view emotional skills, abilities, and intelligence as forms of expertise (Sternberg, 1999b) that develop through learning and experience, although they are likely influenced by genetic factors as well.

Some authors write about emotional intelligence as encompassing social skills. This makes sense in so far as emotional processes influence social interactions, and emotional and social skills are closely intertwined when it comes to managing emotions in interpersonal situations. Nonetheless, we think it is useful to view emotional and social skills as distinct although partially overlapping constructs, because aggregating them yields an excessively broad and ill-defined construct that is unwieldy for research. In this chapter, we use the term *social skills* to refer to skills that help people to interact effectively with others and do not fall strictly under the realms of emotional or analytical intelligence. For example, social skills might include using cues related to power differences, proximity, and dress to interpret social situations; using perspective taking to understand other people's intentions; or using one's knowledge of social norms and human nature to navigate interpersonal encounters.

Four Abilities Underlying Emotional Intelligence

The theory of emotional intelligence proposed by Salovey and Mayer (1990; Mayer & Salovey, 1997) encompasses four interrelated abilities: perceiving, using, understanding, and managing emotions. The first ability involves identifying emotions in oneself and others as well as in objects of art and other stimuli. It entails identifying information conveyed by facial expressions, tone of voice, gestures, body posture, color, rhythm, bodily sensations, and other cues. It also involves the capacity to express emotions effectively using such cues. The ability to decode emotional information helps one to appraise important situations, whereas the ability to express emotions contributes to effective communication.

The second ability involves using emotions to facilitate thinking. This entails a capacity to generate, use, and feel emotion in order to focus attention, reason, and communicate. It entails the capacity to associate mental images and emotions and knowing how emotions influence cognitive processes such as deductive reasoning, problem solving, creativity, and communication. This ability may contribute to the quality of decision making, among other processes.

The third ability involves understanding emotional processes. This entails understanding what events are likely to trigger different emotions, how emotions combine to form complex blends of feelings, and how emotions progress over time, sometimes generating a chain of emotional reactions. A deep understanding of emotional processes may help one to judge how other people might respond to different situations—or to different negotiation strategies, for example.

The fourth and last ability has to do with managing emotions in oneself and in emotionally challenging interpersonal situations. It entails modulating the experience and expression of emotions within oneself and in the context of interpersonal interactions, in order to achieve one's goals. This could mean reframing a bad experience to make it seem more bearable; telling a funny story to keep one's colleagues in good spirits; playing up one's anger to make sure that a subordinate gets the message; or dampening one's exhilaration about a promotion if a colleague who is sitting nearby did not even get a bonus. This ability may help people to expand their social networks, get others excited about a project, provide performance feedback without hurting others' feelings, and diffuse conflicts in a team.

ASSESSING EMOTIONAL ABILITIES

Most studies of emotional intelligence in the workplace conducted to date have relied on self-report measures of emotional intelligence that have several limitations. Some of the most widely used self-report measures do not discriminate perceived emotional abilities from personality traits (Brackett & Mayer, 2003), raising concerns that emotional intelligence measures are reinventing the wheel. Self-report measures are also prone to self-deceptive enhancement and deliberate faking and tend to correlate weakly with ability tests (e.g., Brackett & Mayer, 2003; Mabe & West, 1982; Paulhus, Lysy, & Yik, 1998).

Imagine that you need to select job candidates with strong cognitive abilities. You can ask candidates to rate their own abilities by indicating their agreement with statements such as, "I am very good at solving logical problems." Yet one candidate may exaggerate his or her abilities more than another, and therefore these responses may be a poor indicator of their actual abilities. A better approach would be to administer ability tests to all candidates and select the candidates with the highest scores. The same idea applies to emotional intelligence.

Ability tests of emotional intelligence were developed in an effort to overcome the limitations of self-reports of emotional intelligence and provide a more objective assessment of people's actual rather than self-perceived abilities. The most recently developed performance measure is the Mayer–Salovey–Caruso Emotional Intelligence Test (MSCEIT; Mayer, Salovey, & Caruso, 2002). This test assesses people's performance on the four dimensions of emotional intelligence, using two tasks for each dimension. The tasks include decoding the emotional information conveyed by facial expressions and designs, evaluating what moods facilitate performance on various tasks, understanding blends of emotions and emotional dynamics, and evaluating the effectiveness of strategies for regulating emotions in various situations. The MSCEIT takes about 45 min to complete and can be scored in two ways. Expert scores reflect the degree of agreement between an individual's responses and those of a panel of 21 experts, drawn from an international society of emotion researchers. Consensus scores reflect the extent to which the test taker's responses agree with those of a normative sample of 5,000 individuals. Because experts tend to endorse consensual responses, expert and consensus scores correlate highly on the MSCEIT ($r > .90$; Mayer et al., 2003).

The MSCEIT is reliable—split-half reliabilities range from .76 to .91 for the four branches (Mayer et al., 2003). Confirmatory factor analyses indicate that the eight tasks comprising this test represent four distinct but interrelated abilities, which can also be subsumed under a single general factor of emotional intelligence (Mayer et al., 2003). These findings support the four-branch model of emotional intelligence. MSCEIT scores are unrelated to current mood or to people's tendency to provide socially acceptable answers (Barchard, 2001; Lopes, Salovey, & Straus, 2003).

Cultural differences among Western nations do not seem to distort seriously people's responses to this test. There are both universal elements and cultural differences in the experience and expression of emotion (e.g., Ekman, 1972, 1994; Izard, 1971; Markus & Kitayama, 1991; Mesquita & Frijda, 1992; Russell, 1994; Scherer & Wallbott, 1994). The MSCEIT was designed to tap into the more universal aspects of emotional experience. For example, there was high agreement between the pattern of responses provided by a German sample and that of the mostly North American normative sample (correlations ranged from .86 to .93 for the four branches; Lopes, Brackett, Nezleck, Schütz, Sellin, & Salovey, 2004). Women tend to score slightly higher than men on the MSCEIT (Mayer et al., 2002), as they do on other measures of interpersonal sensitivity and social skills (e.g., Hall & Bernieri, 2001). Ethnic differences are slight, and no one group scores systematically higher or lower than others on all the branches of emotional intelligence (Mayer et al., 2002). Evidence of the predictive validity of emotional intelligence is accumulating rapidly, as reviewed subsequently.

Anyone intending to use measures of emotional intelligence in the workplace needs to understand the strengths and limitations of these measures. The main advantage of performance measures is that they may yield an objective assessment of people's actual rather than self-perceived emotional abilities. This is an important consideration for recruitment purposes. Additionally, performance measures share limited overlap with personality traits and have the potential to yield a deeper understanding of emotional processes, which makes them particularly valuable for research. Yet performance measures of emotional intelligence also have limitations.

With regard to managing emotions, for example, a test such as the MSCEIT is likely to tap into knowledge of appropriate responses rather than into people's actual capacity to implement these responses in real life. A paper-based test such as the MSCEIT cannot assess all there is to emotional intelligence. Moreover, there are no absolute right and wrong answers to many emotionally challenging situations. This raises questions about the interpretation of test scores (Matthews, Zeidner, & Roberts, 2002). A similar problem arises in the assessment of practical, creative, and other abilities (Sternberg et al., 2000). Current ability measures of emotional intelligence deal with this problem by assessing the degree to which one's responses agree with expert and consensus norms. This makes sense in so far as emotional abilities must necessarily reflect attunement to social norms and expectations, and experts seem to agree with consensual opinion. At the same time, this type of scoring penalizes original responses. If some people develop unusual strategies for managing emotionally charged situations, they may receive lower scores on the MSCEIT even if they actually manage emotional situations effectively in real life. For example, in one study we found that a sample of MBA students who had been selected for their interpersonal skills, among other criteria, scored significantly lower than the mean of the average population on the Perceiving and Managing Emotions subscales of the MSCEIT (Hagerty, Lopes, & Salovey, 2002). In this case, we do not know to what extent lower scores reflect lesser ability or merely a different style of handling emotionally charged situations. This highlights the need to exercise extreme caution in interpreting test scores. We also urge caution in using these measures for recruitment purposes until they are further validated in different work settings.

HOW CAN EMOTIONAL ABILITIES CONTRIBUTE TO JOB PERFORMANCE?

Emotional abilities can help people to achieve their goals in life (Salovey, Mayer, & Caruso, 2002). These goals might include establishing good relationships with others, maintaining a healthy emotional balance, and being successful at work. How people use their abilities depends on their motivations, however. Emotional abilities could also be used for exploitative or dishonest purposes that undermine organizational goals, for example.

Several authors have argued that workers' overall performance encompasses both task performance and other, more indirect, contributions (e.g., Motowidlo & Van Scotter, 1994; Rotundo & Sackett, 2002). Task performance involves activities that are formally recognized as part of a job. It entails proficiency in job-specific tasks for which employees are directly responsible. Yet productive employees support organizational goals in many other ways. For example, they cooperate with other coworkers, make constructive suggestions, facilitate team performance, and contribute to a positive work environment and group morale. These other dimensions have often been labeled organizational citizenship behavior. Interpersonal facilitation refers to a specific type of organizational citizenship behaviors, involving interpersonally oriented behaviors that contribute to organizational goals (Van Scotter & Motowidlo, 1996).

We propose that emotional abilities contribute to both task performance and interpersonal facilitation. For example, the ability to manage emotions may help people to perform effectively and make sound decisions under pressure. It may buffer employees against emotional burnout and help them to remain productive and motivated during stressful periods of organizational change. Emotional abilities may be particularly important for interpersonal facilitation because emotions play a crucial role in social interaction. Organizations increasingly assign duties to teams and rely on informal networks rather than a rigid chain of command. Emotional abilities may help individuals to negotiate the challenges of teamwork and navigate all the interpersonal interactions involved in getting their job done (e.g., Caruso et al., 2002; Côté & Morgan, 2002). People's capacity to nurture positive relationships at work may also help them to accumulate social capital, that is, connections and goodwill that one can draw on for support, advice, and other resources when needed. In turn, social capital helps workers achieve success in so far as they depend on interpersonal relationships to achieve their goals (Seibert, Kraimer, & Liden, 2001). Emotional abilities may help workers adapt to structural changes in organizations, such as when companies adopt matrix structures (Sy & Côté, in press). Emotional abilities may also help people to communicate effectively and influence others to get what they want, thereby enhancing their performance.

Various lines of research suggest that emotion plays a crucial role in social interaction. First, expressions of emotion signal one's goals and intentions to others (Ekman, 1993; Keltner & Haidt, 1999, 2001). For example, expressions of guilt signal that one has violated the norm of reciprocity and intends to engage in remedial actions that reestablish reciprocity (Tangney, 1991). Second, individuals may use others' displays of emotions as guides for their own behavior. For example, individuals respond to other people's sadness with empathic and helpful behavior (Clark, Pataki, & Carver, 1996; Eisenberg et al., 1989). Third, individuals can be influenced by the emotional states of the people they interact with, through a largely subconscious process of emotional contagion (Barsade, 2002; Hatfield, Cacioppo, & Rapson, 1994). Fourth, unregulated negative emotions can undermine the smooth orchestration of complex skills involved in social interaction (e.g., Baumeister & Tice, 1990; Csikszentmihalyi, 1992). Fifth, and related to the previous findings, there is evidence that positive emotions enhance sociability and elicit positive responses from others, whereas unregulated negative emotions can drive other people away (e.g., Argyle & Lu, 1990; Furr & Funder, 1998).

Several authors have also suggested that emotional intelligence contributes to leadership (e.g., Ashkanasy & Tse, 2000; Caruso et al., 2002; George, 2000). Leaders need to inspire and motivate others, and emotions are powerful motivational forces. Leaders therefore need to use and manage emotions intelligently to communicate effectively and influence others.

RESEARCH FINDINGS BASED ON ABILITY MEASURES OF EMOTIONAL INTELLIGENCE

Here we report findings from a series of studies conducted with performance measures of emotional intelligence that help us to understand the role of emotional abilities in the workplace. This research avoids some of the limitations of studies based on self-report measures of emotional intelligence, including inaccurate self-assessment, faking, and overlap with personality traits (Brackett & Mayer, 2003). In fact, scores on performance measures of emotional intelligence seem unrelated to socially desirable responding (Barchard, 2001; Lopes, Salovey, & Straus, 2003). This suggests that performance scores are less influenced by impression management and social desirability bias than self-report scores. Performance measures also reveal little overlap with well-established measures of personality traits and intelligence. This suggests that ability measures of emotional intelligence are assessing something new, rather than reinventing the wheel. Scores on the MSCEIT tend to be weakly correlated with the Big Five personality traits of emotional instability, social extraversion, agreeableness, conscientiousness, and openness to experience or intellect (Barchard, 2001; Brackett & Mayer, 2003; Lopes, Salovey, & Straus, 2003). The highest correlation is with agreeableness (in the .3 range), suggesting that more emotionally intelligent individuals tend to be more prosocial and less hostile than others. Correlations between emotional abilities and various indicators of cognitive ability or IQ also tend to be low (Barchard, 2001; Brackett & Mayer, 2003; Lopes, Salovey, & Straus, 2003; Roberts, Zeidner, & Matthews, 2001). The strongest relation observed involved understanding emotions and verbal ability, as expected, because this part of the test relies on knowledge of emotional vocabulary ($r = .39$ in a college student sample; Lopes, Salovey, & Straus, 2003).

Emotional Abilities, Prosocial Behavior, and Quality of Interpersonal Relationships

Evidence is accumulating that emotional abilities are associated with empathy, prosocial behavior, and the quality of interpersonal relationships. Early findings with a test similar to the MSCEIT provided evidence for the link between emotional intelligence and self-reported empathy (Ciarrochi, Chan, & Caputi, 2000; Mayer, Caruso, & Salovey, 1999; Rubin, 1999). The association with the personality trait of agreeableness has been confirmed by a number of researchers using the MSCEIT (Barchard, 2001; Brackett & Mayer, 2003; Lopes, Salovey, & Straus, 2003), suggesting that emotionally intelligent people are more prosocial than their counterparts. Adolescents scoring higher on emotional intelligence were also rated by their peers as less aggressive, and by their teachers as more prosocial, than students scoring lower on emotional intelligence (Rubin, 1999). Male college students scoring higher on the MSCEIT also reported engaging less frequently in behaviors such as physical violence and vandalism (Brackett, Mayer, & Warner, 2004). All these findings support the relation between emotional intelligence and prosocial behavior.

Several studies indicate that the ability to manage emotions is associated with both the self-perceived quality of interpersonal relationships and whether people are viewed favorably by others. In a sample of 103 American college students, scores on the Managing Emotions subscale of the MSCEIT were associated with self-reports of the global quality of interpersonal relationships. Higher Managing Emotions scores were also associated with self-reports of more supportive relationships with parents and less conflictive relationships with a close friend (Lopes, Salovey, & Straus, 2003). In another study, higher Managing Emotions scores were positively related to the quality of interactions with friends, evaluated separately by participants and two friends (Lopes, Brackett, et al., 2004; Study 1). In a study with German college students, participants reported on their social interactions every day for 2 weeks. Individuals with higher scores on Managing Emotions tended to be more satisfied with their daily interactions with people of the opposite sex, which are likely to be more emotionally arousing. They also perceived themselves to be more successful at impression management in daily social interactions (Lopes, Brackett, et al., 2004; Study 2). Another study asked college students to rate themselves and nominate up to eight colleagues living in their residential college in response to a questionnaire spanning a broad range of social and emotional attributes. Those scoring higher on the Managing Emotions branch of the MSCEIT reported higher self-perceived interpersonal sensitivity and were more favorably viewed by their residential college classmates (Lopes, Salovey, Côté, & Beers, in press). In particular, they received a higher proportion of positive versus negative peer nominations as well more peer nominations for interpersonal sensitivity and reciprocal friendship and liking.

In these last four studies, emotional abilities were related to various indicators of quality of interpersonal relationships over and above the Big Five personality traits. Two of these studies controlled statistically for academic intelligence as well. This suggests that emotional abilities are associated with important outcomes in life, over and above personality traits and academic intelligence. Yet personality traits were also significant predictors of the quality of interpersonal relationships. This suggests that we need to take into account both emotional abilities and personality traits to understand social functioning.

In a separate line of investigation, Brackett and Mayer (2003) found that emotional abilities were positively associated with self-reported interpersonal competence, measured by the Emotional Quotient Inventory (Bar-On, 1997; $r = .28$ for MSCEIT total scores). They also assessed the quality of interpersonal relationships by asking participants to report the number of times that they engaged in particular behaviors, such as having a long conversation with a friend, and the number of times that certain events happened to them, such as getting screamed at by a friend (Brackett, Mayer, &

Warner, 2004). Emotional intelligence was associated with more positive and fewer negative interpersonal events.

Research findings linking emotional intelligence to high-quality social relationships have implications for the performance of employees in organizations. First, the results suggest that emotionally intelligent individuals may engage in more extra-role behaviors such as helping coworkers and spreading goodwill about the organization than their counterparts. Second, emotionally intelligent individuals may garner more social capital than their counterparts, and social capital is, in turn, related to career success. Third, people may generally have favorable attitudes about emotionally intelligent individuals, and as a consequence emotionally intelligent individuals may receive better advice, more social support, and higher performance evaluations than their counterparts. Finally, the ability to manage emotions appears to be more strongly and consistently associated with the quality of social interactions than the other branches of emotional intelligence. This suggests that programs of emotional skills training aimed at enhancing people's capacity to interact with others should probably emphasize skills related to managing emotions.

Emotional Abilities and Work Performance

Research using ability measures of emotional intelligence in the workplace has a short history. Nonetheless, preliminary findings suggest that emotional abilities are associated with various work-related outcomes. The outcomes evaluated encompass overall performance, teamwork, decision making, leadership, interpersonal facilitation, and stress tolerance.

The relation between emotional abilities and leadership qualities was explored in a study involving management students working on a 10-week project in small groups (Côté, Lopes, & Salovey, 2004). Individuals scoring highly on the MSCEIT were rated by their peers as proposing more compelling goals and ideas for their group project. This relation was statistically significant after controlling for personality traits and demographic characteristics. These findings suggests that emotionally intelligent individuals may be more successful in producing and communicating inspiring visions or in generating enthusiasm and hope for their ideas. Thus, emotionally intelligent leaders may perform better than their counterparts.

A study conducted for the U.S. Navy looked at performance in four group exercises simulating activities relevant to job performance (Graves, 1999). The study design emulated the recruitment process at an assessment center. The study involved 148 people aged 17 to 30. The exercises included a consensual group decision-making activity, a leaderless group discussion simulating the selection of job candidates, a task that required the sharing of information for effective group performance, and a task involving intergroup competition. The four group exercises lasted 3 hr. Participants' performance was rated by four observers as well as by their peers, on 12 dimensions including social sensitivity, teamwork, oral communication, judgment, behavioral flexibility, leadership, initiative, and organization and planning. Emotional intelligence scores predicted aggregate scores for both assessor and peer ratings. These findings remained significant after controlling for a composite measure of cognitive ability. This study suggests that emotional abilities may contribute to effective performance in group decision making and other group activities, over and above IQ.

Another study looked at 69 undergraduate students working part-time jobs. There was a positive relation between emotional intelligence scores and supervisor ratings of job performance (Janovics & Christiansen, 2001). The results remained statistically significant after controlling for cognitive ability, assessed by the Wonderlic Personnel Test (Wonderlic & Associates, 1992), although not after controlling for the personality trait of conscientiousness.

A study conducted in the financial services center of a large insurance company involved 164 staff grouped in 26 teams. Teams with higher average scores for managing emotions received higher performance rankings from managers, especially for customer service (Rice, 1999). Team leaders scoring higher on perceiving, understanding, and managing emotions also received higher performance rankings from departmental managers. This study suggests that emotional abilities contribute to team effectiveness and work performance.

A study of 42 high school teachers in Spain found significant relations between managing emotions ability, on the one hand, and burnout and mental health, on the other (Extremera, Fernández-Berrocal, Lopes, & Salovey, 2004). Scores on the Managing Emotions subscale of the MSCEIT were positively related to self-reports of mental health assessing happiness, nervousness, and depression over the previous 4 weeks. Managing Emotions scores were also negatively associated with the Depersonalization subscale of the Maslach Burnout Inventory (Maslach & Jackson, 1986) and positively associated with the Personal Accomplishment subscale. The ability to manage emotions, assessed by the MSCEIT, explained significant variance in these criteria even when controlling for age and gender as well as for the self-perceived ability to repair negative moods.

Hard data supporting the criterion validity of emotional intelligence in the workplace were provided by a recent study conducted at a Fortune 400 insurance company in the northeastern United States (Lopes, Côté, Grewal, Kadis, Gall, & Salovey, 2003). The sample consisted of 44 analysts and administrative/clerical staff. Here, emotional abilities were associated with percent merit increases and company rank as well as with peer and supervisor ratings. Higher emotional intelligence scores were associated with higher peer ratings of interpersonal sensitivity, sociability, contribution to a positive work environment, and positive mood. Emotional intelligence scores were also positively related to supervisor ratings of interpersonal sensitivity, sociability, liking, contribution to a positive work environment, stress tolerance, and leadership potential. These relations generally remained statistically significant when controlling for other predictors, including education, demographics, personality, and verbal ability, one at a time. Because the sample was small, we have to be careful about drawing inferences from this study. More generally, we note that many of the findings in this section are not yet published and need to be replicated.

When Emotional Abilities May Be Associated With Negative Outcomes

When we evaluate the role of emotional intelligence in the workplace, emotional abilities may not always be associated with positive outcomes. Emotionally intelligent behavior may sometimes entail trade-offs. For example, in the insurance company study conducted by Rice (1999), team leaders' scores for understanding emotions were associated with higher manager ratings of customer service but lower ratings of team productivity. It is possible that team leaders who were better at understanding emotions paid more attention to customer service and less attention to productivity. For customer claims teams, there may be a trade-off between customer service and productivity.

In another study, college students engaged in a half-hour negotiation exercise simulating a company meeting where they had to allocate a limited sum of bonus money to several candidates (Lopes, Salovey, Nezlek, & Straus, 2003). Each participant represented a different candidate. Participants who scored higher on the Perceiving Emotions subscale of the MSCEIT were better able to identify the emotions that their colleagues actually experienced during the negotiation. Nevertheless, they were rated by their peers as less warm and likable. It is possible that people who are better at decoding facial expressions of emotion also tend to be more observant. They may prefer to sit back and watch others rather than jump into the heat of an argument—especially when faced with a zero-sum game, as in this case. As a result, they may come across as somewhat cold and distant in a first encounter. This highlights the importance of striving for flexibility, balance, and attunement to the social context when using or training emotional skills.

IDEAS FOR TRAINING EMOTIONAL SKILLS

The evidence gathered so far suggests that emotional abilities are associated with various positive outcomes likely to contribute to work performance. Although the studies reviewed in the previous section do not disentangle cause and effect, they suggest the possibility that training emotional skills may enhance work performance. Experiential learning involving interpersonal interaction and quality feedback may be very useful for developing both social and emotional skills. This approach is used in a number of executive training seminars. In this section we discuss other possible ways to train emotional skills in the workplace and other settings, based on the ability model of emotional intelligence described previously.

We do not know of any training programs based on this model that have been rigorously evaluated. In fact, there seems to be a dearth of quality research evaluating the effectiveness of emotional skills training for adults. Nonetheless, studies that track people's development over the years suggest that emotional skills can be developed (e.g., Kagan, 1998; Vaillant, 2000). School-based programs of social and emotional learning for children and adolescents have been found to yield beneficial effects (e.g., Hawkins, Catalano, Kosterman, Abbott, & Hill, 1999; Kusché & Greenberg, 2001). Evaluations of worksite stress management interventions also provide some optimism (see Ivancevich, Matteson, Freedman, & Phillips, 1990, for a review).

Because it may be difficult to change people in a short time, we think that emotional skills training may be most beneficial if it enables and motivates people to learn from everyday experience beyond the training period. What people learn during a workshop may contribute directly to their work performance. However, the extent to which a workshop fuels people's motivation to learn from everyday experience and helps them to do so may be even more important in the long run. Training is likely to be most effective if it induces participants to pay more attention to the feelings and concerns of others and thereby enhances participants' understanding of others' motives and behavior. If that happens, training programs may generate accrued benefits over time as people learn to interact more effectively with others. Organizations may also reap short-term benefits from the boost in motivation and morale that such programs can provide.

Perceiving and Communicating Emotion

Emotions are associated with specific displays that involve facial muscle action, bodily movement, and vocal signals, among others (Ekman, 1993; Keltner & Haidt, 1999). Training people to read facial displays associated with emotions like anger, fear, and happiness may help them to identify and pay more attention to subtle expressions of emotion in real life. For example, people can be trained to identify the difference between a real and a fake smile. A fake smile involves mostly movement of the muscles around the corners of the mouth. A real smile, known as the Duchenne smile, is difficult to fake because it involves movement of the muscles around the eyes in addition to the muscles around the mouth. Ekman and O'Sullivan

(1991) showed videotapes of individuals who were either lying or telling the truth to U.S. secret service agents, federal polygraphers, robbery investigators, judges, psychiatrists, students in a course on deceit, and college students. Only one of the groups was able to detect lies at a rate higher than chance: U.S. secret service agents. These were relatively successful because they examined facial signals of emotion as well as the content of the communication, whereas others focused mostly on the content. Detecting deception is difficult because the relevant cues are often ambiguous or unreliable. Nonetheless, training individuals to attend to emotional cues could enhance decoding accuracy and, more generally, induce them to pay more attention to others.

Real-life situations, films, and photographs can be used for training purposes. The Interpersonal Perception Task (IPT; Archer, Costanzo, & Akert, 2001) has been widely used in educational settings. One is asked to evaluate filmed sequences of interpersonal situations lasting a few minutes each. After watching a brief conversation, for example, one has to identify who is the boss and who is the supervisee. To judge these situations, one can draw on verbal and nonverbal cues. The latter include facial expressions of emotion, tone of voice, body posture, gestures, how far apart two people are sitting, how they are dressed, which one seems to be paying more attention to the other, and so forth. Discussing what cues might convey relevant information in various situations may raise people's awareness about different processes of nonverbal communicati on.

Using Emotion to Facilitate Thinking

Emotions influence thinking in many ways. For example, the emotions people experience at the time of a decision influence how much risk people take (see Loewenstein et al., 2001, for a review). Happiness can stimulate creative thinking. When people are in a happy mood, they generate more unusual responses to a word association task and perform better on problems requiring creativity, for example (Isen, 1999). In contrast, sad individuals process information more systematically (Schwarz, 2001). For instance, sad individuals discriminate best between strong and weak arguments in a persuasive message (Bless et al., 1996). Also, anger and happiness increase risk taking by increasing certainty over the outcomes of one's actions, whereas fear has the opposite effect (Lerner & Keltner, 2001). Understanding the consequences of emotion might enhance one's ability to use emotion to guide thinking and decision making. Emotionally intelligent individuals, for example, might forgo making important decisions when angry, knowing that their decisions may involve unreasonable degrees of risk.

Understanding Emotion

There are several possibilities for improving workers' understanding of emotion. First, one could discuss how emotions combine, progress, and transition from one to the other. Concrete examples may be useful. For example, we may get mad at some colleagues because of some remarks they made and lash out at them but then start thinking that we overreacted and feel guilty about it. Second, one could discuss similarities and differences among emotions. For example, what are the differences between rage, anger, irritation, annoyance, and frustration? Finally, one could discuss what triggers different emotions. Events are appraised along dimensions such as valence (i.e., pleasant vs. unpleasant), self-relevance (i.e., "To what extent does this event further or undermine my goals?"), and control (i.e., "How much personal control do I have over the event?"). This pattern of appraisals determines what emotion is felt (Frijda, 1986; Lazarus, 1991; Roseman & Smith, 2001). For example, appraising an event as unpleasant, important, certain, caused by another person, and requiring high effort elicits anger (Smith & Ellsworth, 1985). Such knowledge might enhance workers' ability to predict and understand their own and others' emotions.

Managing Emotions

Helping people to broaden their repertoire of coping strategies and try out new ways of handling emotionally charged situations may be a good way to enhance emotional management skills. This might involve discussing coping strategies and ways to handle particular situations to raise awareness about alternative strategies. Asking people to role play challenging situations could provide useful practice. Filming interactions to help people understand how they handle stressful situations and what they might do differently would be an interesting way to provide more individualized feedback.

A discussion of coping strategies might start with problem-focused coping. If a problem is bothering us, the best response may be to fix it rather than try to cope with the frustration. To this end, it may be useful to train people to address interpersonal problems and negotiate conflicts effectively. This could involve training staff to evaluate problems from other people's points of view, listen to what others have to say, pay attention to others' feelings and concerns, and try to come up with mutually beneficial solutions. Such training could combine emotional and negotiation skills, for example.

When problems cannot be easily or immediately fixed, there are a number of emotion-focused coping strategies that might help people to handle temporary feelings of anxiety, sadness, or frustration. One strategy is to re-evaluate the problem to make it seem less disturbing or otherwise reframe it in a more positive light. This could entail reframing a difficult situation as an opportunity to learn and finding meaning or wisdom in adversity. Another strategy is to engage in activities that are both absorbing and rewarding to take the problem off one's mind. One could also seek help and emotional support from others or engage in physical activity or meditation to relax.

In contrast, some strategies are likely to be maladaptive. Systematically avoiding or denying problems or turning to drugs (Carver, Scheier, & Weintraub, 1989) is likely to exacerbate problems in the long run. Deliberately trying to suppress negative thoughts does not work because suppressed thoughts seem to resurface in full force after a while (Wegner & Zanakos, 1994). Ruminating endlessly about a problem without doing anything about it may exacerbate a negative cycle leading to depression (Lyubomirsky & Nolen-Hoeksema, 1993, 1995).

Gross (1998) distinguished between antecedent-focused emotion regulation and response-focused emotion regulation. Antecedent-focused emotion regulation takes place before an emotion occurs. Individuals can change the way they evaluate events to alter their emotional impact. For example, an employee can evaluate a boss' criticism as a challenge to overcome instead of a sign of low ability. Response-focused emotion regulation takes place after an emotion occurs. Individuals can modify the way an emotion is displayed to others. For example, employees can amplify displays of happiness to coworkers and customers. Research suggests that antecedent-focused emotion regulation has more favorable consequences for workers than response-focused emotion regulation (Grandey, 2003; Gross, 1998; Richards & Gross, 2000). Accordingly, optimistic salespeople who evaluate rejections as challenges instead of failures are more likely to remain on the job and to attain high performance than pessimistic salespeople (Seligman & Schulman, 1985). Employees can thus be trained to regulate their emotions by changing the way they appraise events.

Because emotions are intimately associated with cognitive and social processes, there may be many ways to enhance workers' capacity to handle emotional problems. For example, training people to dispute overly negative thoughts may help to prevent the sort of rumination and catastrophizing that fuel anxiety, hopelessness, and depression (Seligman, 1990). Relaxation training involving deep breathing exercises may help people to face problems with some calm and peace of mind. Inspiring people to use mature defenses such as humor, and asking team leaders to set the example, might also be useful. Inspiring people to nurture a positive work atmosphere and savor good moments with colleagues may also help them to get over negative emotions more easily (Fredrickson, 2000). Nurturing a sense of shared meaning and purpose within teams, and keeping people focused on important goals, may help staff to endure minor setbacks and frustrations. Training managers to nurture workers' intrinsic motivation by providing challenges to match their level of skill and reinforcing their sense of autonomy and competence (Csikszentmihalyi, 1992) may help to buffer people against stress. Finally, providing opportunities for staff to bond and get rid of tension (through retreats, parties, sports, or outdoor activities) may help people to expand the network of relationships that they can draw on to solve problems at work. All these strategies could help people to capitalize on positive emotions and cope with negative emotions, thereby enhancing motivation and job satisfaction.

CHALLENGES AND IMPLICATIONS FOR TRAINING

We have argued that it may be useful to train emotional skills in the workplace and suggested a number ways of doing so. But exactly how should such training programs be designed (and tailored to different groups) to be most effective? What sort of results can companies expect from these training programs? Are these programs likely to be more or less effective than alternative types of training? We still do not have good answers to these questions. Nevertheless, in this section we synthesize findings from various lines of research to help readers assess the potential and limitations of emotional skills training. We focus on managing emotions because this ability seems to be particularly important for interpersonal interaction. Yet we also broaden our discussion to encompass social skills because managing emotions in interpersonal situations requires both social and emotional skills.

A number of challenges involved in the training of emotional skills have implications for the design or choice of training programs. First, there are many ways that people can manage their emotions and handle interpersonal challenges. What works for some people may not work for others. What works in some situations may not work in other circumstances. Adaptive emotional regulation entails attunement to context and flexibility. Introverts and extroverts may use different strategies to cope with stressful interpersonal situations. This suggests that in training emotional skills, we should respect individual differences, avoid simplistic recommendations, and strive to broaden people's repertoire of coping resources rather than drill a narrow set of skills.

General emotional dispositions, such as the tendency to be cheerful or anxious, for example, seem to be fairly stable and hard to change (e.g., Diener & Lucas, 1999; Watson, 2000). These dispositions may be partly heritable. They mold the development of personality and have a broad influence on social and emotional functioning throughout life (Caspi, 2000; Eisenberg et al., 2000; Watson, 2000). Nonetheless, there is some room for change (Kagan, 1998; Heatherton & Weinberger, 1994; Vaillant, 2000; Watson, 2000). Individuals may develop coping strategies to counter temperamental dispositions and thereby become less shy over the years, for example (Kagan, 1998). Studies tracking people over the life span suggest that most individuals learn to use more adaptive coping strategies, such as humor and sublimation (i.e., investing energy in more fruitful or acceptable goals), as they grow older (Vaillant, 2000). Although broad personality dispositions are hard to change, it is possible to change skills, habits, and attitudes (Costa & McCrae, 1994; Helson, & Stewart, 1994). These can make a big difference in the quality of one's interpersonal relationships, for example. In other words, it is difficult to change temperament, but people can learn to manage their emotions better and thereby improve their relationships with colleagues, clients, and supervisors.

Coping habits are often deeply entrenched and hard to change, because we tend to enact the same responses over and over, to the point that they become nearly automatic. As a result, it may require deliberate effort, repeated practice, and time to change deeply engraved reactions. Accordingly, we should not expect emotional skills training to raise people's emotional intelligence in a few days. Developing skills takes time, as evidenced by the fact that experts in any field typically spend 10 years in intensive training and practice before they reach true expert status (Ericsson & Charness, 1994; Ericsson, Krampe, & Tesch-Römer, 1993). What short training programs can do is raise awareness, help people to learn from everyday experience, and get them started in the right direction.

One of the challenges we face in developing social and emotional skills is that we rarely receive clear and objective feedback about our interactions with others. Research on coaching and expertise suggests that people learn most effectively when they receive prompt, clear, and objective feedback about their performance (Ericsson & Charness, 1994; Ericsson et al., 1993). Although annual performance evaluations and 360° assessments may provide useful feedback, they may not tell people exactly what they are doing wrong or how to improve. One way to make feedback more informative would be to hold periodic meetings where team members discuss interpersonal dynamics and provide specific and constructive suggestions to colleagues. Another way to help people learn would be to videotape interpersonal interactions or group exercises and have participants review and discuss their performance with a qualified observer.

Work on practical intelligence and tacit knowledge suggests that clarifying some of the unspoken rules of interpersonal dynamics in the workplace may also facilitate learning (Sternberg et al., 2000; Sternberg & Hedlund, 2002; Wagner & Sternberg, 1985). Tacit knowledge embodies the sort of know-how and common sense that are usually acquired through experience and allow people to handle problems effectively in the workplace. This knowledge is difficult to acquire precisely because it does not come in books and is usually not explicitly taught. Discussing tacit knowledge about interpersonal dynamics, group norms, and other processes openly may help people to manage interpersonal situations more effectively in the workplace.

Researchers studying social intelligence have generally found that different social skills are weakly interrelated (for reviews, see Cantor & Kihlstrom, 1987; Sternberg et al., 2000). People draw on many different skills when interacting with others, and these skills do not always go together. For example, skills used to decode different types of social and emotional information correlate poorly (Archer et al., 2001; Hall, 2001; Nowicki & Duke, 2001), presumably because people attend to different cues when decoding various types of social and emotional information. As a result, social skills training may fail to generalize across situations (La Greca, 1993). This limits the potential of explicit training and suggests the need to capitalize on informal learning, or learning from experience. For all these reasons, we think that emotional skills training should emphasize raising awareness, broadening people's coping repertoire, and helping people to learn from experience, rather than drilling a narrow set of skills over and over again (e.g., Caruso & Salovey, 2004).

CONCLUSIONS

We view emotional intelligence as a set of interrelated abilities that help people to process emotional information. These abilities develop through learning and experience and are amenable to training. They can be assessed through a performance test that reveals minimal overlap with important personality traits and IQ and that is not susceptible to faking. Such a test holds promise for corporate selection and recruitment, although further research is needed to clarify the benefits of screening emotional abilities for various types of jobs. So far, research suggests that emotional abilities are associated with empathy, agreeableness, prosocial behavior, and quality of interpersonal relationships. Preliminary findings further suggest that emotional abilities are related to stress tolerance, teamwork, group decision making, leadership potential, and overall work performance. Work performance was indexed by supervisor ratings, merit increases, and company rank. Further research is needed to replicate these results.

Emotional capacities may be partly influenced by genetic factors and early development, but there is room for learning. We believe that helping staff to develop emotional skills may yield organizational benefits that accrue over time. The effectiveness of such training programs has yet to be rigorously evaluated. Given the stability of personality traits and deeply entrenched coping habits, we should not expect emotional training to yield rapid change. However, training can raise awareness about the importance of emotional skills and motivate people to learn from their everyday experiences. Organizations may benefit from such training over time as people learn to interact more effectively with others and cope with stress. Organizations may also reap short-term benefits if training programs instill in participants a sense of personal growth and motivation, contributing to a positive work atmosphere.

ACKNOWLEDGMENTS

We thank the following individuals for their comments on earlier drafts of this chapter: Natalio Extremera, Hallvard Follesdal, Maria João Galvão, Pedro Galvão, and Helena Lopes.

We also acknowledge support from Portugal's *Fundação para a Ciência e a Tecnologia* and the European Social Fund to Paulo Lopes; the Social Science and Human Research Council of Canada to Stéphane Côté; and the National Cancer Institute (R01-CA68427), National Institute of Mental Health (P01-MH/DA56826), National Institute on Drug Abuse (PSO-DA13334), and Donaghue Women's Health Investigator Program at Yale to Peter Salovey.

REFERENCES

Archer, D., Costanzo, M., & Akert, R. (2001). The Interpersonal Perception Task (IPT): Alternative approaches to problems of theory and design. In J. A. Hall & F. J. Bernieri (Eds.), *Interpersonal sensitivity: Theory and measurement* (pp. 161–182). Mahwah, NJ: Lawrence Erlbaum Associates.

Argyle, M., & Lu, L. (1990). Happiness and social skills. *Personality and Individual Differences, 11*, 1255–1261.

Ashkanasy, N., & Tse, B. (2000). Transformational leadership as management of emotion. In N. Ashkanasy, C. E. J. Härtel, & W. J. Zerbe (Eds.), *Emotions in the workplace: Research, theory, and practice* (pp. 221–235). Westport, CT: Quorum Books.

Barchard, K. A. (2001). *Emotional and social intelligence: Examining its place in the nomological network.* Unpublished doctoral dissertation, University of British Columbia, Canada.

Bar-On, R. (1997). *Bar-On Emotional Quotient Inventory (EQ-i): A test of emotional intelligence.* Toronto, Canada: Multi-Health Systems.

Bar-On, R. (2000). Emotional and social intelligence: Insights from the Emotional Quotient Inventory. In R. Bar-On & J. D. A. Parker (Eds.), *The handbook of emotional intelligence* (pp. 363–388). San Francisco: Jossey-Bass.

Barrick, M. R., & Mount, M. K. (1991). The Big Five personality dimensions and job performance: A meta-analysis. *Personnel Psychology, 44*, 1–26.

Barsade, S. G. (2002). The ripple effect: Emotional contagion and its influence on group behavior. *Administrative Science Quarterly, 47*, 644–675.

Barsade, S. G., Brief, A. P., & Spataro, S. E. (2003). The affective revolution in organizational behavior: The emergence of a paradigm. In J. Greenberg (Ed.), *Organizational behavior: The state of the science* (2nd ed., pp. 3–52). Mahwah, NJ: Lawrence Erlbaum Associates.

Baumeister, R. F., & Tice, D. M. (1990). Anxiety and social exclusion. *Journal of Social and Clinical Psychology, 9*, 165–195.

Bless, H., Clore, G. L., Schwarz, N., Golisano, V., Rabe, C., & Wölk, M. (1996). Mood and the use of scripts: Does a happy mood really lead to mindlessness? *Journal of Personality and Social Psychology, 71*, 665–679.

Boyatzis, R. E., Goleman, D., & Rhee, K. S. (2000). Clustering competence in emotional intelligence: Insights from the emotional competence inventory. In R. Bar-On & J. D. A. Parker (Eds.), *The handbook of emotional intelligence* (pp. 343–362). San Francisco: Jossey-Bass.

Brackett, M. A., & Mayer, J. D. (2003). Convergent, discriminant, and incremental validity of competing measures of emotional intelligence. *Personality and Social Psychology Bulletin, 29*, 1147–1158.

Brackett, M. A., Mayer, J. D., & Warner, R. M. (2004). Emotional intelligence and its relation to everyday behavior. *Personality and Individual Differences, 36*, 1387–1402.

Cantor, N., & Kihlstrom, J. F. (1987). *Personality and social intelligence.* Englewood Cliffs, NJ: Prentice-Hall.

Carroll, J. B. (1993). *Human cognitive abilities: A survey of factor-analytic studies.* New York: Cambridge University Press.

Caruso, D. R., Mayer, J. D., & Salovey, P. (2002). Emotional intelligence and emotional leadership. In R. Riggio, S. Murphy, & F. J. Pirozzolo (Eds.), *Multiple intelligences and leadership* (pp. 55–74). Mahwah, NJ: Lawrence Erlbaum Associates.

Caruso, D. R., & Salovey, P. (2004). *The emotionally intelligent manager.* San Francisco: Jossey-Bass.

Carver, C. S., Scheier, M. F., & Weintraub, J. K. (1989). Assessing coping strategies: A theoretically based approach. *Journal of Personality and Social Psychology, 56*, 267–283.

Caspi, A. (2000). The child is father to the man: Personality continuities from childhood to adulthood. *Journal of Personality and Social Psychology, 78*, 158–172.

Ciarrochi, J. V., Chan, A. Y. C., & Caputi, P. (2000). A critical evaluation of the emotional intelligence construct. *Personality and Individual Differences, 28*, 539–561.

Clark, M. S., Pataki, S. P., & Carver, V. H. (1996). Some thoughts and findings on self-presentation of emotions in relationships. In G. J. O. Fletcher & J. Fitness (Eds.), *Knowledge structures in close relationships: A social psychological approach* (pp. 247–274). Mahwah, NJ: Lawrence Erlbaum Associates.

Costa, P. T., Jr., & McCrae, R. R. (1994). Set like plaster? Evidence for the stability of adult personality. In T. F. Heatherton & J. L. Weinberger (Eds.), *Can personality change?* (pp. 21–40). Washington, DC: American Psychological Association.

Côté, S., Lopes, P. N., & Salovey, P. (2004). *Emotional intelligence and vision formulation and articulation.* Manuscript submitted for publication.

Côté, S., & Morgan, L. M. (2002). A longitudinal analysis of the association between emotion regulation, job satisfaction, and intentions to quit. *Journal of Organizational Behavior, 23*, 947–962.

Csikszentmihalyi, M. (1992). *Flow—The psychology of happiness.* New York: Harper & Row.

Darwin, C. (1965). *The expression of emotion in man and animals.* Chicago: University of Chicago Press. (Original work published 1872)

Diener, E., & Lucas, R. E. (1999). Personality and subjective well-being. In D. Kahneman, E. Diener, & N. Schwarz (Eds.), *Well-being: The foundations of hedonic psychology* (pp. 213–229). New York: Russell Sage.

Eisenberg, N., Fabes, R. A., Guthrie, I. K., & Reiser, M. (2000). Dispositional emotionality and regulation: Their role in predicting quality of social functioning. *Journal of Personality and Social Psychology, 78,* 136–157.

Eisenberg, N., Fabes, R. A., Miller, P. A., Fultz, J., Shell, R., Mathy, R. M., & Reno, R. R. (1989). Relation of sympathy and distress to prosocial behavior: A multi-method study. *Journal of Personal and Social Psychology, 57,* 55–66.

Ekman, P. (1972). Universals and cultural differences in facial expressions of emotion. In J. Cole (Ed.), *Nebraska Symposium on Motivation, 1971* (Vol. 19, pp. 207–282). Lincoln: University of Nebraska Press.

Ekman, P. (1993). Facial expression and emotion. *American Psychologist, 48,* 384–392.

Ekman, P. (1994). Strong evidence for universals in facial expressions: A reply to Russell's mistaken critique. *Psychological Bulletin, 115,* 268–287.

Ekman, P., & O'Sullivan, M. (1991). Who can catch a liar? *American Psychologist, 46,* 913–920.

Ericsson, K. A., & Charness, N. (1994). Expert performance—Its structure and acquisition. *American Psychologist, 49,* 725–747.

Ericsson, K. A., Krampe, R. T., & Tesch-Römer, C. (1993). The role of deliberate practice in the acquisition of expert performance. *Psychological Review, 100,* 363–406.

Extremera, N., Fernández-Berrocal, P., Lopes, P. N., & Salovey, P. (2004). *Evidence that emotional intelligence is related to burnout and mental health among secondary school teachers.* Manuscript in preparation.

Fredrickson, B. L. (2000). Cultivating positive emotions to optimize health and well-being. *Prevention and Treatment, 3,* np.

Frijda, N. H. (1986). *The emotions.* Cambridge, England: Cambridge University Press.

Furr, R. M., & Funder, D. C. (1998). A multimodal analysis of personal negativity. *Journal of Personality and Social Psychology, 74,* 1580–1591.

Gardner, H. (1983). *Frames of mind—The theory of multiple intelligences.* New York: Basic Books.

George, J. M. (2000). Emotions and leadership: The role of emotional intelligence. *Human Relations, 53,* 1027–1055.

Goleman, D. (1995). *Emotional intelligence.* New York: Bantam.

Goleman, D. (1998). *Working with emotional intelligence.* New York: Bantam.

Grandey, A. (2003). When the "show must go on": Surface and deep acting as determinants of emotional exhaustion and peer-rated service delivery. *Academy of Management Journal, 46,* 86–96.

Graves, J. G. (1999). *Emotional intelligence and cognitive ability: Predicting performance in job-simulated activities.* Unpublished doctoral dissertation, California School of Professional Psychology, San Diego.

Gross, J. J. (1998). Antecedent- and response-focused emotion regulation: Divergent consequences for experience, expression, and physiology. *Journal of Personality and Social Psychology, 74,* 224–237.

Hagerty, M., Lopes, P. N., & Salovey, P. (2002). *Emotional abilities among MBA students.* Unpublished raw data.

Hall, J. A. (2001). The PONS test and the psychometric approach to measuring interpersonal sensitivity. In J. A. Hall & F. J. Bernieri (Eds.), *Interpersonal sensitivity: Theory and measurement* (pp. 143–160). Mahwah, NJ: Lawrence Erlbaum Associates.

Hall, J. A., & Bernieri, F. J. (2001). *Interpersonal sensitivity: Theory and measurement.* Mahwah, NJ: Lawrence Erlbaum Associates.

Hatfield, E., Cacioppo, J. T., & Rapson, R. L. (1994). *Emotional contagion.* New York: Cambridge University Press.

Hawkins, J. D., Catalano, R. F., Kosterman, R., Abbott, R., & Hill, K. G. (1999). Preventing adolescent health-risk behaviors by strengthening protection during childhood. *Archives of Pediatric and Adolescent Medicine, 153,* 226–334.

Heatherton, T. F., & Weinberger, J. L. (Eds.). (1994). *Can personality change?* Washington, DC: American Psychological Association.

Helson, R., & Stewart, A. (1994). Personality change in adulthood. In T. F. Heatherton & J. L. Weinberger (Eds.), *Can personality change?* (pp. 201–225). Washington, DC: American Psychological Association.

Herrnstein, R. J., & Murray, C. (1994). *The bell curve.* New York: Free Press.

Ivancevich, J. M., Matteson, M. T., Freedman, S. M., & Phillips, J. S. (1990). Worksite stress management interventions. *American Psychologist, 45,* 252–261.

Isen, A. M. (1987). Positive affect, cognitive processes, and social behavior. *Advances in Experimental Social Psychology, 20,* 203–253.

Isen, A. M. (1999). Positive affect. In T. Dagleish & M. Power (Eds.), *Handbook of cognition and emotion* (pp. 521–539). New York: Wiley.

Isen, A. M., & Daubman, K. A. (1984). The influence of affect on categorization. *Journal of Personality and Social Psychology, 47,* 1206–1217.

Isen, A. M., Daubman, K. A., & Nowicki, G. P. (1987). Positive affect facilitates creative problem solving. *Journal of Personality and Social Psychology, 52,* 1122–1131.

Izard, C. E. (1971). *The face of emotion.* New York: Appleton-Century-Crofts.

Janovics, J., & Christiansen, N. D. (2001, April). *Emotional intelligence in the workplace.* Paper presented at the 16th Annual Conference of the Society of Industrial and Organizational Psychology, San Diego.

Kagan, J. (1998). *Galen's prophecy.* Boulder, CO: Westview Press.

Keltner, D., & Haidt, J. (1999). Social functions of emotions at four levels of analysis. *Cognition and Emotion, 13,* 505–521.

Keltner, D., & Haidt, J. (2001). Social functions of emotions. In T. J. Mayne & G. A. Bonanno (Eds.), *Emotions: Current issues and future directions* (pp. 192–213). New York: Guilford.

Kusché, C. A., & Greenberg, M. T. (2001). PATHS in your classroom: Promoting emotional literacy and alleviating emotional distress. In J. Cohen (Ed.), *Social emotional learning and the elementary school child: A guide for educators* (pp. 140–161). New York: Teachers College Press.

La Greca, A. M. (1993). Social skills training with children: Where do we go from here? *Journal of Clinical Child Psychology, 22,* 288–298.

Lazarus, R. S. (1991). *Emotion and adaptation.* New York: Oxford University Press.

Leeper, R. W. (1948). A motivational theory of emotions to replace "emotions as disorganized response." *Psychological Review, 55,* 5–21.

Lerner, J. S., & Keltner, D. (2001). Fear, anger, and risk. *Journal of Personality and Social Psychology, 81,* 146–159.

Loewenstein, G. F., Weber, E. U., Hsee, C. K., & Welch, N. (2001). Risk as feelings. *Psychological Bulletin, 127,* 267–286.

Lopes, P. N., Brackett, M. A., Nezlek, J., Schütz, A., Sellin, I., & Salovey, P. (2004). Emotional intelligence and social interaction. *Personality and Social Psychology Bulletin, 30,* 1018–1034.

Lopes, P. N., Côté, S., Grewal, D., Salovey, P., Kadis, J., & Gall, M. (2004). *Emotional intelligence and positive work outcomes.* Manuscript submitted for publication.

Lopes, P. N., Salovey, P., & Beers, M. (in press). Emotion regulation ability and the quality of social interaction. *Emotion.*

Lopes, P. N., Salovey, P., Nezlek, J., & Straus, R. (2003). *Emotional intelligence: A negotiation study.* Unpublished data, Yale University.

Lopes, P. N., Salovey, P., & Straus, R. (2003). Emotional intelligence, personality, and the perceived quality of social relationships. *Personality and Individual Differences, 35,* 641–658.

Lyubomirsky, S., & Nolen-Hoeksema, S. (1993). Self-perpetuating properties of dysphoric rumination. *Journal of Personality and Social Psychology, 65,* 339–349.

Lyubomirsky, S., & Nolen-Hoeksema, S. (1995). Effects of self-focused rumination on negative thinking and interpersonal problem solving. *Journal of Personality and Social Psychology, 69,* 176–190.

Mabe, P. A., & West, S. G. (1982). Validity of self-evaluation of ability: A review and meta-analysis. *Journal of Applied Psychology, 67,* 280–296.

Markus, H. R., & Kitayama, S. (1991). Culture and the self: Implications for cognition, emotion, and motivation. *Psychological Review, 98,* 224–253.

Maslach, C., & Jackson, S. (1986). *Maslach Burnout Inventory Manual* (2nd ed.). Palo Alto, CA: Consulting Psychologists.

Matthews, G., Zeidner, M., & Roberts, R. D. (2002). *Emotional intelligence: Science and myth.* Cambridge, MA: MIT Press.

Mayer, J. D., Caruso, D. R., & Salovey, P. (1999). Emotional intelligence meets traditional standards for an intelligence. *Intelligence, 27,* 267–298.

Mayer, J. D., & Salovey, P. (1997). What is emotional intelligence? In P. Salovey & D. Sluyter (Eds.), *Emotional development and emotional intelligence: Implications for educators* (pp. 3–31). New York: Basic Books.

Mayer, J. D., Salovey, P., & Caruso, D. R. (2000). Models of emotional intelligence. In R. Sternberg (Ed.), *Handbook of intelligence* (pp. 396–420). New York: Cambridge University Press.

Mayer, J. D., Salovey, P., & Caruso, D. (2002). *Mayer-Salovey-Caruso Emotional Intelligence Test (MSCEIT): User's manual.* Toronto: Multi-Health Systems.

Mayer, J. D., Salovey, P., Caruso, D. R., & Sitarenios, G. (2003). Measuring emotional intelligence with the MSCEIT V2.0. *Emotion, 3,* 97–105.

Mesquita, B., & Frijda, N. H. (1992). Cultural variations in emotions: A review. *Psychological Bulletin, 112,* 179–204.

Motowidlo, S. J., & Van Scotter, J. R. (1994). Evidence that task performance should be distinguished from contextual performance. *Journal of Applied Psychology, 79,* 475–480.

Nowicki, S., Jr., & Duke, M. P. (2001). Nonverbal receptivity: The Diagnostic Analysis of Nonverbal Accuracy (DANVA). In J. A. Hall & F. J. Bernieri (Eds.), *Interpersonal sensitivity: Theory and measurement* (pp. 183–198). Mahwah, NJ: Lawrence Erlbaum Associates.

Palfai, T. P., & P. Salovey. (1993). The influence of depressed and elated mood on deductive and inductive reasoning. *Imagination, Cognition and Personality, 13,* 57–71.

Paulhus, D. L., Lysy, D. C., & Yik, M. S. M. (1998). Self-report measures of intelligence: Are they useful as proxy IQ tests? *Journal of Personality, 66,* 525–554.

Publilius Syrus. (100BC/1961). Sententiae. In J. W. Duff & A. M. Duff (Eds.), *Minor latin poets.* Cambridge, MA: Harvard University Press.

Rice, C. L. (1999). *A quantitative study of emotional intelligence and its impact on team performance.* Unpublished master's thesis, Pepperdine University, Malibu, CA.

Richards, J. M., & Gross, J. J. (2000). Emotion regulation and memory: The cognitive costs of keeping one's cool. *Journal of Personality and Social Psychology, 79,* 410–424.

Roberts, R. D., Zeidner, M., & Matthews, G. (2001). Does emotional intelligence meet traditional standards for an intelligence? Some new data and conclusions. *Emotion, 1,* 196–231.

Roseman, I. J., & Smith, C. A. (2001). Appraisal theory. In K. R. Scherer, A. Schorr, & T. Johnstone (Eds.), *Appraisal processes in emotion* (pp. 3–19). New York: Oxford University Press.

Rotundo, M., & Sackett, P. R. (2002). The relative importance of task, citizenship, and counterproductive performance to global ratings of job performance: A policy-capturing approach. *Journal of Applied Psychology, 87,* 66–80.

Rubin, M. M. (1999). *Emotional intelligence and its role in mitigating aggression: A correlational study of the relationship between emotional intelligence and aggression in urban adolescents.* Unpublished dissertation, Immaculata College, Immaculata, PA.

Russell, J. A. (1994). Is there universal recognition of emotion from facial expression? A review of the cross-cultural studies. *Psychological Bulletin, 115,* 102–141.

Salovey, P., & Mayer, J. D. (1990). Emotional intelligence. *Imagination, Cognition, and Personality, 9*, 185–211.

Salovey, P., Mayer, J. D., & Caruso, D. (2002). The positive psychology of emotional intelligence. In C. R. Snyder & S. J. Lopez (Eds.), *The handbook of positive psychology* (pp. 159–171). New York: Oxford University Press.

Salovey, P., Woolery, A., & Mayer, J. D. (2001). Emotional intelligence: Conceptualization and measurement. In G. J. O. Fletcher & M. S. Clark (Eds.), *Blackwell handbook of social psychology: Interpersonal processes* (pp. 279–307). Malden, MA: Blackwell.

Scherer, K. R., & Wallbott, H. G. (1994). Evidence for universality and cultural variation of differential emotional response patterning. *Journal of Personality and Social Psychology, 66*, 310–328.

Schmidt, F. L., & Hunter, J. E. (1998). The validity and utility of selection methods in personnel psychology: Practical and theoretical implications of 85 years of research findings. *Psychological Bulletin, 124*, 262–274.

Schwarz, N. (1990). Feelings as information: Information and motivational functions of affective states. In E. T. Higgins & R. M. Sorrentino (Eds.), *Handbook of motivation and cognition* (Vol. 2, pp. 527–561). New York: Guilford Press.

Schwarz, N. (2001). Feelings as information: Implications for affective influences on information processing. In L. L. Martin & G. L. Clore (Eds.), *Theories of mood and cognition* (pp. 159–176). Mahwah, NJ: Lawrence Erlbaum Associates.

Schwarz, N., & Clore, G. L. (1996). Feelings and phenomenal experiences. In E. T. Higgins & A. W. Kruglanski (Eds.), *Social psychology: Handbook of basic principles* (pp. 433–465). New York: Guilford Press.

Seibert, S. E., Kraimer, M. L., & Liden, R. C. (2001). A social capital theory of career success. *Academy of Management Journal, 44*, 219–237.

Seligman, M. E. (1990). *Learned optimism.* New York: Pocket Books.

Seligman, M. E., & Schulman, P. (1985). Explanatory style as a predictor of productivity and quitting among life insurance sales agents. *Journal of Personality and Social Psychology, 50*, 832–838.

Smith, C. A., & Ellsworth, P. C. (1985). Patterns of cognitive appraisal in emotion. *Journal of Personality and Social Psychology, 48*, 813–838.

Sternberg, R. J. (1999a). The theory of successful intelligence. *Review of General Psychology, 3*, 292–316.

Sternberg, R. J. (1999b). Intelligence as developing expertise. *Contemporary Educational Psychology, 24*, 359–375.

Sternberg, R. J., Forsythe, G. B., Hedlund, J., Horvath, J. A., Wagner, R. K., Williams, W. M., Snook, S. A., & Grigorenko, E. L. (2000). *Practical intelligence in everyday life.* New York: Cambridge University Press.

Sternberg, R. J., & Hedlund, J. (2002). Practical intelligence, g, and work psychology. *Human Performance, 15*, 143–160.

Sy, T., & Côté, S. (in press). Emotional intelligence: A key ability to succeed in the matrix organization. *Journal of Management Development.*

Tangney, J. P. (1991). Moral affect: The good, the bad, and the ugly. *Journal of Personality and Social Psychology, 61*, 598–607.

Tett, R. P., Jackson, D. N., & Rothstein, M. (1991). Personality measures as predictors of job performance: A meta-analytic review. *Personnel Psychology, 44*, 703–742.

Vaillant, G. E. (2000). Adaptive mental mechanisms: Their role in a positive psychology. *American Psychologist, 55*, 89–98.

Van Scotter, J. R., & Motowidlo, S. L. (1996). Interpersonal facilitation and job dedication as separate facets of contextual performance. *Journal of Applied Psychology, 81*, 525–531.

Wagner, R. K., & Sternberg, R. J. (1985). Practical intelligence in real-world pursuits: The role of tacit knowledge. *Journal of Personality and Social Psychology, 49*, 436–458.

Watson, D. (2000). *Mood and temperament*. New York: Guilford Press.

Wegner, D. M., & Zanakos, S. (1994). Chronic thought suppression. *Journal of Personality, 62,* 615–640.

Wonderlic, Inc. (1999). *Wonderlic Personnel Test & Scholastic Level Exam user's manual.* Libertyville, IL: Author.

Chapter 4

Core Competencies in Coaching Others to Overcome Dysfunctional Behavior

Richard E. Boyatzis
Case Western Reserve University

Coaching, or more accurately executive coaching, is one of the few rapid growth industries of the last few years. First accepted as a practice in executive development, it has spawned tens of thousands of practitioners. As a measure of its popularity, a Google web search on December 12, 2002, revealed more than 99,400 Web sites using the phrase "executive coaching." Human resources development and organization development internal and external consultants, psychotherapists, psychologists, social workers, teachers, and other professionals (e.g., lawyers, accountants, and nurses) have had business cards printed and promote themselves as executive or life coaches. Even in countries where management training and executive development are awkward because they threaten the public image of a person's competence and authority, such as in Italy (P. Altomare, personal communication), Spain (R. Serlavos, personal communication), and Japan (Voigt, 2002), coaching is the fastest growing sector of the human resource development business.

Although the practice of executive coaching has expanded dramatically, the writing about it has only expanded at a modest pace. Most of the literature is anecdotal from practitioners or wisdom from those who have provided such services for years (Kampa-Kokesch & Anderson, 2001; Kilburg, 1996, 2000). Except for the use of multisource feedback (i.e., 360), there has not been a stream of empirical research in any of the aspects of executive coaching.

Research on effectiveness, style, and techniques in athletic coaching and psychotherapy has grown. But the less formally prepared providers of executive or managerial coaching services still have little theory or research to advise their development or practice. A review of the few empirical studies and the anecdotal literature reveal confusion about the outcome of coaching. Many explorations focus on effectiveness of coaching. But few studies aim to predict client behavior change. Many use satisfaction with coaches and the coaching experience, the perception of progress, or help from the person being coached as an indicator of effectiveness (Hall, Otazo, & Hollenbeck, 1999; Kampa-Kokesch & Anderson, 2001). Unfortunately, these are really measures of the quality of the relationship with the coach and not necessarily the effectiveness of the coaching. If the latter were the dependent variable of such studies (i.e., attainment of the intended outcome of the process), sustained change in a person's behavior, style, and performance could be measured and predicted.

To offer insight into effective coach behavior, this chapter reviews a series of studies of people acting like coaches in a difficult arena, that of counseling people with alcoholism and substance abuse problems (Boyatzis & Burruss, 1979; Burruss & Boyatzis, 1981). These constitute some of the few empirical studies examining the coach/counselor competencies related to positive behavioral change in clients. These studies were designed to determine the competencies of alcoholism counselors that predicted the work performance of their clients after they had returned to work. The first study used critical incident interviews to inductively develop a coach competency model. The second study differentiated a set of competencies of effective versus less effective coaches/counselors with tests. In an extension of the second study, the tests were then used to predict work performance of the counselor/coaches' clients.

Theory: What Behaviors Support Coach Effectiveness?

Rogers (1951, 1961) articulated a troika of characteristics he deemed critical for effective "helping" behavior emerging from his work on psychotherapy: empathy, unconditional positive regard, and genuineness. Truax and Carkhuff (1967) and Carkhuff (1969) continued to expand, clarify, and develop these concepts and methods. Although developers or proponents of various approaches to psychotherapy would modify Roger's list (e.g., Perls emphasized giving voice to the unspoken, and Ellis emphasized pragmatism), the quest for effective helping behavior has continuously led to the importance of specific "helper" characteristics. Research on psychotherapy and counseling suggested that characteristics of the helper were more important in determining level of effectiveness than differences in schools of thought or the approach to psychotherapy in which the counselor was trained (Emrick, 1974). For example, a few studies have found "empathy" to be critical to counselor effectiveness (Bohart & Greenberg, 1997; Hall &

Bernieri, 2001). Other studies have found other characteristics found to be relevant; for example, Gendlin and colleagues found counselor "focusing ability" to be associated with effectiveness (Gendlin, Beebe, Cassens, Klein, & Oberlandes, 1968).

A conceptual synthesis of competency studies conducted to identify the competencies that support the effectiveness of roles within the human resource field (Brotman, Liberi, & Wasylyshyn, 1998; Goleman, 1998; Spencer & Spencer, 1993) suggests that emotional intelligence (EI) and several cognitive competencies are likely to be important to coach/counselor effectiveness. However, we are left wondering if empirical and predictive testing of such hypotheses would support this analysis or send researchers in another direction in trying to explain why some coaches seem to be effective at helping others whereas some are not.

Periodically, the competencies demonstrated by effective counselors has emerged as a research interest In the alcoholism and substance abuse fields, it emerged from three sources. First, critical reviews of research on the effectiveness of treatment for alcoholics suggested that particular treatment techniques used did not account for differences in outcome measures, such as the behavior of patients following treatment (Emrick, 1974). Second, evaluation literature in the field of psychotherapy suggested that characteristics of therapists account for substantial differences in outcome measures (Burruss, 1977; Glass, 1976; Truax & Carkhoff, 1967; Whitehorn & Betz, 1954). Third, there was a movement, supported by the government, to establish a national body to certify alcoholism counselors and establish credentials that indicate the attainment of a professional level of competence in conducting therapy and counseling alcoholics.

The latter will likely emerge as a concern in the coming years for executive coaches. A need for some form of quality assurance has already appeared in the form of an association-based certification for executive coaches. The International Federation of Coaches currently has the most active and widely known program for certification other than consulting firms or authors of programs privately "certifying" practitioners in their proprietary methods or techniques.

METHODS

Predicting Client Work Performance

For alcoholism counselors in the U.S. Navy, the most objective measure of their effectiveness is the work performance of their clients following treatment. A work performance measure can be considered conservative (i.e., more difficult on which to show change) and a more difficult treatment goal than abstinence because it requires changes in the client's behavior, ways of dealing with others, and drinking behavior.

First, a list of all clients admitted to U.S. Naval alcohol rehabilitation facilities in the continental United States was produced. The clients were listed by facility. Second, the list was sent to each facility. All counselors currently working at each facility were asked to complete a form. If they had worked as a counselor at the facility, they would circle the name of each client with whom they had worked. Each client spent a substantial amount of time with a particular counselor in individual and group therapy, meetings, and other activities.

The social security numbers of clients were used by the U.S. Navy Bureau of Personnel to identify each client's work performance for the 6 months following treatment. This measure was a rating on a 3-point scale: 1 indicated that the person received a general discharge, received an undesirable discharge, received an honorable discharge but was considered unsuitable or unfit, was still on active duty but had a recommendation against reenlistment, or had a medical discharge with a recommendation against reenlistment; 2 indicated that the person received a medical discharge but no recommendation against reenlistment; 3 indicated that the person was still on active duty 6 months after treatment and had not received a recommendation against reenlistment, had received an honorable discharge with no recommendation against reenlistment, or was released to reserve status or to nondisability retirement.

Of the 65 counselors in the system, only 47 were available to be tested at the time of the studies (Boyatzis & Burruss, 1979; Burruss & Boyatzis, 1981). The minimum number of client records required for inclusion was 10. The average number of clients per counselor was 49, with the maximum of 167. The resultant sample was 45 counselors and 2,212 clients.

Discovering Key Competencies

A two-step process was used to identify the competencies of superior performing counselors. In the first step, an extreme case design was used to inductively discover the competencies that were likely to have an impact on client work performance following treatment. Nominations of those viewed as "outstanding" were collected about the 45 counselors in the final sample who had worked more than 2 years.

Twenty-six counselors from three of the largest Naval alcohol rehabilitation facilities were asked to list the names of zero, one, two, or three people currently working as alcoholism counselors in the Navy who they thought were superior alcoholism counselors. A total of 10 counselors were listed as superior by at least two counselors from the three sites. A sample of counselors not nominated by anyone was randomly chosen from the remaining list to serve as a comparison sample of average counselors. The final sample consisted of 26 counselors, including 10 superior counselors and 16 average counselors.

The Behavioral Event Interview (Boyatzis, 1982; Spencer & Spencer, 1993), a variation on the critical incident interview (Flanagan, 1954), was conducted with the 26 counselors. A thematic analysis (Boyatzis, 1998) of the interview transcripts led to the identification of a set of competencies believed to differentiate the outstanding from average counselors. A codebook of these competencies with competency labels, definitions, and indicators was developed and given to two coders who were blind to the outstanding or average categorization of each leader. This coding provided evidence of intercoder reliability for each code and frequency counts of how often each counselor's transcript showed evidence of a particular competency. At the end of these analyses, eight competencies were found to be demonstrated significantly more often in the transcripts of the "outstanding" as opposed to "average" counselors. They were (a) optimism about people's ability to change, considered part of the self-management cluster of EI competencies; (b) initiative, considered part of the self-management cluster of EI competencies; (c) pattern recognition, considered part of a cognitive cluster of competencies (see Boyatzis, 1982); (d) client awareness, considered a part of the social awareness cluster of EI competencies; (e) accurate self-assessment, considered part of the self-awareness cluster of EI competencies; (f) ego maturity, considered a part of the self-management cluster of EI competencies; (g) empathy, considered a part of the social awareness cluster of EI competencies; and (h) emotional self-awareness, considered part of the self-awareness cluster of EI competencies.

To test the validity of the list for predicting counselor success, tests were selected or developed for each of the eight competencies. Several of the competencies were thought to exist within a person at multiple levels (i.e., trait and skill levels of the competency); these include initiative, accurate self-assessment, and empathy. All tests used are discussed subsequently.

Optimism. Counselor optimism about people's ability to change, initiative, and accurate self-assessment were tested with an instrument called the Scenarios Test, which was developed specifically for this study. It consisted of eight scenarios of counseling situations adapted from actual events in the interviews. In this test, the test taker is asked to imagine himself or herself in each situation and to select, in order of preference, 2 of 10 possible responses he or she would be likely to choose. A subset of responses for each category was theoretically designed to assess optimism, initiative, and accurate self-assessment. These were weighted by multipliers of 2 and 1 according to whether they were first or second choices, respectively. This test required approximately 40 min to administer.

Initiative. A trait level of the initiative competency was assessed with an operant test by coding cognitive self-definition from the Picture Story Exercise according to the coding system developed by Stewart and Winter (1977) to reflect whether a person habitually thinks of him- or herself in terms of causes and outcomes or whether a person sees the self as an ineffective victim of events that have an unknown cause. The Picture Story Exercise is a modified version of the Thematic Apperception Test (TAT) originally developed by Murray (1943). A person is asked to spend about 5 min writing a story in response to each of six pictures. People coding this measure had reliability with expert scorers above 90%.

To address possible method variance issues, a second trait level measure of initiative was selected. The Nowicki–Strickland Locus of Control Scale, a forced-choice, respondent measure consisting of 40 questions, was also used as another trait-level respondent measure of initiative. A high score indicates an external orientation (Nowicki & Strickland, 1973).

To assess the skill level of the initiative, a scale in the Scenarios Test was developed (see previous description of the Scenarios Test).

Pattern Recognition. The Test of Thematic Analysis is a measure of the cognitive competency called pattern recognition (Boyatzis, Cowen, & Kolb, 1995). This is thought to be essential in diagnosing problems and understanding others. Presented with two different groups of information, the test taker is asked to describe the differences and similarities in any manner that he or she likes. The two groups of information used in this study were six counseling situations derived from the interviews. A person can receive a score from −3 to +6. The more a person demonstrates critical diagnostic thinking, the more positive the score will be (Winter & McClelland, 1978).

Client Awareness. In addition to one scale in the Scenarios Test, the programmed case was also used to assess client awareness. It is a series of 21 episodes of a true life history. Each episode is accompanied by a set of four alternative future episodes of which only one actually happened. The person being tested is asked to guess which of the four alternatives occurred. A specially designed answer sheet indicates whether he is right or wrong after each guess and he is instructed to keep guessing until he finds the correct alternative. An important aspect of this instrument is that the person has more information as a result of each guess and, therefore, should have a better understanding or "feeling for" the biographical character. To assess client awareness, a counselor's responses on the programmed case were scored according to his overall performance (i.e., the standardized score of 21 minus the number of guesses made before finding the correct one).

Accurate Self-Assessment. Besides a scale from the Scenarios Test, the Helping Resources Inventory was used to assess a counselor's willingness and resourcefulness in using help to work with clients. The Helping Resources Inventory was adapted from the Activities Questionnaire used by McClelland (1975). The respondent was asked to rate, on a scale of 10, "how likely" she would be to consult each of 11 different sources of help (e.g., minister, psychologist, AA sponsor, friend, supervisor, etc.). The mean response per source was then taken to be an index of the person's willingness to seek help. The person was then asked to indicate whether she has actually sought help from each of those same 11 sources within the past month, 6 months, or year. The mean response to this question, weighted in the direction of recency, was used as an indicator of the person's actual use of help. This questionnaire required approximately 10 min to administer.

Ego Maturity. To assess ego maturity, the Picture Story Exercise was also scored for stages of ego development, developed by Abigail Stewart and discussed by McClelland (1975). Persons coding the stages have reliability with expert scorers above 90%. The stories were scored for imagery in four stages. These stage scores were then combined into a single measure with the following formula (as described in McClelland, 1975): [Stage I + 2 (Stage II) + 3 (Stage III) + 4 (Stage IV)] divided by [Stage I + Stage II + Stage III + Stage IV].

Empathy. The Picture Story Exercise was also used to code a trait level of the empathy competency. The stories were scored by trained scorers, who have scoring reliability with expert scorers above the 90% level, according to the system described in Atkinson (1958) for need for affiliation and that developed by Winter (1973) for need for power and activity inhibition (McClelland, Davis, Kalin, & Wanner, 1972). These three scores were adjusted for number of words written with a correction factor developed by Winter (1979). The standardized power score was subtracted from the standardized affiliation score and the difference was multiplied by the square root of the Activity Inhibition score plus one to construct a single variable. The variable, called the Caring Motive Profile, reflects a greater concern for close relationships to people than for having an impact on them while having a high degree of impulse control.

To assess the skill level of the empathy competency, the programmed cases technique was used in a different way than earlier described. An improvement score was calculated as the increase or decrease in the accuracy of subjects' guesses on the later half of the episodes versus the first half (see preceding description of the programmed case test). The improvement score was adjusted for level of accuracy of early responses.

Emotional Self-Awareness. A modified version of the Focusing Ability, as originally designed by Gendlin et al. (1968), was used to assess emotional self-awareness. Prerecorded instructions asked the person to first relax for a moment and then focus on some meaningful personal problem. The instructions continued at brief intervals to guide the person through an exploration of his or her feelings concerning that problem over a 10-min period. At the end of the 10 min, the person was asked to answer, into an individually held tape recorder, specific questions about the experience. Two judges independently rated 43 of the 47 recordings on a 4-point scale from *definitely did not focus* to *definitely did focus* with an interrater reliability of $r = .79$. (The first four recordings were used to establish initial agreement on the scale definitions.) Disagreements were discussed and the final score was agreed. This score is referred to in this report simply as Focusing Ability. It was intended to be a measure of emotional self-awareness because the "focusing" a person may demonstrate during this exercise is one of identifying her feelings and delving deeper into what they are and describing them. This instrument required approximately 20 min to administer.

Variables Other than Competencies

In addition to the preceding measures of counselor characteristics, the Ward Atmosphere Scale (WAS) was administered to assess the climate of the treatment facility. This instrument, developed by Moos (1974), is a 100-item questionnaire concerning important characteristics of the social environment. The 10 subscales were combined by summing eight of them and subtracting Anger and Aggression and Staff Control, which were scored in the opposite direction. The resultant variable, climate, was intended to account for impact of treatment facility on client outcome.

RESULTS

Counselors were classified as superior or average on the basis of a median split on the mean work performance rating of the clients with whom they worked. The average counselors had mean client work performance ratings ranging from 2.20 to 2.56; the percentage of clients with a rating of 3 ranged from 64% to 78% with an average of 70.5%. The superior counselors had mean client work performance ratings ranging from 2.60 to 3.00; the percentage of clients with a rating of 3 ranged from 75% to 100% (one of the superior counselors had 75%; the rest had 80% or better) with an average of 87.2%.

TABLE 4.1
Comparison of 15 Superior and 14 Average Counselors

Variable	Average Counselors	Superior Counselors	t	Significance Level
Optimism:				
Scenarios/optimism	2.29	2.53	.32	NS
Initiative:				
Cognitive self-definition	−6.65	−4.30	1.56	.066
Nowicki–Strickland	16.86	15.67	−1.08	NS
Scenarios/initiative	.57	.80	.37	NS
Pattern recognition:				
Thematic analysis	.43	.93	2.01	.025
Client awareness:				
Programmed case performance	55.36	58.85	1.45	.079
Empathy:				
Caring motive	−.92	.32	1.63	.058
Programmed case/improvement	2.34	15.76	1.68	.054
Accurate self-assessment:				
Scenarios/accurate self-assessment	7.29	5.00	−2.16	.02
Helping Resources Inventory/seeking help	6.08	6.53	.72	NS
Helping Resources Inventory/using help	2.23	2.42	.69	NS
Ego maturity:				
Ego development	2.43	2.44	.08	NS
Emotional self-awareness:				
Focusing	1.71	2.64	2.55	.005

Note. One-tailed significance levels are reported. NS = not significant.

T tests were computed on each of the measures comparing average and superior counselors. The results, shown in Table 4.1 (Table 2 from Boyatzis & Burruss, 1979, p. 25) are the that superior counselors had significantly higher scores on the thematic analysis score, the programmed case: improvement score, and the focusing score. They also had near significantly higher scores on the caring motive profile, cognitive self-definition score, and the programmed case: performance score. The use of resources score was statistically significant, but opposite to the predicted direction; average counselors showed higher scores than superior counselors. All other differences were nonsignificant.

On the basis of these *t* tests, the six measures indicated that four of the EI competencies and the cognitive competency could be considered valid differentiators of superior versus average counseling performance. They were (a) empathy at both the trait and skill levels as measured by the caring motive profile and the programmed case: improvement score, respectively; (b) initiative as measured by cognitive self-definition; (c) pattern recognition as measured by the thematic analysis score; (d) client awareness as measured by the programmed case: performance score; and (e) emotional self-awareness, as measured by the focusing ability.

The findings reveal that one or more competencies from each of the four clusters assessed were needed for effectiveness. These competencies were from the self-awareness, self-management, and social awareness clusters of EI and the pattern recognition of the cognitive cluster.

A discriminant function analysis (DFA) was run on the six measures and the derived function used to assign counselors by groups. It was chosen as the multivariate statistical routine to perform this function due to the categorical nature of the client outcome data. The results are shown in Table 4.2 (Table 4 from Boyatzis & Burruss, 1979, p. 29). The combination of the six measures yielded a high canonical correlation ($r = .677$) and correctly classified 83% of the counselors (correctly classified 87% of the superior counselors). A DFA was also run on the sum of the standardized scores on each of the measures, yielding an even higher canonical correlation ($r = .898$) and correctly classified 83% of the counselors (correctly classified 80% of the superior counselors). A third DFA was run on the number of competencies possessed by a counselor. This was computed by giving a counselor a +1 for each measure on which his standardized score was positive and 0 for each measure on which his standardized score was negative. The sum was computed as the number of competencies possessed by the counselor. This DFA yielded a high canonical correlation ($r = .633$) and correctly classified 83% of the counselors (correctly classified 87% of the superior counselors).

The Impact of Situational Variables

Because the counselors worked in different treatment facilities, it was possible that organizational climate of the facility may affect their performance. The correlation between the Moos Climate Score and client outcome (mean performance rating) was not significant ($r = -.106$, $n = 29$). A t test of the climate in which superior counselors worked versus the average counselors worked was also not significant, with means of 50.00 and 49.93, re-

TABLE 4.2
Discriminant Function Analysis of the Model

Variables	Canonical Correlate	% Counselors Correctly Classified ($n = 29$)	% Superior Counselors Correctly Classified ($n = 15$)
Caring motive profile, programmed case: improvement & performance	.677	83	87
Focusing, thematic analysis, cognitive self-definition sum of standard scores on all 6 variables	.898	83	80
Number of competencies possessed	.633	83	87

spectively ($t = .03$, $n = 29$). Another situational characteristic that could possibly have an impact on counselor effectiveness was the age of their clients. The correlation of mean work performance rating with the percent of clients over 25 years old was not significant ($r = -.038$, $n = 29$). Average counselors had a mean of 51.06% of their clients over 25, whereas superior counselors had a mean of 49.66% of their clients over 25. This difference is not significant ($t = -.39$, $n = 29$).

As a further check, correlations were computed of the Moos Climate Score and percent clients over 25 against each of the competency measures. None of the correlations with percent clients over 25 was significant. None of the correlations with the Moos Climate Score was significant.

Predicting Client Work Performance

A multiple regression was conducted with the average client work performance rating per counselor as the criterion available (work performance) and the six competency test scores as the predictor variables. Because days of a client's active service after treatment and the work performance measure were related ($r = .378$, $df = 43$, $p < .01$), it was decided to control for the confounding effects of unequal time periods between treatment-discharge and service-discharge dates. A seventh independent variable was included, representing the average number of days between treatment and discharge from the service for each counselor's sample of clients.

The multiple regression showed a significant multiple correlation ($R = .562$) in predicting work performance from the competencies, as shown in Table 4.3 (Tables 1 and 3 from Burruss & Boyatzis, 1981, pp. 9 and 12). A

TABLE 4.3
Predicting Work Performance: Summary ($n = 45$)

Analysis	df	Sum of Squares	Mean Squares	F
Regression	7	.426	.061	2.437
Residual	37	.924	.025	

Multiple $R = .562$, $R^2 = .316$, Standard error = .158

Variable	Multiple R	R^2	R^2 Change	Simple R	Beta	F
Days of service	.378	.142	.143	.378	.459	9.567
Caring motive	.380	.144	.001	−.025	−.015	0.011
Programmed case: performance	.380	.144	.000	.027	−.002	0.000
Programmed case: improvement	.506	.256	.112	.307	.331	5.117
Cognitive self-definition	.507	.257	.000	.192	−.049	0.094
Focusing	.554	.306	.050	.174	.254	3.113
Thematic analysis	.562	.316	.009	−.053	−.101	0.495

test of curvilinearity ($F = .474$, p = nonsignificant) demonstrated no significant deviation from linearity. A detailed analysis of the individual contribution of each variable revealed, however, that the primary contributors to that relation were days of service, empathy as measured by the programmed case: improvement score, and emotional self-awareness, as measured by the focusing measure. Because days of service was stepped into the equation first to eliminate its contaminating effects on predicting work performance, the data suggest that two competencies, empathy and emotional self-awareness, are more important than others in predicting the effectiveness of counselors.

DISCUSSION

The superior counselors appeared different from the average counselors. This does not imply any difference in the dedication or compassion of the individual counselors but reflects a difference in their effectiveness. Given the relatively high effectiveness of the Navy alcoholism treatment programs as a whole (Bucky, 1977), the differences discussed represent the difference between superior and average counselors and not between adequate and inadequate counselors.

Two competencies, empathy and emotional self-awareness, distinguished effective counseling and predicted work performance. Another competency, pattern recognition, appeared to contribute to the overall effectiveness of a counselor but did not add unique or distinctive capability as reflected in the regression analysis. Two others, initiative and client awareness, also appeared to contribute to the overall effectiveness, but not as strongly, and did not add unique variance in the regression analysis.

Application of these results to executive coaching would confirm what most coaches, and their clients, know—empathy or sensitivity to the client is the key characteristic of effective coaches. Coaches, like counselors, cannot proceed without listening to and understanding the client and his issues, problems, and situation at work and at home. If the client is viewed as merely a "problem-bearing platform," the coach will focus on the problems and tasks, not the person. In the process, she may miss underlying issues or factors contributing to sustaining current behavior and impact. The coach must be sensitive to changes in the client and his process of change to tailor comments and suggestions to that person's needs at that point in time.

This brings us to the second critical competency revealed in this study, emotional self-awareness. A coach, like a counselor, cannot focus on the client and understanding her situation if the coach is preoccupied with his own challenges. Similarly, awareness of transference, countertransference, and projection must be an integral aspect of the functioning of an executive coach. Coaches must be able to separate their own feelings and values from those of the client. This is not to say that the coach's feelings and values are not important; they are. But the coach has the responsibility to be able to identify and manage his or her feelings and reactions. Whether the coach uses this information as part of understanding the client or as a vehicle for suspending his own needs and anxieties, managing oneself is difficult if not impossible without a high degree of self-monitoring, or emotional self-awareness.

The analyses strongly suggest that counselor competencies account for the majority of variance in effectiveness with clients. Situational factors do not seem to account for variation in client outcome. Although this study did not include a control for type of treatment technique, it is important to indicate that all of the Navy programs were heavily based on practices and procedures of Alcoholics Anonymous and peer coaching. A variety of other techniques are used in their programs, such as psychodrama, education, group and individual therapy, and so forth. Three of the 14 average counselors were civilian (21%), and 5 of the 15 superior counselors were civilian (33%), suggesting no differential impact coming from civilian status. Five of the 14 average counselors (35%) and 6 of the 15 superior counselors (40%) were not trained in the Alcohol Treatment Specialist program, suggesting no differential impact from the Navy's counselor training program.

It is important to note that the "success rate" of the average Navy alcoholism counselors (70.5%) is almost identical to the 67% found in most psychotherapy outcome studies conducted (see Burruss, 1977). This suggests that these counselors are doing at least as well as any other treatment group. The considerably higher success rate of the superior counselors (87.2%), on the other hand, highlights the efficacy of increasing the number of counselors who possess and use specific competencies as a way of improving the overall effectiveness of counseling.

SUMMARY AND IMPLICATIONS

The results showed that two competencies appeared to have a substantial and significant impact on a counselors' effectiveness. To be effective as a counselor, and by extension an executive coach, a person must be sensitive to others. To be sensitive to others, coaches must be sensitive to themselves. These critically important competencies were emotional self-awareness from the self-awareness cluster of EI competencies and empathy from the social awareness cluster of EI competencies. Both of these were significant at the skill level. This implies that training or developing these competencies may be more feasible than if they were at the trait or motive level of personality.

Regardless of the organizational climate of the various facilities in which counselors worked, type of training received to prepare for their role, and the age demographics of their clients, these competencies explained why some counselors were more effective than others.

To extend these findings into the arena of executive coaching, we can infer that a similar set of competencies would help us to understand why some coaches are more effective than others. Specifically, we can also hypothesize that the most critical competencies will come from a wide variety of the clusters and that emotional self-awareness and empathy are most likely to be two of the competencies critical to coaching effectiveness. We need a parallel study to those reviewed here conducted with executive coaches and their clients to determine the precise competencies and their impact. We need to expand the sample size to generalize to all forms of executive and life coaching.

REFERENCES

Atkinson, J. W. (Ed.). (1958). *Motives in fantasy, action, and society.* Princeton, NJ: Van Nostrand.

Bohart, A. C., & Greenberg, L. S. (1997). *Empathy reconsidered: New directions in psychotherapy.* Washington, DC: American Psychological Association.

Boyatzis, R. E. (1982). *The competent manager: A model for effective performance.* New York: Wiley.

Boyatzis, R. E. (1998). *Transforming qualitative information: Thematic analysis and code development.* San Francisco: Sage.

Boyatzis, R. E., & Burruss, J. A. (1979). *Validation of a competency model for alcoholism counselors in the navy.* Final Report on Contract Number N00123-77-C-0499.

Boyatzis, R. E., Cowen, S. S., & Kolb, D. A. (1995). *Innovations in professional education: Steps on a journey from teaching to learning.* San Francisco: Jossey-Bass.

Brotman, L. E., Liberi, W. P., & Wasylyshyn, K. M. (1998). Executive coaching: The need for standards of competence. *Consulting Psychology Journal: Practice and Research, 50*(1), 40–46.

Bucky, S. F. (1977). *The 1976 evaluation of the Navy's alcohol rehabilitation programs.* Unpublished study, Naval Alcohol Rehabilitation Center, San Diego.

Burruss, J. A. (1977). *Evaluating therapists' effectiveness.* Unpublished doctoral dissertation, Harvard University, Cambridge, MA.

Burruss, J. A., & Boyatzis, R. E. (1981). *Continued validation of a competency model for alcoholism counselors in the Navy.* Final Report on Contract Number N002 44-80-C-0521.

Carkhuff, R. R. (1969). *Helping and human relations: A primer for lay and professional helpers.* New York: Holt, Rinehart & Winston.

Emrick, C. D. (1974). A review of psychologically oriented treatment of alcoholism. *Quarterly Journal of Studies on Alcohol, 35,* 523–549.

Flanagan, J. C. (1954). The critical incident technique. *Psychological Bulletin, 51,* 327–335.

Gendlin, E. T., Beebe, J., III, Cassens, S., Klein, M., & Oberlandes, M. (1968). Focusing ability in psychotherapy, personality and creativity. *Research in Psychotherapy, 3,* 217–241.

Glass, G. V. (1976). *Primary, secondary, and meta analysis of research.* Paper presented at the annual meeting of the American Educational Research Association, San Francisco.

Goleman, D. (1998). *Workng with emotional intelligence.* New York: Bantam.

Hall, D. T., Otazo, K. L., & Hollenbeck, G. P. (1999). Behind closed doors: What really happens in executive coaching. *Organizational Dynamics, 27*(3), 39–53.

Hall, J. A., & Bernieri, F. J. (2001). *Interpersonal sensitivity: Theory and measurement.* Mahwah, NJ: Lawrence Erlbaum Associates.

Kampa-Kokesch, S., & Anderson, A. Z. (2001). Executive coaching: A comprehensive review of the literature. *Consulting Psychology Journal: Practice and Research, 53*(4), 205–228.

Kilburg, R. R. (1996). Toward a conceptual understanding and definition of executive coaching. *Consulting Psychology Journal: Practice and Research, 48*(2), 134–144.

Kilburg, R. R. (2000). *Executive coaching: Developing managerial wisdom in a world of chaos.* Washington, DC: American Psychological Association.

McClelland, D. C. (1975). *Power: The inner experience.* New York: Irvington Press.

McClelland, D. C., Davis, W. N., Kalin, R., & Wanner, E. (1972). *The drinking man.* New York: Free Press.

Moos, R. (1974). *Evaluating treatment environments: A social ecological approach.* New York: Wiley.

Murray, H. A. (1943). *Thematic apperception test.* Cambridge, MA: Harvard University Press.

Nowicki, S., & Strickland, B. R. (1973). The locus of control scale for children. *Journal of Consulting and Clinical Psychology, 3*(40), 148–154.

Rogers, C. R. (1961). *On becoming a person: A therapist's view of psychotherapy.* Boston: Houghton Mifflin.

Rogers, C. R. (1951). *Client-centered therapy: Its current practice, implications, and theory.* Cambridge, MA: The Riverside Press (republished 1965, Boston: Houghton Mifflin)

Spencer, L. M., Jr., & Spencer, S. (1993). *Competence at work: Models for superior performance.* New York: Wiley.

Stewart, A. J., & Winter, D. G. (1977). Self-definition and social definition in women. *Journal of Personality, 42,* 238–259.

Truax, D. B., & Carkhuff, R. R. (1967). *Toward effective counseling and psychotherapy.* Chicago: Aldine.

Voigt, K. (2002). Job coaches catch on in Asia. *Wall Street Journal (European edition),* November 12, p. A11.

Whitehorn, J. C., & Betz, B. J. (1954). A study of psychotherapeutic relationships between physicians and schizophrenic patients. *American Journal of Psychiatry, 111,* 321–331.

Winter, D. G. (1973). *The power motive.* New York: Free Press.

Winter, D. G. (1979). *Correcting projective test scores for the effect of significant correlation with length of protocol* (unpublished technical note). Boston: McBer.

Winter, D. G., & McClelland, D. C. (1978). Thematic analysis: An empirically derived measure of effects of liberal arts education. *Journal of Educational Psychology, 70*(1), 8–16.

Chapter 5

The Role of Emotional Intelligence in Developing International Business Capability: EI Provides Traction

Gerald Mount
Grand Valley State University

In an increasingly competitive global environment, organizations are showing a renewed interest in understanding how employees create and sustain the organizational performance necessary for competitive advantage (Becker & Gerhart, 1996). In her 1994 article, "Competencies: The Precious Seeds of Growth?" Wisher recognized the significance of understanding the larger contextual environment of international business when she noted the growing power of companies to transcend borders of nation states in an era of "technical and commercial revolution" resulting in many businesses that literally have no boundaries (Wisher, 1994). This trend suggests a need for human resource assessments that can identify the characteristics of executives who successfully transcend international borders. The absence of information about the behavioral characteristics that support executive success and the context in which those behaviors are practiced in international business is a major gap in the theoretical and practical literature. Therefore, this chapter presents research designed to identify the individual competencies that are linked to executive success in a multinational setting. I argue that organizations with executives who possess these competencies build an international organizational capability.

A competency is defined as an underlying characteristic of an individual that is causally related to effective or superior performance and is empirically determined to be a performance differentiator in a given role or job responsibility. A competency may be a motive, trait, skill, self-image component, social role, or a body of knowledge used by the person (Boyatzis,

1982). An organizational capability is the collective ability of the organization to execute its marketplace strategy successfully (Ulrich & Lake, 1990). Typically, organizational capabilities describe actions or internal processes of a business, not assets or products. They are difficult for competitors to copy and consequently may be viewed by competitors as the black box that enables an organizational system to deliver the performance required to execute a given strategy. A proposition discussed in this chapter is that the pattern of competencies that differentiate outstanding individual performance from average performance in a value chain of functional roles can create an organizational capability necessary for strategic international business performance.

The research presented in this chapter examines the competencies required for success in five separate functional roles operating in an international setting. My purpose was to evaluate the contribution of individual human characteristics (competencies) to superior performance in each role. The results from these five separate studies allow us to understand how an organizational capability for conducting international business in a capital-intensive, asset-based corporation can be developed from the pattern of individual competencies that differentiate superior performance. Because the competencies examined in this research include emotional intelligence competencies (see Goleman, 1998), this research also helps to clarify the role of emotional intelligence competencies in achieving both individual and organizational performance in international business.

STUDYING COMPETENCIES

The value of identifying the characteristics and actions that contribute to high performance in an organizational setting has been debated for some time. In the past, scholars criticized this form of research because it ignored social capability in favor of a reliance on technical competence. As Mayo summarized these concerns, "We have failed to train students in the study of social situations; we have thought that first-class technical training was sufficient in a modern mechanical age. As a consequence we are technically competent as no other age in history has been, and we combine this with our utter social incompetence" (Mayo, 1945, p. 120). More recently, Vaill (1989) criticized competency research saying that it produced lists of characteristics that identified the main factors of a manager's job but missed the more complex issues. He believed that understanding the complexity of the job required studying the subtle interrelations of competencies and capturing the fluidity needed to successfully function in complex, dynamic environments. He also argued that the more complex the organization and the more turbulent the environment, the greater the need for interdependence among factors affecting performance and more fluid managerial capabilities. (Vaill, 1983, 1989).

A considerable body of knowledge exists regarding competency modeling methodology as a means of identifying characteristics that differentiate high performance in a given role or job responsibility. The roots of this methodology predate the 1973 article, "Testing for Competence Rather than for 'Intelligence' " (McClelland, 1973), which is often cited as the beginning of the competency movement. In 1941, Flanagan and his colleagues in the United States Army Air Force's Aviation Psychology Program established the *critical incident technique* as a means for collecting direct observations of human behavior to identify critical behavioral requirements based on factual incidents associated with a particular role or function. This procedure was initially used for understanding the criteria associated with being a successful pilot using critical incident interviews. During the period from 1941 to 1946, the validity of the critical incident technique for identifying accurate descriptions of the characteristics associated with job performance was established through a series of studies conducted in the Army Aviation Psychology Program. These studies demonstrated that the critical incident technique could be used to identify characteristics and actions that made the difference between success and failure in a particular role or job (Flanagan, 1954).

THE ROLE OF EMOTIONAL INTELLIGENCE

Discussions about the relation of emotion to an individual's intelligence, especially in the context of logical thought or decision making, have been ongoing since Plato stated, "We should hold fast to the sacred cord of reason" and Aristotle asserted that emotions were part of our complex thinking process (Cytowic, 1996, p. 294). "Ever since the ancient Greeks, philosophers elevated the rational side of the mind above the emotional and saw the two as separate, this concept has been profoundly influential in western thought; indeed it has shaped some of our most basic institutions and beliefs" (Greenspan, 1997, p. 2). This view has persisted as societies and organizations have valued the "cool head" who can make decisions unencumbered by emotions. As technology made the world more efficient, productive, and smaller, the value of a detached, logical, nonemotional thought process triumphed. Which one of us cannot recall the matter-of-fact, unemotional conversations between NASA's astronauts and mission control? Have we not been impressed by their test-pilot discipline, which allows them to report facts, figures, and data in a cool, detached manner while their lives are on the line and the world and their families watch and listen on television?

Although much has been theorized and discussed about the role of emotional intelligence in life and work success, research is just beginning to uncover the role of EI and EI competencies in organizational contexts (Dulewicz & Higgs, 1998). A goal of the study presented in this chapter is to add to our understanding of how emotional intelligence competencies contribute to performance in an organizational context.

Goleman completed a post hoc analysis of empirically derived competency studies across a broad range of industries and found that 67% of the competencies determined to differentiate performance could be categorized as emotional intelligence characteristics (Goleman, 1998). Emotional intelligence as defined by Goleman is "the capacity for recognizing our own feelings and those of others, for motivating ourselves, and for managing emotions well in ourselves and in our relationships" (Goleman, 1998, p. 317). Salovey and Mayer's definition of emotional intelligence includes the dimension of action: "the subset of social intelligence that involves the ability to monitor one's own and other's feelings and emotions, to discriminate among them and to use this information to guide one's thinking and actions" (Salovey & Mayer, 1990). An emotionally intelligent individual recognizes and understands not only his or her emotional state but also the emotional state of others and is able to use that intelligence to regulate behavior (either their own, that of others, or both) to solve problems (Huy, 1999). However, the role of emotions in organizational contexts has not traditionally been understood or valued, especially in capital-intensive situations where the display of emotions could be viewed as inappropriate for sustaining a desired organizational image (Huy, 1999). According to Huy, (1999), the value of this emotional capability and its ability to unleash emotional energy has been underestimated and viewed as nonrelevant.

The aim of this chapter and the study presented here is to improve understanding of the role that emotional intelligence competencies play in the chain of events between individual behavior (competencies) and organizational performance (organizational capability). Part of the study's significance is that the results are from an industry that traditionally has not placed a high value on the human components of organizational performance. Industries that operate in a high-technology capital-intensive environment, such as the petroleum industry, traditionally do not view the importance of human capabilities the same as they do technical or financial skills. Industries that are relatively labor intensive have a greater awareness of the potential for humans to affect organizational performance and have demonstrated higher correlations between human selection practices and firm performance than capital-intensive industries (Terpstra & Rozelle, 1993). However, this does not mean that human interactive capabilities are not important in a capital-intensive asset-based environment; rather it may mean the value of their contribution has not been as fully understood as the cognitive, technical, and financial expertise capabilities.

Therefore, the study was designed to answer five specific research questions: Which competencies differentiate superior performance when compared with average performance in international business? What are the differences between competencies perceived to be important from survey and focus group data and competencies empirically found through interview data? Is there a relation between emotional intelligence competencies and performance? Can an organizational capability, such as the ability to accomplish international business, be identified and built from a pattern of individual competencies? What is the relationship between IQ and emotional quotient (EQ) in the roles studied?

METHOD

Research Setting

The research was conducted in a major international petroleum corporation with extensive international operations. The five work roles studied were corporate strategist, international business developer, international negotiator, international business services manager, and international asset construction project manager. Although not the only functional roles that contributed to the execution of international business, these roles represent the work process from strategic idea conceptualization to the seamless transition of operational performance and revenue realization in the capital-intensive, asset-based, international petroleum industry (Fig. 5.1). When viewed together as a value chain of responsibilities, these roles represent an organizational capability necessary to accomplish international business.

Strategists (Conceptual Ideas)
+
Business Developers (Concrete Opportunities)
+
Negotiators (Contractual Obligations)
+
Business Service Managers (Infrastructure Builders)
+
Project Managers (Hard Asset Construction)

EQUALS

International Business Organizational Capability

FIG. 5.1.   Value chain of functional roles.

Overview of Competency Methodology

For each of the five roles, a classic competency assessment approach was employed that used multiple methods for data collection and analysis of qualitative interview data and quantitative statistical data to identify the competencies that differentiated the superior-performing employees from the average-performing employees (Spencer & Spencer, 1993). The steps associated with this approach are as follows:

1. Appropriate performance criteria are identified for use in selecting a criterion sample of role incumbents for in-depth critical incident interviews. These performance criteria can be obtained from hard data such as profit reports, performance measures, productivity accomplishments, focus group discussions with executives, supervisors, and role incumbents, or anonymous executive, supervisor, and peer nominations.

2. Using the performance effectiveness criteria from Step 1, criterion samples are selected that represent "superior" performers in the role and good, solid, "typical" performers in the role.

3. Data collection involves, first, focus group discussions with the role's leadership team, position incumbents, and, in some cases, customers to identify critical challenges facing the role and performance outcomes needed to meet those challenge. Second are critical incident research interviews of 2 to 3 hr duration with members of the criterion samples selected in Step 2 in which participants identify critical situations experienced on the job in sufficient depth and detail to reveal who was involved, what the interviewee did, the results, what they were thinking and feeling during the event, and what they wanted to accomplish in dealing with the situation. These interviews enable the researcher to have insight into the interviewee's personality and cognitive style. The third method involves surveys of the populations of employees in the role. Respondents rank ordered the importance of each competency and selected the behavioral characteristics for each competency as related to superior and typical performance based on standardized competency dictionary that was provided.

Sample Selection/Description

The following is a description of the five functional roles analyzed for the study:

1. Strategists—The strategist population consisted of 40 individuals who had responsibility to advise senior corporate management on current and future economic issues regarding the portfolio of businesses that operated across all sectors of the corporation. In the past, this role had been called

"corporate planning" with the major responsibility being to support senior management's decision-making processes by providing economic forecasts of world crude oil prices and analyses of various situations that could, both positively and negatively, affect worldwide crude and refined oil prices. Just prior to the execution of this study, the role of these individuals evolved from "planner" to "strategist." The primary difference was that the role of strategist was proactive as it challenged and engaged senior managers in discussions across a wide range of issues such as risk assessment, decision options, scenario planning, and competitor intelligence with a skill set that could evaluate dynamic environmental events and compare them to the corporation's strategies. The expectation was that individuals in the role would influence corporate decision making by challenging conventional wisdom, building credibility with senior executives, and establishing a partnering relationship with business groups. Study data were derived from a sample of 26 individual interviews, five focus group sessions, and a competency questionnaire administered to the full population of 40 with a 63% response.

2. International business developers—The international business developers population totaled 40 individuals in a newly created department charged with searching out downstream worldwide refining and marketing opportunities. Their role was to identify and screen strategically aligned opportunities, investigate and pursue alliances and joint ventures to capture the opportunity, secure executive approvals, negotiate the deal, and execute the processes to commercialize the opportunity. Study data were derived from a sample of 19 interviews, one focus group session, and a competency questionnaire administered to the population of 40 with a 63% response.

3. International deal makers—These were 106 individuals to negotiate for access to domestic and international oil and gas exploration rights for the upstream (exploration) side of the corporation. This group had been in existence for a number of years. Over time, however, its composition evolved from primarily international attorneys and later MBAs to a more diverse population with a variety of backgrounds as the host country environment for negotiating oil and gas exploration rights changed. Study data were derived from a sample of 23 interviews, four focus group sessions, and a competency questionnaire administered to the population of 106 with a 65% response.

4. International business service managers—These were 127 individuals who were part of a department providing services to operating business units (primarily in the upstream side of the business) to create the administrative infrastructure needed in foreign locations to transition new opportunities to functioning operations. Study data were derived from a sample of 16 interviews, four focus group sessions, and a competency questionnaire administered to the population of 127 with a 51% response.

5. Asset construction project managers—The asset construction project manager population of 74 individuals was a role in transition. Traditionally project management had been viewed as an engineering role focused primarily on the technical process of construction management. More recently, however, the focus of the role changed from a tactical perspective to one that was more strategically oriented and aligned with business unit needs and aspirations. This role was a service group that partnered with business units from all corporate operating sectors (upstream exploration, downstream refining/marketing, pipeline, transportation, and petrochemical manufacturing) to evaluate the feasibility of a capital asset project and to manage the construction process so the projects were operationally onstream in a cost-efficient, safe, and reliable manner. Successful worldwide project management contributed to the competitive advantage of the business unit partners. Study data were derived from a sample of 24 interviews, six focus group sessions, and a competency questionnaire administered to the population of 74 with an 85% response.

Data Collection.   Data collected included a total of 108 critical incident interviews (65 superior performers and 43 average performers), 27.9% of the total population of 387 in the five roles studied. Twenty focus group sessions with managers and role incumbents and 251 competency questionnaires (overall 65% response rate) were administered.

Focus Group Sessions.   The 20 focus group sessions were held with six to eight senior members of each role and other role incumbents. Each session lasted approximately 4 hr and followed a standard format designed to describe the study, describe data collection methods, and elicit attendee perceptions of the business challenges facing the role and the individual competencies believed needed by role incumbents to maximize the role's contribution to corporate goals.

Participants in the executive focus group sessions anonymously nominated individuals considered to be superior performers in their respective role for the interview sample. A similar nomination process was used with the peer incumbent focus groups.

Interviews.   The interview sample distribution, compared with the five study population for gender, was female, 10.2% interview sample versus 2.8% overall population, and male, 89.8% interview sample versus 25.1% overall population.

Interviews were conducted by interviewers trained and certified to conduct critical incident interviews. Each interviewee was advised of the purpose of the study and assured of the confidentiality of the interview. Interviews lasted 2 to 3 hr each and were tape-recorded for transcription to facilitate thematic coding and data analysis. Interviewees were asked to recall an incident that had occurred within the past 12 to 18 months that they considered a "high point" story—one in which they felt particularly effective on the job—and to describe the actual events in as much detail as possible. After the high point story, the interviewee was asked to recall a "low point" story—one where he or she felt less effective or frustrated with his or her performance. Interviewers attempted to capture two or three high- and low-point stories from each interview.

Questionnaire. The Hay/McBer Competency Rating Questionnaire (CRQ) was used, which was based on *McBer & Company's JND Scale Competency Dictionary* version 3.1 (1993), which established a generic language describing the competencies found to consistently distinguish superior managers across multiple organizations and functions. The CRQ was distributed to the population of all five roles regardless of individual performance assessment. Each questionnaire contained 24 generic competency descriptions further subdivided into 160 behavioral statements to describe the progression of behavior from lower to higher levels of complexity. Each respondent was asked to score each of the 24 competencies on importance to the role using a 5-point scale (5 = *critically important*) and to identify which behavioral statement defined superior and minimally acceptable performance for each competency.

Data Analysis

Data analysis to identify the differentiating competencies in each role was conducted along three parallel lines:

1. Analysis of focus group data provided perceptions of performance criteria and a description of the demands of the role.
2. Analysis of interview data provided an empirical identification of the competencies found to differentiate performance between superior and typical performers and identified situations where superior performance was critical to the achievement of business performance.
3. Analysis of the CRQ data provided additional insight from the incumbent's perspective on perceived role demands and performance levels for the competency in each role.

Each of the 108 transcribed interviews was analyzed for competencies using the *McBer & Company's JND Scale Competency Dictionary* as the codebook by independent, experienced coders trained in coding techniques and certified to demonstrate an interrater reliability of 85% when compared with an expert coder. Interrater reliability was determined by (a) correctly identifying a competency in an interview text at a level of 0.90, (b) correctly identifying which competency from the generic codebook is demonstrated 85% of the time, and (c) correctly identifying the exact level demonstrated 75% of the time and within (±) one level 85% of the time. The purpose of coding the interview data was to determine the presence of the competencies, the frequency of occurrence, and the exact level of complexity demonstrated for each competency. Coding also identified unique competencies related to performance outcomes but not listed as competencies in the generic dictionary.

Each transcript was independently assessed regarding the performance of the interviewee by the coder and the interviewer, to complement and support the organization's assessment of superior or typical performance conducted in the sample nominating process. From these assessments, a typical/superior grouping was developed, and the frequency of occurrence and demonstrated complexity levels for each competency were identified by individual performance category. This enabled us to determine the pattern of competencies associated with high performance outcomes.

The triangular analysis of the data streams (focus group, interview, and questionnaire) provided different perspectives of what was required to differentiate performance in each role. Once the competencies associated with superior performance from the interviews were isolated and the behavioral level that differentiated within each competency was clarified, interview transcript sections corresponding to a competency at the differentiating level were selected to provide "snapshot" examples of critical situations and the competency being demonstrated on the job.

RESULTS

Research Question 1

Which competencies differentiate superior performance when compared with average performance in international business?

The competencies found to differentiate superior performance were used to create a final competency model for each role. Twenty-two competencies were found to differentiate performance across the five roles. Because each role was a significant contributor to international business, the aggregate of these competencies could be viewed as the competencies that support organizational performance. This number of competencies was too large to provide clarity to the question, so a simple aggregation of the competencies from each study was not appropriate. Although data from each study provided a compelling argument for the differentiating competencies in each role, an additional process was needed to make sense of the composite data. Using a convergence of data approach, I found that 10 of the 22 competencies in the generic McBer & Company's competency dictionary occurred more frequently (at least 60% of the time) across the various roles. These 10 competencies represent the core competencies that differentiate performance in international business. The core competencies were categorized in three areas: behaviors associated with cognitive intelligence (IQ), behaviors associated with emotional intelligence (EQ), and behaviors associated with skills and knowledge (expertise). This three-bucket categorization facilitated an inspection of the role of emotional intelligence behaviors in the critical situation snapshots of the differentiating level of the competency in action as taken from the interview transcripts.

Table 5.1 lists the 10 core competencies and the six unique characteristics by role. A two-tailed t test of statistical significance was applied to typical versus superior performance across all functional roles to provide further clarification regarding the strength of the differentiating competencies (see Table 5.2). The competencies of achievement motivation, impact and influence, and information seeking were found to be statistically significant for superior performers. Typical performers scored statistically higher on the competencies of analytical thinking and organizational awareness. The second important finding emerging from the analysis was the identification of the behavioral complexity that distinguished the superior performance. These descriptive levels identified a pattern of behavior that persisted across all functional roles. Table 5.3 lists the core competency and the descriptive behavior associated with the competency that differentiated performance across all roles.

Research Question 2

What are the differences between competencies perceived to be important from survey and focus group data and competencies empirically found by interview data?

The CRQ listed all of the competencies in the *McBer & Company's JND Scale Competency Dictionary* that respondents scored for importance to their role on a 5-point scale. Although different responsibilities for each functional role affected the rank ordering of the competencies, the data did indicate certain trends. Specifically, roles dependent on a successful customer relationship (e.g., business services and asset project manager) for their perceived performance success rated teamwork and cooperation as more important than the roles focused on bigger picture strategic outcomes. Table 5.4 compares the interview data that empirically identified core competencies to the CRQ data frequency of identification for that competency as one of the 10 most important across all of the functional studies.

TABLE 5.1
Competencies and Unique Characteristics Found From Interviews to Differentiate Performance in Roles Related to International Business

Competency/Characteristic & Level	Strategist	International Business Developer	International Deal Maker	International Business Services	Worldwide Project Manager	Core (Number of Times Found in Models)
Achievement motivation[a]	X	X	X	X	X	5 of 5
Impact and influence[a]	X	X	X	X	X	5 of 5
Self-confidence	X	X	—	X	X	4 of 5
Analytical thinking	X	X	X	X	—	4 of 5
Conceptual thinking	X	X	X	X	—	4 of 5
Information seeking	X	X	X	X	—	4 of 5
Empathy	X	—	X	X	—	3 of 5
Organizational awareness	X	X	X	—	—	3 of 5
Teamwork & cooperation	X	—	—	X	X	3 of 5
International flexibility/adaptability	—	X	—	X	—	3 of 5
Unique competencies[a]						
Business expertise/perspective	X	—	—	—	X	2 of 5
Negotiations	—	X	X	—	—	2 of 5
Balancing home & local organizations	—	X	X	—	—	2 of 5
Multicultural sensitivity	—	—	—	X	—	2 of 5
Strategic orientation	X	—	—	—	—	1 of 5
International acumen	—	X	—	—	—	1 of 5

[a]Competencies found to differentiate in all functional roles.

TABLE 5.2
Mean Behavioral Scale Values

Competency	Superior Performer ($n = 64$)	Typical Performer ($n = 43$)	Significance Level of t Test
Analytical thinking	2.8	3.0	6.71*
Conceptual thinking	2.9	2.6	1.47
Information seeking	3.7	3.1	2.65*
Achievement motivation	3.8	2.9	3.21*
Impact & influence	4.4	3.5	4.69*
Self-confidence	3.1	2.8	0.71
Teamwork & cooperation	3.1	2.9	0.94
Organizational awareness	2.8	3.4	4.41*
Flexibility/adaptability	2.1	1.4	1.6
Empathy	2.7	2.8	0.53

*$p < .05$.

TABLE 5.3
Core Competency and Behavioral Descriptions
(*McBer & Company JND Scale Competency Dictionary* version 3.1)

Core Competency	Behavioral Complexity Description
Achievement motivation	Improves performance: Makes specific changes in the system or in own work methods to improve performance (e.g., does something better, faster, at lower cost, more efficiently; improves quality, customer satisfaction, morale, revenues), without setting any specific goal.
Impact & influence	Calculates a dramatic action: Takes a well-thought-out dramatic or unusual action to win the point or for a specific impact.
Self-confidence	Chooses challenge or conflict: Likes challenging assignments, is excited by a challenge. Looks for and gets new responsibilities. Speaks up when disagrees with management, clients, or others in power but disagrees politely, stating own view clearly and confidently, even in conflict.
Analytical thinking	Sees multiple relations: Breaks down a problem into smaller parts. Makes multiple causal links: Several potential causes of events, several consequences of actions, or multiple-part chains of events (A leads to B leads to C leads to D). Analyzes relations among several parts of a problem or situation. Anticipates obstacles and thinks ahead about next steps.
Conceptual thinking	Clarifies complex data or situations: Makes complex ideas or situations clear, simple, and/or understandable. Assembles ideas, issues, and observations into a clear and useful explanation. Reinstates existing observations or knowledge in a simpler fashion.
Information seeking	Uses nontypical sources of information: Calls on others who are not personally involved, to get their perspective, background information, experience.

(Continued)

TABLE 5.3
(Continued)

Core Competency	Behavioral Complexity Description
Empathy	Understands current, unexpressed or poorly expressed meanings: Understands current unspoken thoughts, concerns, or feelings. Or gets others to willingly take actions desired by the speaker: That is, uses understanding to get others to act the way you want them to.
Organizational awareness	Understands organizational politics: Understands, describes (or uses) ongoing power and political relationships within the organization (alliances, rivalries), with a clear sense of organizational impact.
Teamwork & cooperation	Solicits inputs: Genuinely values others' input and expertise; is willing to learn from others (including subordinates and peers). Solicits ideas and opinions to help form specific decisions or plans. Promotes team cooperation. Wants all members of a group to contribute to a process.
International flexibility/adaptability	Creates network: Demonstrates an ability to cultivate, establish, and utilize local social, political and/or business networks to overcome an obstacle or meet an objective.

The percentage agreement between the top 10 rankings for each functional role to the 10 empirically determined competencies showed that the strategists had the highest agreement (80%), followed by the international business Developers (70%), international negotiators (60%), worldwide project managers (50%), and international business services (40%).

Also of interest in this data is the identification of the competencies that were not valued in the survey data but were found to significantly differentiate the superior and typical performers in the qualitative analysis of the in-depth interview. Conversely, it is also interesting to examine the competencies listed in the survey data as valued but not found to matter in the more empirical in-depth interviews. In the first category (not valued but found), it is interesting that all five roles failed to rank the competency impact and influence as one of the 10 most important. Four roles omitted organizational awareness from the highest rankings, three omitted information seeking, and two omitted achievement motivation, analytical thinking, and conceptual thinking.

On the other hand, competencies valued by respondents but not found in the 10 core competencies were as follows:

Self-control	4 of 5 roles
Customer service orientation	3 of 5 roles
Relationship building	2 of 5 roles
Listening and responding	2 of 5 roles
Team leadership	2 of 5 roles
Initiative	2 of 5 roles

TABLE 5.4
Rank-Ordered Comparison of Interview Data to CRQ Data

Interview Data Core Competencies	CRQ Data—Strategist	CRQ Data—International Business Developer	CRQ Data—International Negotiator	CRQ Data—International Business Services	CRQ Data—Worldwide Project Manager
Achievement motivation[a]	Conceptual thinking	Information seeking	Empathy	Flexibility[b]	Teamwork & cooperation[b]
Impact & influence[a]	Analytical thinking	Flexibility[b]	Relationship building	Teamwork & cooperation[b]	Team leadership
Self-confidence	Adaptability/flexibility[b]	Empathy	Self-confidence	Customer service orientation	Customer service orientation
Analytical thinking	Information seeking	Relationship building	Analytical thinking Flexibility[b]	Developing others Team leadership	Self-control Initiative
Conceptual thinking	Teamwork & cooperation[b]	Teamwork & cooperation[b]	Listening & responding	Empathy	Analytical thinking
Information seeking	Achievement motivation[a]	Customer service orientation	Teamwork & cooperation[b]	Discretionary effort	Flexibility[b]
Empathy	Self-confidence	Achievement motivation[a]	Conceptual thinking	Self-control	Listening & responding
Organizational awareness	Integrity	Conceptual thinking	Self-control	Initiative	Empathy
Teamwork & cooperation[b]	Organizational awareness	Self-confidence	Organizational commitment	Self-confidence	Achievement motivation[a]
International flexibility/adaptability[b]	Empowerment	Self-control			
Percentage agreement to interview data[a]	80%	70%	60%	40%	50%

Note. CRQ = Competency Rating Questionnaire. Interview data rank ordered by frequency as differentiator of performance from interview data. CRQ data rank ordered by importance from incumbent response data.
[a]Interview data competencies common to all roles. [b]CRQ data competencies common to all roles.

111

Finally, the most significant point from these data was the comparison of the common challenges identified in the focus group data to the competencies found to be core across all roles. Only two competencies were empirically found to be differentiators, both from qualitative interview data and statistical analysis in all roles. These were achievement motivation and impact and influence, but they were not universally perceived to be critically important by CRQ respondents. Achievement motivation was ranked as a top 10 competency in only three of the five roles (60%), and impact/influence was not ranked in the top 10 by respondents from any role. Conversely, the competencies of teamwork and cooperation and international flexibility/adaptability were the only ones ranked in the top 10 by respondents in all five studies.

What makes this finding significant is that the challenges identified in each role's focus group data would require both of these competencies (achievement motivation and impact/influence) to be demonstrated by role incumbents to successfully address the issues. Although these challenges varied across the functional roles (i.e., "prioritization of efforts in chasing opportunities," "obtain management commitment to strategy," and "have input from strategists used in senior management's decisions"), the common thread linking these challenges would require behaviors from both of the competencies, yet the behaviors that described the competencies were apparently not valued by the CRQ respondents.

Research Question 3

Is there a relation between emotional intelligence competencies and performance?

The empirically identified 10 core competencies were separated into three categories according to their respective behaviors: (a) cognitive intelligence, (b) emotional intelligence, and (c) skills and expertise. The list of core competencies was also submitted to an expert with knowledge of the *McBer & Company's JND Scale Competency Dictionary* and the emotional intelligence competency categories found in Goleman (1995) to provide an independent validation for this categorization. The agreement between the researcher and the expert was 100%. Three of the 10 core competencies were categorized as characteristics of cognitive intelligence, and the remaining seven were categorized as emotional intelligence characteristics. None of the core competencies were categorized as skills and knowledge. The unique characteristics found to differentiate performance in the various functional roles were placed in this category. Table 5.5 shows the results of the categorization and the percentage distribution by category.

These results favorably compare with studies done by Dulewicz and Higgs (1998) and Goleman (1998), which found emotional intelligence

TABLE 5.5
Categorization of Emotional Intelligence Competencies and Percentage
Distribution Across Three Types of Work Related Competencies

Cognitive Intelligence	Emotional Intelligence	Skills & Knowledge
Analytical thinking	Achievement motivation	Business expertise
Conceptual thinking	Impact & influence	International acumen
Information seeking	Self-confidence	Negotiations
	Teamwork & cooperation	Strategic orientation
	Organizational awareness	Multicultural sensitivity
	Empathy	Balancing home & local organization
	International flexibility	
19%	44%	38%

Note. Competencies separated into categories according to respective behaviors by author and independent expert.

competencies to be 45% and 67% (respectively) of the overall performance differentiating competencies. (Dulewicz & Higgs reported a distribution of 16% skill/knowledge/expertise; 27% cognitive intelligence [IQ]; 36% emotional intelligence; and 21% unknown random factors, which converted to 20% skill/knowledge/expertise; 34% cognitive intelligence [IQ]; and 45% emotional intelligence [EQ] when recalculated without the unknown random factors.)

Table 5.6 shows results of a non-parametric Spearman correlation test performed to determine the correlation between individual performance and competencies. The results showed that superior performers tended to

TABLE 5.6
Individual Performance/Competency Correlation
(Nonparametric Spearman)

Competency (n = 108)	Categorization	r Value	Significance Level
		0.233*	0.036
Analytical thinking	IQ	−0.444**	0.000
Conceptual thinking	IQ	0.147	0.192
Information seeking	IQ	0.289**	0.009
Achievement motivation	EQ	0.391**	0.000
Impact & influence	EQ	0.474**	0.000
Self-confidence	EQ	0.378**	0.000
Teamwork & cooperation	EQ	0.130	0.249
Organizational awareness	EQ	−0.587**	0.000
Flexibility/adaptability	EQ	0.429**	0.000
Empathy	EQ	−0.146	0.194

*Correlation is significant at the 0.05 level (two-tailed); **correlation is significant at the 0.01 level (two-tailed).

score higher than typical on the IQ competency of information seeking and the EQ competencies of achievement motivation, impact and influence, self-confidence, and flexibility/adaptability. Typical performers tended to score higher on the IQ competency of analytical thinking and the EQ competency of organizational awareness.

Research Question 4

Can an organizational capability, such as the ability to accomplish international business, be identified and built from a pattern of individual competencies?

This study revealed that one of the critical issues to be addressed when attempting to create a specific organizational capability is identification of the key roles that have tangential relationships in the area where the capability is to be developed. The interrelation of these roles creates a systemic process of inputs and outcomes that, when understood and organized to work in harmony, is a significant component of building organizational capability. The results of the study establish that the behavioral competencies that differentiated individual performance for a group of interrelated functional roles can be reduced to a manageable core that is common to all. Although a variance of 33% to 81% existed with respect to the number of core competencies that were differentiators in each function, the overall agreement was 58% with a standard deviation of 18%. The results by function were as follows:

Strategists	11 total competencies/9 core	81% agreement
International business services	13 total competencies/9 core	69% agreement
International negotiators	12 total competencies/7 core	58% agreement
International business developers	16 total competencies/8 core	50% agreement
Project managers	12 total competencies/4 core	33% agreement

These data bring to question the criticality of the missing differentiating competencies to the project management role and the impact of less than superior project management to the development of an overall international business capability. Another issue that affects development of an organization-wide capability, which was not part of this study but was nevertheless a factor in the study, is organizational stability. A dysfunctional organizational design in a critical role will have an adverse impact on outcomes, which in turn affects the performance of the entire value chain. It was not possible in this study to determine if development of the core competencies could improve performance within a role and subsequently cascade over to other related roles because the functional organizations were in a constant state of turmoil and reorganization and, in some cases, were completely disbanded during the course of the study. Consequently, further study in an established, unchanging static environment is necessary to answer the question about creating an organizational capability from a pattern of individual competencies, but the results from this study tend to indicate the possibility, recognizing that competencies are only one of a number of components necessary for the development of a capability.

Research Question 5

What is the relationship between IQ and EQ in the roles studied?

The emotional intelligence competencies played two roles in each of the studied functions. First, the competencies of self-confidence, empathy, organizational awareness, international flexibility, and teamwork acted as catalysts that enabled the cognitive intelligence competencies and the individual's skills and knowledge (expertise) competencies to achieve valued results. In other words, the EQ competencies created an environment that allowed the other competencies to be maximized, thereby giving them traction for performance. Second, the EQ behaviors affected performance outcomes whether exhibited internally with corporate colleagues or with others in positions external to the organization.

Examples of emotional intelligence competencies "in action" as a catalyst to enable other competencies are provided from the following interview excerpts. Each example represents the behavior at the level that differentiated superior performance.

Self confidence is defined as a "belief in one's own capability to accomplish a task and select an effective approach to a problem, choosing challenge or conflict . . . likes challenging assignments . . . speaks up when disagrees with management, clients, or others in power."

> When I saw the process was going down the tubes, I spoke up. I told him, "Look, if I'm going to be accountable for fixing this problem, I've got to be in charge of running this." It was going to be quite an undertaking, and I knew it wasn't going to be easy, but it was something that I knew I could do.
>
> International business developers

In this example, the self-confidence competency gave the individual the opportunity to demonstrate other competencies and skills necessary to fix the problem.

The *teamwork and cooperation* competency "implies the intention to work cooperatively with others, to be part of a team as opposed to working separately. Solicits inputs—genuinely values others' inputs and expertise; is willing to learn from others."

My first step in this Latin American office was to find out what contracts we had and the status of each. I called a meeting of all the involved parties. I handed them the list I'd been working on and asked, "Please tell me whether from your point of view I've missed something or don't understand the priority. This is just a start." After that I would walk around the office and ask people from various departments what I needed to do with regard to each contract. I was getting my arms around the whole program.

International business services

International flexibility/adaptability "involves the extent to which a person is energized by working in a challenging and/or unfamiliar environment; it requires an attitude which welcomes opportunity and fosters resilience, adaptability and confidence: Creates a network—Demonstrates an ability to cultivate, establish, and utilize local, social, political and/or business networks to overcome an obstacle or meet an objective."

So my way of thinking is when you're starting new, cast as wide a net as possible and don't exclude things in the beginning. I had nothing to lose by meeting this guy and he turned out to be a wonderful connection. He opened some doors for us, and it's important, I think, to approach things in that way—building relationships—because you are dealing in a country where you don't know what is going on. It's helpful to establish and develop local relationships. I've done it before, I did it there, and it worked.

International business developers

Organizational awareness is "the ability to understand and learn the power of relationships in one's own organization or in other organizations. Understands organizational politics—Understands, describes (or uses) ongoing power and political relationships within the organization with a clear sense of organizational impact."

I jumped in with two feet with a certain resolve to say I don't want to play the politics, but I do want to get enough information to form my own opinion. There was a lot going on below the surface and people seemed to be forming into two camps either behind Mr. X or Mr. Y. All I can do is be above board and if people want my opinion, I'll give it to them.

International business developers

Empathy "implies wanting to understand other people. Understands current, unexpressed or poorly expressed meanings—understands current unspoken thoughts, concerns or feelings. Or gets others to willingly take actions desired by the speaker; that is uses understanding to get others to act the way you want them to."

I recognized his suspicion as normal coming from a guy who has spent all his life, certainly the last 50 years, right in the middle of the Communist Party hierarchy, and he was suspicious of anyone and everyone where $80 million was involved. He wasn't accusing us of any wrongdoing, but he was very suspicious about what had happened to the $80 million.

International negotiators

The second role that competencies from the emotional intelligence sector played was to provide direction and influence over the activities necessary to achieve desired outcomes. This role was accomplished through the behaviors of the achievement motivation and the impact and influence competencies, as shown in the next examples.

Achievement motivation is "a concern for working well or for competing against a standard of excellence. Improves performance—makes specific changes in the system or in own work methods to improve performance (e.g., does something better, faster, at a lower cost, more efficiently; improves quality, customer satisfaction, morale, revenues) without setting any specific goal."

I was observing that people were spending a tremendous amount of effort and energy on this, and it was meaningless. It was an activity that was a waste of time. The whole concept behind the process was flawed. So I immediately started to rethink what we were doing and assigned a champion to improve the process. I told him what my objectives were for this process and made it clear to him which flaws needed to be addressed and fixed.

Strategists

The *impact and influence* competency "implies an intention to persuade, convince, influence or impress others, in order to get them to go along with or to support the speaker's agenda. Calculates a dramatic action—models behavior desired in others or takes a well thought-out or unusual action in order to have a specific impact."

I decided to include the contractor's team (about 100 people) with our company team for the team meetings. To get everyone's involvement, I scheduled the meeting during lunchtime and bought them lunch. I used that time to inform everyone of what's going on and to do some team building. It worked in that it created a sense of belonging and togetherness which was my intention.

Worldwide project managers

What Is the Pattern of IQ–EQ–Skills/Expertise Competencies Across Different Roles?

The composite 16 competencies that represent the differentiating characteristics from all five functional roles are distributed across the three categories of cognitive intelligence, emotional intelligence, and skills and expertise (S/E). This was true for four of the five functional competency models. The only functional area where this was not the case was the role of worldwide project manager. In that case, the cognitive intelligence competencies were not found to be differentiators of superior performance as they were demonstrated by both typical and superior performers. The distribution across the categories was as follows:

- Strategists   64% EQ   27% IQ   9% S/E
- International business developer   50% EQ   19% IQ   31% S/E
- International negotiator   38% EQ   38% IQ   25% S/E
- International business services   54% EQ   23% IQ   23% S/E
- Worldwide project manager   69% EQ   0 IQ   31% S/E

The distribution in the core competency model was 44% EQ, 19% IQ, and 38% S/E. Each of these roles operated in the complex environment of international business, often away from headquarters and without the infrastructure or support normally present in a large corporation. The nature of the functional work also required the individuals to successfully interact with other individuals representing foreign governments and corporations in very complex situations. These data show that to be successful in a complex environment the individual needs to demonstrate behavioral characteristics in all three areas: emotional intelligence, cognitive intelligence, and the skills/expertise needed for the functional role. These findings support those of Katz reported in 1974 and Dulewicz and Higgs in 1998 wherein the characteristics that define a successful person are a combination of the three categories.

DISCUSSION

The study found that it is possible to empirically identify the critical few competencies that distinguish superior performance in a chain of roles. If the organization focuses on the development of these competencies in these roles, they would create a capability valued by the enterprise. The first requirement was a clear definition of the desired capability and identification of the key functional roles that made up the capability. The empirical interview data identified the competencies that differentiated superior performers in each of the roles and provided examples of the competency behavior in the contextual execution of role responsibilities that added face validity to the competencies. Two factors were critical to the success of this cross-functional study. The first was the use of an empirical data collection process that minimized personal bias in the identification of differentiating competencies. The second was standardization of the competency database used to identify, measure, and assess the competencies. As recognized in earlier studies, without a standard language, the competencies associated with each role would be categorized differently and it would have been impossible to resolve the differences or to come up with a common core applicable to all roles (McClelland, 1985). The 10 competencies found by the study to be a core model across all functional roles, in rank order of congruency, were as follows:

1. Achievement motivation
2. Impact and influence
3. Self-confidence
4. Analytical thinking
5. Conceptual thinking
6. Information seeking
7. Empathy
8. Organizational awareness
9. Teamwork and cooperation
10. International flexibility/adaptability

In addition to the 10 core competencies, six characteristics were identified as unique differentiators of performance in various roles:

1. Business expertise/perspective
2. Negotiations orientation
3. Balancing home and local organizations
4. Multicultural sensitivity
5. Strategic orientation
6. International acumen

The comparison of interview-based empirical data to the perceptive-based focus group and questionnaire data underscores McClelland's comment that "the main contribution of the Freudian revolution to personality theory was the demonstration that people's conscious values and unconscious motives are not necessarily the same" (McClelland, 1985, p. 203). The study results reflected this point exactly. The empirically determined competencies of achievement motivation and impact and influence are derivatives of the motives for achievement and power, respectively. Both of these competencies were found to be statistically significant differentiators of superior performance in every functional role. However, questionnaire respondents did not rate achievement motivation as a top 10 in more than three of the five roles and did not rank impact and influence as a top 10 in any of the roles. Either the respondents did not understand the behavioral descriptions for these competencies and could not relate them to the challenges at hand or they valued other characteristics more highly. Two competencies that were rated in the top 10 by respondents for all roles were international flexibility/adaptability and teamwork and cooperation. Apparently these selections reflected the respondents' experience of flexibility in international environments and the need to work cooperatively, with both individuals external to the organization as well as internal teams.

It is interesting that the congruence between the empirical findings to the perceptual rankings was higher for the more abstract roles (strategists, 80%; international business developers, 70%; international negotiators, 60%) than the more concrete, technically grounded roles (worldwide project managers, 50%; international business services, 40%). This could mean that individuals in the more complex roles had a truer understanding of the complex behaviors associated with performance and consequently selected them in the survey.

The competencies of analytical thinking and organizational awareness were found to have higher values for typical than superior performers in both the correlation and t tests. This is not a surprise as the petroleum industry is technically grounded and science-based and encourages an analytical approach. The ability to think analytically is a baseline requirement for many of the functional roles in the study. It is believed that the superior performers demonstrated a capability for systemic thinking by balancing analytical, detailed thinking with strategic conceptual thinking, whereas typical performers were biased primarily toward analytical thinking. The organizational awareness scores may be a reflection of the political environment surrounding these functional roles. In every role there was a significant political component (either internally, externally, or both), and typical performers may have been overly focused on getting things accomplished "through the system" whereas the superior performers were focused on influencing the decision-making progress toward desired business results. This assessment is supported by the higher values for superior performers on achievement motivation and impact and influence competencies in both the qualitative and quantitative analyses.

Other competencies frequently identified in the questionnaire but not substantiated by the empirical data were self-control and customer service orientation. These ratings may reflect that the studied roles were service providers to business units rather than revenue producers. As a consequence, customer satisfaction was an important consideration in the way business units valued each role and individuals rated it accordingly. These data indicate that individuals participating in perceptive assessments can do a good job of identifying legitimate business challenges and issues but are not as good at recognizing the behaviors needed to address those challenges. The competency of impact and influence was found to be an important component of accomplishing the outcomes desired by business units for all roles and a key component in creating customer satisfaction, but the value of these behaviors' contribution was apparently not understood by questionnaire respondents. The difference between the perceived competencies and the empirical competencies may be less of an issue of correctness than one of depth. The competencies perceived to be most important may have been selected because of political correctness or because the associated behaviors were more easily understood; therefore, their relation to critical issues and desired outcomes was clearer than psychological-sounding competency names and behavioral descriptions.

The 10 core competencies were categorized as cognitive (IQ) based, emotional (EQ) based, or skills/expertise based in order to observe the EQ competencies in isolation. Of the 10, 3 (analytical thinking, conceptual thinking, and information seeking) were categorized as IQ based and the remaining seven were categorized as EQ based. The six unique characteristics were categorized as skills/expertise based (see Table 5.5). It was found, however, that although the competencies can be categorized, they constantly interacted and commingled during the course of daily events as individuals executed their roles in complex environments. In this reality it was found that EQ competencies played two roles in contributing to performance. First, they often operated as the catalyst that provided leverage to the individual's cognitive capabilities and expertise. Cognitive ability enabled individuals to develop the skills and expertise needed for a particular role, but their emotional intelligence competencies enabled them to leverage those capabilities. In some cases, the desired outcomes were only achieved as a result of the EQ competencies. In other cases, the EQ competencies created a circumstance wherein the individuals achieved the desired outcomes through application of their IQ and expertise competencies. Second, through achievement motivation and impact and influence, the EQ competencies provided both the direction of effort through goal setting and the influence and control over the activities necessary to cause desired outcomes. The EQ competencies provided the traction necessary for performance, in all roles, by enabling individual cognitive ability, knowledge, skill, and expertise to be maximized in the crucible of human interactions that made up the international environment.

This relation of IQ, EQ, and skills/expertise could be viewed as a series of steps or plateaus related to superior performance, as shown in Fig. 5.2.

Contribution of the Research

The recurring theme emerging from the data is (a) the importance of the achievement and power motive competencies to individual performance outcomes and (b) the need for competencies from all categories (IQ, EQ,

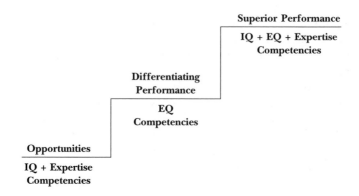

FIG. 5.2.   Relation of EQ competencies to performance.

and expertise) to be successful in the complex environments in which people live and work. It is not enough to just be smart, or to be smart and have great skills, or to have great empathy and emotional intelligence. In today's complex environments, an individual needs to personally develop in all three categories.

This chapter has attempted to remove some of the fogginess about the role of emotional intelligence in critical functions. Significant discussion in the popular press has identified the contribution that EQ competencies make to interpersonal relationships which has been substantiated by these findings. But, in addition to that contribution, EQ competencies describe the behaviors that provide the sense of direction and the means to leverage other capabilities to affect and influence outcomes, self-confidently in a way that is personally satisfying. The hidden value of EQ is the foundation for performance that is provided by the motives of n. achievement and n. power. When the power motive is focused to power for people versus power over people (socialized power), the combined effect of the stimulation of these two motives (need for achievement [n.Ach] and need for socialized power [N. Pow.s]) can result in significant accomplishment.

Organization development operates in the intersection of organizations, individuals, and the social sciences of economics, psychology, political science, sociology, and management. This chapter helps to clarify how individual behaviors can create an organizational capability for performance in an economically valued direction by taking a hermeneutic approach across the social sciences. It attempts to fit pieces of information together from a variety of sources to better understand the relation of individual behavior that has been characterized as emotional intelligence to organizational settings, so that this knowledge can help individuals and organizations grow in a way that is beneficial to both.

Limitations

The study was conducted before the e-commence revolution in international business applications. Although I believe that the competencies identified as differentiators of performance in international business are robust enough to persist in the current environment, the skills and expertise competencies may be different.

Second, the data were collected from a single industry sector and reflected the international business situations of a very specialized and highly technical industry. The issues surrounding the accomplishment of international business in this industry may well be different from what is currently the case in other industries.

Finally, the data are skewed toward White males as a consequence of the industry. Although competencies have been found to be more representative of the characteristics of superior performers, regardless of gender or ethnic background (superior performers share common characteristics more than they share gender or ethnic characteristics), this study was unbalanced in that regard.

These considerations not withstanding, the study presents a clear description of the IQ, EQ, and expertise characteristics that differentiate performance in the functional roles of international business in a capital-intensive, asset-based industry. It provides a rationale for the development of all of these categories as well as an improved understanding of the role EQ competencies play in creating an international capability. It uncovers the need for organizations, through their leaders, to create and sustain environments that stimulate the achievement and power motives so that individuals have a valid sense of direction with the opportunity to exhibit a sense of control over their activities in the complex environment of international business. The recognition that creating a stimulating environment is one of the most important, if not the most important, contributions a leader can make will help organizations prepare for the globalize, e-commerce-generated future. As service and professional organizations migrate to virtual corporations of knowledge merchants electronically linked but physically separated, understanding how to create value from a network of dislocated human assets will become a critical capability. The role that emotional intelligence competencies can play in creating such a capability is an opportunity for valuable future research.

REFERENCES

Becker, B., & Gerhart, B. (1996). The impact of human resource management on organizational performance: Progress and prospects. *Academy of Management Journal, 39*(4), 779–801.

Boyatzis, R. E. (1982). *The competent manager: A model for effective performance.* New York: Wiley.

Cytowic, R. E. (1996). *The neurological side of neuropsychology.* Cambridge, MA: MIT Press.

Dulewicz, V., & Higgs, M. (1998). Emotional intelligence: Can it be measured reliably and validly using competency data? *Competency, 6*(1), 28–37.

Flanagan, J. C. (1954, July). Critical incident technique. *Psychological Bulletin, 51*(4), 327–358.

Goleman, D. (1995). *Emotional intelligence.* New York: Bantam.

Goleman, D. (1998). *Working with emotional intelligence.* New York: Bantam.

Greenspan, S. I. (1997). *The growth of the mind and the endangered origins of intelligence.* Reading, MA: Merloyd Lawrence.

Huy, Q. N. (1999). Emotional capability, emotional intelligence, and radical change. *Academy of Management Review, 24*(2), 325–345.

Katz, R. L. (1974, September–October). Skills of an effective administrator. *Harvard Business Review.* Reprinted in *Business Classics: Fifteen Key Concepts for Managerial Success, Harvard Business Review,* 1998.

Mayo, E. (1945). *The social problems of an industrial civilization.* Graduate School of Business Administration, Harvard University, Boston.

McBer & Company's JND Scale Competency Dictionary version 3.1. (1993). Boston: McBer & Company.

McClelland, D. C. (1973). Testing for competence rather than for "intelligence." *American Psychologist, 28,* 1–14.

McClelland, D. C. (1985). *Human motivation.* Glenview, IL: Scott, Foresman.

Salovey, P., & Mayer, J. D. (1990). Emotional intelligence. *Imagination, Cognition and Personality, 9*(3), 185–211.

Spencer, L. M., Jr., & Spencer, S. M. (1993). *Competence at work.* New York: Wiley.

Terpstra, D., & Rozelle, E. (1993). The relationship of staffing practices to organizational level measures of performance *Personnel Psychology, 46,* 27–48.

Ulrich, D., & Lake, D. (1990). *Organizational capability: Competing from the inside out.* New York: Wiley.

Vaill, P. B. (1983). The theory of managing in the managerial competency movement *Exchange: The Organizational Behavior Teaching Journal, 8*(2), 50–56.

Vaill, P. B. (1989). *Managing as a performing art.* San Francisco: Jossey-Bass.

Wisher, V. (1994, July). Competencies: The precious seeds of growth? *Personnel Management,* 36–39.

Chapter 6

The International Business Case: Emotional Intelligence Competencies and Important Business Outcomes

Fabio Sala
Millennium Pharmaceuticals, Inc.

The concept of emotional intelligence (EI) speaks to many business issues that managers/executives and practitioners/consultants face every day. Some issues are common across organizations, industries, and cultures; for example, How do I get my direct reports motivated around an initiative? How can I competitively reduce turnover? How can I be a more effective leader? What makes our top performers excel and how are they different from poor or average performers? How can we improve customer service and loyalty? How can we prepare our managers for future leadership roles? Although these issues are quite broad, their universal relevance to many business contexts may explain why emotional intelligence makes such intuitive sense to those in the business world. Emotional intelligence, applied to the workplace, is not a cure-all but rather a convenient way to conceptualize the dynamic impact of emotion on behavior and how understanding and managing emotion in the workplace can help address the previously mentioned issues and problems.

Although the term *emotional intelligence* was coined relatively recently, people have understood the value of these skills and abilities for a long time (Cherniss, 2000, outlined the long history of efforts to help workers improve their emotional intelligence). Today, we have seen a growth in programs that are designed to increase awareness of the value of emotional intelligence at work, assess managers' and executives' level of EI competence, and develop behaviors that are consistent with and characteristic of emotionally intelligent leadership. In fact, well-developed principles have been identified to promote effective training and development of EI competencies (Cherniss & Goleman, 2001). Because the concept of emotional intelligence resonates in the business world, practitioners have been eager to implement it to resolve important workplace issues. During this period of growth in application, many have called for more research that (a) clearly conceptualizes emotional intelligence and (b) demonstrates a firm relation between emotional intelligence and actual workplace performance outcomes. Indeed, practitioners and applied researchers alike have called for more evidence demonstrating a link between emotional intelligence and performance-based assessments (Kaufman & Kaufman, 2001). To date, very little research has demonstrated criterion-related predictive validity with outcomes directly relevant to the workplace. This chapter attempts to address both concerns. Using a competency approach for the assessment of emotional intelligence (Boyatzis, 1982; Boyatzis & Sala, 2004; Spencer & Spencer, 1993), I clarify the EI competency framework, outline its theoretical foundation, and provide evidence for a relation between EI competency ratings and measures of performance in workplace contexts.

This chapter makes a case for the value of emotional intelligence competencies in the workplace. Findings are synthesized from three empirical studies that examined the relation between emotional intelligence competencies and work performance across a variety of functional, organizational, and cultural contexts. To assess emotional intelligence competence, the Emotional Competence Inventory (ECI; Boyatzis, Goleman, & Hay Group, 1999) was administered to three samples: South African call center agents from a large life insurance organization, Bass Brewers sales agents covering the entire United Kingdom, and Turkish business school graduates working in a variety of fields for more than 11 years. Measures of workplace performance were obtained for all three groups. Results are synthesized and presented as evidence for the importance and role of emotional intelligence competence on work performance in a variety of roles, organizations, and cultural settings.

MEASUREMENT OF EMOTIONAL INTELLIGENCE COMPETENCIES

The ECI was used to assess EI competencies for each sample. The ECI is a multirater survey instrument that assesses self-ratings, manager ratings, direct report, peer ratings, and client ratings on a series of behavioral indicators of emotional intelligence competencies (Goleman, Boyatzis, & Hay Group, 1999). Previous research has demonstrated acceptable reliability and validity evidence for the ECI (Sala, 2002). From the competency perspective, emotional intelligence is defined as the capacity for recognizing our own feelings and those of others, for motivating ourselves, and for managing emotions effectively in ourselves and others. A competency is more generally defined as a characteristic of an individual that is causally related to criterion-referenced effective or superior performance in a job or situation (Boyatzis, 1982; Spencer & Spencer, 1993). An emotional intelligence competency, however, is an ability to recognize, understand, and use emotional information about oneself or others that leads to or causes effective or superior performance (Boyatzis & Sala, 2004). A more simple definition of emotional intelligence may be that emotional intelligence is the intelligent use of emotions. EI can also be defined as how people handle themselves and their relationships (Goleman, Boyatzis, & McKee, 2002).

The ECI measures 18 competencies organized into four clusters (see Appendixes A and B): self-awareness (emotional self-awareness, accurate self-assessment, self-confidence), self-management (emotional self-control, transparency, conscientiousness, adaptability, achievement, initiative, optimism), social awareness (empathy, organizational awareness, service orientation), and relationship management (developing others, inspirational leadership, influence, change catalyst, conflict management, teamwork & collaboration). See Goleman et al. (2002) for a more detailed description of this framework.

EMOTIONAL INTELLIGENCE AND SOUTH AFRICAN CALL CENTER AGENTS

Organizations that employ call center agents are faced with difficult challenges. Turnover and absenteeism are high in these positions, and therefore staff selection and training are imperative to success. The abilities to focus on customer needs, to handle oneself with frustrated customers, and to convey genuine enthusiasm for products and services are among the key attributes of successful call center agents.

Using the ECI, Heidemarie Nel (2001) conducted a study to examine the relation between emotional intelligence competencies and job performance with a sample of call center agents from a major life insurance agency in South Africa. These front-line professionals are in high-stress roles. The call center personnel have extensive customer contact with current clients (e.g., policyholders), police officers, physicians, and other health care professionals. Maintaining customer satisfaction and loyalty involves managing all these relationships smoothly. This role requires being aware of one's emotions, staying composed and poised in stressful situations, focusing on the customer's needs, and providing solutions and helping to solve clients' problems.

Aside from general computer skills, product knowledge, and policy procedures, success in this role is thought to be largely based on "people skills."

Agents are responsible for making sales proposals to both existing and new clients, providing ongoing customer relations with existing clients, and maintaining customer satisfaction. Agents are responsible for closing proposals and transactions, and to be successful they need to work effectively with other team members to provide fluid services to clients.

Nel (2001) administered the ECI to a sample of call center agents working at the headquarters of a major life insurance agency located in the Western Cape, South Africa. Participants were randomly selected from three call center functions: client services, sales, and administration. These roles are not independent: All three perform relatively similar functions (e.g., transaction services, technology support, customer service inquiries). Client services agents respond to existing policyholders; sales agents primarily work to generate new business by cross-selling; and administration agents focus on internal clients (e.g., health care professionals and physicians) and collections. One hundred fifty-three "self" versions of the ECI were administered, and 135 were completed and returned (response rate = 88.2%). Participants were also rated by 31 team leaders (4.9 participants per team leader). The call center agents were divided as follows: 33% ($n = 44$) client services, 34% ($n = 47$) sales, and 33% ($n = 44$) administration. Each agent was rated on the ECI by the team leader.

A major strength of this study is the quality of the performance measures—or how success was determined. An agent's job performance was an objective overall rating that was provided by the participating organization. Agents' performance ratings were based on the following computerized, objective assessments: (a) closing rate, which is the percentage of successful sales transactions in relation to the amount of decision makers they have spoken to within a specific time period; (b) lapse index, which is the amount of transactions processed within a period of time; (c) production time, the actual logged-in time whereby agents are ready to receive calls (agents are expected to be logged into the system for specific amount of time per day); and (d) quality of conversation, which is based on the blind content analysis of randomly recorded conversations. For the purposes of this study, only overall total performance ratings were available for each agent; individual scores for each assessment could not be obtained.

Table 6.1 reports the study results, which found significant correlations between agents' ECI ratings and measures of call center performance. Results suggest a strong relation between agents' competency ratings and performance within all three call center environments. Self-confidence, trustworthiness, conscientiousness, initiative, influence, change catalyst, and conflict management were strongly correlated with performance across all three groups. Consistent with what would be expected from proposed EI model, competencies from the self-management and social skills (relationship management) clusters seem most significantly related to performance.

TABLE 6.1
Correlations Between ECI 1.0 Scores and Performance
for Call Center Agents by Department (Nel, 2001)

ECI Cluster	Emotional Intelligence (ECI) Competence Managerial Ratings	Call Center Department		
		Client Services (n = 44)	Sales (n = 47)	Administration (n = 44)
Self-awareness	Emotional self-awareness	.23	.33	.46
	Accurate self-assessment	.38	.33	.46
	Self-confidence	.61	.47	.73*
Self-management	Self-control	.17	.26	.48
	Trustworthiness	.66*	.53*	.45
	Conscientiousness	.49*	.45	.57*
	Adaptability	.37	.31	.58*
	Achievement orientation	.64*	.35	.63*
	Initiative	.58*	.42	.72*
Social awareness	Empathy	.22	.42	.45
	Organizational awareness	.49*	.25	.48
	Service orientation	.27	.39	.46
Social skills	Developing others	.30	.30	.68*
	Inspirational leadership	.49*	.26	.62*
	Communication	.41	.32	.46
	Influence	.53*	.37	.63*
	Change catalyst	.57*	.43	.58*
	Conflict management	.45	.26	.59*
	Building bonds	.35	.48	.55*
	Teamwork & collaboration	.44	.41	.57*

Note. ECI = Emotional Competence Inventory.
*$p < .05$.

The self-awareness competencies (i.e., knowing oneself and knowing others) may lead to superior performance by providing a foundation for the appropriate use of self-management and relationship management competencies. For example, an empathic response to a problem that the customer is having may lead to higher satisfaction in a call center context. When a person calls because he or she is frustrated by the insurance company's lack of responsiveness, an empathic response might be, "I'm sorry about that, I can understand how you would be irritated and dissatisfied." A high-performing agent will "hear" the distress (empathy), care enough to do something (achievement or initiative), and then be able to reassure this person that he or she will handle the situation and not discontinue the business relationship (influence, conflict management).

For agents in this study, self-confidence and trustworthiness may be essential to establishing and maintaining rapport with clients—gaining their trust and confidence through the quality of phone conversations. Conscientiousness, initiative, achievement orientation, and influence may facilitate various aspects of performance. For example, initiative (i.e., acts on and creates opportunities) and achievement (i.e., concern with improving performance, setting challenging goals) may help agents increase production time and improve lapse indexes. These likely lead to better performance outcomes through high levels of customer satisfaction.

EMOTIONAL INTELLIGENCE AND SALES PERFORMANCE

What does it take to be an effective salesperson? Are those who are good at closing sales higher in emotional intelligence competencies? Although some think of sales as a rational transaction of goods and services, it is very much an emotional and relational transaction. What are the characteristics that turn us off as clients and consumers? Aggressiveness, a self-interest orientation (i.e., the salesperson will put his or her sales targets above your interests), untrustworthy (e.g., distorting the truth or even lying to get you to buy), lacking integrity, and poor listening skills are a few characteristics that might undermine sales effectiveness. Perhaps a skilled salesperson adapts him- or herself to the perceived preferences of the audience. In professional services organizations, for example, we know that those who are good at sales gain the trust of their clients and deliver high-quality service (Maister, Green, & Galford, 2000).

Using the ECI 2.0 (see Sala, 2002), Lloyd (2001) conducted a study to determine whether emotional intelligence competencies were associated with various measures of performance for sales agents at Bass Brewers in the United Kingdom. The sample consisted of 33 area development manager (ADM) sales agents at Bass Brewers. Covering the entire United Kingdom, the Bass sales force consists of 54 ADMs who are organized into seven regional teams led by seven field sales managers (FSM). These teams are responsible for building volume and profit, implementing national promotional activity, and resolving customer service issues. Essentially, the job requires the ability to sell and deliver high-quality service.

Similar to the study previously discussed, the strength of this research rests in the care Lloyd took in assessing performance for these sales agents. His current role as national account director and his previous ADM position provided him with a thorough understanding of the metrics that identify success in this role at Bass. Understanding the influence of ADM area changes, position changes, market conditions, and centrally negotiated business delivered by national account managers, he argued, "One or two simple hard financial measures such as volume and profit could indicate variances/relationships not necessarily attributable to a particular ADM and indeed their emotional intelligence" (Lloyd, 2001, p. 21). To address this issue, an overall performance measure (OPM) was developed that consisted of hard, soft, and personal development indicators. The OPM included the following measures (see Lloyd, 2001, for greater detail):

- A "ready for promotion" rating. ADMs were rated by FSMs on the following 5-point scale: (5) *ready for promotion*, (4) *promotion within 2 years*, (3) *lateral move next*, (3) *correct level and correct job*, (2) *wrong level*, and (1) *wrong job.*
- Average number of new brand installations per quarter per fiscal year. The ADMs are responsible for increased branding within their regions.
- Average number of new accounts gained per quarter per fiscal year. This is their hard sales targets. ADMs must increase the number of vendors who directly sell Bass.
- Customer service audit. Customer satisfaction surveys are randomly sent to customers every quarter by an independent telemarketing agency.
- Annual performance rating. This was based on mutually agreed appraisal targets that are updated quarterly. Using company performance appraisal policy, FSMs rate ADMs on a 5-point scale: (5) *superior performance*, (4) *commendable*, (3) *on-target*, (2) *improvable*, and (1) *unacceptable.*
- Number of job band changes. This is the number of job band changes (promotions) at Bass divided by the number of years served.

This study was designed to assess the predictive criterion validity for the ECI and to find out whether emotional intelligence competencies might underlie some of the behaviors that lead to better performance in this role. Performance data were assessed 6 months after emotional intelligence competency ratings were obtained. ADMs provided self-ratings on the ECI, and they were also rated by their managers (i.e., FSMs). This helps to establish a causal connection between exhibiting emotional intelligence competencies and future performance; it also helps to reduce some of the common-source bias in the study.

Lloyd (2001) found strong relations between ECI self- and managerial ratings and sales agent performance; ADMs with higher overall competency ratings averaged across all competencies performed best. ECI self-ratings were positively associated with the OPM (which captures all performance indicators). In terms of the individual performance indicators, ECI self-ratings were also associated with the number of new distribution points achieved, the number of new accounts sold year to date, and career progression/band changes (promotions). Similar patterns were found for managerial ratings (FSM): ECI ratings were significantly associated with overall performance and number of new accounts sold. Respectable effect sizes were found between ECI FSM ratings and number of new distribution points, customer service ratings, and annual performance ratings; however, ECI self-ratings were not predictive of customer service ratings and annual performance ratings.

These findings may be due to the nature of the performance indicators and limitations of self-assessments. For example, self-ratings have been shown to be less predictive of performance (Church, 2000; Harris & Schaubroech, 1988; Sala & Dwight, 2002), and they typically demonstrate a leniency bias (Church, 1997; Podsakoff & Organ, 1986; Van Velsor et al., 1993). Therefore, self-ratings may have correlated more strongly with number of new accounts sold and number of new distribution points because those measures are more transparent—that is, people regularly track and monitor those indicators. Customer service ratings and annual performance ratings, however, are more elusive and subjective; it's harder to know whether your customers and your manager are satisfied with your work. This is the paradox of emotional intelligence: If people are not very good at assessing their own strengths and limits, it will be difficult for them to accurately rate themselves on the EI competencies against performance, and similarly, it will be more difficult for them to "see" themselves as others see them.

Interestingly, tenure at Bass and years of sales experience are not associated with performance or EI competency ratings. The data suggest a true performance culture at Bass with clarity between sales agents and managers. The strong relation between performance and EI competence suggests that individual effort, rather than tenure, leads to performance. Furthermore, the fact that self-ratings are correlated with managerial ratings suggests dialogue between agents and managers, because previous research has shown that ratings from these rater groups tend to diverge (Sala & Dwight, 2002). Indeed, quarterly updated appraisal targets for annual performance reviews likely contributed to superior performance management.

ROLE OF EMOTIONAL INTELLIGENCE
AFTER BUSINESS SCHOOL

Emotional intelligence competencies theoretically ought to be associated with all kinds of life outcomes. Mastery of emotional self-control, for example, should help people navigate a variety of social interactions as well as manage their own reactions to stress. It's been clearly documented that a higher experience of stress can have negative physical consequences. The focus of this chapter, of course, is on the relation between EI competencies and workplace outcomes. Levent Sevinc (2001), a researcher at Istanbul

TABLE 6.2

Correlations Between Bass Brewers (Lloyd, 2001) Sales Agents Overall ECI 1.0 Ratings and Measures of Performance ($N = 33$)

Bass Brewers Assessment	1	2	3	4	5	6	7	8	9	10
1. ECI self-rating	—									
2. ECI manager rating	.59***	—								
3. Overall performance	.62***	.51***	—							
4. Number of new dist. pts.	.40**	.28	.85***	—						
5. Number of new accounts	.57***	.43**	.92***	.78***	—					
6. Customer service	.04	.25	.38**	.35**	.16	—				
7. Annual performance rating	.08	.23	.31*	.40**	.15	.58***	—			
8. Years Bass service	.09	.04	.04	.07	.07	.01	.26	—		
9. Career progression	.39**	.23	.51***	.32*	.33*	.01	.10	.20	—	
10. Years of sales experience	-.27	.07	.02	.04	.01	.04	.17	.73***	.13	—

Note. ECI = Emotional Competence Inventory.
*$p < .10$. **$p < .05$. ***$p < .01$.

University, was interested in broadening the conceptualization of workplace "performance" to include both objective and subjective measures of career success. He conducted a study using the ECI with a sample of Turkish business school graduates working in various industries and functions for more than 11 years after graduation. Participants were graduates of Istanbul University, Department of Business Administration in 1990; they were contacted in 2001 through a university alumni association.

One hundred twenty graduates were contacted and 71 returned self-scored ECI surveys (response rate = 59%). Participants were 58% (41) male and 42% (30) female and were between the ages of 31 and 36. The majority (97%) worked for private organizations, whereas only two (3%) worked in the public sector. As you might imagine, graduates were working in a variety of fields and functions. The majority (62%) were in finance (i.e., banking, insurance, securities, etc.), and others were in service industries (14%), manufacturing (14%), and other industries (10%). Sales positions, marketing, general management, accounting, and finance were represented. Participants also were provided with two copies of the ECI-360 to be completed and returned by either a peer, direct report, or manager. Forty participants returned ECI-360 ratings (response rate = 44%), and the majority (90%) of those returned were completed by one rater.

For each participant, Sevinc also obtained several measures of self-reported objective and subjective indicators of career success. Self-reported objective measures of success included current salary, managerial level (first-, mid-, and senior-level management), and number of promotions. Subjective career and life satisfaction was reliably assessed with a self-report survey (Chay, Aryee, & Tan, 1994; Gattiker & Larwood, 1986) that included the following components: financial satisfaction (e.g., I am earning as much as I think my work is worth, I am satisfied with progress toward meeting goals for income); hierarchical satisfaction (e.g., I am pleased with the promotions I have received so far, I am satisfied with success achieved in career or line of work); interpersonal satisfaction (e.g., I am respected by my peers); job satisfaction (e.g., I am in a job which offers me the chance to learn new skills); and life success (e.g., I am happy with my private life, I am happy with life overall).

Results showed a relatively consistent pattern between career success and ECI ratings for both rater groups (i.e., self and other). As one might expect, significant relations between self-reported career satisfaction and self-reported ECI ratings were more frequent and robust than those between self-reported career satisfaction and ECI other-ratings. Table 6.3 shows correlations between ECI self-rating cluster scores and work/life career success/job satisfaction and measures of objective career success. Those who rated themselves high in emotional intelligence competencies also reported the following:

TABLE 6.3
Relation Between ECI 1.0 Self-Ratings and Objective
and Subjective Career Satisfaction With a Sample
of Turkish Business Professionals (Sevinc, 2001)

		Emotional Intelligence Clusters (Self-Rating)			
Self-Reported		Self-Awareness	Self-Management	Social Awareness	Social Skills
Objective	Salary ($n = 68$)	.43**	.37**	.37**	.41**
career	Managerial level ($n = 71$)	.15	.16	.10	.22*
success	Number of promotions ($n = 59$)	−.13	−.14	−.12	−.17
Subjective	Job satisfaction ($n = 71$)	.32**	.37**	.28**	.43**
career/life	Financial satisfaction ($n = 71$)	−.04	−.07	−.01	.01
satisfaction	Hierarchical satisfaction ($n = 71$)	.14	.21*	.16	.24**
	Interpersonal satisfaction ($n = 71$)	.48**	.47**	.40**	.53**
	Life satisfaction ($n = 71$)	.24**	.29**	.14	.35**

Note. ECI = Emotional Competence Inventory.
*$p < .10$. *$p < .05$.

- Higher salaries.
- Higher job satisfaction: They felt more supported by management in their work, and they felt challenged, responsible, and accountable in their work.
- Higher hierarchical satisfaction: They were more satisfied with career goals, promotion, and achievements.
- Higher interpersonal satisfaction: They felt more respected and accepted by peers and superiors.
- Higher life satisfaction: They reported being happier and more satisfied with their private life.

Table 6.4 shows correlations between ECI other-rating cluster scores and work/life career success/job satisfaction and measures of objective career success. Significant correlations were less frequent with total other-ratings than with ECI self-ratings. Although significant correlations between total other-ratings and success measures were less frequent, these findings may be more informative and reliable because the sources of data (i.e., self-reported success/satisfaction and ECI ratings by others) are independent from one another. Those who were rated by others as high in emotional intelligence reported having higher salaries, higher job satisfaction, and higher life satisfaction.

The consistent relation between salary and ECI self- and other-ratings suggests that EI competencies are associated with financial success. It was

TABLE 6.4
Correlations Between ECI 1.0 Total Others Ratings and Objective
and Subjective Career Satisfaction With a Sample
of Turkish Business Professionals (Sevinc, 2001)

		Emotional Intelligence Clusters (Total Others Ratings)			
Self-Reported		Self-Awareness	Self-Management	Social Awareness	Social Skills
Objective	Salary ($n = 38$)	.30*	.37**	.43**	.40**
career	Managerial level ($n = 40$)	.09	.10	.19	.29*
success	Number of promotions ($n = 29$)	.03	−.06	−.17	−.10
Subjective	Job satisfaction ($n = 40$)	.12	.33**	.26*	.34**
career/life	Financial satisfaction ($n = 40$)	−.21	−.07	−.16	−.15
satisfaction	Hierarchical satisfaction ($n = 40$)	−.02	.16	.05	.01
	Interpersonal satisfaction ($n = 40$)	.00	.17	.01	.10
	Life satisfaction ($n = 40$)	.29*	.46**	.38**	.46**

Note. ECI = Emotional Competence Inventory.
*$p < .10$. **$p < .05$.

concluded that those who are successful in Turkish finance and service industry organizations must possess certain analytical skills; however, it is believed that those who excel (vs. those who are average) also possess certain interpersonal skills that help them work more effectively with others. The ability to persuade someone to invest their money in mutual funds at your bank is not wholly related to your ability to demonstrate your technical competence in investment funds. Most customers have no way of evaluating these skills (much like you don't know if your auto mechanic is going to cheat you based on your evaluation of his or her technical skill—which you may also have trouble evaluating). So, in part, we make decisions based on the interpersonal and largely emotional dynamic and subtle nonverbal interaction with the service provider.

CONCLUSIONS

The research in this chapter provides evidence for the association between EI competency ratings and workplace performance. The results reveal that emotional intelligence competency behaviors are linked to performance in a variety of jobs, organizations, and cultures. Competencies that demonstrate the ability to manage one's emotions and the emotions of others were found to be an important determinant of success at work in a variety of situations and cultures. Emotional intelligence competencies helped African call center agents be more effective in their role; important indicators of performance were linked to how well they were able to understand and manage emotions. Bass sales agents' hard performance measures were linked to their emotional intelligence competence ratings. Finally, important objective and subjective measures of career success and satisfaction were found to be linked to emotional intelligence competencies for Turkish business school graduates.

The world of work is emotional—our emotions influence how we perceive and interpret information and how we respond to others. Many of the implicit and deliberate decisions we make are largely based on emotion. Connecting and establishing rapport with colleagues and clients, being comfortable in one's own skin, understanding the dispositions of others and adjusting one's approach accordingly, and engaging and energizing ourselves and others are all in part influenced by our emotions. As shown by the studies presented in this chapter and those presented in the chapters throughout this volume, there is increasing evidence that learning to become more aware of our ourselves and our emotions, more accurate at perceiving and interpreting emotion in others, and better at managing emotion in ourselves and others can have a significant positive influence on our work effectiveness.

Future Research

There are a number of methodological limitations to the research presented in this chapter. Because the research is mostly empirically based, future work might establish a clear link between the theoretical foundation of EI competencies and performance within each organizational domain. For example, hypothesis testing may help us better understand exactly how competencies drive performance in the workplace. The studies discussed here are largely descriptive; a more detailed understanding of the demands of each role presented might further explain why EI competencies drive performance and how they lead to better outcomes. Rich qualitative research might also uncover greater detail about how the emotional competencies in which superior performers engage actually lead to superior results.

The design of the South African call center study may have inflated correlations between ECI ratings and performance metrics. Call center agents' managers likely had some knowledge of each agent's performance, which may have influenced a tendency toward more desirable ratings. Although ECI rating by team leaders is probably the most important vantage point, using ratings only from this group limits the reliability of ECI assessments. Future work might include assessments from clients and might also attempt to ensure that rater groups are blind to agents' performance. Also, for both the South African call center and the Bass studies, performance measures were not independent. Future work might increase sample sizes and use independent assessments—in other words, managers in these studies rated more than one participant in the study.

Another limitation of the Bass study is that two of the measures (ECI and annual performance rating) were directly assessed by the manager. Also, managers likely had knowledge of ADMs' scores on customer service audits, their career progression, and their number of new accounts and distribution points. This common source bias may have inflated the correlations between ECI manager ratings and performance. A future study might improve on the current design by using 3 years worth of performance data, by assessing EI competencies from other perspectives, or by using stronger predictive designs where the manager is blind to any past performance. The current study was partially predictive (performance was assessed 6 months after ECI ratings were collected), but there is likely some inflation.

Analyses were conducted to explore the extent of this bias. First, manager ECI ratings were not significantly correlated with annual performance ratings ($r = .23$, $p =$ not significant). This suggests that the common source bias may not be very strong. Furthermore, the ECI manager rating was only significantly correlated to one measure (i.e., number of new accounts). Partial correlations were run between ECI manager ratings and the overall performance measure and number of new accounts while controlling for the ADMs' annual performance rating as rated by their manager. The correlations remained significant and were only slightly reduced. All this suggests that the relations found between ECI ratings and performance are robust and not compromised by common source bias.

Although direct report ECI ratings could not be obtained in the Bass study (ADMs do not have subordinates), 61% (33 of 54 ADMs) of the population was sampled. Lloyd (2001) also used excellent measures of performance. His role and solid understanding of sales and production at Bass Brewers allowed him access to data that are not often obtained in applied behavioral research. The intercorrelations reveal relatively independent performance indicators. Future work might increase sample size and attempt to understand the complex causal relations among all variables using structural equation modeling.

The relations among emotional intelligence competency behaviors, work satisfaction, and objective outcomes in the study of Turkish business school graduates need further exploration. For example, consistent with the results, we would not expect to find a relation between managerial level and

ECI ratings. Raters tend to calibrate their ratings within levels. In other words, raters' judgments are based on, and calibrated against, the standards and expectations within the target role they are rating. Therefore, we would not expect that higher level managers receive higher ratings than lower level managers because they are not judged on the same criteria. For example, on a 360 instrument, senior executives and CEOs might get similar absolute competency scores as did those working in the mailroom. Why? Because it would be inappropriate and unfair to rate the behavior of the mailroom person against the expectations and standards of the executive. Similarly, number of promotions during their 11-year careers was not associated with current ECI ratings. This finding may be due to variance in organizational size; no relation was found between salary and number of promotions ($r = -.03$, $p = .85$).

To better study the relation between promotion and EI competence, future work might look at individuals who have recently been promoted against those in similar situations who were not promoted. What did those who got promoted do differently than those who did not? I imagine that emotional intelligence competencies play a role. Similarly, with managerial level, what are the expectations between levels that lead to success? That is, what kinds of emotional intelligence behaviors lead to success for the same role at different levels?

IMPLICATIONS FOR PRACTICE AND IMPLEMENTATION

The research evidence here and throughout this book suggests the need to select wisely and invest in employee development. Selection instruments and procedures can be used to help better predict which candidates will likely be outstanding performers. Structured interviews, situational judgment tests, role playing exercises, and assessment center simulations can be used to aid in selection. In compliance with adverse impact laws, these tools and methods can help organizations make more informed hiring decisions. Of course, an organization would first start with identifying the competencies (i.e., create a competency model) that lead to outstanding performance for the particular job it is hiring. Research-based and performance-driven methods can greatly ensure that new hires are successful. Once people are hired, a number of developmental tools exist for increasing emotional intelligence competence. Multirater survey instruments can be used to assess strengths and areas for improvement. Managers can also work closely with subordinates to create plans for long-term development that are consistent with the requirements of the job.

APPENDIX A

Cluster	Competency	Sample Item
Self-awareness	Accurate self-assessment	Acknowledges own strengths and weaknesses
	Emotional self-awareness	Knows how one's feelings affect one's actions
	Self-confidence	Presents self in an assured manner
Self-management	Achievement orientation	Seeks ways to improve performance
	Adaptability	Handles unexpected demands well
	Emotional self-control	Gets impatient or shows frustration
	Initiative	Initiates actions to create possibilities
	Optimism	Stays positive despite setbacks
	Transparency	Acts on own values even when there is a personal cost
Social awareness	Empathy	Listens attentively
	Organizational awareness	Understands the organization's unspoken rules
	Service orientation	Matches customer or client needs to services or products
Relationship management	Change catalyst	Is reluctant to change or make changes
	Conflict management	Avoids conflicts
	Developing others	Recognizes specific strengths of others
	Influence	Gets support from key people
	Inspirational leadership	Articulates a compelling vision
	Teamwork and collaboration	Does not cooperate with others

APPENDIX B

Competency	Brief Explanation
Accurate self-assessment	Knowing one's inner resources, abilities, and limits
Emotional self-awareness	Recognizing how one's emotions affect performance
Self-confidence	A strong sense of one's self-worth and capabilities
Achievement orientation	Striving to improve or meeting a standard of excellence
Adaptability	Flexibility in handling change
Emotional self-control	Keeping disruptive emotions and impulses in check
Initiative	Readiness to act on opportunities
Optimism	Persistence in pursuing goals despite obstacles and setbacks
Transparency	Maintaining integrity, acting congruently with one's values
Empathy	Sensing others' feelings and perspectives and taking an active interest in their concerns
Organizational awareness	Reading a group's emotional currents and power relationships
Service orientation	Anticipating, recognizing, and meeting customers' or clients' needs
Change catalyst	Initiating or managing change
Conflict management	Negotiating and resolving disagreements
Developing others	Sensing others' development needs and bolstering their abilities
Influence	Having impact on others
Inspirational leadership	Inspiring and guiding individuals and groups
Teamwork and collaboration	Working with others toward a shared goal; creating group synergy in pursuing collective goals

REFERENCES

Boyatzis, R. (1982). *The competent manager: A model for effective performance.* New York: Wiley.

Boyatzis, R. E., Goleman, D., & Hay Group. (1999). *The Emotional Competence Inventory.* Boston: Hay Group.

Boyatzis, R. E., & Sala, F. (2004). Assessing emotional intelligence competencies. In G. Geher (Ed.), *The measurement of emotional intelligence.* Hauppauge, NY: Nova Science.

Chay, Y. W., Aryee, S., & Tan, H. H. (1994). An examination of the antecedents of subjective career success among a managerial sample in Singapore. *Human Relations, 47*(5), 487–509.

Cherniss, C. (2000). Social and emotional competence in the workplace. In R. Bar-On & J. D. Parker (Eds.), *The handbook of emotional intelligence: Theory, development, assessment, and application at home, school, and in the workplace.* San Francisco: Jossey-Bass.

Cherniss, C., & Goleman, D. (2001). Training for emotional intelligence. In C. Cherniss & D. Goleman (Eds.), *The emotionally intelligent workplace.* San Francisco: Jossey-Bass.

Church, A. H. (2000). Do higher performing managers actually receive better ratings? A validation of multi-rater assessment methodology. *Consulting Psychology Journal: Practice and Research, 54*(3), 166–172.

Gattiker, U. E., & Larwood, L. (1986). Subjective career success: A study on managers and support personnel. *Journal of Business and Psychology, 1*(2), 78–94.

Goleman, D. (1998). *Working with emotional intelligence.* New York: Bantam Books.

Goleman, D., Boyatzis, R., & McKee, A. (2002). *Primal leadership: Realizing the power of emotional intelligence.* Boston: Harvard Business School Press.

Gowing, M. K. (2001). Measurement of individual emotional competence. In C. Cherniss & D. Goleman (Eds.), *The emotionally intelligent workplace.* San Francisco: Jossey-Bass.

Harris, M., & Schaubroech, J. (1988). A meta-analysis of self-supervisor, self-peer, and peer-supervisor ratings. *Personnel Psychology, 41*, 43–62.

Kaufman, A. S., & Kaufman, J. C. (2001). Emotional intelligence as an aspect of general intelligence: What would David Wechsler say? *Emotion, 1*(3), 258–264.

Lloyd, M. (2001). *Emotional intelligence and Bass Brewers Ltd.* Unpublished doctoral dissertation, Nottingham Business School, The Nottingham Trent University.

Maister, D. H., Green, C. H., & Galford, R. M. (2000). *The trusted advisor.* New York: Free Press.

Nel, H. (2001). *An industrial psychological investigation into the relationship between emotional intelligence and performance in the call centre environment.* Unpublished master's thesis, University of Stellenbosch, Department of Industrial Psychology, South Africa.

Podsakoff, P., & Organ, D. (1986). Self-reports in organizational research: Problems & prospects. *Journal of Management, 12*, 86–94.

Roberts, R. D., Zeidner, M., & Matthews, G. (2001). Does emotional intelligence meet traditional standards for an intelligence? Some new data and conclusions. *Emotion, 1*(3), 196–231.

Sala, F. (2002). Emotional Competence Inventory: Technical manual. Hay Group. Retrieved December 9, 2002, from http://www.eiconsortium.org/.

Sala, F. (2003). Executive blind spots: Discrepancies between self-other ratings. *Journal of Consulting Psychology: Research and Practice, 54*(4), 222–229.

Sala, F., & Dwight, S. A. (2002). Predicting executive performance with multi-rater surveys: Whom you ask makes a difference. *Consulting Psychology Journal: Practice and Research, 54*(3), 166–172.

Sevinc, L. (2001). *The effect of emotional intelligence on career success: Research on the graduates of Business Administration Faculty of Istanbul University in 1990.* Unpublished master's thesis, Istanbul University.

Spencer, L., & Spencer, S. (1993). *Competence at work: Models for superior performance.* New York: Wiley.

Van Velsor, E., Taylor, S., & Leslie, J. B. (1993). An examination of the relationships among self-perception accuracy, self-awareness, gender, and leader effectiveness. *Human Resource Management, 32*(2–3), 249–263.

Part II

EMOTIONAL INTELLIGENCE IN GROUPS AND GROUP EFFECTIVENESS

Chapter 7

Emotional Intelligence, Emotional Self-Awareness, and Team Effectiveness

Peter J. Jordan
Griffith Business School
Griffith University

Neal M. Ashkanasy
UQ Business School
The University of Queensland

An issue at the forefront of recent emotional intelligence debates revolves around whether emotional intelligence can be linked to work performance. Although many authors continue to develop new and improved measures of emotional intelligence (e.g., Mayer, Caruso, & Salovey, 2001) to give us a better understanding of emotional intelligence, the links to performance in work settings, especially in the context of group effectiveness, have received much less attention. In this chapter, we present the results of a study in which we examined the role of emotional self-awareness and emotional intelligence as a predictor of group effectiveness. The study also addressed the utility of self- and peer assessment in measuring emotional self-awareness and emotional intelligence. In particular, we looked at the extent to which emotional self-awareness and emotional intelligence are predictors of team goal focus and process effectiveness related to achieving those goals. Both goal setting and effective team processes contribute to team performance (see Campion, Medsker, & Higgs, 1993; Marks, Mathieu, & Zaccaro, 2001; West, 1994). We also look at the practical implications of our research for managers and suggest how emotional intelligence and self-awareness can improve team effectiveness.

Although recent studies have started to explore the effects of emotional intelligence on work performance (e.g., Bachman, Stein, Campbell, & Sita-renios, 2000; Fox & Spector, 2000; Jordan, Ashkanasy, Härtel, & Hooper, 2002), a great deal of work still needs to be done to confirm the efficacy of emotional intelligence in this respect. The importance of this issue is reinforced in chapters throughout this volume. Chapter 1, by Bar-On, Handley, and Fund, for example, outlines a study of emotional intelligence and its impact on the performance of military personnel, whereas Mount (chap. 5, this volume) describes a study that links emotional intelligence to individual performance in industry. In this chapter, we contribute to this work by outlining a study in which a self- and peer assessment measure of emotional intelligence is tested for its ability to predict team effectiveness.

EMOTIONAL INTELLIGENCE AND THE ROLE OF EMOTIONAL SELF-AWARENESS

Salovey and Mayer (1990) proposed initially that emotional intelligence comprised a set of social skills and abilities akin to, but distinct from, intellectual intelligence. Since then, interest in emotional intelligence has increased dramatically, including popular books on the topic, such as Goleman's (1995) best-seller. Driven in large part by the popularity of Goleman's book, interest in emotional intelligence has extended into management literature, with recent books focusing on the contribution of emotional intelligence to management in organizational settings (e.g., Cherniss & Adler, 2001; Cooper & Sawaf, 1997; Goleman, 1998; Weisinger, 1998).

The number and diversity of definitions of emotional intelligence have, however, caused a good deal of confusion in relation to the validity of the construct (see Jordan, Ashkanasy, & Härtel, 2003). In our research, we have conformed to the original concept as defined by Salovey and Mayer. In the most recent version of this model, Mayer and Salovey (1997) postulated four abilities (or "branches") that contribute to emotional intelligence: perception, assimilation, understanding, and management of emotion. According to Mayer and Salovey, the four branches involve the following skills: (a) accurate verbal and nonverbal expression and appraisal of emotion; (b) generation of emotions to assist in problem solving; (c) acquisition of emotional knowledge designed to promote intellectual and emotional growth; and (d) regulation of emotion in self and in others. These skills are seen by Mayer and Salovey to be iterative, rather than linear. In other words, each contributes to emotional intelligence, but they are not necessarily sequential. Rather, each ability assists in the development of other abilities.

To illustrate this in a team situation, as team members experience other team members' emotions they may gain more knowledge about emotions through their observations. This in turn may make them more emotionally aware of their own behavior and the emotion that influences this behavior. For instance, if they witness an emotional outburst by a fellow team member, they may, on reflection, realize that they are also prone to this type of behavior. Subsequently, this may lead to improved emotional regulation during stressful episodes as that individual attempts to modify his or her behavior. On the other hand, experiences of emotional regulation may assist team members to gain a greater knowledge of their own emotions and thus contribute to their emotional knowledge. For example, during a crisis, team members may draw on emotional strengths and abilities that they were unaware they possessed. In this case, during a stressful episode an individual may react in a calm manner using this skill to calm others and assist them to focus on resolving the task at hand. The picture that emerges from this conceptualization of emotional intelligence in teams is one of inherent complexity. Within teams, this complexity is magnified as the complexity and diversity of the team are added to this equation.

To try to improve our understanding of this complex interaction, we argue that there may be some benefit in examining smaller aspects of emotional intelligence. In this chapter we examine the concept of emotional self-awareness and argue that this is a fundamental factor of emotional intelligence. Indeed, we argue that emotional self-awareness may provide a key to operationalizing the construct in teams and may have an impact on team effectiveness.

Sosik and Megerian (1999) also suggested that self-awareness may lie at the core of emotional intelligence, a view supported by Cherniss and Goleman (1998). In developing a program to implement emotional intelligence in organizations, Cherniss and Goleman (1998) identified self-awareness as an essential emotional and social competency. Mayer, Salovey, and Caruso (2000) also discussed the centrality of self-knowledge and the accuracy with which people report emotions as being an important factor in determining emotional intelligence. Based on this literature, our aim in the study we outline in this chapter was to investigate the role of emotional self-awareness in the emotional intelligence–performance nexus.

At this point, it is important also to note that, although emotional self-awareness forms one component of emotional intelligence (cf. Mayer & Salovey, 1997), it is not necessarily synonymous with high emotional intelligence. Thus, individuals can have high or low self-assessed emotional intelligence and still have accurate emotional self-awareness in comparison to how others see them. Variations in emotional self-awareness emerge from overestimation or underestimation by the respondent of his or her abilities (Lindeman, Sundvik, & Rouhiainen, 1995), not from having high or low emotional intelligence per se. Consequently, we included measures of both accurate emotional self-awareness and emotional intelligence in our study.

Drawing on our identification of emotional self-awareness as a cornerstone of emotional intelligence, we hypothesize specifically that team members who accurately assess their own emotional abilities will contribute to their team being more effective than teams whose members have an inaccurate perception of their emotional abilities. Our focus on team effectiveness, rather than individual performance in teams, reflects the reality that teams are an increasingly common method of organizing work and achieving goals (Beyerlein, Johnson, & Beyerlein, 1997).

EMOTIONAL INTELLIGENCE AND TEAM EFFECTIVENESS

The purpose of organizing work around teams is to gain performance benefits (Beyerlein et al., 1997). Research demonstrates that a number of factors influence group performance, including organizational culture (Ashforth, 1985), similarity-attraction effects (Snyder, 1979), stages in team development (Gersick, 1991; Tuckman, 1965), and team processes (Marks et al., 2001). Other factors that can influence team performance are team diversity (Simons, Pelled, & Smith, 1999), length of tenure of the team (Pelled, 1996), and the homogeneity and heterogeneity of the team (Swezey, Meltzer, & Salas, 1994). In essence, high team performance emerges from the interaction between team members and the working relationships established in the team (Tuckman, 1965). These interactions and relationships produce processes that enable teams to perform at a higher level than individuals. Consequently, and as Campion et al. (1993) reported, team performance depends ultimately on the effectiveness of team processes (see also Marks et al., 2001).

Furthermore, and on the basis of work by Weiss and Cropanzano (1996), we argue that interactions in work settings are inherently emotional. As team performance emerges from a process of team member interaction (Campion et al., 1993; Marks et al., 2001), it follows that high team effeciveness (and resulting high performance) must also have an emotional genesis. Weiss and Cropanzano also noted that the episodic and situationally specific nature of emotions can both engender and decrease personal effectiveness in business settings. Clearly, this must also carry over to teams. For instance, emotions such as enthusiasm in a problem-solving situation can provide positive energy within a team that will invigorate others and lead to greater creativity (Barsade, 1997). On the other hand, when linked to dysfunctional conflict, emotions can result in team members being distracted from their current work and focusing instead on their feelings about the conflict (Jordan & Troth, 2002). An example of this occurs when team members are subject to a potential restructure or realignment of their tasks and spend an inordinate amount of time discussing potential outcomes as means to alleviate their anxiety. Individuals who have high emotional self-awareness or high emotional intelligence might be able to avoid this (Jordan, Ashkanasy, & Härtel, 2002).

Previous research has shown that behaviors that engender team effectiveness include constructive controversy (Alper, Tjosvold, & Law, 1998), cooperative behaviors (Eby & Dobbins, 1997), trust (Porter, 1997), and social approval (Eby & Dobbins, 1997). These behaviors, although not intrinsically emotional in nature, can be linked to emotional intelligence because they involve the control of emotional expression, being able to understand others' emotions, emotional awareness, and emotional knowledge.

An examination of one of these factors, constructive controversy, in greater detail demonstrates the link between emotional intelligence and team process effectiveness. The development of constructive controversy in teams involves the ability to see a problem from other team members' perspectives and also to understand and to address any underlying emotions that may be attached to those perspectives (Alper et al., 1998). Constructive controversy also requires the imposition of emotional self-control as any controversy in a team has the potential to be an extremely emotional event. As an emotional event, controversy can also be a source of dysfunctional conflict in organizations, particularly if the controversy results in the unrestrained expression of emotion (Fitness, 2000). In other words, if team members allow issues to become personalized, the conflict can move away from the issues at hand to focus on individual personalities. In this case, emotional awareness, knowledge, and management are required to deal with this conflict constructively and to prevent the conflict escalating. We argue that the application of these skills is an indicator of a concomitant high level of emotional intelligence.

EMOTIONAL SELF-AWARENESS
AND TEAM EFFECTIVENESS

One of the key premises of managing teams is that feedback improves effectiveness and therefore performance. In other words, increasing individuals' understanding of their strengths and weaknesses allows them to take corrective action to change their behavior and to become more effective. The underlying assumption here is that being aware of existing behavior allows individuals to undertake a diagnosis of their skill levels and abilities and work to improve any deficiencies. This is particularly the case for team members who are trying to adapt their suite of skills to fit into the team's needs.

We argued earlier that working in teams is an inherently emotional experience. Furthermore, as Tuckman (1965) observed, when working in teams, individuals have to work toward a common objective that may require them to suppress their own desire for achievement to work toward a common goal. In other words, the personal interactions that occur in teams as a result of striving for collaborative goals often require individuals to compromise their own personal goals, leading to an affective response (Weiss & Cropanzano, 1996). We posit that emotional self-awareness can have a positive impact on individual team members' contributions to performance and thus on team effectiveness as it allows these team members to resolve their own feelings about their personal goals being subsumed into team goals.

One of the most useful tools consultants use when examining self-awareness is the Johari Window (Luft, 1970). The Johari Window is based on the premise that self-awareness of an individual's behaviors and traits can be understood by the intersection of four factors: things we know about ourselves, things we don't know about ourselves, things others know about us, and things others don't know about us. Consideration of these four factors provides not only an understanding of an individual's own personality but also an insight into the personality of others, and an explanation of their motivations and behaviors. The Johari Window raises the question of how we can increase or become better acquainted with our own level of emotional self-awareness. Clearly, peer assessment and feedback are one source of insight into emotional self-awareness (see Boyatzis & Goleman, 1999).

Note, however, that we diverge from others (e.g., Boyatzis & Goleman, 1999) who have used peer assessment measures of emotional intelligence and who argue that peer assessment can be used as a proxy measure for emotional intelligence. Our position is that comparative analysis of self-reports and peer reports can be used as an indicator of emotional self-awareness but that this should be used for developmental purposes only. In other words, a measure of emotional self-awareness can be used to provide feedback to the respondents on others' perceptions of their emotional abilities with the aim of improving their emotional self-awareness but not as a reliable measure of emotional intelligence per se.

To explore these issues further in our study, we tested the proposition that high levels of emotional intelligence and self-awareness are associated with team effectiveness, measured in terms of team members' ability to maintain a focus on achieving goals and the effectiveness of the processes used to achieve those goals within the team. To measure emotional self-awareness in our study we use peer assessment. The use of peer assessment, however, raises another set of issues that we now address.

PEER ASSESSMENT IN TEAMS

Peer ratings have been commonly used in organizations to measure performance (Barclay & Harland, 1995). Additionally, a considerable amount of research has been conducted into peer–self assessment within organizations, including peer evaluation in self-managing work groups (Saavedra & Kwun, 1993), self-monitoring and performance appraisal in project teams (Miller & Cardy, 2000), factors affecting the convergence of self– peer ratings on contextual and task performance (Mersman & Donaldson, 2000), and the influence of self-ratings versus peer ratings on supervisors' performance judgments (Makiney & Levy, 1998). Taken as a whole, this research has demonstrated that members constantly compare themselves with others in their work group.

Although much of the research conducted into peer assessment of personality has provided low positive correlations with self-assessment (D'Augelli, 1973; Powell, 1948; Shore, Tetrick, & Shore, 1998), each of these studies required peers to assess complex psychometric constructs such as personality adjustment and personality traits. Ready, Clark, Watson, and Westerhouse (2000), in a study of peer–self agreement, found that peer ratings moderately agreed with self-ratings and that the level of agreement increased in proportion to the length of the relationship. What Ready and her colleagues also found was that agreement varied depending on how difficult the trait was to judge. Where peers were asked to assess difficult or complex traits, they invariably based their judgments on their own personality. It may be that by asking peers to recall specific behaviors, a more accurate response can be obtained.

In developing a method of peer rating in teams, three broad issues need to be addressed. The first issue relates to the accuracy of data collected from peers. The second concerns the implications of peer ratings for the coherence of the team and future performance of the team. The final issue relates to the statistical preconditions required to ensure valid analysis of difference scores.

Accuracy of Peer Ratings

Murphy and Blazer (1989) and Imada (1982) noted that rater accuracy and rater error must be addressed when using peer ratings. Factors that influence accurate peer rating include intragroup reliability, the possibility that a varying standard is chosen by group members to determine ratings (Saavedra & Kwun, 1993), lack of willingness to provide peer ratings (Murphy & Cleveland, 1991), and the impact of the rater's own performance (Murphy & Cleveland, 1991). For instance, Murphy and Cleveland (1991) found that low performers adjusted their ratings of others to reflect their own poor performance, whereas high achievers rated in relation to the high standards they set for themselves.

In addition, as Lindeman et al. (1995) noted, the complex interaction of overestimation and underestimation of abilities when assessing self-awareness can mask the relations between variables. This observation is supported when you examine peer-assessed measures of personality and realize that these traditionally achieve low overall correlations with self-assessed measures (e.g., see Shore et al., 1998). Concerns over the reliability and validity of the peer ratings (Murphy & Blazer, 1989) mean that researchers and managers need to be careful in their use of peer ratings. In combination, our lack of understanding of the implications of over- and underestimation of abilities may mean that the links between emotional self-awareness and team effectiveness can only be accurately assessed for those with high emotional self-awareness.

To address this issue in our study, we combined the peer reports themselves to corroborate team members' self-reports of emotional intelligence. A discrepancy between peer-assessed and self-assessed emotional intelligence was taken to be an indicator of low emotional self-awareness. As we were unable to determine the source of this inaccuracy (inaccurate self-assessment or inaccurate peer assessment) these individuals were excluded from our test of the self-awareness hypothesis. We did this based on the premise that individuals with low emotional self-awareness are, by definition, least able to report accurately on their own emotional intelligence or on the emotional intelligence of their teammates.

Interaction With Team Performance

Another difficulty associated with peer ratings is that the ratings may affect team relationships and therefore the future performance of the work team. Liden and Mitchell (1983) found that differential ratings can disturb a positive work group climate. Although this issue is not of particular concern in the present study, because the teams in our study were ad hoc project teams, an ethical responsibility existed to ensure that any future working relationship of the team members was not jeopardized. This, however, is a much larger issue that needs to be addressed by managers who are working with established work teams. Managers need to be made aware that the results of peer assessment can have implications for team members' ongoing relationships and, by extension, the teams' performance. Steps to minimize the impact of both peer rating accuracy and future team performance were addressed in the research design phase of this study and are outlined in the methodology section of this chapter.

Use of Difference Scores

A third issue is a statistical issue revolving around the use of difference scores to assess the relation between self- and peer ratings. Although difference scores provide the most convenient method to measure differences between self-assessment and peer assessment, statistical concerns exist over the use of difference scores. For instance, Zimmerman (1997) noted that psychometricians have questioned the reliability and validity of difference scores. In response, he maintained that there are specific conditions under which difference scores can be made more reliable. Issues noted by Zimmerman, and addressed in our study, include an examination of the reliabilities of component scores as well as correlations between components and reliabilities of criterion variables.

METHOD

Sample

Participants in this study were 140 Australian students enrolled in a business communication course. Their ages ranged from 17 years to 46 years, with a mean of 20.5 years (SD = 2.54 years). Females made up 62.3% of the sample, and 93% reported full-time or part-time work experience.

Procedure

Participants were randomly assigned to 35 teams. The size of the teams varied between three and seven people. The teams worked together weekly for 10 weeks using a problem-based learning model (Engel, 1993) to undertake self-directed study. The typical meeting lasted between 2 and 3 hr. The personal relationships and dependencies that emerged from this style of work correspond to a work setting where teams are formed to undertake specific projects and to achieve specific goals working within broad parameters (West, 1994). We anticipated that the relationships formed over the 10 weeks would enable team members to observe the behavior of their fellow team members during group work with the aim of improving the accuracy of the peer assessment (see also Jordan, Ashkanasy, Härtel, & Hooper, 2002).

The goals set at the team meetings and the processes the teams used to achieve these goals were at the discretion of the groups. Although overall objectives were stated in the course syllabus, the teams independently set their own weekly goals and devised their own methods of undertaking the work.

The teams were asked to submit weekly reports of their team meetings detailing the goals the team had set each week and the processes that contributed to their learning. Teams were also asked to detail in their report team member interactions, team processes, and any other factors that affect team effectiveness and performance, such as general moods, work environment, and diversions experienced by the team during their meeting. Typical processes used during these meetings included (but were not restricted to) role playing, general discussion, debates, group analysis, mind mapping, and brainstorming. These reports formed a part of the assessment for the course and were graded.

Measures of Emotional Intelligence

The Workgroup Emotional Intelligence Profile (WEIP; Jordan, Ashkanasy, Härtel, & Hooper, 2002) is a team-based measure of emotional intelligence that was developed on the premise that employee behavior, and consequently performance, can be predicted accurately using a contextual measure of emotional intelligence. Essentially, Jordan and his colleagues argued that variance in behavior and performance emerges as a result of differing prior experiences and differing affective reactions, which are triggered by the situation individuals encounter.

This framework conforms to Sternberg (1985), who posits that three criteria determine the existence of intelligence. First, intelligence should reflect behavior in the real world, relevant to the culture in which the individual lives. Second, it should be purposive or directed toward goals. Third, it should involve either adaptation to the environment (fluid intelligence) or the automation of high-level processes (crystallized ability). In essence, Sternberg's (1985) point was that the hallmark of intelligence is the ability to predict situational performance.

Dawda and Hart (2000) argued that multiple methods of data collection constitute a way to deal with measurement error in emotional intelligence instruments. Murphy and Cleveland (1995) similarly justify 360° performance evaluation as a means to reduce error. The WEIP contains both a self-reporting and a peer reporting measure.

Self-WEIP. The self-report version of the WEIP contains 52 items measured in a 7-point response format, ranging from 1 (*strongly disagree*) to 7 (*strongly agree*). Jordan, Ashkanasy, Härtel, and Hooper (2002) outlined five factors that contribute to the construct. The focus of the current study is emotional self-awareness, so we used the self-WEIP as a unitary measure of emotional intelligence. The alpha for this scale was .85. Typical items in the self-WEIP include, "I can explain the emotions I feel to team members," "When I am angry with a member of my team, I can overcome that emotion quickly," and "My enthusiasm can be contagious for members of my team."

Because we were interested in assessing emotional self-awareness using difference scores, the unitary measure of self-assessed emotional intelligence we used drew only on items from the self-WEIP that directly matched the items in the peer-WEIP. This decision was made to address concerns over the use of difference scores that we noted earlier. The resulting scale contained 17 items and had an alpha reliability of .81.

Peer-WEIP. The peer report version of the WEIP consists of 24 items measured on 7-point Likert-type scales where 1 = *strongly disagree* and 7 = *strongly agree.* The scale was based on the self-WEIP, with items chosen for their parsimony, reliability, and focus on observable behavioral manifestations (e.g., control of anger). To complete the peer-WEIP, respondents are asked to assess the emotional skills and abilities of each of the other individuals in their work team. Typical items include, "This team member can explain the emotions he/she feels to team members," "When this team member is angry he/she can overcome that emotion quickly," and "This team member's enthusiasm can be contagious for members of my team." Again, in line with our earlier discussion, the peer report was reduced to 17 items with a resulting alpha reliability of .82.

To address the issues of peer-assessment accuracy, participants were informed that peer feedback for each individual was to be averaged across all members of the team to ensure the anonymity of the rater. This method also dealt with three possible confounding effects: (a) ratings that may have diverged as a result of the performance of the rater (self–other agreement), (b) underlying personality clashes, and (c) each rater adopting a different standard of comparison. Thus, if a single discrepant score existed in rating a particular team member, then taking an average effectively attenuated the variance contributed by the discrepant score. To ensure this effect, peer data were used only for teams where three or more members in the group completed the evaluation on each team member.

The peer-WEIP was administered after the teams had been working together for 10 weeks. This gave each team member time to experience a range of behaviors of fellow team members during team meetings. Finally, the results of the peer assessment were only available after the team had completed their project, so that effects on team interactions and performance were minimized.

Team Effectiveness Data

Effectiveness data were drawn from analysis of the teams' regular meeting reports. In these reports, team members recorded the goals set by the team and the processes used to achieve those goals. The reports also documented team members' interpersonal interactions, including emotional states such as boredom, enthusiasm, and frustration. Three independent raters assessed the written reports of the team meetings using six criteria: three relating to the team's process effectiveness and three assessing the team's goal focus. Typical items in the team process effectiveness criteria included, "How concerned was the group with monitoring its own application of the processes?" and "How appropriate were the processes used for learning about the content?" Team goal focus criteria dealt with the generation of appropriate goals and the focus the team had on goal attainment. Typical items used for assessing team goal focus included, "Are the goals clearly articulated in this session?" and "Does the group remain focused on the goals in this session?" Team process effectiveness criteria reflected quality, understanding, and attention to team processes. Team goal focus criteria dealt with the generation of appropriate goals and the focus the team had on goal attainment. The raters scored the reports using 7-point Likert-type scales. Computed alphas were .74 for team process effectiveness and .75 for team goal focus. Interrater reliability of the effectiveness data, also assessed using alpha reliability, was .91.

RESULTS

The reliability of the matching items from both the self-WEIP and the peer-WEIP scores (17 items) were tested to ensure that these did not interfere with the results of the difference score data (Zimmerman, 1997). The mean, standard deviations, correlations, and alphas for the scales are given in Table 7.1. Analysis of the standard deviations of mean scores for both the self-WEIP and peer-WEIP (Table 7.1) revealed that the scores were comparable and therefore were suitable for analysis as difference score data.

In terms of self- and peer-WEIP scores, there was a significant correlation between the measures, $r(140) = .18$, $p < .05$. This correlation between self- and peer reports was comparable to that reported in research by D'Augelli (1973) and Shore et al. (1998).

In respect to a link between emotional intelligence and team effectiveness, there were only weak correlations between the peer-WEIP and goal focus and the peer-WEIP and team effectiveness, $r(140) = .17$, $p < .05$, in each instance. Our results did not support any correlation between self-assessed emotional intelligence and the team effectiveness measures. To examine this further, we decided to examine the difference between peer-assessed and self-assessed scores as an indicator of emotional self-awareness.

There are basically three ways to calculate differences: raw (signed) difference scores, absolute (unsigned) difference scores, or squared difference scores. For this analysis, it was deemed appropriate to use absolute (unsigned) differences, because the focus of this study was on the accuracy of self-assessment, not whether the respondent overestimated or underestimated his or her ability (see Ashkanasy & O'Connor, 1997). In this respect, raw differences provided an index of accuracy of assessment, consistent with the construct of accurate self-awareness. No correlation was found be-

TABLE 7.1
Means, Standard Deviations, Correlations, and Cronbach Alphas ($N = 140$)

	Mean	SD	1	2	3	4	5	6	7
1 Process effectiveness	4.97	1.48	1.00	(.74)					
2 Goal focus	4.74	1.29	.85**	1.00	(.75)				
3 Team effectiveness	9.71	2.66	.97**	.95**	1.00	(.75)			
4 Self-WEIP	77.26	9.45	.12	.15	.14	1.00	(.81)		
5 Peer-WEIP	74.89	8.59	.15	.17*	.17*	.18*	1.00	(.82)	
6 Emotional self-awareness—as raw difference score	2.38	11.55	-.01	.00	-.01	.68**	-.59**	1.00	
7 Emotional self-awareness—as absolute difference score	9.23	7.29	-.07	-.07	-.08	.19*	-.26**	.35**	1.00

Note. WEIP = Workgroup Emotional Intelligence Profile. Cronbach alphas coefficients are listed on the diagonal.
*r ($p < .05$). **r ($p < .01$).

TABLE 7.2
Correlations for Team Effectiveness, Self-WEIP, Peer-WEIP, and Absolute
Difference Scores for Respondents With High Self-Awareness ($n = 35$)

		Mean	SD	1	2	3	4	5	6
1	Process effectiveness	5.17	1.43	1.00					
2	Goal focus	5.00	1.21	.85**	1.00				
3	Team effectiveness	10.17	2.53	.96**	.95**	1.00			
4	Self-WEIP	76.65	5.38	.01	.09	.05	1.00		
5	Peer-WEIP	76.59	5.39	.07	.14	.11	.90**	1.00	
6	Emotional self-awareness— as absolute difference scores	1.91	1.37	.33*	.49**	.42**	.25	.26	1.00

Note. WEIP = Workgroup Emotional Intelligence Profile.
*r ($p < .05$). **r ($p < .01$).

tween the difference scores and process effectiveness or goal focus for the full sample.

As we noted earlier, a problem with self-awareness is that respondents with low self-awareness scores are intrinsically unreliable. In other words, they are less able to accurately report regarding their own emotional intelligence or the emotional intelligence of others. To overcome this problem, we conducted an analysis using only a subsample of respondents deemed to have accurate emotional self-awareness respondents (i.e., with low absolute difference scores).

The results of this analysis are shown in Table 7.2. This indicates significant correlations between self-awareness (unsigned difference scores) and goal focus, $r(35) = .49$, $p < .01$, and between self-awareness and team effectiveness, $r(35) = .42$, $p < .01$. There was also a significant correlation between self-awareness and process effectiveness, $r(35) = .33$, $p < .05$. These results provide strong support for our argument that team effectiveness is related to emotional self-awareness. As we anticipated, however, this effect was only evident in the subsample of accurate self-assessors.

DISCUSSION

In this chapter, we wanted to explore the relation between emotional intelligence, emotional self-awareness, and team effectiveness as a precursor of team performance (Marks et al., 2001). A weak relation was found between the peer-assessed measure of emotional intelligence and team effectiveness, and no relation was found between the self-assessed measure of emotional intelligence and team effectiveness. These results must be considered in the light of both self-report and peer report measures being proxy measures of emotional intelligence, as the number of items in both measures had been reduced to address issues relating to the self-awareness section of our study. As a result, no firm conclusions can be drawn from these data.

The results of our study, however, demonstrated that high emotional self-awareness predicted team effectiveness. Notably, however, this result emerged only when we used scores from individuals high on self-awareness (i.e., low absolute difference between self- and peer assessment). Our study has also demonstrated that a peer-assessed measure of emotional awareness is useful for enhancing the information gained from a self-assessed measure.

We acknowledge that there are three limitations inherent in our study. Two of them, lack of insight into the complex interactions inherent in emotional intelligence, and the problems of self-assessment, peer-assessment, and difference scores, have already been discussed. The third limitation of our study is that it was based on ad hoc student project teams who had only worked together for a relatively short period of time. As Ready et al. (2000) noted, teams who have worked together for longer periods of time may be expected to achieve a greater correlation between self- and peer assessment.

IMPLICATIONS FOR MANAGERS

Several implications for managers emerge from our study. In particular, we stress the importance of emotional self-awareness as a predictor of team effectiveness and, by extension, team performance. Although emotional intelligence has attracted considerable attention in relation to potential performance gains (e.g., Goleman, 1998), there has also been a great deal of controversy over the extent of variance in performance that can be attributed to emotional intelligence. On the other hand, self-awareness has been a focal point of performance improvement over a lengthy period of time. From this point of view, focusing on emotional self-awareness in the context of teamwork, where team member interactions are inherently emotional (Weiss & Cropanzano, 1996), has potential to provide clear performance benefits in terms of team effectiveness (cf. Marks et al., 2001). This is an area that managers may do well to address in the future.

Another aspect of emotional intelligence that managers will need to pay attention to is the inherent complexity of emotional intelligence, a construct that consists of four abilities (or branches) that have varying methods of interaction. How these abilities interact has not been made fully clear by empirical research, although the potential contribution of emotional intelligence to performance is clear (Jordan et al., 2003). There are also differing opinions on how to train workers to increase emotional intelligence.

On the other hand, examining self-awareness is much easier. Indeed, managers looking for a means to improve team effectiveness may wish to focus on improving emotional self-awareness as a relatively quicker way to improve team skills.

The final issue for managers and researchers to be aware of from our research involves the difficulties likely to be encountered when one uses peer assessment in teams. Although this method of data collection can provide valuable insights into the behavior of team members, the onus is on the manager to ensure that the method of collection of peer data does not affect the future performance of the team. Managers also need to ensure that the procedures used to collect the data contribute to the accuracy of those data and to be aware of the self–other reporting biases that can occur.

CONCLUSION

This study has demonstrated that high self-awareness of emotional abilities is a predictor of the effectiveness in teams. Thus, although a peer-assessed measure of emotional intelligence was weakly related to measures of team effectiveness, self-awareness was strongly related to team effectiveness for the accurate self-assessors in the sample.

Our principal findings relate to emotional self-awareness rather than emotional intelligence per se. Nonetheless, the finding that self-awareness is related to a measure of team effectiveness provides insight into the role of emotional intelligence in work settings. In essence, our work supports authors such as Goleman (1998) and Mayer et al. (2000), who argue that emotional intelligence is based, at its core, on personal self-awareness.

ACKNOWLEDGMENT

The research in this chapter was funded with a grant from the Australian Research Council.

REFERENCES

Alper, S., Tjosvold, D., & Law, K. S. (1998). Interdependence and controversy in group decision making: Antecedents to effective self-managing teams. *Organizational Behavior and Human Decision Processes, 74,* 33–52.

Ashforth, B. E. (1985). Climate formation: Issues and extensions. *Academy of Management Review, 10,* 837–847.

Ashkanasy, N. M., & O'Connor, C. (1997). Value congruence in leader-member exchange. *Journal of Social Psychology, 137,* 647–662.

Bachman, J., Stein, S., Campbell, K., & Sitarenios, G. (2000). Emotional intelligence in the collection of debt. *International Journal of Selection and Assessment, 8,* 176–182.

Barclay, J. H., & Harland, L. K. (1995). Peer performance appraisals: The impact of rater competence, rater location, and rating correctability on fairness perceptions. *Group and Organization Management, 20,* 39–60.

Barsade, S. G. (2002). The ripple effect: Emotional contagion in groups. *Administrative Science Quarterly, 47*(4), 644–675.

Beyerlein, M. M., Johnson, D. A., & Beyerlein, S. T. (Eds.). (1997). *Advances in interdisciplinary studies of work teams.* Greenwich, CT: JAI.

Boyatzis, R., & Goleman, D. (1999). *Emotional Competence Inventory 360 (ECI 360).* Retrieved December 10, 2002, from http://www.eiconsortium.org/eci_360.htm.

Campion, M. A., Medsker, G. J., & Higgs, A. C. (1993). Relations between work group characteristics and effectiveness: Implications for designing effective work teams. *Personnel Psychology, 46,* 823–850.

Cherniss, C., & Adler, M. (2001). *Promoting emotional intelligence in organizations.* Alexandria, VA: American Society for Training & Development.

Cherniss, C., & Goleman, D. (1998). *Bringing emotional intelligence to the workplace* (technical report). Piscataway, NJ: Rutgers University: The Consortium for Research on Emotional Intelligence in Organizations. Retrieved December 1, 2002, from http://www.eiconsortium.org/technical_report.htm.

Cooper, R. K., & Sawaf, A. (1997). *Executive EQ: Emotional intelligence in leadership and organizations.* New York: Grossett/Putnam.

D'Augelli, A. R. (1973). The assessment of interpersonal skills: A comparison of observer, peer, and self-ratings. *Journal of Community Psychology, 1,* 177–179.

Dawda, D., & Hart, S. D. (2000). Assessing emotional intelligence: Reliability and validity of the Bar-On Emotional Quotient Inventory (EQ-i) in university students. *Personality and Individual Differences, 28,* 797–812.

Eby, L. T., & Dobbins, G. H. (1997). Collectivistic orientation in teams: An individual and group-level analysis. *Journal of Organizational Behavior, 18,* 275–295.

Engel, C. E. (1993). Not just a method but a way of learning. In D. Bond & G. Felletti (Eds.), *The challenge of problem based learning* (pp. 23–33). London: Kogan Page.

Fitness, J. (2000). Anger in the workplace: An emotion script approach to anger episodes between workers and their superiors, co-workers and subordinates. *Journal of Organizational Behavior, 21,* 147–162.

Fox, S., & Spector, P. E. (2000). Relations of emotional intelligence, practical intelligence, general intelligence, and trait affectivity with interview outcomes: It's not all just 'G'. *Journal of Organizational Behavior, 21,* 203–220.

Gersick, C. J. (1991). Revolutionary change theories: A multilevel exploration of the punctuated equilibrium paradigm. *Academy of Management Review, 16,* 10–36.

Goleman, D. (1995). *Emotional intelligence: Why it can matter more than IQ.* New York: Bantam.

Goleman, D. (1998). *Working with emotional intelligence.* New York: Bantam.

Imada, A. S. (1982). Social interaction, observation, and stereotypes as determinants of differentiation in peer ratings. *Organizational Behavior and Human Decision Processes, 29,* 397–415.

Jordan, P. J., Ashkanasy, N. M., & Härtel, C. E. J. (2002). Emotional intelligence as a moderator of emotional and behavioral reactions to job insecurity. *Academy of Management Review, 37,* 361–372.

Jordan, P. J., Ashkanasy, N. M., & Härtel, C. E. J. (2003). The case for emotional intelligence in organizational behavior research. *Academy of Management Review, 40,* 195–197.

Jordan, P. J., Ashkanasy, N. M., Härtel, C. E. J., & Hooper, G. S. (2002). Workgroup emotional intelligence: Scale development and relationship to team process effectiveness and goal focus. *Human Resource Management Review, 12,* 195–214.

Jordan, P. J., & Troth, A. C. (2002). Emotional intelligence and conflict resolution: Implications for human resource development. *Advances in Developing Human Resources, Special Edition: Perspectives of Emotion and Organizational Change, 4*(1), pp. 62–79.

Liden, R. C., & Mitchell, T. R. (1983). The effects of group interdependence on supervisor performance evaluations. *Personnel Psychology, 36,* 289–299.

Lindeman, M., Sundvik, L., & Rouhiainen, P. (1995). Under- or overestimation of self? Person variables and self-assessment accuracy in work settings. *Journal of Social Behavior and Personality, 10,* 123–134.

Luft, J. (1970). *Group processes: An introduction to group dynamics.* Palo Alto, CA: National.

Makiney, J. D., & Levy, P. E. (1998). The influence of self-ratings versus peer ratings on supervisors' performance judgments. *Organizational Behavior and Human Decision Processes, 74,* 212–228.

Marks, M. A., Mathieu, J. E., & Zaccaro, S. J. (2001). A temporally based framework and taxonomy of team processes. *Academy of Management Review, 26,* 356–376.

Mayer, J. D., Caruso, D. R., & Salovey, P. (2001). Selecting a measure of emotional intelligence: The case for ability scales. In R. Bar-On & J. D. A. Parker (Eds.), *The handbook of emotional intelligence: Theory, development, assessment, and application at home, school, and in the workplace* (pp. 320–342). San Francisco: Jossey-Bass.

Mayer, J., & Salovey, P. (1997). What is emotional intelligence? In P. Salovey & D. Sluyter (Eds.), *Emotional development and emotional intelligence: Implications for educators* (pp. 3–31). New York: Basic Books.

Mayer, J. D., Salovey, P., & Caruso, D. R. (2000). Competing models of emotional intelligence. In R. Sternberg (Ed.), *Handbook of intelligence* (pp. 396–420). New York: Cambridge University Press.

Mersman, J. L., & Donaldson, S. I. (2000). Factors affecting the convergence of self-peer ratings on contextual and task performance. *Human Performance, 13,* 299–322.

Miller, J. S., & Cardy, R. L. (2000). Self-monitoring and performance appraisal: Rating outcomes in project teams. *Journal of Organizational Behavior, 21,* 609–626.

Murphy, K. R., & Blazer, W. K. (1989). Rater errors and rater accuracy. *Journal of Applied Psychology, 74,* 619–624.

Murphy, K. R., & Cleveland, J. N. (1991). *Performance appraisal: An organizational perspective.* Boston: Allyn & Bacon.

Murphy, K. R., & Cleveland, J. N. (1995). *Understanding performance appraisal: Social, organizational, and goal based perspectives.* Thousand Oaks, CA: Sage.

Pelled, L. H. (1996). Demographic diversity, conflict, and work group outcomes: An intervening process theory. *Organization Science, 7,* 615–631.

Porter, G. (1997). Trust in teams: Member perceptions and the added concern of cross-cultural interpretations. In M. M. Beyerlein, D. A. Johnson, & S. T. Beyerlein (Eds.), *Advances in interdisciplinary studies of work teams* (Vol. 4, pp. 45–77). Greenwich, CT: JAI.

Powell, M. G. (1948). Comparisons of self-rating, peer-ratings, and expert's-ratings of personality adjustment. *Educational and Psychological Measurement, 8,* 225–234.

Ready, R. E., Clark, L. A., Watson, D., & Westerhouse, K. (2000). Self- and peer-related personality: Agreement, trait ratability, and the "self-based heuristic." *Journal of Research in Personality, 34,* 208–224.

Saavedra, R., & Kwun, S. K. (1993). Peer evaluation in self-managing work groups. *Journal of Applied Psychology, 78,* 450–462.

Salovey, P., & Mayer, J. D. (1990). Emotional intelligence. *Imagination, Cognition and Personality, 9,* 185–211.

Shore, L. M., Tetrick, L. E., & Shore, T. H. (1998). A comparison of self, peer, and assessor evaluations of managerial potential. *Journal of Social Behavior and Personality, 13,* 85–101.

Simons, T., Pelled, L. H., & Smith, K. A. (1999). Making use of difference: Diversity, debate, and decision comprehensiveness in top management teams. *Academy of Management Journal, 42,* 662–673.

Sosik, J. J., & Megerian, L. E. (1999). Understanding leader emotional intelligence and performance: The role of self-other agreement on transformational leadership perceptions. *Group and Organization Management, 24,* 367–390.

Snyder, R. A. (1979). Individual differences and the similarity/attraction relationship: Effects of level of similarity-dissimilarity. *Perceptual and Motor Skills, 49,* 1003–1008.

Swezey, R. W., Meltzer, A. L., & Salas, E. (1994). Some issues involved in motivating teams. In H. F. O'Neil, Jr., & M. Drillings (Eds.), *Motivation: Theory and research* (pp. 141–169). Hillsdale, NJ: Lawrence Erlbaum Associates.

Sternberg, R. J. (1985). *Beyond IQ: A triarchic theory of human intelligence.* New York: Cambridge University Press.

Tuckman, B. W. (1965). Developmental sequence in small groups. *Psychological Bulletin, 63,* 384–399.

Weisinger, H. (1998). *Emotional intelligence at work.* San Francisco: Jossey-Bass.

Weiss, H., & Cropanzano, R. (1996). Affective events theory: A theoretical discussion of the structure, causes and consequences of affective experiences at work. *Research in Organizational Behavior, 18,* 1–74.

West, M. A. (1994). *Effective teamwork.* Leicester, England: BPS Books.

Zimmerman, D. W. (1997). A geometric interpretation of the validity and reliability of difference scores. *British Journal of Mathematical and Statistical Psychology, 50,* 73–80.

Chapter 8

Team Emotional Intelligence: What It Can Mean and How It Can Affect Performance

Hillary Anger Elfenbein
University of California at Berkeley

We are only just beginning to understand the consequences of emotional intelligence (EI) for work groups in organizational settings. High among the benefits emphasized for emotionally intelligent individuals has been greater effectiveness in working together with colleagues. Thus, EI could be a crucial component of high-functioning teamwork. However, little academic research has examined the impact that EI can make for teams. The goal of this chapter is to review evidence documenting that the emotional intelligence of teams is a substantial predictor of effective team performance.

I begin by emphasizing that there are two very different ways of thinking about the EI of teams: first, by examining the EI of the individual members on the team, and second, by examining how much emotional intelligence team members display in their interactions with each other. These perspectives do not compete with each other. Rather, both are valuable, and each provides different insights and opportunities for both researchers and practitioners. After briefly outlining these two perspectives, I describe the design of a recent study that provides data relevant to each perspective. Then, I review in greater detail the evidence for emotional intelligence as an important predictor of team effectiveness.

WHAT DO WE MEAN BY "TEAM EMOTIONAL INTELLIGENCE"?

What does it mean for a work group to be emotionally intelligent? There is more than one way to think about the emotional intelligence of groups. This chapter reviews the two main perspectives addressing this question. First, we can consider the emotional intelligence of the individual members of the team. A team may be more effective if its members have greater emotional intelligence, which is an *individual resource* that each person can use in his or her work. Second, we can consider the degree of emotional intelligence that team members appear to use when they interact with each other. It is reasonable to expect an emotionally intelligent team to have healthy and effective emotional dynamics and to use emotion productively to conduct their work with each other. Instead of considering EI as an individual resource that members can use, the second method looks at emotional intelligence as a set of norms or patterns about the way people behave with each other.

Although these two perspectives may at first seem very similar, there can be important differences. Many of us have worked on teams in which the whole was more—or less—than the sum of its parts. A team with emotionally average members might have a spark that ignites them toward exceptional sensitivity and adeptness in how they relate to each other. Members of some teams just "get" each other—sometimes after working together extensively or perhaps after a shared experience, and sometimes right from the start. Conversely, some teams fall short of their promise, when individuals who are normally quite effective on their own appear to be "off" when they work with each other.

The major difference between the two perspectives is the focus on the resources that a team has versus the style of interacting that a team uses. In the first perspective, examining the EI of individual team members allows us to understand the individual emotional resources that members have available for teamwork—that is, the sum of the parts. By contrast, in the second perspective, examining how teams actually use their emotional skills when working together allows us to understand the dynamics of a work group—that is, the "whole" or the team emotional intelligence that may or may not be the same as the sum of its parts.

These two perspectives complement each other rather than compete with each other. Figure 8.1 summarizes the perspectives, with detail to be filled in over the course of this chapter, and highlights how they each ask very different questions about teams. Before presenting the research evidence that team EI predicts greater effectiveness, I first describe the design of a recent study conducted to examine both perspectives on what it means to study emotional intelligence in teams.

DATA LINKING TEAM EMOTIONAL INTELLIGENCE AND EFFECTIVENESS

For these two perspectives on group emotional intelligence, I next discuss relevant examples of previous research. Recent work has documented links between effective teamwork and team emotional intelligence as measured

Perspective	Insights
I. EI of individuals in the team *Examining the individuals who make up the team*	
Team-level average EI	Does this team generally **have** the emotional resources to be productive?
Team-level minimum EI	Does this team **have** anyone left behind?
Team-level maximum EI	Does this team **have** a member who could jumpstart emotional effectiveness?
Team-level diversity of EI	Does this team **have** members who speak the same "emotional language"?
II. "Team EI" *A team as more than the sum of its parts*	
Observational and self-report measures of the emotional savvy in interactions among team members	Does this team **use** emotion effectively in its work?

FIG. 8.1.   Perspectives on emotional intelligence in teams.

by both perspectives. To compare and contrast the perspectives more directly, I highlight data from a new multimethod longitudinal study that I conducted along with colleagues Nalini Ambady from the Department of Psychology at Harvard and Jeff Polzer from the Harvard Business School. This is the first project to examine group EI using both perspectives—examining the EI that individuals have and also the EI that team members use with each other. This study demonstrates that groups' emotional intelligence is an important predictor of a range of team-level performance measures, including ratings by senior staff members, retention, and self-reported outcomes such as performance, liking of colleagues, and team learning.

Why Examine Accuracy in Communicating Emotion?

In the longitudinal study that I discuss next, the particular aspect of emotional intelligence that I examined was accuracy in the communication of emotion. That is, to what extent can team members understand their colleagues' emotional expressions? Likewise, to what extent can team members express their own emotions clearly? At first this skill may seem out of place in a business setting, but in fact we use it continually to get our work done. For example, a supervisor might believe that an employee has just made an excellent presentation. In that case, does the employee correctly perceive the supervisor's positive reaction to the presentation—or, instead, is the employee uncertain what the supervisor thinks, or perhaps does the employee even believe that the supervisor did not like the presentation at all? In this example, note that the emotional content is related directly to the work itself, where the employee needs to understand the supervisor's emotional reaction as a form of feedback.

The longitudinal study focused on emotional communication skill for three reasons. First, the ability to use emotion as a channel of communication is a core component of emotional intelligence (Mayer, Caruso, & Salovey, 1999; Mayer, DiPaolo, & Salovey, 1990), and so far some of the best scientific evidence for the importance of EI in the workplace has come from the positive relation between job performance and emotion recognition accuracy (Elfenbein, Marsh, & Ambady, 2002). For example, in one study, business executives and Foreign Service officers who were better at identifying the emotional content expressed in voice samples and video clips also achieved greater performance ratings and were promoted to higher level positions (Rosenthal, Hall, DiMatteo, Rogers, & Archer, 1979). This is because we need to be able to judge our colleagues' reactions, intentions, preferences, and likely future behaviors to work productively with them.

The second reason to focus on the effective use of emotion as a communication tool is that, among the various components of EI, it is one of the most inherently social aspects. Communication—unlike emotion regulation, for example—simply cannot occur alone. Thus, it is particularly relevant to teams.

The third reason for focusing on the communication of emotion is that it has the most valid, reliable, and sophisticated set of measurements available within the field of emotional intelligence. When a new area fascinates researchers and managers, it can take many years to reach the level of scientific standards associated with psychological research. However, the communication of emotion has been a topic of scientific study for several decades. During that time, researchers have validated methods for measuring how accurate communication is—using judgments of photographs, audio recordings of the voice, and video recordings of body movement. These types of measures are more valid and reliable than self-report and written test measures (Ciarrochi, Chan, & Caputi, 2000; Davies, Stankov, & Roberts, 1998; Roberts, Zeidner, & Matthews, 2001). Self-report measures are often limited because, even when people try to describe themselves honestly, they can vary greatly in how much self-awareness they have about their own emotional skills. Pencil-and-paper performance questions (Mayer et al., 1999) that have a "correct" answer are also limited because it can be challenging to capture accurately in words the richness of emotional intelligence. By contrast, 360° performance appraisals can be extremely valuable when the appraisers have had extensive contact and experience with the person they are rating. However, these methods are also vulnerable to rating bias and subjectivity and are less applicable for initial screening and hiring. Despite these challenges, I am optimistic that further developments within the field will enable the measurement of other components of EI to catch up with the several decades "head start" for psychologists studying the communication of emotion.

A Study of Group Emotional Intelligence in Teams

To examine the effects of team-level emotional intelligence, my colleagues Nalini Ambady, Jeff Polzer, and I recently conducted a large-scale longitudinal study of work groups (for more detail, see Elfenbein & Ambady, 2002; Elfenbein, Polzer, & Ambady, 2004). Participants were members of a nonprofit public service organization based in a medium-sized city in the northeastern United States. The organization is part of the national service program Americorps, which serves as the domestic version of the United States Peace Corps, providing community service in underprivileged neighborhoods. Team members were young adults between 17 and 23 years of age serving as full-time employees for one academic year. Members worked in teams to perform a variety of public service jobs such as serving as assistant teachers, after-school and day-camp counselors, disaster relief workers, assistants to local community charities, and in many other public service roles working mostly with "at-risk" societal groups. The organization paid them modest compensation and benefits in addition to university scholarships if they completed the challenging year-long program.

This organization was an ideal environment in which to study emotional intelligence in teams. First, the organizational design made it easy to study teams over time, beginning when they were first formed. The groups conducted all of their work in teams, with 16 teams total and five to six active members each. Teammates were unacquainted before the program began. Senior staff members determined team composition using a random assignment process that maximized the demographic diversity of team members. Second, members conducted difficult work that made emotional skills an important ingredient for their individual and team effectiveness. The organization is demographically diverse, including a wide range of ethnic and educational backgrounds.

Participants completed a range of measures associated with the different perspectives on emotional intelligence in teams. Next I describe the specific measures as well as the results.

TWO MODELS OF "TEAM EMOTIONAL INTELLIGENCE"

The two methods to conceptualize emotional intelligence in groups each provide a valuable—yet distinct—perspective. In this section, I review the underpinnings and evidence for thinking about team EI both in terms of the EI that individual members have and also in terms of the degree of emotional intelligence that team members appear to use when they interact with each other.

Emotional Intelligence of Individual Group Members

Because we know that emotional intelligence has important consequences for individuals in the workplace, we suspect—but do not necessarily know—that the emotional intelligence of individual members should also have consequences for teams. Indeed, researchers often find it valuable to think about work groups in terms of the individuals who are in the group. Emotional tendencies can be considered as individual traits, and these traits of individuals combine and create the emotional composition of a group (Kelly & Barsade, 2001). The emotional composition of a team not only involves the average value for each team member but also includes the maximum value, the minimum value, and the diversity in values across teammates, each of which I discuss here.

Group-Level Average of Emotional Intelligence. The most common method of thinking about a psychological phenomenon at the team level is to take an average value, which "aggregates" individual-level scores into a single score for the group. The underlying assumption is that emotional intelligence can be viewed a resource that team members draw on and that members of the team can pool their abilities to share and compensate for one another. Thus, a higher average level of EI among the individuals in a team provides a benefit to the team's performance.

Before I go into the research evidence showing that teams with higher average EI outperform teams with lower average EI, it is worth taking a brief detour to address an academic debate about whether it is meaningful to use an average value across individuals to describe a team as a whole. Scholars have debated extensively about whether it is necessary first to demonstrate that there is a high degree of similarity among team members before calculating an average value (e.g., Chan, 1998; Klein, Dansereau, & Hall, 1994; Rousseau, 1985). In the case of emotional intelligence, I argue that this requirement does not apply. Demonstrating similarity can be a worthwhile safeguard when examining psychological phenomena such as attitudes or group culture, because it is difficult to say that group attitudes or cultures exist if colleagues cannot agree upon them. However, emotional intelligence is different in the sense that it can be viewed as a kind of individual resource. This analogy makes it clear that it is meaningful to compare teams with high versus low average values, whether or not individual team members are similar to each other in EI.

Past research has documented performance consequences for group-level averages across emotional personality traits. Jennifer George (1990) studied the emotional tendencies of individuals in teams and defined *affective tone* as consistent emotional reactions by members of a work group. She found that groups with more positive affective tone tended to have lower absenteeism, and groups with less negative tone tended to have greater helping behavior among members. Likewise, Bouchard (1969) found that group problem-solving performance was higher in groups that had more sociable members. More recently, Neuman and Wright (1999) found that teams whose members had positive, "agreeable" personalities were better able to work cooperatively toward team objectives. Their social skills allowed the team to communicate openly and to resolve conflicts and disruptions.

Although this past work documented the effects of group averages with personality traits rather than emotional intelligence, it strongly suggested that this would be a valuable method of examining team EI. Along with colleagues Jeff Polzer and Anita Williams Woolley at the Harvard Business School, I recently studied teams of MBA students participating in business plan competitions (Elfenbein, Polzer, & Woolley, 2002). The work of these teams is more than just a course project—approximately one third of the teams involved in this contest are developing their plan as the roadmap for a new business venture. At the beginning of the contest, participants completed a survey that included a long-standing test of emotion recognition called the Diagnostic Analysis of Nonverbal Accuracy (DANVA; Nowicki & Duke, 2001). They viewed a series of photographs of facial expressions, and they indicated the emotion that they thought was best represented in the photo. The photos included expressions of happiness, sadness, fear, and anger. This test has been used for nearly a decade in many dozens of studies by researchers across areas of psychology. It strongly predicts important elements of life functioning such as academic success and social adjustment among children and adolescents, and in more recent studies it has also predicted workplace success among adults. For example, Nalini Ambady and I found that individuals with higher total scores in recognizing the emotional expressions on the DANVA test also had higher performance appraisals from both supervisors and peers (Elfenbein & Ambady, 2002c).

At the end of the business plan competition—but before the official contest results had been announced—participants completed another survey that included questions about the way their team had functioned during their work together. We found that teams whose members had higher average scores on the DANVA reported that they felt greater psychological safety with each other, had lower levels of conflict, made decisions more collaboratively together, and experienced greater team learning over the course of their project. These results argue for the effectiveness of teams with individuals high in emotional intelligence.

In the large-scale longitudinal study of emotional intelligence in teams that I conducted along with Nalini Ambady and Jeff Polzer, described previously, we documented a similar pattern of findings. This replication is helpful because the two studies examined work groups in very different contexts. The members of business plan contest teams were older, they had more work experience, and they were students at a prestigious business school. Most important, they chose their own teammates. By contrast, members of the public service group were younger and less experienced, and they were full-time employees working with their teammates daily. They were randomly assigned to their teams. An additional difference is that we were able to give the public service participants a longer version of the DANVA test, which included vocal tones in addition to photographs of facial expressions.

Yet, in both cases, teams with greater average emotional intelligence also experienced better team functioning. At our public service group, these teams with high average DANVA scores reported that they had accomplished more in their work together, and they also had greater retention of their members throughout the challenging year-long program. Thus, teams with higher average levels of individual emotional intelligence appear consistently to outperform teams with lower average levels.

Group-Level Minimum and Maximum Emotional Intelligence. Although a group average is valuable as a single measure to summarize the overall emotional intelligence of a group, the average value is not the only worthwhile number. Depending on the type of group task, other values may be more appropriate to describe important features of the group. Closely related to the average value are several other mathematical functions, such as the maximum and the minimum value in a team (Barsade & Gibson, 1998).

In 1972, Steiner outlined a typology of group tasks that is helpful to consider for this purpose. The group average is most useful for examining "additive" tasks, in which each group member's contribution is added together into a common pool of output. Emotional intelligence serves as a resource for teams, and for many types of tasks it may not matter how that resource is distributed across individuals—as long as it is available for use.

By contrast, a group's maximum level of EI among individuals is useful for exploring what Steiner called "conjunctive" tasks, in which a group output represents the performance of its strongest member. For some types of work, having one teammate with exceptionally high emotional intelligence may be sufficient to assist the entire team. For example, in a negotiation setting with multiple representatives from each party, one person who is particularly adept at sensing the interests and tone of the other party can share this information with teammates, so that the entire group can act appropriately. In other settings, it is possible for a "good-cop–bad-cop" routine to develop in which the teammate acting as a "good cop" can undo any emotional tension caused in the process of productive work by the "bad cop." In other cases, one colleague with very high EI can serve as a lightning rod to detect and dissipate tensions that can arise during a team's work.

Few researchers have examined the impact on team effectiveness of the highest level of skill among team members. In a notable exception, Williams and Sternberg (1988) conducted a study using teams of students working on difficult marketing assignments that required analysis and creativity. The researchers tested a type of social intelligence—an unwillingness to participate in socially unpleasant tasks—and found that the maximum level was highly predictive of team effectiveness. In the study of business plan competitions that I conducted with Jeff Polzer and Anita Williams Woolley, teams that had a very large maximum level did not necessarily appear to benefit from that exceptional skill of one or more individuals. These teams did report that they relied less on rules and procedures to govern their work interactions, and they were less overwhelmed by the day-to-day work in their teams. However, they reported that they had somewhat less satisfying relationships among colleagues. This suggests that individuals who were very highly skilled found it challenging to use their exceptional skill for the benefit of the whole team. Perhaps a single individual who stands out from teammates in EI has greater difficulty integrating socially with them. For the public service group that I examined with colleagues Nalini Ambady and Jeff Polzer, by contrast, no pattern appeared to emerge for the highest scores for each team.

The minimum level of EI among individuals in a group is most useful for exploring what Steiner called "disjunctive" tasks, in which a group performance is only as strong as its weakest link. In the case of emotional intelligence, this may be true for certain types of teams, for example, those that represent their organization to outside stakeholders, such as a sales team with a goal of 100% customer satisfaction. In these teams, individual behavior that is emotionally inappropriate and lacking can reflect poorly on the entire group. Barsade and Gibson (1998) also noted that the lowest value can be important if individuals may be able to infect their colleagues with their negativity.

Some evidence suggests the benefits for teams that have a high minimum level of emotional intelligence. In Williams and Sternberg's (1988) teams working on marketing problems, the minimum value of their social intelligence measure did not predict team performance. By contrast, in our business plan study (Elfenbein, Polzer, & Woolley, 2002), it appeared that there was a large benefit for teams that had a high minimum score. These are teams in which no one is left behind, in which each member has a relatively strong level of emotion recognition. In these teams, the minimum standard was high, and the benefit to team performance for having a high minimum standard was even greater than the benefit of having a high average level. Similarly, in the longitudinal study of our public service group, groups with a higher minimum level of emotion recognition skill reported a somewhat greater sense that they accomplished their goals, although this effect was relatively small.

In summary, the research findings demonstrate that a high average level of individual emotional intelligence of team members predicts stronger team performance. Teams also appeared to benefit from having a high minimum standard of EI across individuals. However, teams did not necessarily appear to benefit from the exceptionally high skill of any one individual. The research results regarding minimum and maximum skill levels appear to be promising but showed some inconsistencies across studies that suggest a degree of caution in interpreting the findings. However, the results for high average levels of emotional intelligence were consistent and robust.

Group-Level Diversity in Emotional Intelligence. An additional way to examine EI at the team level is to consider the amount of diversity, or variability, across individual scores in a group. The underlying assumption is that emotional intelligence can also be viewed as a trait and that members of the team who are similar may fit together more smoothly and may be better able to coordinate their activities.

This perspective draws on research examining diversity in terms of personality traits, workplace goals and values, demographic characteristics, and functional background and training—which shows that diversity provides helpful perspectives but unfortunately can be accompanied by greater challenges as well. Whether team diversity helps or hinders team performance depends on the type of diversity as well as the context and environment of the work group. Although diversity along dimensions such as personality and technical skills can be beneficial, diversity along demographic characteristics such as ethnicity and gender is often associated with poorer group functioning and performance (Williams & O'Reilly, 1998).

In general, one would expect that greater similarity in emotional intelligence among team members could benefit team performance. Psychologists frequently find that people show favoritism toward others who they believe are similar to themselves (Byrne, 1971). Barsade and Gibson (1998) applied this finding specifically to similarity along emotional characteristics. Thus, they argued that individuals may work better with colleagues who share their own emotional styles. Barsade, Ward, Turner, and Sonnenfeld (2000) recently documented evidence that emotional diversity presents a challenge for the effective functioning of top management teams. In their study of Fortune 500 companies, top management teams benefited both from higher levels of positive affect as well as from greater similarity in their emotional tendencies. Emotional similarity was associated with better financial performance of the company as well as more effective group processes. Furthermore, these two effects interacted with each other, so that the very worst performers in their study were those teams with both low average positive affect and high affective diversity.

Although emotional diversity might generally pose a challenge to effective team functioning, there may also be some contexts and environments in which emotional diversity could be valuable. Emotional diversity could help teams to succeed if it provides differences in perspective that are helpful for the team's work and if the diversity is accompanied by a supportive organizational climate that respects the differences among individuals. Particularly for personality and other social traits, teams can benefit from a mix of styles. Sometimes, having a group that is homogeneous can be "too much of a good thing." As early as the 1950s and 1960s, researchers found that participants preferred working with colleagues with complementary—rather than similar—personality traits (Haythorn, 1968; Hoffman & Maier, 1961; Rychlak, 1965). More recently, researchers have found that this is particularly true for extraversion, so that individuals benefit from having colleagues who differ from themselves (Barry & Stewart, 1997; Kristof-Brown, Barrick, & Steven, 2001). Although some similarity can be helpful, researchers found that it was overload to have colleagues who were all exceptionally outgoing and gregarious.

These findings, taken together, argue for the importance of examining the impact of diversity in emotional intelligence among individuals in a team. When expressing important messages, people use nonverbal methods of communicating just as much—or more—than verbal methods. Thus, the way that we use emotions in the workplace can function like a language that we speak simultaneously with our spoken language. Using this metaphor, diversity in the levels of emotional intelligence among teammates can serve as a language barrier. If some members are skilled with—and, consequently, accustomed to—using their emotions as a channel for communicating and coordinating with others, then it may be challenging for them to work with others who prefer a different method. In this case, diversity can imply that some colleagues speak one language and other colleagues speak another.

This suggests that diversity in emotional intelligence is likely to hinder team effectiveness. Indeed, recent evidence shows that this is the case. In our survey examining Harvard Business School students writing business plans, described previously, we also examined the level of diversity in emotional intelligence. High levels of emotional diversity in the team predicted poorer team functioning. Teams with more variability in emotion recognition levels reported that they felt less psychological safety and had more conflict with their teammates, did not collaborate on decisions as well together, and experienced less team learning. This suggests that teams with diverse levels of emotional intelligence can find it more challenging to work together.

Our longitudinal study of public service teams, described earlier, also found that affective diversity presented challenges for group effectiveness. Teams with less similarity in levels of emotional intelligence reported that they had accomplished less in their work together, had lower retention through the end of the year-long program, and were rated less highly by senior staff members at the organization.

Interestingly, these trends were stronger for the section of the DANVA test of emotion recognition that included photographs of facial expressions—more so than the section using audiotapes of vocal tones. Researchers studying the communication of emotion often distinguish among the various "channels" of the body through which we express ourselves—facial expressions, vocal tones, and body movements. Among these, the face is considered the most controllable. That is, we can more easily control our own facial expressions, and we generally pay more attention to facial expressions than to other types of emotional expressions (DePaulo, 1992; Elfenbein, Marsh, & Ambady, 2002; Ekman & Friesen, 1969; Rosenthal et al., 1979). By contrast, the voice is considered the most "leaky." That is, it is relatively more difficult to control our vocal tone, and often our true feelings can leak out through our voice. This is why some newer lie detection machines use stress analysis to examine small vocal tremors. The differences across channels of communication suggest that facial expressions are the expressions of emotion that are the most likely to be noticed, acknowledged, and discussed in a work group setting. Therefore, differences among teammates in accuracy with facial expressions would be particularly detrimental. One person may act on, and attempt to discuss, a signal that another colleague did not even notice. If some members are more sensitive than others, it can be as if they are speaking a different language. Correspondingly, in the case of our public service group, teams that were very diverse in understanding facial expressions had lower liking among colleagues, whereas teams diverse in understanding vocal tones did not have the same difficulty.

These results argue for the complexity of emotional intelligence and for the need to assess EI using a range of methods that assess multiple components. Although teams appear to experience greater functioning and effectiveness when their members are highly emotionally intelligent, teams also appear to work better when members have similar levels of emotional intelligence. The detrimental effects of "affective diversity" are particularly strong for the components of emotional intelligence that are the most public and discussable among team members.

Team EI: Using Emotional Skills When Working in a Team

The evidence already reviewed focuses on the emotional intelligence of a team by examining the emotional intelligence of individual group members—their average value, their minimum value, their maximum value, or the diversity in their values. However, this is not the only way to focus on the emotional intelligence of a team, and it is not always necessary to measure the scores of individual team members. The second main perspective for examining EI at the team level is to examine the emotional savvy exhibited when the team members interact with each other. I refer to this second perspective as "team EI."

The underlying assumption of the second perspective is that emotional intelligence can be viewed as a process and that this process can differ across interaction partners. That is, one person may display more emotionally intelligent behavior when interacting with colleague A than with colleague B. A person may display more emotionally intelligent behavior in situation A than in situation B. We each have a unique emotional style, and the style we use fits better with certain people and with certain contexts than it does with others—even after accounting for the individual's general level of emotional intelligence. Thus, it can be worthwhile to examine the team-specific emotional intelligence—that is, the emotional quality of interactions in the team context. Researchers have often used this perspective by administering surveys that tap into the use of effective interpersonal processes among teammates. Researchers can also engage in participant observation and can conduct controlled exercises with intact teams. The core distinction between this perspective and the perspective used in the work with results described previously is the focus on how much emotional intelligence is displayed and actually used in the interactions among teammates—rather than the fixed individual attributes of teammates—as a predictor of team performance.

This approach to examining team EI is a natural extension to the definition of intelligence. Psychologist Robert Sternberg (1984) defined intelligence as "adaptation to, selection of, and shaping of real-world environments relevant to one's life" (p. 285). This suggests that the intelligence of a group should be the ability of that group to collaborate and work interdependently. This is the "functional intelligence of a group of people working as a unit" (Williams & Sternberg, 1988, p. 356). By examining the group as a whole, rather than the individuals who are in it, we can gain an important perspective on what it means to be emotionally intelligent.

Previous research has validated the importance of thinking about the emotional intelligence of groups in terms of effective functioning. Vanessa Urch Druskat and colleagues (e.g., Druskat & Kayes, 1999; Druskat & Wolff, 2001) have investigated team EI in a variety of contexts. They found that many of the elements of effective emotional functioning in teams came from norms that team members developed with each other rather than from the intelligence of the particular individuals. That is, team emotional intelligence was often a matter of effective interpersonal behaviors rather than unchangeable traits. The whole was more than just an average of the parts, because teams tend to take on their own unique character. Teams acted in the most emotionally intelligent manner when they had mutual trust among members, a sense of group identity, and a sense of group efficacy. Note that these norms do not focus on soft areas such as being happy and friendly, but rather they focus on the conditions for communicating openly even under difficult circumstances. Although individuals can contribute toward building or destroying the necessary factors, it is the group as a whole that shapes norms. Druskat and Wolff found that individuals with high levels of emotional intelligence tended to be more effective at fostering healthy norms for teamwork. However, once in place these norms took on a life of their own and no longer depended on the individual group members.

Another source of evidence for the importance of examining team EI— in terms of the interactions among teammates rather than the EI of individuals in the team—comes from research on the linkage of moods among colleagues. When one person in a team experiences an emotion or mood, that person's teammates are often influenced and can take on some of that emotion or mood as well. Jennifer George's (1990) study, reviewed earlier, found evidence that colleagues tended to be consistent in describing the emotional tone of their team, which provides evidence that emotional tone is an important part of team culture, with implications for performance. Totterdell, Kellett, Teuchmann, and Briener (1998) demonstrated that individuals are influenced by the emotional tone of their teammates, and over time they tend to shift their own moods toward those of their colleagues. In a study that used naturalistic observations rather than surveys, Caroline Bartel and Richard Saavedra (2000) found further evidence that members of work groups generally converge to develop similar moods. Team members tended to develop their similar moods through a process known as "emotional contagion"—so that people who are nearby tend to "catch" the moods of others. Sigal Barsade (2002) investigated this process of emotional contagion more closely. In her research, she found that the contagion of positive emotion led to greater team effectiveness, in the form of greater cooperation and performance as well as lower levels of conflict. Thus, the ability of team members to share positive mood with each other is a form of emotionally intelligent behavior that promotes greater team effectiveness.

Thus, there appears to be strong evidence for the importance of emotionally intelligent interactions among colleagues in predicting the success of teams. Nalini Ambady, Jeff Polzer, and I examined this issue further in our own longitudinal study of public service teams. We used an exercise that measured how accurate colleagues were in mutually understanding each other's emotional expressions. This exercise had two parts. First, I conducted a one-on-one interview with each individual joining the organization. We discussed previous occasions during which they had felt strong emotions in a workplace or school setting and in which they wanted others to know how they felt. Each participant described a separate incident each for anger, fear, amusement, happiness, and sadness. I asked them to repeat what they had said during the incident and to describe how they expressed themselves. If they had not said anything at the time of the incident, I asked them what they wish they had said or what they might have said. Although this interview was a reenactment, after participants described the incidents and the words that they had used, the interviews took on a strong emotional tone. I videotaped the interviews and edited them to create brief 5-sec video clips containing naturalistic samples of their emotional expressions. These video clips used segments with words that did not give away the emotion and did not violate the participant's privacy.

In the second stage of this exercise, colleagues viewed these video clips within 1 week of the team being formed. I created a separate cassette for each team so that they could view the video clips from each of their new colleagues. Colleagues made multiple-choice judgments regarding which emotion had been expressed in each video clip. Several additional measures served to validate this video clip exercise. At the end of this process, we had a measure of how well each team's members could understand their colleagues' workplace-relevant expressions of emotion. Note that this exercise did not merely measure the skill of individuals on the team, because it tapped into their skill in understanding their specific teammates—which we demonstrated was distinct from their general skill in understanding other people's emotions. This is because people express themselves in a range of different styles, and it is easier to understand a style with which we are more familiar.

We were surprised by the strength of this exercise in predicting team effectiveness over the course of the year. In fact, the ability of team members to understand each colleague's emotional expressions explained 40% of the variance in team performance (with an adjusted R^2 of 28%), which is rare for research on psychological processes. However, these results also showed that sometimes less is more: Greater accuracy in understanding colleagues' positive emotions predicted better team performance, whereas greater accuracy with negative emotions actually predicted worse team performance. Teams whose members easily understood each other's expressions of amusement and happiness reported greater success in accomplishing their service goals and greater interest in working with each other again. By contrast, teams adept in understanding colleagues' anger, fear, and sadness reported lower evaluations of their team's work, less liking for each other, and less interest in working together again. While spending time with the groups that were very perceptive at understanding each other's negativity, I found that they were unable to translate this sensitivity into productive use. These teams got into spirals of negative energy.

The results of this study do not necessarily argue that the mutual ability to understand negative emotion is always unproductive. There are many situations in which we need negative feedback among teammates in order to improve—and in which failing to understand negative emotion would be a roadblock for learning. In this study, the public service teams consisted of young adults largely in their first full-time job, and they appeared not to have the skills to use negative emotion productively. Rather than perceiving negative emotions in colleagues as a warning sign to reevaluate the work they were doing or to reflect on their style of team interaction, they reacted defensively and escalated conflict. Overall, these results emphasize the complex interaction among the various components of emotional intelligence. In the absence of effective emotion regulation skills, it may be better not to have strong emotional perception skills. A balance among skills is important for emotionally intelligent behavior in teams. It is worthwhile to make an effort to achieve this balance, in light of the promise of greater team effectiveness.

IMPLICATIONS AND FUTURE WORK

It is an exciting time to study emotional intelligence. However, it can also be a challenging time as well, because the research findings often do not stretch far enough to make recommendations that are as firm and unambiguous as managers and practitioners will ultimately need to make productive use of this research.

The initial evidence is very promising, suggesting strongly that greater emotional intelligence benefits work groups in organizational settings. This chapter emphasizes that there are two very different ways of thinking about what it means for a team to be emotionally intelligent: first, by examining the EI of individual members, and second by examining the EI displayed in interactions among team members. The two perspectives, summarized in Fig. 8.1, complement each other by asking different questions about teams and thus provide different insights and opportunities for researchers and practitioners.

The first perspective—examining the EI of individual members—offers the chance to make predictions about team performance before a team is formed. For this reason, it is the only practical method that can be useful for choosing team members. By contrast, you cannot examine the team EI displayed in interactions among team members until the team is formed. Thus, the second perspective on team EI would be prohibitively expensive for choosing team members because team EI is more than the combination of its parts. And, in many cases, team membership must be driven by specific needs for the functional backgrounds and availability of individual members and cannot be adjusted based on emotional capabilities.

However, Vanessa Urch Druskat and Steve Wolff's work (chap. 11, this volume) shows us that the second perspective on team emotional intelligence should still be crucial at the time of team formation: Rather than using EI as a selection tool to choose team members, managers can use it as a development tool to help foster emotionally effective norms from the first meeting onward. Creating the conditions for teams to communicate openly can help to build trust, a group spirit, and a can-do attitude. Thus, emotionally intelligent behavior can develop in teams, regardless of the test scores achieved by individuals.

Both perspectives on the emotional intelligence of teams can be useful in crafting interventions once a team has already formed. When a problem arises that appears related to the interpersonal dynamics among colleagues, it is worthwhile to ask each of the questions on the right side of Fig. 8.1. Whether a team generally has the emotional resources that it needs, whether the team has anyone left behind in terms of emotional competencies, whether the team has anyone with exceptional skill who could help to build a more effective environment, and whether the team has members who speak the same emotional language all offer a chance to pinpoint possibilities for team coaching or altering team membership. It is also important to ask, encouraged by the second perspective, whether a team uses emotion effectively in its work. If the answer is no, then there is rich potential for intervention by a manager or qualified coach to develop more effective norms for emotional behaviors.

The first step in using emotional intelligence as a tool for improving team performance is to consider carefully the nature of the team's goals and contexts. Some teams work in environments that are more emotionally charged, sensitive, or sophisticated than others—for example, a negotiating team that represents a company to outside interests would most likely benefit more from emotional intelligence than a manufacturing team internal to the company. Likewise, a team that is responding to a set of system failures may benefit more than a team installing standardized new systems. Thus, it helps to decide when it is worthwhile to intervene in the emotional intelligence of a team. It will not always be the case—the research reviewed here should convince you that emotional intelligence is valuable, but complicated, in its impact on teams.

It is important for scholars to accumulate more evidence for the connection between the emotional intelligence of teams and effective performance. For example, what are the consequences when emotional processes such as the understanding of emotional expressions are interrupted, which can happen during telecommuting, during electronic communication, or in virtual teams? More research would be particularly helpful in examining critically and scientifically the results of strategies for intervening. We are only now at the stage where we have documented the likely impact of emotional intelligence in workplace settings, and we need to be careful and judicious with attempts to alter a team's emotional landscape. However, the current research suggests cause for optimism, as there could be great benefits for teams that can harness effectively the power of emotional intelligence.

ACKNOWLEDGMENTS

I thank Nalini Ambady, Sigal Barsade, Jeff Polzer, and Anita Williams Woolley for their contributions to this chapter and to the research it describes.

REFERENCES

Barry, B., & Stewart, G. (1997). Composition, process, and performance in self-managed groups: The role of personality. *Journal of Applied Psychology, 82,* 62–78.

Barsade, S. G. (2002). The ripple effect: Emotional contagion in groups. *Administrative Sciences Quarterly, 47,* 644–675.

Barsade, S. G., & Gibson, D. E. (1998). Group emotion: A view from top to bottom. In D. H. Gruenfeld, B. Mannix, & M. Neale (Eds.), *Research on managing groups and teams: Composition* (Vol. 1, pp. 81–102). Greenwich, CT: JAI.

Barsade, S. G., Ward, A. J., Turner, J. D., & Sonnenfeld, J. A. (2000). To your heart's content: A model of affective diversity in top management teams. *Administrative Science Quarterly, 45,* 802–836.

Bartel, C. A., & Saavedra, R. (2000). The collective construction of work group moods. *Administrative Science Quarterly, 45,* 197–231.

Bouchard, T. J., Jr. (1969). Personality, problem-solving procedure, and performance in small groups. *Journal of Applied Psychology, 53,* 1–29.

Byrne, D. (1971). *The attraction paradigm.* New York: Academic Press.

Chan, D. (1998). Functional relations among constructs in the same content domain at different levels of analysis: A typology of composition models. *Journal of Applied Psychology, 83,* 234–246.

Ciarrochi, J. V., Chan, A. Y. C., & Caputi, P. (2000). A critical evaluation of the emotional intelligence construct. *Personality and Individual Differences, 28,* 539–561.

Davies, M., Stankov, L., & Roberts, R. D. (1998). Emotional intelligence: In search of an elusive construct. *Journal of Personality and Social Psychology, 75,* 989–1015.

DePaulo, B. M. (1992). Nonverbal behavior and self-presentation. *Psychological Bulletin, 11,* 203–243.

Druskat, V. U., & Kayes, D. C. (1999). The antecedents of team competence: Toward a fine-grained model of self-managing team effectiveness. *Research on Managing Groups and Teams, 2,* 201–231.

Druskat, V. U., & Wolff, S. B. (2001, March). Building the emotional intelligence of groups. *Harvard Business Review,* pp. 81–90.

Ekman, P., & Friesen, W. V. (1969). Nonverbal leakage and clues to deception. *Psychiatry, 32,* 88–106.

Elfenbein, H. A., & Ambady, N. (2002). Predicting workplace outcomes from the ability to eavesdrop on feelings. *Journal of Applied Psychology, 87,* 963–971.

Elfenbein, H. A., Marsh, A., & Ambady, N. (2002). Emotional intelligence and the recognition of emotion from the face. In L. F. Barrett & P. Salovey (Eds.), *The wisdom of feelings: Processes underlying emotional intelligence* (pp. 37–59). New York: Guilford.

Elfenbein, H. A., Polzer, J. T., & Ambady, N. (2004). *Emotional skills as team competencies: The case of recognizing others' emotions.* Manuscript submitted for publication.

Elfenbein, H. A., Polzer, J., & Woolley, A. W. (2002). *Team process and team success: A survey study of business plan competitions.* Manuscript in preparation.

George, J. M. (1990). Personality, affect, and behavior in groups. *Journal of Applied Psychology, 75,* 107–116.

Haythorn, W. W. (1968). The composition of groups: A review of the literature. *Acta Psychologica, 28,* 97–128.

Hoffman, L. R., & Maier, N. R. (1961). Quality and acceptance of problem solutions by members of homogeneous and heterogeneous groups. *Journal of Abnormal and Social Psychology, 62,* 401–407.

Kelly, J. R., & Barsade, S. G. (2001). Mood and emotions in small groups and work teams. *Organizational Behavior and Human Decision Processes, 86,* 99–130.

Klein, K. J., Dansereau, R. G., & Hall, R. J. (1994). Levels issues in theory development, data collection, and analysis. *Academy of Management Review, 19,* 195–229.

Kristof-Brown, A., Barrick, M. R., & Steven, C. K. (2001, August). *A test of competing models of person-team fit on extraversion.* Paper presented at the Annual Meeting of the Academy of Management, Washington, DC.

Mayer, J. D., Caruso, D. R., & Salovey, P. (1999). Emotional intelligence meets traditional standards for an intelligence. *Intelligence, 27,* 267–298.

Mayer, J. D., DiPaolo, M., & Salovey, P. (1990). Perceiving affective content in ambiguous visual stimuli: A component of emotional intelligence. *Journal of Personality Assessment, 54,* 772–781.

Neuman, G. A., & Wright, J. (1999). Team effectiveness: Beyond skills and cognitive ability. *Journal of Applied Psychology, 84,* 376–389.

Nowicki, S., Jr., & Duke, M. P. (2001). Nonverbal receptivity: The diagnostic analysis of nonverbal accuracy (DANVA). In J. A. Hall & F. J. Bernieri (Eds.), *Interpersonal sensitivity theory and measurement* (pp. 183–198). Mahwah, NJ: Lawrence Erlbaum Associates.

Roberts, R. D., Zeidner, M., & Matthews, G. (2001). Does emotional intelligence meet traditional standards for an intelligence? Some new data and conclusions. *Emotion, 1,* 196–231.

Rosenthal, R., Hall, J. A., DiMatteo, M. R., Rogers, P. L., & Archer, D. (1979). *Sensitivity to nonverbal communication: The PONS test.* Baltimore: Johns Hopkins University Press.

Rousseau, D. M. (1985). Issues of level in organizational research: Multi-level and cross-level perspectives. *Research in Organizational Behavior, 7,* 1–37.

Rychlak, J. F. (1965). The similarity, compatibility, or incompatibility of needs in interpersonal selection. *Journal of Personality and Social Psychology, 2,* 334–340.

Steiner, I. D. (1972). *Group process and productivity.* New York: Academic Press.

Sternberg, R. J. (1984). Toward a triarchic theory of human intelligence. *Behavioral and Brain Sciences, 7,* 269–315.

Totterdell, P., Kellett, S., Teuchmann, K., & Briener, R. B. (1998). Evidence of mood linkage in work groups. *Journal of Personality and Social Psychology, 74,* 1504–1515.

Williams, K. Y., & O'Reilly, C. A. (1998). Demography and diversity in organizations: A review of 40 years of research. In L. Cummings & B. Staw (Eds.), *Research in organizational behavior* (Vol. 20, pp. 77–140). Greenwich, CT: JAI.

Williams, W. M., & Sternberg, R. J. (1988). Group intelligence: Why some groups are better than others. *Intelligence, 12,* 351–377.

Chapter 9

About the "I" in the EI Construct:
A More Social Approach to Intelligence and Its Performance Implications

A. Alexandra Michel
Marshall School of Business
University of Southern California

Karen A. Jehn
Social and Organizational Psychology
Leiden University

The emotional intelligence (EI) approach investigates how people can use their emotional resources effectively from the theoretical perspective of intelligence; this chapter complements emotional intelligence research by studying the effective use of emotional resources from the theoretical perspective of the self. An emotional intelligence perspective entails studying how people can respond more appropriately to their social context when they apply abstract reasoning to their emotions, when they "think about feeling" (Salovey & Mayer, 1990). The self-perspective we develop is based on the observation that emotions always work together with cognition and motivation to help the person act appropriately in relation to the social context, or self-regulate (Carver & Scheier, 1981, 1990; Higgins, 1996a). This self-perspective differs from an emotional intelligence perspective in two principal respects. First, it posits that emotions need to be understood in the context of this self-system as a self-regulatory process. This also means that emotions cannot be studied separately from other self-regulatory processes, namely cognition and motivation. Second, it suggests that responding effectively is not necessarily a matter of managing emotions through abstract thought—an "outside-in" process in that it is self-reflexive or about the self—but rather is a matter of facilitating the natural functioning of the self-system—an "inside-out" process. In fact, this inside-out approach we advocate often involves clearing away a reflexive preoccupation with the self to reorient emotion, cognition, and motivation toward the social situation (Michel & Jehn, 2003; Michel & Wortham, 2002).

Section 1 summarizes our argument and motivates it theoretically. In Section 2, we present ethnographic data from a 2-year study of two comparable Wall Street investment banks. These data illustrate two main implications for emotional intelligence researchers and organizational practitioners. First, the data suggest that emotional intelligence can have unintended negative performance consequences. We explain why they arise and how they can be avoided. Second, we show how our self-based approach affords a more social perspective on emotions and their effective deployment and why a more social approach matters. Section 3 concludes with recommendations for EI research and practice.

SECTION 1: THEORETICAL BACKGROUND

Studying the effective use of emotional resources from the perspective of intelligence means studying how people can apply abstract reasoning to their emotions. The preeminent intelligence researcher Robert Sternberg (2001) stated that, "Although definitions of intelligence differ . . . , virtually all of these definitions view intelligence as the ability to adapt to the environment" (p. 361). Intelligence researchers conceive of this ability in terms of carrying out "abstract reasoning" (Mayer & Salovey, 2002). According to Mayer and Salovey (2002), a focus on this ability for abstract reasoning unites different types of intelligences; they differ primarily in the domain to which abstract reasoning is applied. For the EI construct this domain is emotion: EI involves "thinking about feeling" (Salovey & Mayer, 1990) to facilitate adaptation to the social environment, or social intelligence (Thorndike, 1920; cf. Goleman, 2001a). When people understand and monitor emotions—their own and others'—they learn to marshal emotions as resources to meet social goals and problems (e.g., Bar-On, 2000). This perspective on emotion as a potential support versus a necessary impediment to social intelligence represents an important contribution of the EI approach (Mayer & Salovey, 2002).

This chapter also examines social intelligence, which we define as effective adaptation to the social context, as an outcome and the role of emotions in achieving it. But we argue that "thinking about feeling"—that is, applying abstract reasoning to emotion—can unintentionally impede rather than facilitate the social intelligence of individuals and groups. These unintended negative consequences become visible when one studies emotions from the perspective of the self. Studying emotions from the perspective of the self also shows how these negative consequences can be avoided. The following summarizes our self-based perspective and its relevance to emotional intelligence research.

A Self-Based Perspective

What does it mean to study emotions from the perspective of the self? Emotions are part of an abstract standpoint that the individual takes toward the social context to assess consequences for the self (cf. Ben-Ze'ev, 2000; Nussbaum, 2001). The psychological literature often uses the terms *self, self-concept,* and *identity* synonymously (Higgins, 1996b). These terms all refer to abstract-cognitive knowledge that an individual stores about his or her relation to the social context (Andersen, Reznik, & Chen, 1997; Higgins, 1996b). On the basis of this knowledge, the individual regulates interactions with the social context to promote self-relevant goals. Emotional and cognitive processes participate in this self-regulation through homeostatic mechanisms that compare the current situations to the self-relevant goals (e.g., Carver & Scheier, 1990, 1981; Higgins, 1989b). Unpleasant emotions, for example, inform the individual of discrepancies between the current situation and self-relevant goals and compel the person to eliminate this discrepancy. Whenever people experience emotion, they also experience other processes of the self, including personal goals (motivation) and cognitive processes that monitor the context in relation to these goals (Carver & Scheier, 1981, 1990). Studying emotions from the perspective of the self means studying emotions from a (a) systemic and (b) functional perspective (cf. Higgins, 1996b), that is, from the perspective of how they (a) cooperate with cognitive and motivational processes to (b) serve the self.

We propose that this self-based perspective provides emotional intelligence researchers with a different point of view on adaptation or social intelligence, which hinges on the following insight: When emotions are activated, that is, when people experience emotions, the entire self—that is, the self-concept with its cognitive and motivational processes—is activated. By "activation" we mean that these concepts and processes are made ready for use; they then mediate the individual's interactions with the social context (Andersen & Berk, 1998; McCall & Simmons, 1978). In this chapter we draw on our own data and on research in the areas of sociocognitive development (Higgins, Loeb, & Ruble, 1995; Ruble, 1994), transference (Andersen & Berk, 1998; Andersen & Cole, 1990; Andersen, Glassman, Chen, & Cole, 1995; Andersen, Reznik, & Chen, 1997), automaticity (Bargh, 1982, 1989, 1996; Hull, Slone, Meteyer, & Matthews, 2002), self-focused attention (Schwarzer & Wicklund, 1991), and symbolic self-completion (Wicklund & Gollwitzer, 1982). Together, these data indicate that the activation of the self can decrease social intelligence because it interferes with the processing of relevant situational information and because it causes the individual to supply irrelevant information to the situation.

We highlight the following explanatory mechanism that is implicit in this existing research but, according to our opinion, incompletely understood: The activation of the self compels people to abstract. According to social psychology, the self summarizes the person's relation to the context in an abstract manner (e.g., Higgins, 1996b; Markus, 1980). Following *Webster's* (1996), we use *abstract* to refer to "an idea or term considered apart from concrete realities, specific objects, or actual instances." An abstract self-concept, for example, contains one's mental representation of one's essential qualities, such as "humorous" or "warmth." These qualities are abstract in that they summarize the various instances in which the individual behaves wittily or warmly. When the self is activated, the person experiences the social context in relation to this more general self-relevant information and, therefore, is necessarily removed from "the unique and idiosyncratic properties of specific objects and events to which [the person] is dynamically responding" (Higgins, 1996a, p. 1078). Our colloquial language use implicitly acknowledges the impediment that the abstract poses to concrete experience by also defining "abstract" as "diverting or drawing attention away"—here from the concrete social context that the abstract summarizes (*Webster's*, 1996). Note that distraction, in the form of "inattention and mental absorption," is the very definition of *abstraction* (*Webster's*, 1996)— versus a mere side-effect that can potentially be avoided. This means that, according to our socially shared understanding, the one necessarily entails the other.

The cognitive–developmental literature shows that when people find themselves in an unfamiliar situation, they enter the *construction* stage, in which they actively seek out concrete information. As they become familiar with the situation, they progress through a *consolidation* to an *integration* stage (e.g., Higgins et al., 1995; Ruble, 1994). These latter two stages of what we refer to as the CCI model are characterized by a progression toward (a) more abstract representation of the social context; (b) more schematic processing of information; (c) an increasing interest in drawing self-relevant conclusions, which implies that the self-concept is activated; and (d) a "reduced receptivity" to new information (Ruble, 1994). Schematic processing means that "information is organized in terms of existing conclusions and information consistent with these conclusions is more easily retrieved" (Ruble, 1994, p. 168). We coded all three correlates of abstract representations (i.e., schematic processing, emphasis on self-relevant versus situation-relevant conclusions, reduced receptivity) as forms of distractions from what is relevant to a given situation.

Experimental research by Wood and Bandura (1989) implies causality. The researchers observed managers in a business simulation. They found that when the managers first approached the simulation, they tried to understand the task and responded to concrete task-related cues. But over time the managers derived a sense of who they were in relation to the task. From then on, this abstract relation between self and task (vs. the more concrete task-related cues) guided their efforts. This experimental research is consistent with our proposition that the activation of the self may not merely be a correlate of abstraction-induced distraction but might be its very cause.

We are not suggesting that abstract thinking is bad per se. Indiscriminate abstraction, we propose, is the problem. According to Piaget (1929), effective adaptation—or in the terms of our model, high social intelligence—requires a balance between abstract or "top-down" and concrete or "bottom-up" processing (Bobrow & Norman, 1975) that is dictated by the demands of the situation. For example, to be effective, people should rely relatively more on bottom-up processing in response to novel aspects. However, the CCI model suggests that people often resort to abstraction not because of what a given situation requires but because of what the person's cognitive–developmental stage affords.

This cognitive–developmental research is consistent with our data in that it associates the activation of the self with a progression toward reduced receptivity to situation-specific information. But our data show that this prior research overgeneralizes. The progression toward reduced receptivity to information that, according to the CCI model, characterizes the last two stages of learning (consolidation and integration) is only one—albeit ubiquitous—way in which people can learn. Our data indicate that specific socialization processes can diminish the likelihood that the self-concept is activated. The data further suggest that when the self-concept is not activated, people continue to engage the context with such concrete, situation-oriented processes that characterize the CCI model's construction period. We label this engagement with the concrete aspects of the context *direct involvement*. With "direct" we mean that this involvement is not mediated by constant reference to the self-concept.

Some researchers have proposed that a progression toward reduced receptivity of concrete situational information is functional because an ongoing openness might impede goal-directed activity and, therefore, undermine mastery (e.g., Deci & Ryan, 1987; Ruble & Frey, 1991; March, 1991). We explain how direct involvement expands the cognitive resources the individual uses from a primary reliance on mental resources to a flexible use of both mental and social resources, including task structures, other people, and objects. It thereby expands the load that this cognitive resource system, which includes but is not limited to the individual, can support (e.g., Michel & Jehn, 2003). Consequently, we posit that the system's ongoing receptiveness to information causes enhanced performance, versus impeded performance, as existing research suggests.

Implications for EI Research and Practice

The self-based perspective proposes that one fundamental obstacle to social intelligence—an important outcome variable in relation to emotional intelligence—is the activation of the person's self with its abstract concepts. In addition, our argument relates to emotional intelligence because emotional intelligence is itself an abstract reasoning process (cf. Mayer & Salovey, 2002) that by definition (see *Webster's*, 1996, as cited previously) distracts the individual from unique aspects of the social situation and, therefore, potentially diminishes the person's ability to act effectively in the situation. Emotional intelligence also is an operation that the person performs on a self-process— namely emotions—and that is, therefore, likely to activate the self. Bargh, Bond, Lombardi, and Tota (1986) demonstrated that different sources that influence the activation of the self and its concept have independent effects (cf. Andersen et al., 1995). We propose that emotional intelligence is an independent source of activating the self—in the form of "thinking about feeling"—and, therefore, potentially an additional cause of distortions and distractions. Consequently, emotional intelligence might unwittingly decrease rather than increase social intelligence. We believe that emotional intelligence researchers should study the undisputed positive effects of emotional intelligence together with these unintended negative effects to better predict individual and group performance consequences.

Committed to an abstract–cognitive approach to thinking, the social psychological literature, including EI research, currently has no framework for how people can regulate themselves without constant reference to an abstract self-concept and without the abstract–cognitive processing of information (Berkowitz & Devine, 1995). From observing more direct ways in which people engaged the social context, we inductively developed such a framework. The mechanisms we posit are consistent with more associationistic social psychological constructs, including social facilitation (F. H. Allport, 1924; Zajonc, 1965) as well as suggestion and imitation (G. W. Allport, 1985; Jackson, 1988). Similar direct mechanisms have also been detailed in ecological and phenomenological approaches to psychology (Bateson, 1972; Dreyfus, 1999; Heidegger, 1962).

The direct involvement construct affords explicit comparison between more and less abstract ways of relating to the social context and their differential consequences for social intelligence, which we code as one aspect of individual and group performance. Consistent with other research on intelligence, we define social intelligence as effective adaptation to the social context. In contrast to this other research, we do not include "abstract reasoning" as part of our definition of intelligence but as an independent variable. We compare the effectiveness of a mode of relating that places a primacy on abstract reasoning, including "thinking about feeling," to a mode of relating that places a primacy on concrete perception, namely direct involvement. With "primacy" we refer to the temporal ordering of different ways of relating to the social context. Cognitive social psychology, including the EI approach, only studies ways of relating that place a primacy on abstract cognition. In these ways people approach the social context with abstract concepts (Fiske & Taylor, 1991), such as the abstract–cognitive aspects of emotion (Ben-Ze'ev, 2000).

Our data show that when people approached the context in these relatively abstract ways, individual and group social intelligence—one aspect of performance—suffered because the concepts that the individuals supplied to the situation were often not relevant. In contrast, we show that the people who exhibited direct involvement performed better because they first used concrete–perceptual processes and then, if at all, drew on the relevant abstract concepts. Consequently, their behavior was directed relatively more by the concrete constraints of the objective social situation (vs. by their psychological situation), including the behavior of other people or the structures provided by artifacts, such as data, technology, objects, and tasks. This observation provides the basis for what we argue is a more social approach to social intelligence. It is more social in that it takes account of how the social context can effectively substitute for a person's mind in accomplishing cognitive activity. We argue that when people are aware of how social resources can complement mental resources, they harness both types of resources more effectively. Therefore, individual performance and group performance benefit.

To practitioners, this analysis recommends different kinds of interventions, as compared with those recommended by the EI approach. To summarize these differences, which we discuss in detail in Section 3, our self-based perspective proposes that practitioners can enhance social intelligence when they avoid the activation of the self and, thereby, remove its mediating influence in social interactions. But in contrast to this strategy that we recommend, we argue that EI adds even more structure to this abstract self-concept—the person's "I"—in the form of an abstract reasoning process that monitors emotions—the "I" in the EI construct. The ambiguous referent of the "I" in our title alludes to the intimate but neglected connection between these two "I's" ("i"ntelligence and the self's "I") and to the obfuscation that this connection can cause.

SECTION 2: ANALYSIS AND RESULTS

Developing a Self-Based Approach to Social Intelligence

This section introduces our self-based perspective by guiding the reader through our empirical discovery process. We developed this self-based approach to social intelligence in response to ethnographic data that pointed to limiting assumptions that the EI approach and social psychological research hold about the self. First, we outline what these assumptions are and how they influence our understanding of social intelligence. Next, we present the data that question these assumptions.

Identity-Induced Involvement and Direct Involvement

Emotions and emotional intelligence are self-regulatory processes and, we argue, should be studied as such. When one studies these processes within the context of their psychological functioning, one discovers a potential problem for EI research:

> Regulating in relation to [the self], precisely because it summarizes one's general interrelatedness with the world, necessarily removes oneself from the here and now, from the unique and idiosyncratic properties of specific objects and events. . . . The self is only one aspect of a broader process of organismic integration which includes other intrinsic growth processes (Deci & Ryan, 1991). Indeed, using the self . . . for self-regulation could even undermine certain intrinsic engagement processes. (Higgins, 1996b, pp. 1078–1079)

Our data suggest that, similar to other self-regulatory processes, the abstract reasoning processes of emotional intelligence can unintentionally "remove" the individual from the immediate social situation and that the activation of the self that results from "thinking about feeling" can lead to distortions. To evaluate this problem, EI researchers need to understand the nature and the dynamics of the self. One type of understanding that we encourage relates to what we argue are limiting assumptions that EI research implicitly adopts from the social psychological tradition. These limiting assumptions relate to a relatively narrow understanding of "self." We revise these assumptions by introducing a more social perspective on the self to social psychological research and to the EI approach. We then return to the potential problems we flagged by showing how this more social perspective on the self can help resolve them.

Consistent with Higgins' previous quote, we propose that the problems caused by regulating toward the self can be resolved by encouraging a different kind of "intrinsic engagement"—namely direct involvement—in which the individual regulates toward the social situation. Even though social psychology has documented the value of some intrinsic regulatory processes, such as intrinsic motivation (Amabile, 1996; Deci & Ryan, 1987, 1991), we believe that these alternative regulatory processes are currently incompletely understood. In particular, we propose that the social psychological literature has a narrow sense of what it means for these regulatory processes to be intrinsic to a situation (vs. to an individual) or "social." This

TABLE 9.1
Attributes of Identity-Induced Involvement
and Direct Involvement

	Identity-Induced Involvement	Direct Involvement
Self-interpretation	Identity, agency	Participating in concrete situation, resource
Self-regulatory locus	"Within" individual	Socially distributed
Self-regulatory focus	Identity	Concrete situation

Note. Regulatory locus and focus refer to the locus and focus of emotional, cognitive, and motivational processes.

narrow conception, in turn, stems from the assumption that the self is restricted to the biological individual.

The social psychological literature restricts the self to the biological individual in three related ways. First, it places the self in the individual's "head" as an identity (see Table 9.1), an abstract concept that the individual has about his or her relation to the social context (Higgins, 1996b). Related assumptions include that (a) self-regulatory processes are also individual properties in the form of mental faculties (inner mind as a regulatory locus, see Table 9.1) and (b) that these mental faculties serve the interests of this individual by monitoring the social context with respect to the individual's identity goals (identity as a regulatory focus, see Table 9.1; e.g., Higgins, 1996b). We refer to this social psychological model as an identity-induced involvement approach to highlight how identities mediate social involvement. EI implicitly adopts these assumptions by conceiving of emotion and emotional intelligence as individual-level processes and by relegating the social to an independently existing context to which the individual adapts.

In contrast, we argue that the self is not a natural object but something that people enact (Schafer, 1992). We found that some people enacted a more social type of self that did not refer to a mentally represented (id)entity that describes the biological individual but to the activity of participating (see Table 9.1) in a social resource system. This system includes but is not limited to the resources of the biological individual. It also includes the objects, tasks, and people the individual engages. In this more social type of self that characterizes direct involvement, the regulatory processes of emotion, cognition, and motivation are not mental faculties that serve the individual but properties of the situation (locus; see Table 9.1) that serve the social situation (focus; see Table 9.1).

We do not argue that social psychological theory is wrong. In fact, our data show that most of the people for most of the time enact the kind of abstract, individual-based self that social psychology assumes to be universal. When the people we observed enacted this kind of self, emotions often functioned in the distracting and distorting ways documented by the social psychological literature on the self we reviewed previously. We merely propose that social psychological theory, and the EI approach that is based on it, is incomplete. It is incomplete because it assumes what needs to be investigated: The form that the self takes should not be an assumption but a variable. The following presents the data that support and elaborate this claim.

Summary of Methods

For 2 years, we studied two of Wall Street's highly successful investment banking departments, Organization Bank and People Bank. Organization Bank and People Bank were comparable in terms of number and type of employee (about 60 undergraduates and MBAs who were selected from elite universities with an average of zero and about 2 years of work experience for undergraduates and MBAs, respectively), type of client (Fortune 100 companies), nature of the task (financial advisory services), approximate size and structure of remuneration (base salary plus performance-contingent bonus), and human resource (HR) processes (e.g., 360° feedback).

We used four overlapping data sources: overt participant and nonparticipant observation (about 7,000 hr); 136 formal, semistructured interviews that lasted between 30 and 45 min; informal interviews of 120 informants; and analysis of company materials. We triangulated the data obtained from these various sources to increase the confidence in our interpretations (Eisenhardt, 1989; Jick, 1979; Yin, 1984). In addition, we had access to nonperceptual performance measures that included monthly league table standing and quarterly departmental profitability for both departments. For more detail, see Michel (2003).

Why the Self Should Be a Variable

Our time spent in these two highly successful Wall Street investment banking departments (People Bank and Organization Bank) led us to understand the importance of studying the self as a way of understanding social intelligence (see Michel & Jehn, 2003). As we illustrate next, relative to the People Bankers, the Organization Bankers exhibited exceptionally high social intelligence. We found that these bankers differed primarily in the kind of self they enacted. We initially believed that the high social intelligence we observed in the Organization Bankers represented a well-studied kind of social self: a social identity. The literature differentiates between personal identities and social identities. The former refer to the individual's representation of personal attributes, such as "warm" or "witty"; the latter represent the individual's representation of attributes as a group member or a role occupant, such as "mother" or "banker."

Current research assumes that a social identity has positive performance implications because people presumably regulate toward a more expanded self, one that goes beyond the narrow interests of the biological individual to encompass the social collective the individual identifies with (e.g., Albert, Ashforth, & Dutton, 2000; Dutton, Dukerich, & Harquail, 1994; Elsbach, 1999; O'Reilly & Chatman, 1996; Pratt, 1998). Steeped in this perspective, we hypothesized that the Organization Bankers' higher social intelligence could be explained by their identification with the social context, such as their group, the department, or the bank. We tested this hypothesis by administering different measures of social identification to the People and the Organization Bankers (see Appendix A).

Dimensions of Studying the Self: Content Versus Frequency of Activation

In this process, we noticed some puzzling differences between People Bankers and Organization Bankers when we administered measures of social identification that required self-description (e.g., Measures 3 and 7, Appendix A). To our surprise, even though the Organization Bankers we interviewed described deal-related situations with fine nuance, these eloquent bankers had great difficulty in answering such self-descriptive questions as, "How would you describe your 'actual self'? By 'actual self' we mean the attributes that you actually possess," or "How would you describe your 'ideal self'? By 'ideal self' we mean the attributes that you ideally wish or hope to possess." We had adopted these items from Moretti and Higgins' (1999b) measure of identification (see Appendix A, Measure 7). In contrast, the People Bankers answered these self-descriptive questions quickly and with elaboration.

For example, one People Banker answered to the first question: "I am a rainmaker, that's my job. So I am aggressive, always on top of my clients, always calling with new ideas, never one to give up. That's the way we are around here, gruffy, fighting, with personality, not like those clones at [Organization Bank]." "Rainmaker" is the People Bankers' term for relationship managers or RMs. RMs are responsible for bringing in business. We coded the banker's self-description in terms of his social role as evidence for social identification. Also consistent with the social identification literature (Turner, 1981, 1975), the banker classified himself as part of an ingroup ("the way we are around here"), which he separated from a denigrated out-group, namely Organization Bank.

One Organization Banker fumbled to the same question: "Hmm, attributes like what? Like what I am doing to get the job done? (pause) You know that really depends on the situation. (pause) Do you want me to give you examples?" This answer is representative (see Table 9.1) in that the Organization Banker thought about the self not in terms of the generalized attributes of an (id)entity but in terms of participating in activity ("doing") and in terms of specific instances and examples ("depends on the situation"). When we asked the Organization Bankers why they had such difficulty answering these questions, most bankers replied along the lines of, "I guess I just don't think about these issues [i.e., my own attributes] a lot."

According to the social psychological literature (e.g., Higgins, 1996b; Markus, 1980), people who do not often think of themselves with reference to a particular attribute, such as shyness, are *aschematic* on that particular attribute. Self-schemata are ways in which people represent and organize their own behaviors. These schemata develop from "repeated categorizations and evaluations of oneself in similar ways by both oneself and others. Such repetition produces a clear idea of the kind of person one is in a particular domain" (Higgins, 1996b, p. 1067; Markus, 1980). Because the person does not reflect on the self with relation to shyness and because schemata only form through repeated reflection, the person's self-concept is unlikely to contain shyness-related schemata.

Our interviews with Organization Bankers pointed to an expanded application of this construct: Perhaps people do not only differ in terms of the particular attributes along which they classify the self (i.e., in terms of their self-concept's content); perhaps people also differ in terms of the relative frequency with which they reflect on—and, therefore, activate—the self-concept. We interpreted these findings to imply that the Organization Bankers were relatively aschematic on the self, meaning that their self-concept did not consist of well-formed schema because, according to the bankers, they rarely reflected on and, therefore, rarely activated the abstract attributes that constitute the self-concept. We then tested this interpretation by investigating the following research question: Are Organization Bankers aschematic about the self?

We found this research question difficult to test with existing measures, which generally test individual differences in the content of the self-concept. These measures assess people's differential propensity to construe their selves in terms of a particular set of attributes ("How would you describe your self?") but not people's differential propensity to reflect on the self in terms of abstract attributes ("How often do you think about your self?"). More than that, current measures—including the questions we had posed to our subjects—might in fact prime subjects to think about the self in terms of abstract attributes who otherwise would not. For example, Higgins's Selves Questionnaire, which is a well-validated and frequently used measure, is typically administered as a paper-and-pencil test (e.g., Higgins, Bond, Klein, & Strauman, 1986). Like the Organization Bankers we interviewed, the subjects who fill out the Selves Questionnaire might be eager to cooperate and to produce answers.

But from merely inspecting the written responses, the psychologist who scores the Selves Questionnaire will not notice difficulties that some subjects might have in answering self-defining questions, which, in turn, would indicate that these questions lack validity in terms of the subject's experience. Our assumption here is that it is easier for people to find words for experiences that they have thought or talked about more frequently before. We are, of course, not insinuating that these existing measures lack scientific validity. We are not questioning whether subjects, when prompted to reflect on the self, are able to classify their own attributes and tendencies accurately, such as the extent to which they behave shyly. We are merely suggesting that these measures and the theories they are based on neglect a potentially important dimension of studying the self—beyond differences in self-concept content—that relates to the relative frequency with which people reference the self-concept.

Testing for Aschematicity

To test the possibility that Organization Bankers were aschematic on the self, we asked both Organization Bankers and People Bankers to respond to eight items that included the following: "I don't really think a lot about my personal attributes"; "I don't really think a lot about my emotions"; "I spend a great deal of time taking stock of my positive and negative attributes" (reverse coded); "I spent a great deal of time thinking about my emotions" (reverse coded). We modified these items from Kruglanski et al. (2000). Consistent with the self-regulatory literature (Carver & Scheier, 1990; Higgins, 1996a), we coded emotions as a process of and, therefore, an aspect of the self. We also interpreted the questions on emotions as self-reported measures of emotional intelligence, based on Salovey and Mayer's (1990) definition of emotional intelligence as "thinking about feeling." We triangulated these self-reported measures with our field notes.

In addition, we measured the response latency to the question, "Which attributes do you consider self-defining or important?" Low response latency is a frequently used indicator for the presence of well-developed schemas. It is based on the assumption that people respond faster on issues about which they have thought a lot because they supposedly have stored these prior thought processes as part of a mental schema that they can simply activate in response to a relevant stimulus. This activation process saves time because people only need to engage in a limited amount of new cognitive activity. We interpreted longer response latencies as indicating a higher extent of aschematicity (cf. Festinger, 1943). Our results on all three measures (self-report, field notes, and response latency) were consistent with the hypothesis that, compared with the People Bankers, Organization Bankers were relatively aschematic on the self.

With respect to emotional intelligence, our data showed that the People Bankers thought a lot about their emotions because they recognized that such emotions as anxiety and anger often interfered with their performance. This is consistent with Wicklund (1986), who argued that people develop language concepts around issues that are problematic to them because language facilitates finding problem-solving strategies. We argue that because the Organization Bankers did not experience such problematic emotions, they did not need the language concepts.

At a later stage in our research, we became aware of the work by Pennebaker and his colleagues (e.g., Pennebaker & Francis, 1999; Pennebaker & King, 1999), who had developed a different approach to natural language use than the one we had been following up to that point. By natural language use we mean "relatively open-ended responses to questions, natural interactions, and written or spoken text" (Pennebaker, Mehl, & Niederhoffer, 2003, p. 549). Studying how people naturally use self-representations avoids the previously described priming effects that in our opinion have misled past research on the self. To study natural language use, we had so far followed approaches that assumed that language use is contextual, that one can infer social and psychological processes not from the words people use but from how they used them in this instance—that is, from what people mean (Schiffrin, 1994).

The work by Pennebaker and his colleagues was of interest to us because of a striking set of findings for which they had no conceptual explanations (Pennebaker et al., 2003) but which was compatible with the explanatory model that emerged during our research. The researchers found that the most powerful predictor of a wide variety of emotional styles and of psychological well-being was the relative frequency with which people used verbal representations of the self, such as *I*, *me*, and *mine*, independent of the context in which people used these representations or their meaning. The simple counting of these self-representations, a frequency of activation measure, outperformed measures that used emotion words as predictors of emotional style, a content measure (Pennebaker et al., 2003). For example, Pennebaker and his colleagues found that poets whose poetry contained more self-representations were more likely to kill themselves (Pennebaker, 2002; Stirman & Pennebaker, 2001). We interpreted the higher suicide rate as a higher propensity to experience disruptive emotions. Conceptually, this work bolstered our developing sense that to understand the psychological processes we were interested in, including emotion, it was important not only to study people's differential constructions of the self's content but to also study people's differential tendencies to refer to—and, therefore, activate—their self-concept.

Methodologically, this work suggests that the simple counting of self-representations could be a powerful predictor of psychological processes we were interested in, including emotion. We consequently counted the use of *I* by People Bankers and Organization Bankers. We did not count *me*, *my*, and *mine* because some prior research suggested that these might be less powerful predictors (Bucci & Freeman, 1981, as cited in Pennebaker et al., 2003). Hymes (1974) suggested that speech acts can be classified along eight dimensions. Following his classifications as far as possible, we tried to match text samples from People Bankers and Organization Bankers according to salient attributes of the speaker and the audience, type of interaction (e.g., public speech, informal conversation, meeting), and general content/goal of interaction. We analyzed 100 comparable texts, 50 from each bank. The averages for our sample were 4.5% for People Bankers and 2.7% for Organization Bankers. These findings are consistent with our proposition that the Organization Bankers are relatively aschematic on the self. Schemata form through repetition. People who evoke the self less frequently are likely to have less well-developed schema on the self.

We also compared 36 texts from 10 People Bankers and 10 Organization Bankers whom we had observed frequently across different situations. We found that the frequency with which a given People Banker used *I* remained relatively stable across different situations. This is consistent with Pennebaker and King's (1999) finding that "language use is a reliable individual difference" (p. 1305). However, in contrast, the frequency with which a given Organization Banker used *I* varied across situations. We use this finding to argue that the *I* use of the Organization Bankers, which is one aspect of their direct involvement, cannot be conceived of as an individual difference variable. This is one important difference between the direct involvement construct and other social approaches to the self, including social identities (Albert et al., 2000), flow (Csikszentmihalyi, 1990, 1993), and collectivism (Markus & Kitayama, 2001; Triandis, 1995).

This set of data questions current social psychological assumptions concerning what the self is and how people self-regulate. Researchers infer what the self is by observing how it works (e.g., Higgins, 1996b). The self directs or regulates the individual's behavior. Its content constitutes high-priority goals (motivation), which serve as behavioral standards. People monitor each situation cognitively with respect to how it meets these goals. They experience discrepancies as negative emotions, which by their unpleasantness propel people to act (behavior) on behalf of the goals. This model accurately described how the People Bankers enacted the self and its regulatory processes (Michel, 2003). In contrast, the Organization Bankers did not constantly reference their abstract self-concept. Therefore, these data question the social–psychological assumption that our cognitive, emotional, and motivational faculties as well as our capacity to act effectively necessarily depend on the mediating function of the self-concept. If the self is as the self does, these data also suggest that the self is not necessarily a collection of abstract attributes that mediates behavior, as social psychology currently assumes.

In summary, we propose that there are ways in which people can interpret the self for which there are currently no concepts in social psychological theories. A self-interpretation is a person's implicit sense of what it means to be a self and of how a self relates to the social context. Self-interpretations differ from self-theories (Dweck, 1999) or enactments (Weick, 1995) in that the former are not necessarily based on such mental representations as attitudes or beliefs. Rather, they can be inferred from people's "conspicuous" actions (Dreyfus, 1999; Heidegger, 1962). This is an important distinction because the Organization Bankers exhibited a self-interpretation that differed from their self-reported believes and attitudes. Drawing on such measures as the number of verbal self-interpretations and their response latency to self-descriptive questions, we concluded that the Organization Bankers did not experience the self in terms of abstract attributes that they identified with. Yet, they dutifully answered questions about such abstract attributes.

Self-regulatory theory has no answers to these questions that our data raised: If the Organization Bankers do not draw on the constant guidance of the self-concept, how will these faculties work? What standards guide effective action? And what does the self "look like" if it is not a collection of abstract concepts? We argue that because of this lack of social psychological concepts, EI research misses an important opportunity to study how emotions can naturally function as adaptive social resources when a preoccupation with an abstract self is cleared away. Our next research steps, therefore, aimed to fill this conceptual void in two ways: (a) by examining how regulatory processes can also function without reference to an abstract self-concept (regulatory locus and focus, see Table 9.1) and (b) by inferring the attributes that such a nonabstract kind of self has (self-interpretation, see Table 9.1). These are the two aspects of the construct we introduce: direct involvement. The next section summarizes our findings on these two research questions in comparison to how the self and its regulatory processes function in identity-induced involvement, which is the kind of self that social psychology takes for granted. Our final section posits a model of social intelligence.

Variance in the Self and Its Regulatory Functions: Identity-Induced Involvement and Direct Involvement

Identity and Situation as Alternative Regulatory Loci and Foci

To understand how Organization Bankers might regulate themselves differently, we coded our field notes with an emphasis on how cognition, emotion, motivation, and action were interrelated. We designated the "self" as a variable. In the following example, one Organization Bank vice president (VP) discusses the relation between the variables we were interested in. He read a client document on which an Organization Bank analyst had been working all night and found that the document was of low quality. He told the analyst:

> You are trying too hard. You got to be more task-oriented. Don't worry about what I will say or what the client will think about you. Then you are making bad choices. Here, look at this section. Once you made [that decision], the [other section] should have followed by itself. . . . Take one step and then see where it takes you. . . . Have some fun!

In this quote, the VP contrasted two types of motivations: (a) a task-oriented or task-intrinsic motivation, which involves goals and standards that relate to the task, and (b) a task-extrinsic or self-oriented motivation, which involves the goals and standards that the analyst thought other people had in relation to her self. A social identity consists of those social goals that we have accepted as our own goals (Kelman, 1958; Moretti & Higgins, 1999b). Consequently, we coded the second type of motivation as one aspect of a social identity. The VP located these different motivations within distinct patterns of emotion and cognition. He associated the analyst's self-oriented motivation with the emotion of worry and with "bad choices," a cognitive aspect. He implied that the analyst's worry had distracted her from the guidance that the task was offering. In contrast, he associated a task-oriented motivation with the emotion of fun and cognitive sensitivity to task constraints.

The analyst behaved as the social identity literature would predict. By staying up all night, she had exerted tremendous effort to live up to the social standards she had identified with. But in contrast to what the social identity literature would predict, this enhanced effort did not benefit the organization because the quality of the product was poor. In fact, the VP said that the quality of the product was poor basically because of her social identification. This social identification, according to the VP, had created a psychological situation that was characterized by the emotion of worry and by "bad choices," a cognitive aspect. Consistent with Schwarzer (1986), he implied that this worry had distracted the analyst from the guidance that the task, as a resource, was offering, which we coded as one aspect of low social intelligence. The fourth column of Fig. 9.1 illustrates such distraction by a hatched line crossing the information pathway (the straight line) that connects the person (X) and other resources (x, x).

This example illustrates two aspects of our more general findings. First, similar to the traditional homeostatic model of self-regulation (Carver & Scheier, 1990), the VP conceived of emotion, cognition, and motivation as

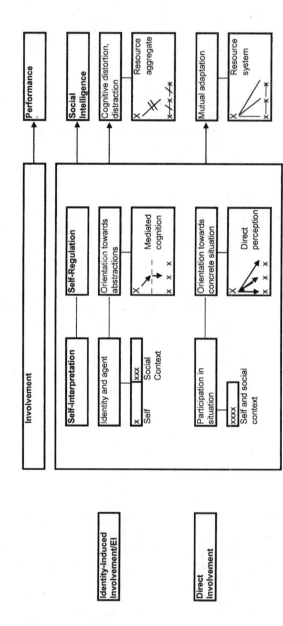

FIG. 9.1. A model of social intelligence. Note: *Self-regulation* refers to emotional, cognitive, and motivational processes.

elements of an interdependent system. Second, in contrast to this model, the VP implied that this system can take one of two mutually exclusive states. It can either collect information about the self, an abstraction (see Fig. 9.1, third column), or about the situation (see Fig. 9.1, third column). If this system does not collect information about the self, people will be more receptive to the guidance that the task-situation provides. In the more theoretical terms of our involvement construct, if people do not collect information about the self, the self-concept is not activated and, therefore, does not mediate people's experience of the situation. Perception is more direct (see Fig. 9.1). The concrete cues of the task fill in the regulatory gap by providing the guidance that otherwise our identity goals would supply.

The notion that the task can guide cognition was an important theme in our Organization Bank data. For example, we participated in a meeting between Organization Bankers and a strategy consulting firm that tried to solicit business at Organization Bank. The consultants kept prodding the attending Organization Bankers to report on the bank's strategies. One of the Bankers answered,

> Strategies, goals, visions, and that stuff don't work here. Our business is too complex for that. You have to take one little step at a time and then see where it gets you before you take the next one.

Another banker evoked a similar process to explain how Organization Bank had come to be known for its strategy in health care investment banking. He said that there had been opportunities in health care that astute Organization Bankers had noticed and seized. "And then at some point we looked back and saw: 'Gee, we have a health care strategy.' " In contrast, as we elaborate later, the People Bankers used exactly the same observation—the complexity of the business—as their reason for why they needed such abstract guides as strategies. Moreover, not only did they not believe that task-cues can substitute for strategic guidance, they did not understand how tasks (vs. people's minds) can guide action meaningfully in the first place. One People Banker instructed me that "all action has a theory underlying it. And theories are things that people think up."

In summary, these data indicated that somehow situational structures, such as task-structures, can do the work that we normally attribute to the person's inner realm. The following explores how the social situation can substitute for the self-concept in guiding cognition and how the self-concept can in fact interfere with guidance from the task. For similar discussions concerning motivation and emotion, please refer to Michel (2003) and Michel and Wortham (2002). The data we present in the following section further suggest that if people recognize the potential contribution of situational structures—if they interpret the self in the more social terms that we describe later ("participation in situation," second column, Fig. 9.1)—they can harness them more effectively, resulting in higher social intelligence. In contrast, if people interpret the self in traditional social–psychological terms ("self as identity and agent," Fig. 9.1)—if they believe that their inner mind is the primary resource for cognitive activity—they will fail to notice situational resources, such as task constraints, and will fail to harness them effectively. These failures result in lower social intelligence and, thus, lower performance.

Distinct Regulatory Loci and Foci: Cognition

Analysis of Cognitive Maps: Data.   Our own understanding of how situational structures can work as one system with a person's mental and behavioral structure was helped along by a quote from Jerome Bruner. This quote generalizes the Organization Bankers' conception of how tasks guide action to a wider variety of creative processes and informed our analysis of cognitive maps.

> You begin to write a poem. Before long, the poem begins to develop metrical, stanzaic, symbolical requirements. You, as the writer of the poem, are serving it—it seems. Or you may be pursuing the task of building a formal model to represent the formal properties of single nerve fibers and their synapses: soon the model takes over. Or we say of an experiment in midstream that *it* needs another control group to cinch the effect. It is at this point in the analysis that we get our creative second wind, at the point where the object takes over. I have asked about a dozen of my most creative and productive friends whether they knew what I meant as far as their own work was concerned. All of them replied with one or another form of sheepishness, most of them commenting that one usually does not talk about this kind of personal thing. "This is when you know you're in and—good or bad—the thing will compel you to finish it. . . ." As one friend, a novelist and critic put it, "If it does not take over and you are foolish enough to go on, what you end up with is contrived and alien." (Bruner, 1962, pp. 25–26)

According to Bruner, the task can guide cognition by embodying social information. For example, through its metrical, stanzaic, and symbolic requirements, a poem points the poet to the specific social and cultural rules that are applicable at each step in the writing process. We believe that our Organization Bank informants referred to a similar process. For example, the VP told the analyst who was working on a client memo, "Once you have made [that decision], the [other section] should have followed by itself." Within the investment banking community, there are socially shared rules of what makes for a good client memo, just as there are socially shared rules of what makes for a good poem. Once the analyst had made a writing choice, the applicable rules had become visible and then could have reminded her about what to do next.

Bruner's reification (e.g., "when the object takes over") illustrates that the task can participate in the writing process like another person. He conceives of the cognitive process as an ongoing conversation between the developing text (the task) and the writer who is sensitive to the guidance that the text, as a resource, provides. We argue that such a heightened sensitivity to available resources constitutes the high social intelligence we observed in the Organization Bankers. Support for this proposition comes partly from an analysis of cognitive process maps. In contrast to the frequently used cognitive maps (e.g., Bougon, 1992), the cognitive process maps we used did not examine intramental processes, what people think, but interactive processes, how people think with the help of available resources. We first established the kinds of tasks that investment bankers engaged in most frequently, such as participating in meetings, preparing presentation books, and conducting financial analyses. We then analyzed how People Bankers and Organization Bankers (a) used different types of resources to complete similar tasks and (b) integrated the input of these resources in different ways.

For example, we sometimes had the opportunity to compare how People Bankers and Organization Bankers competed for business from the same client. In one such situation, the client had invited teams from both banks by sending detailed financial statements with the comment: "We think we need to do something about [division x]." The People Banker team prepared for the client meeting by conducting detailed analyses about various merger alternatives that they assembled in a presentation book with more than 60 pages. The book followed the Bank's standard format. In this, as in most meetings, the structure of the book determined the structure of the meeting. The most senior People Banker spoke almost without interruption for the first half of the meeting, talking the client through the book, section by section. This was typical for the People Bank client meetings we analyzed. The discourse consisted of the abstract language of high finance, as the Banker expounded the implications of the suggested merger alternatives for this type of client, that is, for a firm with a particular type of market capitalization, earnings per share, and cash flow.

In contrast, the Organization Bankers arrived at the meetings with more preliminary analyses in the form of 12 pages of spreadsheet analyses. Although Organization Bank had standard formats, banker teams often used idiosyncratic presentation styles to cater to the clients' preferred presentation format. For example, another banker team had used posters for a client in the media industry who appreciated creative flair. We interpreted this variation as evidence that the Organization Bankers' choice of presentation format was relatively more determined by the needs of the situation versus abstract standards that the bankers brought to a situation. The Organization Banker team opened the conversation by asking the client questions about his comment, "We need to do something with [division x]." They asked who the decision makers were (the "we"), what their respective perspectives were on what should be done with the division (the "something"), and what the history of the division was.

As the client provided the requested information, he used relatively concrete language. In the meeting with People Bank, the client often used *we* to refer to an abstract organization and its general strategies, such as "we want to position ourselves as the preeminent producer of *x*." In the meeting with Organization Bank, he talked about the interests and concerns that specific decision makers had and about the division's specific performance problems ("our best sales people left," "Hank can't get good people for what he can pay them"). The more concrete language that the Organization Bankers had prompted in the client guided the joint decision-making process more than the general language. Hence, it is not merely that the Organization Bankers noticed situational cues that the People Bankers did not notice; in addition, by their engagement with the situation, the Organization Bankers created a different kind of situation, one that is more cue-rich and, therefore, can provide better guidance. Next, the Organization Bankers suggested various financial alternatives. The banker team consisted of merger specialists. But using the information the client presented, they also proposed public market strategies, such as an initial public offering. At that point, more people joined the meeting as the Organization Bankers phoned in corporate finance specialists and as the client asked his treasurer to join.

Interpretation: The Task-Oriented Cognition of Direct Involvement Versus Identity-Induced Cognition.

We argue that in the Organization Bank meeting, the joint situation or task (vs. an individual banker's intention) guided cognition. In terms of the self-regulatory model (see Table 9.1), this is a question of locus: Where are cognitive processes conceptually located? The meeting participants engaged in the kind of dynamic conversation that Bruner and our Organization Bank informants had depicted. The conversation was dynamic in that each conversational contribution transformed the joint perspective to reveal new guidance in the form of constraints that, in turn, pointed to the next steps that were required, including inviting in more perspectives. Figure 9.1 refers to this dynamic conversation between resources as their mutual adaptation. As different participants contributed and compared their lower level or concrete perspectives, more general or higher level trends became visible that eventually pointed to the public market alternative. We propose that this gradual, constrained progression from concrete to more abstract forms of cognition is one reason why direct involvement cognition is so effective.

The client commented on his choice of the public market alternative, stating that he did not feel like he had made a decision: "It was more like paroling the boundaries." This impression supports our position that the participants recognized that the relevant acts of cognition were not the mental processes of particular individuals but the emergent interactive processes of the task system, which included various bankers and client executives. We argue that because of this recognition, they could more effectively facilitate this joint cognitive process. Of course, this does not mean that the participants did not think or that their individual thoughts did not matter. The joint cognitive accomplishment indeed resulted from the thoughts and actions of the participants, but not from an individual design or agency. "To be an agent is to intentionally make things happen by one's actions" (Bandura, 2001, p. 2). In terms of the self-regulatory model (see Table 9.1), issues of agency are issues of focus: How does cognition control goal-directed action? What kinds of goals (i.e., identity- vs. task-goals) is it directed towards?

In contrast, in line with traditional social psychological assumptions, the People Bank client meeting did follow the design of the specific senior People Banker and not that of the task. His personal problem-solving processes, which took place independently before the meeting and which he supplied to the meeting in the form of the book, substituted for the joint and dynamic problem-solving process. The hatched lines in Fig. 9.1, column 4, represent the banker's less active use of the social resources that were available in the situation. As he prepared the book, the People Banker explained to us how he was "covering all the bases," by which he meant that he tried to anticipate the client's comments and have answers ready. Because cognitive accomplishments could be explained in terms of the organization of social resources in the Organization Bank meeting, a situated locus, versus in terms of one individual's mental activity, an inner locus, we argue that the Organization Bankers' form of cognition was more social and that it was more effective because it was more social. But was this preparation in which the People Banker mentally represented the client's perspective not an equivalent form of social cognition?

Many social psychologists would answer affirmatively. For example, following Weber (1967), Tory Higgins (1992, p. 243) argued that cognition is social "when its meaning and orientation takes account of other people," independently of whether these other people are actually present or represented as "inner audiences" (Moretti & Higgins, 1999a). Constructivist approaches have reacted to the mentalism of traditional sociocognitive research and proposed narratives as more social forms of cognition. Nevertheless, representing such a narrative approach, Hermans and Kempen (1993) judged situations in which another person is "present or implied" as equivalent instances of social cognition. In contrast, the data suggest that these instances should be distinguished because they are associated with different antecedents, processes, and outcomes.

By initiating the meeting with questions, the Organization Bankers indicated that they did not understand the client's situation sufficiently to make recommendations. In contrast, the People Banker acted with great confidence on the client's sparse information. He spent significant resources preparing for the meeting and then offered this work as his recommendation without collecting more information from the client. We suggest that because of his role identification, the senior People Banker felt inappropriately familiar with the situation. Because he failed to recognize the situation's uncertainty, he failed to gather needed information from the client. A *role identity* comprises those aspects of the self-concept that the "individual devises for himself as an occupant of a particular social position" (McCall & Simmons, 1978, p. 67). We believe that the salience of his role identity as a senior merger specialist activated his self-concept, which then mediated his cognition and led to inferior performance.

Andersen et al. (1997) demonstrated that mental representations of the self are "bundles of knowledge stored in memory" (p. 241) that encompass such information as skills, experiences, and relations with other people. Because of this bundling effect in memory, when one aspect of the self is activated (e.g., "senior merger specialist") by external cues, other aspects (e.g., merger-related knowledge) are activated automatically and frame the situation according to these self-relevant aspects that might not be relevant to the situation (Andersen & Berk, 1998). *Automatic* here means that the person has no knowledge of this activation and has no ability to control it. This meaning differs from how the term *automatic* is sometimes used to refer to such routinized activities as typing, reading, or walking, activities that are intentional and stoppable. These activated aspects of the self " 'fill in' information missing in the external stimuli. . . . [Consequently], people see things that are not there" (Higgins, 1989a, p. 79). For example, the People Banker experienced the client's vague information as a situation requiring a merger solution. We argue that the People Banker's experience automatically and inappropriately filled in the missing information. In contrast, the Organization Banker recognized the information's vagueness and worked together with the client to fill in the missing information based on fact (vs. based on an interpretation that the banker supplied automatically). This more accurate and complete information could guide the joint decision making by Organization Bankers and client more effectively, which we coded as an aspect of higher group performance.

The person's subjective experience of this automatic activation is a sense of familiarity with the situation. Fodor (1983) referred to such cognitive processes that require only the registration of a familiar stimulus to automatically trigger the entire stimulus pattern in which it is encoded as "input processes." Input processes represent our most basic sensory encoding and form the givens of our consciousness; they are "unavoidable and uncontrollable. For example, try as one might, it is not possible to see the oranges in a bowl as actually purple, or the sky at noon as vivid red" (Bargh, 1989, p. 9). The important point is that the person experiences what is an interpretation as a fact that has the status of "the sky is blue" and, therefore, acts with supreme confidence: "[Automatic] interpretations are not questioned, but are seen as undoubtedly valid sources of information, and are as a result a prime source of judgment and decisions" (Bargh, 1989, p. 11). In other words, we believe that the People Banker did not solicit additional information because he was not aware that his sense of familiarity was the outcome of an interpretive process versus an objective fact. Because he did not experience his inferences as such, he did not seek validation.

A baseline analysis of the People Banker's habitual ways of reasoning supports our interpretation that his performance was influenced by his habitual cognitive patterns. We found that the cognitive stabilities that this People Banker exhibited across diverse situations also occurred with respect to this client situation, which is one piece of evidence that the banker supplied cognitive habits to the situation. In addition, we asked other People Bankers how one should proceed in such situations. We used their judgment as a socially shared standard for what the more objective requirements were in this situation. We also asked these other bankers to read our field notes and to point out discrepancies from this socially shared standard. Together with our research assistants, we found that the majority of these discrepancies from a socially shared standard could be explained in terms of the banker's habitual patterns.

With respect to regulatory locus, we have argued that the Organization Bankers relied more on situationally available resources whereas the People Bankers relied more on their own mental resources. One might question this judgment because the People Banker used significantly more organizational resources as input for the meeting. However, the direct involvement construct is not about heavy resource use per se but about discriminate resource use, about resource use that is appropriate to the situation. We argue that the People Banker's resource usage was indiscriminate, and therefore inefficient, because it was not determined by the actual needs of the situation but by his untested interpretation of the situation. Also, the resources he brought to the situation were not adapted and refined during the meeting. People Bank's business manager agreed with our judgment. She said that such excessive resource usage was a common and costly problem that she believed was "ego-driven": "These guys [would] rather let their team work all night than say in a meeting 'sorry, I don't know, I'll have to ask my colleagues and get back to you.' " Hence, we coded the People Banker's handling of the situation as an instance of ineffective performance. This classification was also based on the client's choice of Organization Bank over People Bank, his comment that the People Bankers "just talked at us," and the judgment of other People Bankers.

In summary, as identification activated the People Banker's expert knowledge ("orientation to abstraction," Fig. 9.1), which is an aspect of the self-concept (Andersen et al., 1997), he believed that he knew what the situation was about. He consequently relied relatively more on his own resource, a relatively less social cognitive process that is conceptually located in a person's mind. The semipermeable line in Fig. 9.1, column 3, denotes the People Bankers' relatively coarse perception of the concrete, social situation. For example, the People Banker related primarily to his abstract conception of a generic or abstract type of client that came in the way of using the concrete, co-present client as a resource. Instead of using the client as a resource, the banker reduced the client to a social stimulus that triggered the banker's preexisting abstract concepts that he then supplied to the situation, independent of how relevant they were. This illustrates our general point that abstraction can get in the way of a person's sensitivity to the situation and thereby impede social intelligence, an aspect of performance.

In contrast, because the Organization Bankers were not sure whether and how their own mental resources might apply, they oriented to the situation for guidance (Fig. 9.1, column 3). Because the Organization Bankers were open to available resources, this social resource system then guided cognition through the processes of mutual adaptation we described (Fig. 9.1, column 4). With the concept of a resource system, we imply that each resource brings out the specifically relevant (e.g., complementary) aspects of another resource—a process that we refer to as mutual constitution—and that this mutual constitution can generate synergy. The contrasting concept of a resource aggregate denotes the absence of such synergy. The concept of synergy implies that by acting as one, resources jointly achieve results that the mere sum of these resources could not achieve. For more detail, see Michel and Jehn (2003) and Michel (2003).

Different Kinds of Selves

What does the preceding discussion of regulatory processes reveal about how the different bankers conceived of the self differently? Our data show that, consistent with the social psychological literature, the People Bankers interpreted the self in terms of an identity (see Table 9.1) that included either personal attributes ("I am smart") or social attributes ("I am a vice president"). Moreover, the People Bankers considered the self an agent (see Table 9.1): they believed that they caused outcomes because of the specific personal attributes they identified with. For example, the People Bank merger specialist thought that, based on his experience and skill, he was responsible for devising an appropriate solution for the client. Hence, people seem to use self-interpretations as a running commentary on how things they care about happen. The self is to people what a unit of analysis is to scientists. It is the locus for all those variables and mechanisms, such as personal attributes, that bring about the kinds of outcomes we are interested in.

In contrast, as illustrated previously, the Organization Bankers who exhibited direct involvement referenced such an abstract self (i.e., "I am") less frequently but referred to the self more in terms of the activities they were participating in (i.e., "doing"—see Fig. 9.1). In identity-induced involvement, bankers focused on their personal attributes (e.g., "I am analytically strong") partly because they saw these attributes as causing their success or failure at organizational tasks, the notion of agency. In contrast, in direct involvement bankers did not interpret the self as an agent but as one of many fungible resources (see Table 9.1). In identity-induced involvement, an agent has inner attributes (locus) that do not depend on the situation and by which he or she realizes personal goals (focus). In contrast, in direct involvement, a resource is defined—that is, exists only in reference to (locus) the situation it is supposed to serve (focus).

Whereas identity-induced involvement locates agency in people, direct involvement is blind with respect to the entity in which the relevant resources are located. Our data (see Michel, 2003) showed that Organization Bankers did not assume a unit of analysis, such as a person, but drew on the principle of equifinality. They recognized that each task can be completed through many different resource combinations in which artifacts can substitute for people. If a banker did not know a piece of information, she could ask any number or combination of colleagues, consult documentation about prior comparable deals, or try to figure out the answer by building a financial model. Because these different structures jointly complete a task, this resource system, the particular manifestation of which varied with each task, is the relevant agent (locus). Because the Organization Bankers believed that their personal attributes were relatively less important for explaining task outcomes, they focused relatively more on an undifferentiated resource pool that included but was not limited to their own resources. The second column of Fig. 9.1 illustrates this interpretation of the self as equivalent with other social resources by representing both self and social context with the same symbol (x) and as part of the same box, which represents a joint resource pool.

We argue that the Organization Bankers interpreted the self as the activity of participating (a process) in such resource activity systems. This means that, in contrast to the People Bankers, the Organization Bankers did not assume that a self is a separate entity that then has to be linked into a social context. For example, similar to social psychology, the People Bankers implicitly assumed two entities, the Banker and the Bank, which they linked cognitively through an overlap of attributes, the process of social identification. Again, self-interpretation is about the explanation of activity. By saying that the Organization Bankers conceived of the self in terms of an activity, we do not mean that they did not think of themselves as people. We are making a distinction between a biological person and a conceptual person. The biological person may be described in attributes such as hair color, weight, gender, intentions, or beliefs. We argue that the Organization Bankers' actions showed that they did not believe that such personal attributes are important explanations for how cognitive outcomes occur. Therefore, when studying the Organization Bankers' self-interpretation, we did not include such personal attributes in the conceptual category "person" or "self." The attributes that were relevant to the conceptual person were attributes that always related to a specific activity they were engaged in.

SECTION 3: CONCLUSION AND DISCUSSION

Our data suggest that the direct involvement theory of self and the social–psychological theory of self, which informs the EI approach, are two contradictory theories about psychological processes that include cognition, motivation, and emotion. The direct involvement theory argues that the social–psychological and the EI approach attribute processes to an inner self that can also be the property of a situation. For example, Salovey and Mayer (1990) explicitly defined emotional intelligence as "the ability to monitor one's own and other's feelings and emotions, to discriminate among them, and to use this information to guide one's thinking and action" (p. 189). Their influential model focuses on this ability in the form of "mental aptitudes." We argue that this model consequently assumes what should be investigated, namely whether emotions and other regulatory processes are the mental attributes of an individual or the attributes of a social situation. William James (1997) argued that the value of a distinction hinges on its practical consequences: "What difference would it practically make to anyone if this notion rather than that notion were true?" (p. 94). We propose that the attribution of self-processes matters because when people interpret the self in these identity-induced involvement ways, they are distracted from the situational resources that could guide their behavior. Consequently, individual and group performance suffers (see Fig. 9.1).

Our argument seems to echo familiar criticisms. For example, the situated cognition literature—a competitor to traditional social psychology (e.g., Anderson, Reder, & Simon, 1996, 1997; Anderson, Greeno, Reder, & Simon, 2000; Greeno, 1997)—also argues that the appropriate unit of analysis should not be the individual but the situated activity system (e.g.,

Greeno, 1998; Hutchins, 1999; Lave & Wenger, 1991). Our approach differs from these other critics in that (a) we are not saying that traditional social psychology and the EI approach are wrong, and (b) we are not suggesting our approach as a competitor to these approaches. Rather, we argue that the direct involvement and the social–psychological theory of self implicit in the EI approach are both accurate descriptions of how psychological processes can function but under different conditions. Consequently, we argue that they should be studied within one theory—the theory of involvement. With respect to the rivalry between social–psychological theory and theories of situated cognition, we argue that both approaches overgeneralize. Both provide correct descriptions of how cognitive accomplishments can happen but fail to specify the contingencies under which their description holds and the distinct consequences. We integrate traditional social–psychological/EI as well as situated perspectives into one paradigm, as two distinct forms of involvement (see Fig. 9.1), and specify contingencies and consequences (Michel, 2003).

We believe that the study of involvement encompasses a paradigm shift because it requires a reinterpretation of data, including the resorting of processes that EI currently attributes to the conceptual category "person" and to the conceptual category "situation"—but also of attributes that situated cognition currently attributes to the "situation" in the category "person." We conduct this sorting process with conventional methodological criteria that relate to how one chooses an appropriate unit of analysis. One chooses a unit of analysis so that it comprises all those processes and mechanisms that vary at the same time for the same reason in relation to the outcome variable of interest (Freeman, 1978). To study problem solving, this means that the appropriate unit of analysis should include all those structures that have input into the process. Social structures have input, in turn, when people are sensitive to them. For example, when the analyst and the poet are sensitive to the evolving task structures, the appropriate unit of analysis includes the writer and the text ("direct involvement," Fig. 9.1); when they ignore the evolving task structures and act on their on their personal conceptions and intentions, the unit of analysis should include primarily the writer's mental structures, an enactment of the social–psychological/EI self or "identity-induced involvement" (Fig. 9.1). In other words, the EI approach is incomplete because it assumes what needs to be demonstrated. Where cognition, motivation, and emotion are located and what they focus on are empirical questions.

Our concern with people's sensitivity to available resources is another important distinction between involvement theory and a situated cognition approach. Reacting to the mentalism of traditional social psychology, a situated approach argues that the way we think is invariably influenced by the social, cultural, and material context. We agree. However, the data suggest that the kind of influence that these social structures have depends on how people approach them. When people frame the social context in light of their identity, they automatically supply the content of their self-concept to the situation and ignore important social cues. Therefore, what was social in origin is now infused with idiosyncratic significance, that is, meaning and importance. This personal meaning (vs. situational guidance) then orients problem solving.

Direct involvement encompasses a more social form of cognition, motivation, and emotion because it is relatively more oriented by the concrete, social resources in a situation (vs. by a person's psychological situation). Our conception of what counts as social differs from other approaches that generally define something as more social when it includes more people (e.g., Weick & Roberts, 1993). In contrast, we propose that whether an interaction is social or not does not depend on the number of people who participate in it. Acts of private reflection, such as the writing of a poem, as well as group interactions can all be more or less social depending on the extent to which the person involved is continuously sensitive to the cues of the relevant social elements.

Implications for EI Research and Practice

The resulting understanding of how this resource system (vs. the biological individual) solves problems matters because it prompts different kinds of research questions and suggests different performance-enhancing interventions. For example, our analysis suggests that research questions about emotions should not be posed separately from questions about self, cognition, and motivation. In our model, emotion, cognition, and motivation are always interdependent as self-processes. This differs from Mayer and Salovey's (1997) influential model, in which the integration between cognitive and emotional processes is a skill that an individual can develop. Also, in their model, questions about intelligence are questions about an individual's aptitude, which is a faculty that is located in the individual and helps the individual, as an agent, to control or regulate behavior. In contrast, in our analysis, questions concerning how to manage emotions effectively do not solely relate to an individual's mind and its resources, such as abstract reasoning, but should relate to how the mind connects with and works together with the extramental resources available in a situation. The processes that emerge from this interaction of resources can control or regulate behavior more effectively than an individual's intention. An understanding of these emergent processes requires an understanding of preconceptual ways of knowing (e.g., Merleau-Ponty, 1962), which is currently missing in the EI literature.

TABLE 9.2
Performance-Enhancing Interventions
of the EI and the Involvement Approach

EI Interventions: Abstract Structures	Involvement Interventions (cf. Michel & Jehn, 2003)
Employee selection: EI skills (Goleman, 2001b)	Avoid hiring experts
Training or education: EI skills and concepts (Goleman, 2001b)	Avoid training that conveys generalized principles
Abstract culture: Shared understandings, values, norms, and standards (Druskat & Wolff, 2001)	Minimize abstract cultures
Organizational design: Performance management systems	Minimize influence of organizational structures

To practitioners, the involvement approach recommends different performance-enhancing interventions compared with the emotional intelligence approach. Currently, EI research recommends organizational interventions that rely on adding abstract structures—that is, structures that do not reference a specific situation—to the individual or the social context (see Table 9.2). For example, the emotional intelligence approach recommends that practitioners should (a) hire people based on EI skills, (b) train people on EI skills and concepts, (c) put performance management systems in place, such as specifying performance goals, and (d) create norms and values that encourage people to display EI skills (e.g., Cherniss & Adler, 2000; Druskat & Wolff, 2001; Goleman, 2001b; Spencer, 2001).

The involvement approach we introduce points to the unintended consequences of such interventions. We argue that these interventions unwittingly impede performance because they focus people on abstract structures and distract them from a more direct involvement with the task. Our data show that performance benefited when organizations minimized the influence of such abstract structures (e.g., Michel, 2003; Michel & Jehn, 2003). The alternative approach to enhancing performance we introduce advocates interventions that clear away abstract structures to strengthen self-organizing processes (cf. March, 1994) or direct involvement. This requires active intervention because many of these structures emerge naturally: People naturally progress from concrete to abstract thinking (e.g., Ruble, 1994), tend toward social identification (e.g., Baumeister & Leary, 1995; Burke, 1937), and enact readily available cultures (e.g., Dreyfus, 1999).

Of course, we do not mean to suggest that abstract thinking, identification, and culture are necessarily bad. Rather, we investigated when and how these structures come in the way of how situational resources can organize themselves, as described by Bruner and our Organization Bank informants.

Our research (e.g., Michel, 2003) illustrates alternatives for managers that involve a primacy on action and perception (vs. abstract thought), employee identification with a concrete situation (vs. with abstract categories), and culture as concrete cues and constraints (vs. abstract principles). For example, Organization Bank (a) hired people based on their relative lack of relevant experience and specific skills, (b) avoided classroom- and systematic on-the-job training, and (c) oriented people away from organizational norms and values to enhance their awareness of situational complexity.

Damasio (1999) argued that our brain comes to identify with the body because it constantly monitors all physiological processes within the body's boundaries. We argue that this is a fundamental principle of how people formulate a self-interpretation. We include as part of our self-boundary all those processes that we need to monitor constantly to solve our daily problems. Because of the situational complexity they constantly experienced, the Organization Bankers continuously brought additional resources to a situation and then monitored these resources as joint problem solving progressed. Following Damasio's (1999) logic, we propose that the complexity that Organization Bank's interventions highlighted caused the bankers to interpret the self in terms of the concrete activity of participation or involvement with these other resources—versus experiencing the self as a distinct object with abstract attributes and processes that constitute an identity—and to experience the combined resources as jointly bringing about task outcomes—versus privileging the self as an agent. We believe that to facilitate these situational self-interpretations, which are at the very heart of organizing, is a practitioner's primary task.

APPENDIX A: MEASURES OF SOCIAL IDENTIFICATION

1. Do you talk up the department as a great place to work for? (O'Reilly & Chatman, 1986)

2. Are you proud to tell others that you are part of the department? (O'Reilly & Chatman, 1986)

3. Do you consider the values, goals, and standards of the department similar to your own? (Measure of internalization: O'Reilly & Chatman, 1986)

4. Do you feel personally insulted when someone criticizes the department? (Mael & Ashforth, 1992)

5. Do you feel personally complimented when someone praises the department? (Mael & Ashforth, 1992)

6. When you talk about the department, do you usually say *we* rather than *they*? (Mael & Ashforth, 1992)

7. Selves Questionnaire (adapted from Moretti & Higgins, 1999b, and Higgins, Bond, Klein, & Strauman, 1986) (a) We asked the bankers to spontaneously generate sets of up to 10 traits or attributes that describe their actual self (i.e., attributes they believe they actually possess) and their self-guides (i.e., attributes that they ideally wish or hope to possess or think they ought to possess). (b) In addition, we asked them to generate lists of attributes that they believe their group and organization hope they possess or think they should possess. We scored the overlap between the two types of lists (self and group/organization) as indicating the extent of a banker's group and organizational identification.

ACKNOWLEDGMENTS

We thank Vanessa Druskat for her insightful suggestions. This research was supported by the Wharton Center for Leadership and Organizational Change.

REFERENCES

Albert, S., Ashforth, B. E., & Dutton, J. E. (2000). Introduction to special topic forum. Organizational identity and identification: Charting new waters and building new bridges. *Academy of Management Review, 25*(1), 13–17.

Allport, F. H. (1924). *Social psychology.* Boston: Houghton Mifflin.

Allport, G. W. (1985). The historical background of social psychology. In G. Lindzey & E. Aronson (Eds.), *Handbook of social psychology* (3rd ed., Vol. 1, pp. 1–46). New York: Random House.

Amabile, T. M. (1996). *Creativity in context. Update to the social psychology of creativity.* New York: Westview Press.

Andersen, S. M., & Berk, M. S. (1998). Transference in everyday experience: Implications of experimental research for relevant clinical phenomena. *Review of General Psychology, 2*(1), 81–120.

Andersen, S. M., & Cole, S. W. (1990). "Do I know you?": The role of significant others in general social perception. *Journal of Personality and Social Psychology, 59,* 384–399.

Andersen, S. M., Glassman, N. S., Chen, S., & Cole, S. W. (1995). Transference in social perception: The role of chronic accessibility in significant-other representations. *Journal of Personality and Social Psychology, 69,* 41–57.

Andersen, S. M., Reznik, I., & Chen, S. (1997). The self and others: Cognitive and motivational underpinnings. In J. G. Snodgrass & R. L. Thompson (Eds.), *The self across psychology: Self-recognition, self-awareness, and the self-concept* (pp. 233–275). New York: New York Academy of Science.

Anderson, J. R., Greeno, J. G., Reder, L. M., & Simon, H. A. (2000). Perspectives on learning, thinking, and activity. *Educational Researcher, 29*(4), 11–13.

Anderson, J. R., Reder, L. M., & Simon, H. A. (1996). Situated learning and education. *Educational Researcher, 25*(4), 5–11.

Anderson, J. R., Reder, L. M., & Simon, H. A. (1997). Situative versus cognitive perspectives: Form versus substance. *Educational Researcher, 26*(1), 18–21.

Bandura, A. (2001). Social cognitive theory: An agentic perspective. *Annual Review of Psychology, 52,* 1–26.

Bargh, J. A. (1982). Attention and automaticity in the processing of self-relevant information. *Journal of Personality and Social Psychology, 43,* 425–436.

Bargh, J. A. (1989). Conditional automaticity: Varieties of automatic influence in social perception and cognition. In J. S. Uleman & J. A. Bargh (Eds.), *Unintended thought* (pp. 3–51). New York: Guilford.

Bargh, J. A. (1996). Automaticity in social psychology. In E. T. Higgins & A. W. Kruglanski (Eds.), *Social psychology—Handbook of basic principles* (pp. 169–183). New York: Guilford.

Bargh, J. A., Bond, R. N., Lombardi, W. L., & Tota, M. E. (1986). The additive nature of chronic and temporary sources of construct accessibility. *Journal of Personality and Social Psychology, 50,* 869–878.

Bar-On, R. (2000). Emotional and social intelligence: Insights from the Emotional Quotient Inventory. In R. Bar-On & J. D. A. Parker (Eds.), *The handbook of emotional intelligence: Theory, development, assessment, and application to home, school, and in the workplace* (pp. 363–388). San Francisco: Jossey-Bass.

Bateson, G. (1972). *Steps to an ecology of mind.* New York: Ballantine.

Baumeister, R., & Leary, M. R. (1995). The need to belong: Desire for interpersonal attachments as a fundamental human motivation. *Psychological Bulletin, 117,* 497–529.

Ben-Ze'ev, A. (2000). *The subtlety of emotions.* Cambridge, MA: MIT Press.

Berkowitz, L., & Devine, P. G. (1995). Has social psychology always been cognitive? What is "cognitive" anyhow? *Personality and Social Psychology Bulletin, 21*(7), 696–703.

Bobrow, D. G., & Norman, D. A. (1975). Some principles of memory schemata. In D. G. Bobrow & A. Collins (Eds.), *Representation and understanding: Studies in cognitive science* (pp. 131–149). New York: Academic Press.

Bougon, M. J. (1992). Congregate cognitive maps: A unified dynamic theory of organization and strategy. *Journal of Management Studies, 29*(3), 367–389.

Bruner, J. S. (1962). *On knowing: Essays for the left hand.* Cambridge, MA: Belknap Press of Harvard University Press.

Burke, K. (1937). *Attitudes towards history.* New York: The New Republic.

Carver, C. S., & Scheier, M. F. (1981). *Attention and self-regulation: A control-theory approach to human behavior.* New York: Springer Verlag.

Carver, C. S., & Scheier, M. F. (1990). Principles of self-regulation: Action and emotion. In E. T. Higgins & R. M. Sorrentino (Eds.), *Handbook of motivation and cognition: Foundations of social behavior* (Vol. 2, pp. 3–52). New York: Guilford.

Cherniss, C., & Adler, M. (2000). *Promoting emotional intelligence in organizations.* Alexandria, VA: American Society for Training and Development.

Csikszentmihalyi, M. (1990). *Flow: The psychology of optimal experience.* New York: Harper & Row.

Csikszentmihalyi, M. (1993). *The evolving self: A psychology for the third millennium.* New York: Harper & Row.

Damasio, A. R. (1999). *The feeling of what happens: Body and emotions in the making of consciousness.* New York: Harcourt Brace.

Deci, E. L., & Ryan, R. M. (1987). The support of autonomy and the control of behavior. *Journal of Personality and Social Psychology, 53,* 1024–1037.

Deci, E. L., & Ryan, R. M. (1991). A motivational approach to the self: Integration in personality. In R. Dienstbier (Ed.), *Nebraska symposium on motivation* (pp. 237–288). Lincoln: University of Nebraska Press.

Dreyfus, H. L. (1999). *Being-in-the-world. A commentary on Heidegger's Being and Time, Division I.* Cambridge, MA: MIT Press.

Druskat, V. U., & Wolff, S. B. (2001). Group emotional intelligence and is influence on group effectiveness. In C. Cherniss & D. Goleman (Eds.), *The emotionally intelligent workplace. How to select for, measure, and improve emotional intelligence, in individuals, groups, and organizations* (pp. 132–155). San Francisco: Jossey-Bass.

Dutton, J. E., Dukerich, J. M., & Harquail, C. V. (1994). Organizational images and member identification. *Administrative Science Quarterly, 39,* 239–263.

Dweck, C. S. (1999). *Self-theories. Their role in motivation, personality, and development.* Philadelphia: Psychology Press.

Eisenhardt, K. M. (1989). Building theory from case study research. *Academy of Management Review, 14,* 532–550.

Elsbach, K. D. (1999). Rewards for professionals: A social identity perspective. In R. C. Dorf (Ed.), *The technology management handbook.* Danvers, MA: CRC Press.

Festinger, L. (1943). Studies in decision. *Journal of Experimental Psychology, 32*(4), 411–423.

Fiske, S. T., & Taylor, S. E. (1991). *Social cognition* (2nd ed.). New York: McGraw-Hill.

Fodor, J. A. (1983). *The modularity of mind.* Cambridge, MA: MIT Press.

Freeman, J. H. (1978). The unit of analysis in organizational research. In M. W. Meyer (Ed.), *Environments and organizations* (pp. 335–351). San Francisco: Jossey-Bass.

Goleman, D. (2001a). Emotional intelligence: Issues in paradigm building. In C. Cherniss & D. Goleman (Eds.), *The emotionally intelligent workplace. How to select, measure, and improve emotional intelligence in individuals, groups, and organizations* (pp. 13–26). San Francisco: Jossey-Bass.

Goleman, D. (2001b). An EI-based theory of performance. In C. Cherniss & D. Goleman (Eds.), *The emotionally intelligent workplace. How to select, measure, and improve emotional intelligence in individuals, groups, and organizations* (pp. 27–45). San Francisco: Jossey-Bass.

Greeno, J. G. (1997). On claims that answer the wrong questions. *Educational Researcher, 26*(1), 5–17.

Greeno, J. G. (1998). The situativity of knowing, learning, and research. *American Psychologist, 53*(1), 5–26.

Heidegger, M. (1962). *Being and time.* New York: Harper & Row.

Hermans, H. J. M., & Kempen, H. J. G. (1993). *The dialogical self. Meaning as movement.* New York: Academic Press.

Higgins, E. T. (1989a). Knowledge accessibility and activation: Subjectivity and suffering from unconscious sources. In J. S. Uleman & J. A. Bargh (Eds.), *Unintended thought* (pp. 75–123). New York: Guilford.

Higgins, E. T. (1989b). Promotion and prevention: Regulatory focus as a motivational principle. *Advances in Experimental Social Psychology, 30,* 1–46.

Higgins, E. T. (1992). Social cognition as a social science: How social action creates meaning. In D. N. Ruble, P. R. Costanzo, & M. E. Oliveri (Eds.), *The social psychology of mental health: Basic mechanisms and applications* (pp. 241–277). New York: Guilford.

Higgins, E. T. (1996a). Emotional experiences: The pains and pleasures of distinct regulatory systems. In R. D. Kavanaugh, B. Zimmerberg, & S. Fein (Eds.), *Emotion—Interdisciplinary perspective* (pp. 203–241). Mahwah, NJ: Lawrence Erlbaum Associates.

Higgins, E. T. (1996b). The "Self Digest": Self-knowledge serving self-regulatory functions. *Journal of Personality and Social Psychology, 71*(6), 1062–1083.

Higgins, E. T., Bond, R. N., Klein, R., & Strauman, T. (1986). Self-discrepancies and emotional vulnerability: How magnitude, accessibility, and type of discrepancy influence affect. *Journal of Personality and Social Psychology, 51,* 5–15.

Higgins, E. T., Loeb, I., & Ruble, D. N. (1995). The four A's of life transition effects: Attention, accessibility, adaptation, and adjustment. *Social Cognition, 13*(3), 215–242.

Hull, J. G., Slone, L. B., Meteyer, K. B., & Matthews, A. R. (2002). The nonconsciousness of self-consciousness. *Journal of Personality and Social Psychology, 83*(2), 406–424.

Hutchins, E. (1999). *Cognition in the wild.* Cambridge, MA: MIT Press.

Hymes, D. (1974). *Foundations of sociolinguistics: An ethnographic approach.* Philadelphia: University of Pennsylvania Press.

Jackson, J. M. (1988). *Social psychology, past and present.* Hillsdale, NJ: Lawrence Erlbaum Associates.

James, W. (1997). What pragmatism means. In L. Menand (Ed.), *Pragmatism. A reader* (pp. 93–111). New York: Random House.

Jick, T. D. (1979). Mixing qualitative and quantitative methods: Triangulation in action. *Administrative Science Quarterly, 24,* 602–661.

Kelman, H. C. (1958). Compliance, identification, and internalization: Three processes of attitude change. *Journal of Conflict Resolution, 2,* 51–60.

Kruglanski, A. W., Thompson, E. P., Higgins, E. T., Atash, M. N., Pierro, A., Shah, J. Y., & Spiegel, S. (2000). To "do the right thing" or to "just do it": Locomotion and assessment as distinct self-regulatory imperatives. *Journal of Personality and Social Psychology, 79*(5), 793–815.

Lave, J., & Wenger, E. (1991). *Situated learning: Legitimate peripheral participation.* Cambridge, England: Cambridge University Press.

Mael, F., & Ashforth, B. E. (1992). Alumni and their alma mater: A partial test of the reformulated model of organizational identification. *Journal of Organizational Behavior, 13,* 103–123.

March, J. G. (1991). Exploration and exploitation in organizational learning. *Organization Science, 2,* 71–87.

March, J. G. (1994). The evolution of evolution. In J. A. C. Baum & J. V. Singh (Eds.), *Evolutionary dynamics of organizations* (pp. 39–49). New York: Oxford University Press.

Markus, H. (1980). The self in thought and memory. In D. M. Wegner & R. R. Wallacher (Eds.), *The self in social psychology* (pp. 102–130). New York: Oxford University Press.

Markus, H. R., & Kitayama, S. (2001). The cultural construction of self and emotion: Implication for social behavior. In W. G. Parrott (Ed.), *Emotions in social psychology* (pp. 119–137). Philadelphia: Taylor & Francis.

Mayer, J. D., & Salovey, P. (1997). What is emotional intelligence. In P. Salovey & D. J. Sluyter (Eds.), *Emotional development and emotional intelligence: Implications for education* (pp. 3–31). New York: Basic Books.

Mayer, J. D., & Salovey, P. (2002, August). *Emotional intelligence: A four-branch model.* Paper presented at the meeting of the American Psychological Association, Chicago.

McCall, G. P., & Simmons, J. L. (1978). *Identities and interactions.* (Rev. ed.). New York: Basic Books.

Merleau-Ponty, M. (1962). *Phenomenology of perception.* London: Routledge & Kegan Paul.

Michel, A. A. (2003). *Kinds of minds: How organizations think and why it matters.* Unpublished doctoral dissertation, Wharton Business School, Universsity of Pennsylvania, Philadelphia.

Michel, A. A., & Jehn, K. A. (2003). The dark side of identification: Overcoming identification-induced performance impediments. In E. Mannix, J. Polzer, & M. Neale (Eds.), *Research on managing groups and teams: Identity issues in groups* (Vol. 5, pp. 189–219). Greenwich, CT: JAI.

Michel, A. A., & Wortham, S. E. F. (2002). Clearing away the self. *Theory & Psychology, 12*(5), 625–650.

Moretti, M. M., & Higgins, E. T. (1999a). Own versus other standpoints in self-regulation: Developmental antecedents and functional consequences. *Review of General Psychology, 3*(3), 188–223.

Moretti, M. M., & Higgins, E. T. (1999b). Internal representations of others in self-regulation: A new look at a classic issue. *Social Cognition, 17*(2), 186–208.

Nussbaum, M. C. (2001). *Upheavals of thought. The intelligence of emotions.* New York: Cambridge University Press.

O'Reilly, C. A., & Chatman, J. A. (1986). Organizational commitment and psychological attachment: The effects of compliance, identification, and internalization on prosocial behavior. *Journal of Applied Psychology, 71*, 492–499.

Pennebaker, J. (2002, August). *Using their words to study the emotions and motives of historical figures.* Paper presented at the meeting of the American Psychological Association, Chicago.

Pennebaker, J. W., & Francis, M. E. (1999). *Linguistic inquiry and word count: LIWC.* Mahwah, NJ: Lawrence Erlbaum Associates.

Pennebaker, J. W., & King, L. A. (1999). Linguistic styles: Language use as an individual difference. *Journal of Personality and Social Psychology, 77*(6), 1296–1312.

Pennebaker, J. W., Mehl, M. R., & Niederhoffer, K. G. (2003). Psychological aspects of natural language use: Our words, our selves. *Annual Review of Psychology, 54*, 547–577.

Piaget, J. (1929). *The child's conception of the world.* New York: Harcourt Brace.

Pratt, M. G. (1998). To be or not to be. Central questions in organizational identification. In D. A. Whetten & P. C. Godfrey (Eds.), *Identity in organizations. Building theory through conversations* (pp. 171–208). Thousand Oaks, CA: Sage.

Ruble, D. N. (1994). A phase model of transitions: Cognitive and motivational consequences. *Advances in Experimental Social Psychology, 26*, 163–214.

Ruble, D. N., & Frey, K. S. (1991). Changing patterns of comparative behavior as skills are acquired: A functional model of self-evaluation. In J. Suls & T. A. Wills (Eds.), *Social comparison: Contemporary theory and research* (pp. 79–113). Hillsdale, NJ: Lawrence Erlbaum Associates.

Salovey, P., & Mayer, J. D. (1990). Emotional intelligence. *Imagination, Cognition, and Personality, 9*, 185–211.

Schafer, R. (1992). *Retelling a life.* New York: Basic Books.

Schiffrin, D. (1994). Approaches to discourse. Cambridge, MA: Blackwell.

Schwarzer, R. (Ed.). (1986). *Self-related cognitions in anxiety and motivation.* Hillsdale, NJ: Lawrence Erlbaum Associates.

Schwarzer, R., & Wicklund, R. A. (Eds.). (1991). *Anxiety and self-focused attention.* New York: Harwood Academic.

Spencer, L. M. (2001). The economic value of emotional intelligence competencies and EIC-based HR programs. In C. Cherniss & D. Goleman (Eds.), *The emotionally intelligent workplace. How to select, measure, and improve emotional intelligence in individuals, groups, and organizations* (pp. 45–82). San Francisco: Jossey-Bass.

Sternberg, R. J. (2001). What is the common thread of creativity?: Its dialectical relation to intelligence and wisdom. *American Psychologist, 56*(4), 360–362.

Stirman, S. W., & Pennebaker, J. W. (2001). Word use in the poetry of suicidal and nonsuicidal poets. *Psychosomatic Medicine, 63*, 517–522.

Thorndike, E. L. (1920). Intelligence and its uses. *Harper's, 140*, 227–235.

Triandis, H. C. (1995). *Individualism and collectivism.* Boulder, CO: Westview Press.

Turner, J. C. (1975). Social comparison and social identity: Some prospects for intergroup behavior. *European Journal of Social Psychology, 5*, 5–34.

Turner, J. C. (1981). The experimental social psychology of intergroup behavior. In J. C. Turner & H. Giles (Eds.), *Intergroup behavior* (pp. 66–101). Cambridge, England: Cambridge University Press.

Weber, M. (1967). Subjective meaning in the social situation. In G. B. Levitas (Ed.), *Culture and consciousness: Perspectives in the social sciences* (pp. 156–169). New York: Braziller.

Webster's New Universal Unabridged Dictionary. (1996). New York: Barnes & Noble.

Weick, K. E. (1995). *Sensemaking in organizations.* Thousand Oaks, CA: Sage.

Weick, K. E., & Roberts, K. H. (1993). Collective mind in organizations: Heedful interrelating on flight decks. *Administrative Science Quarterly, 38*, 357–381.

Wicklund, R. A. (1986). Orientation to the environment versus preoccupation with human potential. In R. M. Sorrentino & E. T. Higgins (Eds.), *Handbook of motivation and cognition: Foundations of social behavior* (pp. 64–95). New York: Guilford.

Wicklund, R. A., & Gollwitzer, P. M. (1982). *Symbolic self-completion*. Hillsdale, NJ: Lawrence Erlbaum Associates.

Wood, R., & Bandura, A. (1989). Social cognitive theory of organizational management. *Academy of Management Review, 14*(3), 361–384.

Yin, R. K. (1984). *Case study research*. Beverly Hills, CA: Sage.

Zajonc, R. B. (1965). Social facilitation. *Science, 149*, 269–274.

Chapter 10

The Link Between Group Emotional Competence and Group Effectiveness

Steven B. Wolff
Innovative Systems Associates

Vanessa Urch Druskat
The University of New Hampshire
Whittemore School of Business
McConnell Hall of Graduate Study

Elizabeth Stubbs Koman
Director of Organizational Improvement
The Stubman Group

Tracey Eira Messer
Weatherhead School of Management
Case Western Reserve University

In a period of about 15 years, participation in work teams has become a standard in most U.S. organizations (Lawler, 1998). In fact, the *Wall Street Journal*'s rank of the criteria used by recruiters seeking to hire MBAs placed "the ability to work well within a team" second; it was right behind "communication and interpersonal skills" (Alsop, 2003).

The speed with which the "team revolution" took over the workplace is one way to explain the results of a recent survey that asked the leaders of 100 of the most innovative companies in the United States (as defined by the Work in America Institute) to name the workplace challenges they most wanted researchers to address. Ninety-five percent of the respondents identified creating and sustaining effective work teams as their number one challenge (Farren, 1999).

Yet, group dynamics and group effectiveness have been studied by academics for more than 6 decades. Some scholars argue that existing theory and research are not behaviorally specific enough to be useful for practicing managers searching for the best way to develop and sustain effective work groups (Cannon-Bowers, Tannenbaum, Salas, & Volpe, 1995; Cohen & Bailey, 1997). Others have argued that scholars can increase understanding of team dynamics and team effectiveness through research and theory on the roles of emotion and relationships in teams (Edmondson, 1999; George, 2002; Keyton, 1999).

We agree with both arguments. Thus, this chapter is about a behaviorally specific model of team effectiveness that emphasizes the role of emotion and relationships on team effectiveness. It is built on our knowledge that social interactions create emotion and that the frequency of required interactions in a group amplifies the need for emotional intelligence in a group setting. It is also built on our understanding of groups as social systems in which interactions among members are the basic building blocks (Morgeson & Hofmann, 1999). This means that group outcomes are determined not by the competence of individual group members but by the competence evident in the patterns of interactions among all members (Poole, 1999; Weick & Roberts, 1993). Therefore, we argue that to be most useful in a group setting, behaviors consistent with emotional intelligence must be manifested at the group level. In other words, a group must have norms or informal rules that support actions and behaviors that acknowledge, recognize, monitor, discriminate, and attend to emotion and that respond constructively to emotional challenge (see Holmer, 1994; Huy, 1999). We refer to these as *emotionally competent* norms. We refer to groups that hold such norms as *emotionally competent groups*.

In this chapter, we define and discuss our theory of group emotional competence and present our research journey as we test the theory, refine our measure, and work to refine the theory. Specifically, we present the results of ongoing research being conducted to test parts of our theory and research begun by Christina Hamme (2003) to develop a reliable and valid survey to measure group emotional competence. Finally, we discuss the implications of our theory for addressing five critical gaps in current knowledge about how to build and sustain group effectiveness.

DEFINITION OF TERMS

Before we begin we define a few terms we use consistently throughout this chapter. We use the terms *group* and *team* interchangeably. We define a group or team as "made up of individuals who see themselves and who are seen by others as a social entity, who are interdependent because of the tasks they perform as members of a group, who are embedded in one or more larger social systems (e.g., community, organization), and who perform tasks that affect others (such as customers or coworkers)" (Guzzo & Dickson, 1996, p. 308). Emotion is defined as the personal display of affected states or emotional arousal (e.g., joy, love, contentment, fear, anger, or embarrassment) and is differentiated from feelings, which involve awareness of the arousal (Fineman, 1991). Group norms are defined as standards or informal rules that groups adopt to regulate and regularize member behavior (Feldman, 1984). As is discussed, norms grow out of repeated interactions through which members come to an implicit agreement about the unique values and expectations by which members of this particular group will operate (i.e., appropriate behaviors).

THE CORE OF THE THEORY: LINKING
EMOTION-FOCUSED AND TASK-FOCUSED NORMS

Despite decades of theory and research suggesting the importance of the role of emotion-focused norms and processes to group outcomes (e.g., Bales, 1950; Homans, 1950; Tuckman, 1965), current theories of group effectiveness (see Ancona & Caldwell, 1992; Guzzo & Dickson, 1996; Hackman, 1987) emphasize the rational task-focused processes and strategies associated with effective work groups (e.g., coordination). They give little explicit attention to the emotional and social norms and rules that must underlie the effective execution of task-focused activities. The following two examples of teams we have studied provide an illustration of the relevance of both emotion-focused and task-focused norms in work groups and show how tightly they are coupled. In one high-technology company, the teams devised an effective task process strategy in which teams would work together to ensure on-time delivery. When one team fell behind schedule, those teams who were ahead of schedule helped it to catch up—without managerial intervention. This strategy required task-focused norms such as managing the task boundary (i.e., who does what) and pooling knowledge and resources. It also required a parallel set of emotion-focused norms. As one team lagged behind and had to request help from another, it had to develop norms for managing the emotion that team members felt when they had to admit they had fallen behind by requesting help. Similarly, those teams providing help had to manage their own displeasure and emotion at having to work harder and longer to lend a hand.

In a second manufacturing firm, self-managing teams decided that to improve their effectiveness all team members would have to become multiply skilled enough to complete all tasks conducted by a team. This required members to learn new skills through training sessions, peer coaching, and the giving and receiving of feedback. In most situations, learning new skills, especially from peers, is known to involve feelings of vulnerability and the fear of evaluation (Schein, 1993); therefore, the groups had to build a sense of trust and safety (see Edmondson, 1999) to enable members to admit mistakes and to feel comfortable providing and receiving honest feedback. In sum, group task and emotional norms were tightly connected.

Our theory of group emotional competence (Druskat & Wolff, 2001a, 2001b; Wolff & Druskat, 2004) contributes to current knowledge on team

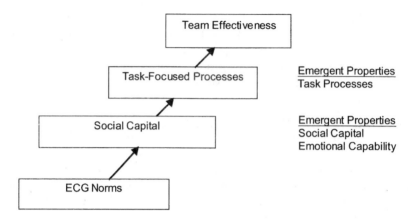

FIG. 10.1.   Simplified socioemotional model of group effectiveness (Druskat & Wolff, 2001a).

effectiveness by clarifying how emotion and relationships underlie engagement in effective task-focused processes (e.g., cooperation, effort, boundary management). Specifically, we argue that engagement in effective task-focused processes is facilitated by constructive group member relationships (i.e., social capital: trust and safety, efficacy, networks), which are supported by a set of emotionally competent group norms (ECG norms; see Fig. 10.1). We elaborate on our theory next.

GROUP EMOTIONAL COMPETENCE

An Emotional Structure

Behavior in groups is not random; it is structured through norms defined as standards or informal rules adopted by group members to ensure predictability in member behavior (Feldman, 1984). The interpersonal interactions and behaviors necessary for group work are the source of many emotions, such as joy, contentment, fear, anger, and embarrassment (Kemper, 1978). This means that emotions have an unavoidable and pervasive effect in groups (Barsade, 2002). In group settings, just as patterns of behavior and interactions are labeled *group dynamics*, patterns of behavior and interactions that arouse, display, or address emotion are labeled *emotional dynamics* (Huy, 1999). Like all behavior in groups, emotional dynamics are not random, they emerge through member interactions, which are restricted by the social context and the range of actions considered admissible by contextual and cultural factors (Morgeson & Hofmann, 1999). Over time, group member back-and-forth interactions, actions, and reactions cause certain emotional dynamics to become routine and to emerge as a collective emotional structure or a set of rules and resources that influence the experience of emotion in the group.

To define the specific norms or rules within a group emotional structure, we draw from two relevant theories. The first is the cognitive appraisal theory of emotion, which delineates the process through which emotion influences behavior (referred to as the emotional process) (Lazarus, 1991). The second theory is the complex systems theory of small-group dynamics, which suggests that dynamics within groups occur at multiple levels including the individual member level, the group level, and the cross-boundary level because groups are open systems (Arrow, McGrath, & Berdahl, 2000).

The cognitive appraisal theory of emotion (see Plutchik, 2003) suggests that there are two phases in the emotion-to-behavior process. Phase 1 of the emotional process begins with an event that stirs emotion and ends with the arousal of specific emotions (e.g., anxiety and excitement). The link between the event and the arousal is moderated by awareness and interpretation of the context surrounding the event, which enables the individual to label the emotion (Ilgen, Fisher, & Taylor, 1979). Phase 2 consists of the choice of a response to the emotion. This response is moderated by one's belief about the appropriate action in that situation (Levy, 1984).

Anthropologists and organizational scholars have found that cultural norms influence (a) an individual's interpretation and awareness of emotion and (b) the individual's belief about the appropriate response to specific emotions (see Ekman, 1980; Martin, Knopoff, & Beckman, 1998). For example, in Tahiti the emotion interpreted as sadness by Western cultures is interpreted as fatigue and the expected appropriate response to this emotion differs (Levy, 1984). Also, research on culture in organizations has shown that newly hired employees watch interpersonal interactions to learn how to interpret emotion-eliciting events and to learn the norms and "display rules" that define socially acceptable responses to specific emotions in that organization (e.g., Louis, 1980; Salancik & Pfeffer, 1978).

Group cultural norms also influence individual awareness and response to emotion in groups. We label the aspect of group culture that influences awareness of emotion and response to emotion as *emotional structure*. Furthermore, because dynamics in a group occur at multiple levels including individual, group, and cross-boundary (Arrow et al., 2000), the emotional structure contains norms that influence awareness and response to emotion at each level. In sum, we propose that the emotional structure has six categories of norms. Each category influences either awareness of emotion or response to emotion at one of three levels: individual, group, or cross-boundary.

Emotionally Competent Group (ECG) Norms

The emotional structure that a group adopts determines a group's level of emotional competence, which has been defined as the willingness to acknowledge, recognize, monitor, discriminate, and attend to emotion and the ability to respond constructively to emotional challenge (see Holmer, 1994; Huy, 1999). As part of a collective emotional structure, emotional competence exists in the behaviors and interactions among group members and in those between members and relevant individuals outside the group.

Emotionally competent norms are rules and expectations within the group emotional structure that have beneficial emotional consequences through their positive influence on the development of group emotional competence and social capital (see Nahapiet & Ghoshal, 1998). Subsequently we define specific ECG norms in each of the six categories of norms we use to define an emotional structure (i.e., awareness of emotion and response to emotion—at each of three levels: individual, group, or cross-boundary). Our theory proposes that these ECG norms are linked to group effectiveness through their positive influence on the development of group social capital and effective task processes. Thus, before we present the specific ECG norms in our theory, we present a brief explanation of social capital and our definition of group effectiveness.

Social Capital

Social capital represents the value added by the structure and quality of social relationships (Nahapiet & Ghoshal, 1998). Unlike other forms of capital (e.g., financial or human), social capital is jointly held by the parties in relationship (Burt, 1992), yet, "like other forms of capital, social capital is productive, making possible the achievement of certain ends that in its absence would not be possible" (Coleman, 1988, p. 98). For example, a group within which there exists a psychological sense of safety (an element of social capital) is able to accomplish more than a comparable group in which safety does not exist.

Nahapiet and Goshal (1998) organized the elements of social capital into three dimensions: structural, relational, and cognitive. The structural dimension represents networks of connections, for example, network ties and the configuration of those ties. The relational dimension represents factors related to the quality of relationships. An example is group psychological safety, defined as the degree to which the social climate in the group is conducive to interpersonal risk (Edmondson, 1999). The cognitive dimension refers to "resources providing shared representations, interpretations, and systems of meaning" (Nahapiet & Ghoshal, 1998, p. 244). An example is group efficacy, defined as the collective belief that a group can be effective (Lindsley, Brass, & Thomas, 1995). Two features are common across all three dimensions of social capital: Each constitutes some aspect of the social structure, and each facilitates interactions that lead to desirable outcomes (Nahapiet & Ghoshal, 1998).

Group Effectiveness

Measures of group effectiveness should consider both current and future performance (Sundstrom, De Meuse, & Futrell, 1990). Groups focused exclusively on current performance run the risk of ignoring team and member well-being and development, which in the long run can impair a group's viability and performance (Hackman, 1987). Hackman (1987) proposed a multidimensional definition that defines team effectiveness as considering both customer satisfaction and a team's ability to continue working together effectively. In the studies reported here, we define group effectiveness as a multidimensional composite of productivity, work quality, performance compared with other groups, the group's ability to be self-directed, and the group's ability to continue working together effectively in the future.

THE LINK BETWEEN EMOTIONALLY COMPETENT NORMS AND GROUP EFFECTIVENESS

In the early conceptualization of our theory of ECG norms, we defined 13 norms that fit into the six categories of behaviors that represent an emotional structure (see Druskat & Wolff, 2001a, 2001b). However, our research, thus far, has examined six norms, one from each of the six categories. Thus, next we define more clearly these six emotionally competent group norms that influence awareness and response to emotion at the individual, group, and cross-boundary levels (interpersonal understanding, confronting members who break norms, team self-evaluation, proactive problem solving, and organizational understanding). We discuss why we believe each norm will be directly associated with group effectiveness.

Group Awareness of Members' Emotion

Interpersonal Understanding. A group norm of interpersonal understanding promotes group awareness of emotions at the individual member level. It encourages behavior that seeks awareness of individual member talents, preferences, needs, and feelings. Research has found that team members who feel their teammates know and understand them receive higher supervisor ratings of creativity and self-report lower levels of absenteeism than members who feel they are not known or understood (Thatcher, 2000). Another recent study found that interpersonal congruence, defined as the degree to which team members feel other members accurately know and understand them personally, was linked to high levels of social integration and group identification within the team and low levels of emotional conflict (Polzer, Milton, Swann, & William, in press). The same study also found that in teams with high levels of interpersonal congruence, team member diversity enhanced creative task performance. McAllister (1995) showed that interpersonally attentive behavior within a group helps build interpersonal trust and safety, which have been found to trigger the cooperation and knowledge sharing (Larkey, 1996; Rousseau, Sitkin, Burt, & Camerer, 1998) that increase group effectiveness (Campion, Medsker, & Higgs, 1993).

Group Management of Members' Emotion

Confronting Members Who Break Norms. A group norm of confronting members who break norms promotes group management of emotion (i.e., response to emotion) at the individual level. It encourages constructive feedback and the candid confrontation of individuals whose actions disturb group operations. The norm helps build the emotional competence and capacity (i.e., the willingness to deal with difficult emotion; see Holmer, 1994) to cope with the difficult feelings that might result from candid feedback. Groups that ignore inappropriate member behavior in an attempt to avoid conflict decrease their ability to solve problems that are often conspicuous. Avoiding conflict frequently results in hostility and reduced performance (Nemeth & Staw, 1989). Murnighan and Conlon (1991) found that members of successful string quartets confronted rather than avoided problematic member behavior. When done skillfully, confronting members who break norms builds trust and safety in the team by promoting honest, trustworthy, predictable behavior, which increases group effectiveness (Campion et al., 1993).

Awareness of Group-Level Emotion

Team Self-Evaluation. A group norm of team self-evaluation promotes group awareness of emotions and issues at the group level. It encourages behavior that seeks awareness of group-level strengths, needs, preferences, and resources. It helps build the emotional competence to address the discomfort or anxiety that often accompanies self-evaluation. A norm of team self-evaluation encourages the surfacing and evaluation of routines or habits that may be compromising team effectiveness. Evaluating the status quo is a prerequisite for positive team development and team effectiveness

(Gersick & Hackman, 1990; Louis & Sutton, 1991). The self-correction and improvement that can come out of a norm of team self-evaluation also help build a group's sense of efficacy and stimulate group effectiveness by encouraging behavior that makes group efficacy self-fulfilling (Lindsley et al., 1995; Shea & Guzzo, 1987).

Management of Group-Level Emotion

Proactive Problem Solving. A group norm of proactive problem solving promotes group management of emotion (i.e., response to emotion) at the group level. It encourages coping with problems, potential problems, or impending difficulties in a "can-do" way. It helps build the emotional competence and capacity to address potentially tough situations proactively rather than rigidly or reactively as often seen in human systems (Staw, Sandelands, & Dutton, 1981). Research has demonstrated a link between proactive behavior in teams and team effectiveness (Ancona & Caldwell, 1992). Proactive problem solving contributes to a group's sense of control over its future and its sense of efficacy, thereby facilitating group effectiveness (Campion et al., 1993; Shea & Guzzo, 1987).

Awareness of Emotion in the External Boundary

Organizational Understanding. A group norm of organizational understanding promotes group awareness of emotions and issues at the cross-boundary level. It encourages behavior that seeks information from the larger organization and that attempts to understand the needs, preferences, perspectives, and behaviors of important individuals and groups outside of the group's boundary. These preferences and feelings may be very different from the group's needs and concerns. Therefore, such behavior helps the group learn the conceptual frameworks and language used by important organizational members, a crucial step toward building networks of external relationships (Tushman & Scanlan, 1981) that can provide information, resources, and support from the larger organization (Ancona & Caldwell, 1992; Yan & Louis, 1999). Theory-building research with self-managing manufacturing teams found that the highest performing teams exhibited a norm of organizational understanding (Druskat, 1996).

Management of Emotion in the External Boundary

Building External Relationships. A group norm of building external relationships takes the awareness gained as a result of organizational understanding and promotes management of emotion when dealing with individuals and groups outside of the group's boundary. Specifically, it encourages emotionally sensitive actions that build relationships with individuals and groups that can help the group achieve its goals. Such actions have been directly linked to team effectiveness (Ancona & Caldwell, 1992; Yan & Louis, 1999). Research reveals that team effectiveness is highest in teams with strategies that involve engaging and working with colleagues in the larger organization to acquire information, resources, and support; effectiveness is lowest in teams with nonaggressive and nonexistent external boundary strategies (Ancona, 1990; Ancona & Caldwell, 1992).

TESTING OUR THEORY

We conducted two studies designed to test our theory. The first study was conducted using 382 full-time master of business administration (MBA) students, comprising 48 groups. This study tested the relation between team effectiveness and the six ECG norms discussed previously (i.e., interpersonal understanding, confronting members who break norms, team self-evaluation, proactive problem solving, organizational understanding, and building external relationships). The norms were measured with a questionnaire that we developed, piloted, and revised with two previous classes of MBA students. Performance was rated by the instructor 1 month after the norm data were collected and again 6 months after the norm data were collected. The performance rating form asked five questions about the quality of the team's work, its performance relative to teams doing similar work, and the team's ability to continue working together effectively in the future.

The results revealed that all ECG norms except confronting members who break norms were correlated with team effectiveness ratings at Time 1 (1 month after the norm measurements were taken). Correlations between ECG norms and team effectiveness ratings ranged from .36 for team self-evaluation to .56 for organizational understanding. Correlations between ECG norms and team effectiveness ratings at Time 2 (6 months after the norm measurements were taken) showed similar results except that team self-evaluation was no longer significantly correlated with performance at Time 2.

In the second study we examined the influence of ECG norms in 119 teams in six organizations located in the midwestern United States, including four Fortune 1000 firms. The sample represented diverse industries including industrial and consumer goods manufacturers, financial services, transportation, and product design and development. The average number of teams per organization was 20.7 with a range of 8 to 40. Teams had a mean of 11.95 team members (range = 4–29; median = 8).

In this study, we examined the second step of our theory. That is, we examined whether group social capital would mediate the relation between the ECG norms and team effectiveness. Specifically, we examined a structural equation model that included five ECG norms (the same as Study 1, but building relationships was not included) leading to a latent variable of social capital, that predicts the observed social capital components (trust/safety, group efficacy, and networks) and team effectiveness. The norms were measured using the same scales used in Study 1, and team effectiveness was measured using two measures: (a) The subjective performance rating scale used in Study 1 was completed by team managers two levels above the teams, and (b) objective performance scores were used (e.g., percentages of team goals met). The model was a good fit. All ECG norms predicted social capital, except that confronting members who break norms had a negative relation to social capital. Social capital predicted team effectiveness. The squared multiple correlation for performance was .25, indicating that one fourth of the variance in performance was explained by the model.

The results of these two studies partially support our group emotional competence theory, with the exception of confronting members who break norms. However, we are not yet willing to give up on this hypothesis. We believe that confronting members effectively may require training that was not provided to the teams in either of our samples. In the absence of such training, group members may have instinctively avoided confrontation or may have inappropriately confronted members.

REFINING THE THEORY AND ITS MEASUREMENT

Since conducting the research just discussed, we have worked to refine our theory and to improve and validate a survey to measure group emotional competence. Although our chapter has, thus far, discussed our examination of six specific ECG norms (i.e., interpersonal understanding, confronting members who break norms, team self-evaluation, proactive problem solving, organizational understanding, and building external relationships), our original theory proposed 13 ECG norms (see Druskat & Wolff, 2001a). The additional seven norms include perspective taking and caring behavior (individual level), seeking feedback, creating resources for working with emotion, and creating an optimistic environment (group level), and intergroup awareness and ambassadorial orientation (cross-boundary level). Thus, our first step toward theory refinement was to develop a questionnaire to measure the 13 norms and to determine, through factor analytic methods, whether they fit within the six proposed categories of norms, that is, awareness of emotion and response to emotion—at each of three levels: (a) individual, (b) group, or (c) cross-boundary.

The survey development and validation was carried out by a graduate student from Rutgers University, Christina Hamme Peterson, under the supervision of her dissertation chair, Cary Cherniss (Hamme, 2003). To develop the survey, Christina began with the items we had used in the two studies discussed earlier. Then, in close collaboration with us to ensure uniformity with the theory, she developed items to test all 13 norms. Factor analytic methods confirmed that, as expected, each of the 13 norms fit within its appropriate category. Again, these categories were composed of awareness of emotion and response to emotion—at each of three levels: (a) individual, (b) group, or (c) cross-boundary. Eight of the 13 scales were found to be reliable. The statistics suggested that we should collapse the 13 norms into nine clear and reliable norms. These nine scales also passed tests of convergent and discriminant validity when compared with other already validated scales examining similar and different team norms and processes. In other words, the ECG norm scales were moderately correlated with scales measuring similar but different group-level constructs, thus confirming the convergent validity of the scales. They also were weakly correlated with scales measuring very different group-level constructs, thus confirming the discriminant validity of the scales. Figure 10.2 presents the nine norms emerging from Christina's analyses (Hamme, 2003). More recently, we have further refined and tested the nine ECG norm scales. Those interested in the survey should contact the first or second author of this chapter.

Three Additional ECG Norms

Thus, three ECG norms have been added to the original six ECG norms defined earlier in this chapter and examined in the studies presented previously: caring behavior, creating resources for working with emotion, and creating an optimistic environment.

Caring Behavior. Caring behavior is defined as communicating positive regard, appreciation, and respect to group members. Through a caring orientation, team members communicate that the team values the presence and contributions of the recipient member. In a study of 67 work groups, Wolff (1998) found that norms of caring behavior in a team contributed to team effectiveness by increasing members' sense of safety, cohesion, and satisfaction, which in turn facilitated member engagement in the task. Kahn (1998) argued that a caring orientation builds workplace relationships that provide a "secure base" for individuals, which allows them to take risks that facilitate personal learning and development. Both Wolff (1998) and Kahn (1998) indicated that caring does not necessitate close personal relationships. It requires member validation and respect.

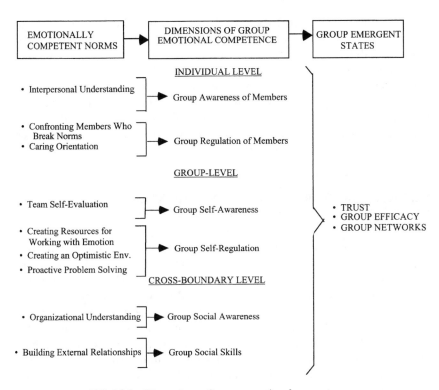

FIG. 10.2. Dimensions of group emotional competence.

Creating Resources for Working With Emotion.   A group can facilitate effective interpretation and response to emotional stimuli by providing resources that legitimize the recognition of emotional stimuli and that help members to discuss feelings (e.g., tools, time, clear mechanisms such as open discussion periods; Levy, 1984). Levy (1984) argued that individuals draw on cultural resources for their ability to process feelings; without such resources the emotion is likely to be ignored or suppressed. In individuals, suppressed emotions lead to dysfunctions such as depression (Kleinman, 1988). In groups, suppressed emotion manifests itself as apathy or lack of motivation. An emotionally competent group accepts emotions as an inherent part of group life. It legitimizes discussion of emotional issues and creates a vocabulary for discussing them.

Creating an Optimistic Environment.   Once a team has created resources for accessing and working with emotion, it must channel its energy to create an optimistic and affirmative environment. Emotions are contagious in a group setting (Barsade, 2002). Thus, constructive, positive images can have an important impact on how emotions are experienced in a group setting. Optimistic environments are defined as those that favor positive images over negative ones, which according to Cooperrider (1990) can result in positive affect, positive behavior, and positive outcomes. For example, in an optimistic environment team members are likely to interpret an unexpected obstacle as a challenge rather than a difficulty and, thus, are likely to mobilize positive energy to manage the obstacle. For example, research by Isen and her colleagues shows that a sense of optimism toward the future predisposes people toward acts that likely support continued positive affect (e.g., helping; Isen & Baron, 1991).

IMPLICATIONS FOR PRACTICE: HELPING TEAMS DEVELOP AND SUSTAIN EFFECTIVENESS

We now examine six major outcomes of augmenting current perspectives on team effectiveness and development with an understanding of group emotional competence. These outcomes include (a) reducing dependence on a manager for health of the team; (b) reducing dependence on a facilitator for development of the team; (c) using interventions that are better able to integrate task processes and emotional processes, which leads to both (d) reducing the time teams must devote to interventions and the degree to which the interventions artificially separate task work from emotional work; (e) reducing the degree to which a team focuses on symptoms of problems (e.g., resolving conflict) rather than building a sound emotional foundation that naturally results in the group's ability to effectively address problems; and (f) enhanced long-term sustainability of the benefits from interventions (i.e., as the proverb goes, the degree to which they will be able to fish rather than rely on outsiders to throw them a fish when they are in need). We examine each of these outcomes next.

Dependence on a Manager

The current paradigm of team effectiveness focuses primarily on the role of an external manager or team leader for maintaining the health of the team. Certainly, an external manager or team leader has a large impact on the team; however, teams must realize that every team member has the responsibility for his or her team's effectiveness. Knowledge about how a manager can create effective teams is vitally important; however, when this is augmented with an understanding of how every team member can help guide his or her team toward greater effectiveness, the leadership ability and energy of every team member are augmented. Group emotional competence theory provides a framework that guides the behavior of every team member including the team leader. When an understanding of group emotional competence is integrated with our understanding of the role of managers and team leaders, we reduce the team's dependency on the leaders for its effectiveness. The behavior of each member contributes to building a set of norms that influence the emotional dynamics in the group and, thus, the ability of the team to effectively accomplish its task.

Dependence on a Facilitator for Team Development

When a team encounters a problem or becomes dysfunctional, the predominant paradigm places an external facilitator at the center of the process of bringing the team back toward health. Certainly there are many cases where issues are so difficult and team members so personally involved that it takes a neutral third party to help the team through its problems. Even small issues may require a neutral facilitator when the team does not have the emotional competence to address them. For example, small differences can get blown out of proportion when the team has not developed the emotionally competent norms of caring and respect. On the other hand, a team that has developed its emotional competence could work through many issues on its own and thus be much less dependent on an outside facilitator to resolve its problems.

Integrating Task Processes and Emotional Processes

In today's extremely fast-paced business environment, we have repeatedly seen that teams are not willing to devote time to team interventions that are not directly related to task accomplishment. The current paradigm of team building generally separates team development from task accomplishment. In other words, teams learn "soft" skills such as conflict resolution or giving feedback in isolation from their actual task. Such skill building is certainly important; however, when it is isolated from actual task performance, team members may not fully grasp the relevance and may not be able to transfer the skills to actual task performance. Group emotional competence theory provides a perspective that suggests that behavior in pursuit of the task influences the development of norms that guide emotional experience. The results of building emotionally competent norms are similar to the outcome of "soft" skills training, that is, more effective interaction and stronger relationships but they are achieved by focusing team members on behavior that occurs during task accomplishment rather than developing them in isolation from the task. Thus, interventions are better able to integrate task and emotional processes.

Focusing on the Task and Not the Intervention

One result of integrating task and emotional processes is that improving task effectiveness becomes synonymous with improving emotional processes. It is not necessary, or desirable, to divert the team's attention from the task to teach them soft skills. Instead, we can teach them task behaviors that simultaneously help them build group emotional competence. This is not necessarily different from current perspectives of team building; however, group emotional competence theory more strongly highlights and reinforces the importance of focusing on the task.

Getting Below the Surface

Many current team building interventions focus on helping a team improve task processes such as decision making or problem solving. In the process, teams may be taught skills in conflict resolution, negotiation, and integrating diverse perspectives. The current paradigm for building team task skills is useful; however, it must be complemented with an understanding that a team first needs to build an emotional foundation. Current interventions, although helpful, tend to focus on the mechanics of task processes but tend to ignore the underlying emotional processes that form the foundation required for a team to use them effectively. For example, a team can be taught the mechanics of decision making and the importance of openly sharing information; however, the effectiveness with which they can carry out these processes depends on their emotional competence. Sharing information requires a degree of trust and safety that results from emotional processes in the group. We believe that much training is not sustainable and fails to meet its potential because the group does not have the emotional competence necessary to make it successful over the long run. Group emotional competence theory helps us understand that we must first build the necessary foundation that task processes need to take hold.

Teaching Teams to Fish

When we create dependence on a manager, team leader, or facilitator and teach task processes without providing the emotional foundation, we fail to provide the team the tools it needs to sustain an ability to continually learn, improve, and address obstacles. We also fail to harness the responsibility of all team members to move the team in an effective direction. When something goes wrong, a leader or facilitator is expected to provide an intervention. It is a reactive process rather than a proactive one. A proactive process would expect the team to be responsible for understanding and working through its issues. It would teach the team the skills to understand its obstacles and move through them on its own. It would teach the team to take responsibility for its own effectiveness. In essence, when the team is emotionally hungry, our current perspectives lead to the proverbial equivalent of throwing it a fish. The theory of group emotional competence helps us understand how to focus the team such that it can satiate its own emotional hunger; that is, it helps us understand how to teach them to fish in the emotional waters inherent in group life and become self-sufficient in meeting its emotional needs. We teach them to recognize their emotional processes and how to build norms that help them build effective task processes and deal with obstacles that hinder performance.

CONCLUSION

We believe our theory takes knowledge of group effectiveness one step closer toward explaining how to build and sustain effective teams. Although several current theories describe the kind of behaviors a group needs to display to be effective, they have not been fully useful for practicing managers interested in knowing how to build those behaviors (Cannon-Bowers et al., 1995; Cohen & Bailey, 1997). We propose that building effective groups requires building group trust/safety, group efficacy, and group networks. We further suggest that the emotional structure a group produces is critical to building these effective emergent states.

Our theory of group emotional competence has clear implications for team development. We define a set of norms that form an emotional structure to guide behavior such that the emotional experience of the group builds social capital. Norms are developed through the behavior and interaction of each and every group member. This implies that every member has a responsibility for the health of his or her team.

Our theory and research suggest that understanding the mechanics of task processes may not be sufficient for developing and sustaining team effectiveness. We reveal that social capital (group trust/safety, group efficacy, and group networks) underlies the ability of the team to efficiently perform the task. Because ECG norms facilitate the emergence of social capital, the interventions required to build team effectiveness become clear. Specifically, our theory and research suggest that before training a team in the mechanical processes necessary for task completion, team members must understand how to build an emotional structure conducive to task accomplishment.

Training a group to develop ECG norms involves training team members to influence group norms. As discussed throughout this chapter, norms represent a habitual way of operating in a team. This means that training should focus on helping teams build effective habits. One means of doing this is to provide them with tools that capture attention and focus behavior on desired patterns of behavior.

REFERENCES

Alsop, R. (2003). MBA programs focus on leadership skills. *College Journal from the Wall Street Journal* [online serial]. Retrieved August 5, 2004, from http://www.collegejournal.com.

Ancona, D. G. (1990). Outward bound: Strategies for team survival in the organization. *Academy of Management Journal, 33,* 334–365.

Ancona, D. G., & Caldwell, D. F. (1992). Bridging the boundary: External activity and performance in organizational teams. *Administrative Science Quarterly, 37,* 634–665.

Arrow, H., McGrath, J. E., & Berdahl, J. L. (2000). *Small groups as complex systems: Formation, coordination, development, and adaptation.* Thousand Oaks, CA: Sage.

Bales, R. F. (1950). *Interaction process analysis: A method for the study of small groups.* Chicago: University of Chicago Press.

Barsade, S. G. (2002). The ripple effect: Emotional contagion in groups. *Administrative Science Quarterly, 47*(4), 644–675.

Burt, R. S. (1992). *Structural holes: The social structure of competition.* Cambridge, MA: Harvard University Press.

Campion, M. A., Medsker, G. J., & Higgs, A. C. (1993). Relations between work group characteristics and effectiveness: Implications for designing effective work groups. *Personnel Psychology, 46,* 823–850.

Cannon-Bowers, J. A., Tannenbaum, S. I., Salas, E., & Volpe, C. E. (1995). Defining competencies and establishing team training requirements. In R. A. Guzzo, E. Salas, & Associates (Eds.), *Team effectiveness and decision making in organizations* (pp. 333–380). San Francisco: Jossey-Bass.

Cohen, S. G., & Bailey, D. E. (1997). What makes teams work: Group effectiveness research from the shop floor to the executive suite. *Journal of Management, 23*(3), 239–290.

Coleman, J. S. (1988). Social capital in the creation of human capital. *American Journal of Sociology, 94,* 95–120.

Cooperrider, D. L. (1990). Positive image, positive action: The affirmative basis of organizing. In S. Srivastva, D. L. Cooperrider, & Associates (Eds.), *Appreciative management and leadership: The power of positive thought and action in organizations* (pp. 91–125). San Francisco: Jossey-Bass.

Druskat, V. U. (1996). *A team competency study of self-managed manufacturing teams.* Unpublished doctoral dissertation, Boston University.

Druskat, V. U., & Wolff, S. B. (2001a). Building the emotional intelligence of groups. *Harvard Business Review, 79*(3), 81–90.

Druskat, V. U., & Wolff, S. B. (2001b). Group emotional competence and its influence on group effectiveness. In C. Cherniss & D. Goleman (Eds.), *Emotional competence in organizations* (pp. 132–155). San Francisco: Jossey-Bass.

Edmondson, A. (1999). Psychological safety and learning behavior in work teams. *Administrative Science Quarterly, 44*(2), 350–383.

Ekman, P. (1980). *The face of man. Expressions of universal emotions in a New Guinea village.* New York: Garland STPM Press.

Farren, C. (1999). A smart team makes the difference. *The Human Resource Professional, 12*(1).

Feldman, D. C. (1984). The development and enforcement of group norms. *Academy of Management Review, 9,* 47–53.

Fineman, S. (1991). *Emotion and organizing.* Thousand Oaks, CA: Sage.

George, J. M. (2002). Affect regulation in groups and teams. In R. G. Lord, R. J. Klimoski, & R. Kanfer (Eds.), *Emotions in the workplace* (pp. 183–217). San Francisco: Jossey-Bass.

Gersick, C. J. G., & Hackman, J. R. (1990). Habitual routines in task-performing groups. *Organizational Behavior and Human Decision Processes, 47,* 65–97.

Guzzo, R. A., & Dickson, M. W. (1996). Teams in organizations: Recent research on performance and effectiveness. *Annual Review of Psychology, 47,* 307–338.

Hackman, J. R. (1987). The design of work teams. In J. W. Lorsch (Ed.), *Handbook of organizational behavior* (pp. 315–342). Englewood Cliffs, NJ: Prentice-Hall.

Hamme, C. (2003). *Group emotional intelligence: The research and development of an assessment instrument.* Unpublished doctoral dissertation, Rutgers University, New Brunswick, NJ.

Holmer, L. L. (1994). Developing emotional capacity and organizational health. In R. H. Kilmann, I. Kilmann, & Associates (Eds.), *Managing ego energy: The transformation of personal meaning into organizational success* (pp. 49–72). San Francisco: Jossey-Bass.

Homans, G. (1950). *The human group.* New York: Harcourt Brace Jovanovich.

Huy, Q. N. (1999). Emotional capability, emotional intelligence, and radical change. *Academy of Management Review, 24*(2), 325–345.

Ilgen, D. R., Fisher, C. D., & Taylor, S. M. (1979). Consequences of individual feedback on behavior in organizations. *Journal of Applied Psychology, 64*(4), 349–371.

Isen, A. M., & Baron, R. A. (1991). Positive affect as a factor in organizational behavior. *Research in Organizational Behavior, 13,* 1–53.

Kahn, W. A. (1998). Relational systems at work. In L. L. Cummings & B. M. Staw (Eds.), *Research in organizational behavior* (Vol. 20, pp. 39–76). Stamford, CT: JAI.

Kemper, T. D. (1978). *A social interactional theory of emotions.* New York: Wiley.

Keyton, J. (1999). Relational communication in groups. In L. F. Frey, D. S. Gouran, & M. S. Poole (Eds.), *The handbook of group communication theory and research* (pp. 192–222). Thousand Oaks, CA: Sage.

Kleinman, A. (1988). *Rethinking psychiatry: From cultural category to personal experience.* New York: Free Press.

Larkey, L. K. (1996). Toward a theory of communicative interactions in culturally diverse workgroups. *Academy of Management Review, 21*(2), 463–491.

Lawler, E. E., III. (1998). *Strategies for high performance organizations.* San Francisco: Jossey-Bass.

Lazarus, R. S. (1991). Progress on a cognitive-motivational-relational theory of emotion. *American Psychologist, 46,* 819–834.

Levy, R. I. (1984). Emotion, knowing, and culture. In R. A. Sweder & R. A. LeVine (Eds.), *Culture theory: Essays on mind, self, and emotion* (pp. 214–237). Cambridge, England: Cambridge University Press.

Lindsley, D. H., Brass, D. J., & Thomas, J. B. (1995). Efficacy performance spirals: A multilevel perspective. *Academy of Management Review, 20*(3), 645–678.

Louis, M. R. (1980). Surprise and sense making: What new-comers experience in entering unfamiliar organizational settings. *Administrative Science Quarterly, 25*(2), 226–251.

Louis, M. R., & Sutton, R. I. (1991). Switching cognitive gears: From habits of mind to active thinking. *Human Relations, 44*(1), 55–76.

Martin, J., Knopoff, K., & Beckman, C. (1998). An alternative to bureaucratic impersonality and emotional labor: Bounded emotionality at The Body Shop. *Administrative Science Quarterly, 43,* 429–469.

McAllister, D. J. (1995). Affect- and cognition-based trust as foundations for interpersonal cooperation in organizations. *Academy of Management Journal, 38*(1), 24–59.

Morgeson, F. P., & Hofmann, D. A. (1999). The structure and function of collective constructs: Implications for multilevel research and theory development. *Academy of Management Review, 24*(2), 249–265.

Murnighan, J. K., & Conlon, D. E. (1991). The dynamics of intense work groups: A study of British string quartets. *Administrative Science Quarterly, 36,* 165–186.

Nahapiet, J., & Ghoshal, S. (1998). Social capital, intellectual capital, and the organizational advantage. *Academy of Management Review, 23*(2), 242–266.

Nemeth, C. J., & Staw, B. M. (1989). The tradeoffs of social control and innovation in groups and organizations. In L. Berkowitz (Ed.), *Advances in experimental social psychology* (Vol. 22, pp. 175–210). New York: Academic.

Plutchik, R. (2003). *Emotions and life: Perspectives from psychology, biology, and evolution.* Washington, DC: American Psychological Association.

Polzer, J. T., Milton, L. P., Swann, J., & William, B. (in press). Capitalizing on diversity: Interpersonal congruence in small work groups. *Administrative Science Quarterly.*

Poole, M. S. (1999). Group communication theory. In L. F. Frey, D. S. Gouran, & M. S. Poole (Eds.), *The handbook of group communication theory and research* (pp. 88–165). Thousand Oaks, CA: Sage.

Rousseau, D. M., Sitkin, S. B., Burt, R. S., & Camerer, C. (1998). Not so different after all: A cross-discipline view of trust. *Academy of Management Review, 23*(3), 393–404.

Salancik, G. R., & Pfeffer, J. (1978). A social information processing approach to job attitudes and task design. *Administrative Science Quarterly, 22,* 427–456.

Schein, E. H. (1993, Winter). How can organizations learn faster? The challenge of entering the green room. *Sloan Management Review,* pp. 85–92.

Shea, G. P., & Guzzo, R. A. (1987). Group effectiveness: What really matters? *Sloan Management Review, 28,* 25–31.

Staw, B. M., Sandelands, L. E., & Dutton, J. E. (1981). Threat-rigidity effects in organizational behavior: A multilevel analysis. *Administrative Science Quarterly, 26,* 501–524.

Sundstrom, E., De Meuse, K. P., & Futrell, D. (1990). Work teams: Applications and effectiveness. *American Psychologist, 45*(2), 120–133.

Thatcher, S. M. B. (2000). *Does it matter if you really know me? The implications of idenity fit on individuals working in diverse organizational teams.* Paper presented at the Annual Meeting of the Academy of Management, Toronto.

Tuckman, B. W. (1965). Developmental sequence in small groups. *Psychological Bulletin, 63,* 384–399.

Tushman, M. L., & Scanlan, T. J. (1981). Boundary spanning individuals: Their role in information transfer and their antecedents. *Academy of Management Journal, 24,* 289–305.

Weick, K. E., & Roberts, K. H. (1993). Collective mind in organizations: Heedful interrelating on flight decks. *Administrative Science Quarterly, 38,* 357–381.

Wolff, S. B. (1998). *The role of caring behavior and peer feedback in creating team effectiveness.* Unpublished dissertation, Boston University.

Wolff, S. B., & Druskat, V. U. (2004). *Toward a socioemotional theory of work group effectiveness.* Unpublished manuscript.

Yan, A., & Louis, M. R. (1999). The migration of organizational functions to the work unit level: Buffering, spanning and bringing up boundaries. *Human Relations, 52*(1), 25–47.

Part III

THE AGENDA FOR FUTURE RESEARCH AND PRACTICE: What We Know and Still Need to Know About the Link Between Emotional Intelligence and Work Performance

Chapter 11

A Practitioner's Research Agenda: Exploring Real-World Applications and Issues

Marilyn K. Gowing
Aon Consulting

Brian S. O'Leary[1]
U.S. Office of Personnel Management

Dottie Brienza
Ethicon

Kathleen Cavallo
Corporate Consulting Group

Ronald Crain[2]
Defense Finance and Accounting Service

It has been our privilege to serve as members of the Consortium for Research on Emotional Intelligence in Organizations (CREIO) largely since its inception by founders and co-chairs Dr. Cary Cherniss and Dr. Daniel Goleman. The first author was initially invited to participate in the consortium as she was serving as director of the Personnel Resources and Development Center of the U.S. Office of Personnel Management (OPM), which was, at the time, the largest civilian psychological research center in the federal government. OPM is the corporate human resource policy office for approximately 1.7 million federal government employees. The second author headed the federal government testing program for many years, overseeing the research in social skill assessment. Dottie Brienza and Ron Crain served as organizational consortium members representing Johnson & Johnson and the Defense Finance and Accounting Service (DFAS), respectively. Ms. Brienza is now with Ethicon, a Johnson & Johnson Company, and Mr. Crain is still the Human

---

[1]The views expressed in this article are those of the author and do not reflect the official policy or views of the U.S. Office of Personnel Management.

[2]The views expressed in this article are those of the author and do not reflect the official policy or views of the Defense Finance and Accounting Service.

Resource Director for DFAS. Dr. Cavallo, while not a member of the EI Consortium, assisted Ms. Brienza and Matthew Mangino, the other J&J representative, with the research presented in this chapter.

Because we are practitioner members on the consortium, other practitioners frequently seek our guidance when a CEO or agency head determines that emotional intelligence (EI) should be integrated into the leadership selection and development programs for their organizations. Earlier chapters of this book have addressed this issue and others; however, in this chapter, we intend to provide practitioners with guidance on what steps need to be taken to bring emotional intelligence into their organizations. We provide descriptions of a series of real-world applications and the resulting business issues that emerged. In each case, let us be clear, that although our focus is on application (i.e., how you do it), there is always an underlying research foundation. We conclude this chapter by providing some recommendations regarding future directions for a practitioner's research agenda.

The CREIO mission is "to aid the advancement of research and practice related to emotional intelligence in organizations." The consortium encourages its organizational members to undertake research projects to chart new territory in the application of emotional intelligence in organizations. In this chapter, we present a number of these research partnerships undertaken by consortium organizational members. These include the following:

- OPM's Senior Executive Service Competency Model
- Johnson & Johnson's (J&J) Leadership Competency Model
- The Defense Finance and Accounting Service's (DFAS) EI Professional and Leadership Certification Program
- OPM's EI Index for Emotionally Intelligent Organizations

OPM'S SENIOR EXECUTIVE SERVICE (SES) COMPETENCY MODEL

Developing the SES Competency Model

In the late 1980s, the U.S. Office of Personnel Management developed a model of quality service suggesting that organizational outputs and outcomes are determined by the individual competencies of the leaders, the workforce, and the organizational culture (see Fig. 11.1). In 1991, OPM reviewed the management and leadership literature from both the public and the private sectors hoping to identify competencies that differentiated effective leaders (Corts & Gowing, 1992) from those that were less effective. The results of this literature review (knowledge, skills and abilities, and associated behaviors) were incorporated into a survey distributed to a strati-

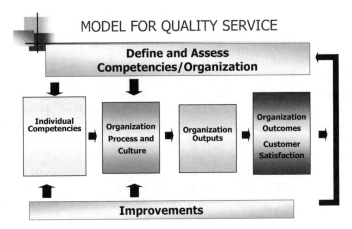

FIG. 11.1. Model for quality service.

fied, random sample of 20,000 supervisors, managers, and executives in the federal government. Responses from 10,000 led to the development of the Leadership Effectiveness Framework with 22 managerial competencies (Gregory & Park, 1992). This framework identified basic competencies that were common to all three management levels, as well as those designated first-level competencies (supervisors), midlevel competencies (managers), and higher level competencies (executives).

In 1996, OPM decided to revisit the Leadership Effectiveness Framework and involved panels of 41 experts from 17 different agencies and departments. These panels resulted in the identification of 27 competencies that were later grouped into five meta-competencies: leading change, leading people, results driven, business acumen, and building coalitions/communication (Eyde, Gregory, Muldrow, & Mergen, 1999; see also Rodriguez, Patel, Bright, Gregory, & Gowing, 2002). These meta-competencies have served as the basis for selecting, developing, and even evaluating the nearly 7,000 members of the Senior Executive Service across more than 100 agencies and departments.

Questioning the Competency Model

Despite the empirical foundation of this competency model, numerous entities have questioned whether the government is measuring the right things (e.g., National Academy of Public Administration, 2003). The National Commission on Public Service (2003) concluded, "In the 21st century, government touches every American's life. It affects, often profoundly, the way we live and work. So we have a deep and growing concern that our public service and the organization of our government are in such disarray" (p. 1). In 2002, OPM distributed the Federal Human Capital Survey to more than 200,000 employees. Of the 106,742 respondents (51% response rate), only 36% said that their leaders "generate high levels of motivation and commitment in the workforce" and 43% held their leaders in high regard. The Gallup Organization, in its revolutionary book, *First, Break All the Rules* (Buckingham & Coffman, 1999), suggested that employee commitment and retention are influenced by the employee's immediate manager. Although a number of factors determine commitment (knowing work expectations, having the needed materials and equipment, having the opportunity to do what I do best every day, having one's opinions count), one item in particular, "Does my supervisor, or someone at work, seem to care about me as a person?" (p. 34) plays an important role. Similarly in Gallup's follow-up study with 80,000 managers appearing in the same book, the authors conclude that "a willingness to individualize" (p. 12) one employee at a time made all the difference in successful leadership. Effective leaders, they concluded, "recognize that each person is motivated differently, that each person has his own way of thinking and his own style of relating to others" (p. 56). This differentiating ability of effective leaders reflects the essence of emotional intelligence.

Aligning the SES Competency Model With the EI Competencies

The first step in aligning any organizational leadership model to the EI competencies is to construct a crosswalk of the two competency frameworks. OPM has done just that and developed a Leadership Competency Crosswalk to Emotional Intelligence (see Fig. 11.2).

This crosswalk suggests that the EI competency model is fully covered by the Senior Executive Service leadership competency model with the one exception of emotional awareness under self-awareness (or "recognizing one's emotions and their effects"). So how do we explain the recent results from the Federal Human Capital Survey if there is almost a perfect crosswalk between the SES Competency Model and the Goleman EI Competency Model?

We can think of several possible explanations and you may think of still others. One possible explanation is that the crosswalk may show some generic linkages across competencies with similar labels while missing important differences and nuances in the behavioral operational definitions of those competencies. A second possible explanation is that the Executive Core Qualifications (ECQs) used to select, train, develop, and evaluate members of the Senior Executive Service are too far removed from the basic competency definitions and no longer reflect the essential behavioral components of emotional intelligence. A third possibility is that although the definitions of the ECQs may have sufficient coverage of the EI competencies, that coverage is lost through the actual selection process for senior execu-

Self-Regulation

EI	OPM
Self-Control	Resilience
Trustworthiness	Integrity/Honesty
Conscientiousness	Accountability
Adaptability	Flexibility
Innovativeness	Creativity and Innovation

Social Skills

EI	OPM
Influence	Influencing/Negotiating
Communication	Oral Communication
	Written Communication
	Interpersonal Skills
Leadership	Team Building
	Vision
Change Catalyst	Vision
	Entrepreneurship
Conflict Management	Conflict management
Building Bonds	Interpersonal Skills Partnering
Collaboration and Cooperation	Team Building
Team Capabilities	Team Building

Self Awareness

EI	OPM
Emotional Awareness	None directly apply
Accurate Self-Assessment	Continual Learning
Self-Confidence	Resilience

Social Awareness

EI	OPM
Empathy	Interpersonal Skills
Service Orientation	Customer Service
Developing Others	Team Building
Leveraging Diversity	Leveraging Diversity
Political Awareness	Political Savvy

Self-Motivation

EI	OPM
Achievement Drive	Accountability
	Continual Learning
Commitment	Service Motivation
Initiative	Entrepreneurship
	Decisiveness
Optimism	Resilience

FIG. 11.2. OPM's Leadership Competency Crosswalk to Emotional Intelligence.

tives. The federal government requires applicants to write summaries of their past experience relating to the ECQs. These descriptions are rated and ranked. Typically, such training and experience ratings are among the least valid of all possible selection procedures (see Table 1 in O'Leary, Lindholm, Whitford, & Freeman, 2002). Table 11.1 reveals that work samples have much greater validity, and with the advent of the information age, it is now possible to construct miniature offices on computer (e-mail, pagers, voice mail, video mail) and on telephone, providing a realistic job preview for candidates and a valid assessment of the leadership competencies of the candidates ("Distractions Make Global Manager a Difficult Role," 2000).

We have hypothesized for a long time that effective administrators require a combination of technical, conceptual, and human skills (Katz, 1974). The research on executives by the Center for Creative Leadership has certainly suggested that intellectual skills are not sufficient to avoid derailment (McCall, 1988). This research was corroborated in a more recent survey of most admired and peer Fortune 500 companies (see Fig. 11.3; Hay, 1999). The work of Gallup and others (Collins, 2001; Goleman, Boyatzis, & McKee, 2002; Rosen, 1996) establishes the relation between the emotional competence of the leader and organizational effectiveness. Clearly, OPM is headed in the right direction by mapping its competencies with those of the EI framework. The next steps must be to ensure the accu-

TABLE 11.1
Validity of Common Selection Procedures
in the Prediction of Overall Job Performance

Assembled Procedures	Validity	Unassembled Procedures	Validity
1. Work sample[a]	.54	1. Peer ratings[a]	.49
2. General mental ability	.51	2. Behavioral consistency or	
3. Structured interview	.51	achievement record	.45
4. Job knowledge[a]	.48	3. Reference checks[a]	.26
5. Job tryout[a]	.44	4. Job experience (years)	.18
6. Integrity	.41	5. Training and experience point	
7. Unstructured interview	.38	method	.11
8. Assessment center	.37	6. Years of education	.10
9. Biodata	.35	7. Interests	.10
10. Conscientiousness	.31	8. Graphology	.02
		9. Age	−.01

Note. Unless otherwise noted, all of the validities in this table are corrected for the downward bias due to measurement error in the measurement of job performance and range restriction on the predictor in incumbent samples relative to applicant populations. From Schmidt and Hunter (1998, Table 1). Copyright 1998 by the American Psychological Association. Adapted with permission of the author.

[a]Corrected only for the downward bias due to measurement error in the measure of job performance. Range restriction data not available. Reproduced from O'Leary et al. (2002).

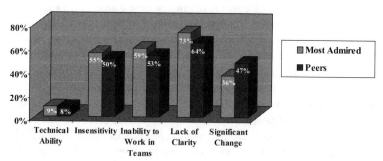

Derailment of Leaders
What has caused or causes your 'High Potentials' to derail (i.e., no longer considered as high potentials)?

- **Hay 1999 Survey of Fortune 500 companies**

FIG. 11.3. Derailment of leaders.

racy of those linkages in terms of specific behaviors and to ensure that the most valid assessments available today are used to evaluate all leadership competencies.

EMOTIONAL INTELLIGENCE AND THE JOHNSON & JOHNSON LEADERSHIP COMPETENCY MODEL

The Johnson & Johnson Consumer and Personal Care Group, a division of Johnson & Johnson, an EI Consortium organizational member, undertook a two year project aimed at determining the significance of EI in leadership success. They also assessed opportunities for integrating the most relevant EI competencies into their Standards of Leadership competency model.

It's important to understand the context within which this project was undertaken. Johnson & Johnson describes itself as a "family of companies." The J&J enterprise is made up of many individual business units, or companies, that operate in a highly decentralized environment established to inspire entrepreneurship and reduce corporate bureaucracy. There is an overarching culture across these companies, based on the well-known J&J Credo, and the Standards of Leadership (SOL). Although each of the individual companies has its own unique "personality," the Credo and SOL function as beacons guiding the organization. The Credo, crafted in the mid 1990s, is J&J's statement of values, ethics, and broad mission that drives decision-making to this day. It is expected that all employees "live" the Credo.

Layered under the Credo are the Standards of Leadership (SOL), an internally developed leadership competency model. The SOL identifies 6 Core Capability Clusters: Credo Values/Business Results, Customer & Marketplace Focus, Complexity & Change, Organizational & People Development, Innovation, and Collaboration. The SOL, like the Credo, was firmly integrated into the assessment, selection, and development activities throughout the organization.

In 1998, Dan Goleman's HBR article, "What Makes a Leader," struck a chord with members of the J&J management board. Ralph Larson, the Chairman of J&J at the time, was highly interested in J&J's leadership having a better understanding of how the EI Competencies that Goleman identified as vital to leadership success, could be capitalized upon. Simultaneously, Human Resources staff and business leaders of the Consumer & Personal Care (C&PC) Group were interested in finding out how Goleman's EI competencies related to the SOL and how they could better identify and develop leaders. The Chairman of the C&PC Group sponsored research in this area.

The research objectives were twofold; first to determine if the EI competencies were captured in the J&J SOL competency model, and second, to assess if the EI competencies did in fact, distinguish high performers as

Goleman and others had suggested. The plan at the outset of the project was to address any gaps in the SOL if the research demonstrated that the EI competencies did distinguish high performers and high potentials.

The project had several distinct phases. In Phase 1, an expert panel was pulled together to conduct a comparison study, a Delphi, between the SOL competency model and the Goleman Model of Emotional Intelligence, to see if the EI Competencies were captured in the SOL. The Delphi technique is a way of structuring the observations or opinions across members of the expert group in order to arrive at a group consensus. Using this procedure, a number of gaps in EI were identified in the SOL model. In phase 2, a multi-rater survey was constructed combining the items or behavioral indices in the SOL model with the items in the research version of the Emotional Competency Inventory (ECI) (Boyatzis, Goleman, & Hay/McBer, 1999). This blending of the two surveys yielded a 183 question multi-rater survey that was distributed to a sample of approximately 450 leaders across the globe. Although participants were randomly selected, the sample was controlled for years of service and gender and regional distribution. Participants had to have a minimum of two years experience in a management position at J&J. Gender and regional distribution of participants was representative of C&PC organizational statistics: 55% were male and 45% female; approximately 20% were from Asia-Pacific, 25% from Europe, 15% from Latin America, and 40% from North America. Participants selected at least one supervisor and four additional raters to complete the multi-rater survey. Data was received on 373 of the 450 leaders (83%). In total, one thousand and thirty (1,030) raters completed the multi-rater survey.

A correlation study between the items from the SOL and the items from the ECI confirmed the Delphi findings that there were several EI gaps in the SOL model. However, before additions to the SOL model were contemplated, it was important to confirm that the EI competencies did distinguish high performers from average performers. Next, we moved into Phase 3 of the study which compared performance and potential ratings with scores on the survey.

Regional human resource representatives provided performance and potential ratings data for a two-year period on the participants. Participants were identified as high performing if their ratings were in the "exceeds expectations" category. In addition, individuals were identified as high potential or not based on their immediate potential to move up 2 or more levels.

The results were supportive of Goleman's suggestion that EI differentiated strong performance. Six (6) competencies were found to distinguish high performing leaders across the three rater groups, Supervisor, Peer, and Direct Report. There was strong inter-rater agreement that the competencies of Self-Confidence, Achievement Orientation, Initiative, Leadership, Influence and Change Catalyst differentiated superior performers.

This finding is strikingly similar to the conclusions reached by McClelland (1998), that found the most powerful leadership differentiators were Self-Confidence, Achievement Drive, Developing Others, Adaptability, Influence and Leadership.

Results further showed that high performing leaders were rated significantly higher by Supervisors and Direct Reports in all four of the EI dimensions: Self-Awareness, Self-Management, Social Awareness, and Social Skills. Peers rated the high performers higher in Self-Awareness and Self-Management. Overall, of the 20 distinct EI competencies measured, Direct Reports rated the high performers higher on 17, the Supervisors rated them higher on 14, and peers rated them higher on 9 (Cavallo & Brienza, 2001).

The results in terms of distinguishing high potential leaders were not as robust across the rater groups. Direct Reports rated high potential managers slightly higher in only 1 of the 20 competencies, Conscientiousness,

TABLE 11.2
J&J Study: Mean Scores on ECI by Performance Rating

Cluster or Competency	Supervisor		Peer		Direct Report	
	Over 4.0	4.0 or Less	Over 4.0	4.0 or Less	Over 4.0	4.0 or Less
Self-awareness	92.6**	83.7**	91.0*	85.6*	91.5*	85.0*
Emotional self-awareness	16.1	15.2	16.0	15.7	15.2	15.2
Accurate self-assessment	34.7*	31.6*	33.4	32.0	33.7	31.9
Self-confidence	40.8*	37.1*	41.8***	37.9***	41.7***	37.8***
Self-management	175.2**	159.4**	171.6**	160.5**	173.8**	160.6**
Self-control	20.8	20.4	21.4	20.7	21.8*	20.1*
Trustworthiness	24.1*	22.5*	22.3	21.9	22.8*	21.3*
Conscientiousness	30.7	28.9	30.0	28.7	30.2	29.0
Adaptability	28.5**	26.3**	27.1	25.8	27.7**	25.8**
Achievement orientation	35.6**	31.4**	34.7**	32.3**	34.8**	32.3**
Initiative	34.8**	31.2**	34.7**	31.4**	34.3**	31.4**
Social awareness	63.0*	57.8*	61.5	59.6	62.8**	57.9**
Empathy	40.2*	36.8*	38.0	37.7	38.9*	35.6*
Organizational awareness	22.6	20.8	23.8***	21.7***	24.0**	22.3**
Social skills	306.3**	273.0**	297.3	284.4	300.4**	272.9**
Developing others	28.4	26.1	28.4*	26.7*	28.4*	26.3*
Service orientation	41.1*	37.3*	39.5	37.6	40.4*	37.6*
Leadership	23.4**	19.6**	22.1**	20.5**	22.0***	19.7***
Influence	39.4**	34.8**	39.2**	36.3**	39.5**	36.0**
Communication	32.0	29.7	33.1*	30.9*	33.4*	31.3*
Change catalyst	40.4***	35.3***	39.4**	35.0**	39.7**	36.6**
Conflict management	27.8*	25.5*	27.4	26.0	27.3*	25.1*
Building bonds	23.5*	21.0*	22.9	21.7	23.5***	21.2***
Teamwork and collaboration	47.2*	43.0*	45.4	43.8	46.1*	42.5*

Note. High Performers received performance ratings of 4.1 or higher on a 5.0 point scale.
$*p < .05$. $**p < .01$. $***p < .001$. K. Cavallo & D. Brienza (2001).

while Peers rated high potentials higher on 6 of the 20 competencies measured, and Supervisors rated the high potentials higher on 13 of the 20 EI competencies. It is likely that Supervisors' ability to recognize high potentials may result from their ongoing involvement in attracting and developing talent, succession planning, and assessment of talent to determine actual potential ratings. It's also likely that high potential individuals make an effort to demonstrate each capability to their Supervisors in an attempt to influence their opinion regarding their promotability and future potential.

Another interesting finding is around gender. Consistent with other research findings, there were few gender differences found. However, Supervisors rated females higher in Adaptability and Service Orientation, while Peers rated Females higher on Emotional Self-Awareness, Conscientiousness, Developing Others, Service Orientation, and Communication. Direct reports scored Males higher in Change Catalyst. Research concerning gender difference in leadership performance has found little evidence to sug-

TABLE 11.3
J&J Study: Mean Ratings on ECI by Potential

Cluster or Competency	Supervisor		Peer		Direct Report	
	High Potential	Average Potential	High Potential	Average Potential	High Potential	Average Potential
Self-awareness	87.6***	80.7***	86.9	84.6	86.5	86.1
Emotional self-awareness	15.8	15.1	15.6	15.8	15.6	15.6
Accurate self-assessment	32.6**	30.7**	32.4	31.6	32.3	32.3
Self-confidence	38.9***	35.0***	39.1**	37.1**	38.7	38.0
Self-management	164.4***	154.9***	162.8*	157.2*	161.6	163.2
Self-control	20.8	20.1	20.4	20.7	20.7	20.2
Trustworthiness	22.4	22.0	21.5	21.6	21.5	21.9
Conscientiousness	29.4	28.4	29.1	28.5	29.6*	28.5*
Adaptability	26.3**	24.6**	26.1	25.6	26.1	26.1
Achievement orientation	32.7***	30.0***	33.1***	31.3***	33.0	32.0
Initiative	32.4***	29.8***	32.2**	30.7**	31.8	31.4
Social awareness	58.5	57.1	59.0	59.2	59.8	58.7
Empathy	37.1	36.7	37.0	37.4	37.0	36.5
Organizational awareness	21.3	20.3	22.1	21.7	22.8	22.2
Social skills	280.7*	264.6*	284.1	278.5	280.7	279.0
Developing others	26.8*	25.2*	26.6	26.3	27.0	26.6
Service orientation	38.1*	36.0*	37.7	37.5	38.7	37.8
Leadership	20.9**	19.3**	21.1**	20.0**	20.5	20.0
Influence	35.9*	33.9*	36.6	36.0	37.2	36.4
Communication	30.6*	28.9*	31.4	30.7	32.1	31.2
Change catalyst	36.8**	34.1**	37.1*	35.5*	37.4	36.7
Conflict management	26.2*	25.0*	26.2	25.4	25.9	25.3
Building bonds	21.9***	20.2***	21.7	21.5	22.0	21.5
Teamwork and collaboration	44.0	42.2	43.7	43.2	43.5	43.2

*$p < .05$. **$p < .01$. ***$p < .001$. K. Cavallo & D. Brienza (2001).

gest that males and females differ in their leadership effectiveness (Landau, 1996; Eagly et al., 1992, 1995; Ragins, 1991). In particular, several studies have demonstrated that there is little to no difference in satisfaction levels of Subordinates of either male or female leaders (Carless, 1998; Ragins, 1991; Osborn & Vicars, 1976). The findings of the current study support this research. However, some studies suggest that the style by which males and females lead has consistently been found to be different. A meta-analysis conducted by Eagly and Johnson (1990) found females to have better social skills and to be described as "interested in other people." Women leaders as a group, when compared to male leaders as a group, tend to be described as more friendly, pleasant, and socially sensitive (as cited in Eagly & Johnson, 1990). This finding is consistent with the current study, showing higher scores for females in several of the interpersonal and social competencies measured.

Based on the results of the research in Phases 1–3, the research moved into Phase 4 of the project, the integration of EI into the SOL model and

TABLE 11.4
J&J Study: Mean Ratings on ECI by Gender

Cluster or Competency	Supervisor		Peer		Direct Report	
	Male	Female	Male	Female	Male	Female
Self-awareness	82.8	85.0	84.5*	87.4*	86.5	86.0
Emotional self-awareness	15.2	15.6	15.3***	16.4***	15.5	15.7
Accurate self-assessment	31.5	31.7	31.8	32.3	32.6	31.9
Self-confidence	36.1	37.6	37.5	38.7	38.4	38.4
Self-management	157.4	161.7	159.5	160.5	162.2	162.6
Self-control	20.3	20.6	20.5	20.5	20.7	20.2
Trustworthiness	22.3	22.0	21.6	21.5	21.7	21.7
Conscientiousness	28.5	29.4	28.3**	29.5**	29.0	29.1
Adaptability	24.9*	26.1*	25.6	26.1	26.2	25.9
Achievement orientation	31.0	31.6	31.9	32.5	32.8	32.1
Initiative	30.7	31.3	31.1	31.9	31.8	31.2
Social awareness	57.5	58.0	58.6	59.9	59.7	58.5
Empathy	36.5	37.3	36.7	38.0	37.0	36.4
Organizational awareness	20.8	20.7	21.7	22.2	22.8	22.1
Social skills	266.8	279.6	278.0	286.2	281.6	277.1
Developing others	25.5	26.6	26.0*	27.0*	27.0	26.6
Service orientation	36.2*	38.0*	36.9*	38.4*	38.4	38.1
Leadership	19.8	20.4	20.3	20.9	20.5	19.8
Influence	34.4	35.4	35.9	36.9	37.1	36.3
Communication	29.8	29.6	30.6*	31.7*	31.9	31.2
Change catalyst	34.6	36.3	36.0	36.5	37.6*	36.2*
Conflict management	25.5	25.8	25.5	26.2	25.9	25.3
Building bonds	20.8	21.2	21.4	21.8	21.8	21.8
Teamwork and collaboration	42.4	43.8	43.1	44.0	43.6	43.0

$*p < .05.$ $**p < .01.$ $***p < .001.$ K. Cavallo & D. Brienza (2001).

the education of employees. The Consumer & Personal Care Group of J&J modified their SOL to include Goleman's emotional intelligence competencies that distinguished successful leaders and that were found to be missing from the SOL model. Additionally, a training program was designed and launched globally to educate employees about EI and introduce the modified SOL model. The enhanced model was integrated into performance management activities and systems. In addition, a new multi-rater feedback survey was developed based on the newly enhanced leadership model.

From a project leadership standpoint, the research team found 5 factors that were critical to the successful completion of this research: 1) Executive sponsorship; 2) Clearly defined benefits and value to the business; 3) Well understood & communicated objectives & roles; 4) Business leadership interest & engagement, including shared provision of resources; 5) Collaborative and trusting internal HR & external Consultant partnership.

The research was a success in that it confirmed the relevance of emotional intelligence to leadership success at Johnson & Johnson and provided the organization with a clear path toward enhancing the leadership model, the SOL, that guides much of the selection, assessment, and development of organizational talent.

THE DEFENSE FINANCE AND ACCOUNTING SERVICE'S (DFAS) EI PROFESSIONAL AND LEADERSHIP CERTIFICATION PROGRAM

Federal agencies are now realizing that there is a growing need for succession planning. Several agencies have already begun career development programs to ensure that a smooth transition will occur as mission critical positions are vacated. One such agency is the Defense Finance and Accounting Service. DFAS was created to perform the accounting and finance mission for all military departments and defense agencies. It is the world's largest finance and accounting operation, disbursing more than 1 billion dollars a day to a variety of customers including vendors, military personnel and defense civilian personnel, and retired annuitants. There is great scrutiny of DFAS management personnel and a great need for accuracy in disbursements. Recently, DFAS was selected as one of a few entities to handle the centralized payroll functions of the federal government.

In November 1998, DFAS developed the Professional and Leadership Certification Program (PLCP). This program was a development initiative providing very high-potential employees with multiple new opportunities to strengthen their leadership, technical, and professional skills. The program was limited to the Financial Management series GS-500 and covered grades

13 to 15, typically team leader, supervisory, and midlevel management jobs in the federal government. Persons selected for the program received priority access to rotational assignments, educational opportunities, and management training to accelerate their professional development and augment their technical credentials and skills. Candidates who successfully completed the certification program were eligible for noncompetitive promotion to the next higher grade level. Certification, which follows successful completion of the training plan, is the public recognition of professional achievements and demonstrated leadership proficiency. Certification provides a framework for developing a professional leadership cadre prepared to address the challenges the agency faces as it enters the 21st century.

Applicants for the program are assessed through an accomplishment record that is scored using an automated application scoring program and through a structured interview. The accomplishment record scoring and the structured interview were developed using the executive core qualifications and leadership competencies identified in OPM's leadership study described earlier in this chapter (Eyde et al., 1999). The applicant scoring program measured both the five meta leadership competencies and functional knowledge. A panel of three senior DFAS managers familiar with the content and goals of the PLCP conducted the structured interview for each candidate. Multiple leadership competencies are assessed during the interview. Twenty-two of the 54 applicants were selected through a competitive process in April 1999.

As a first step in the program, each participant is required to construct an individual development plan (IDP). These plans are central to the program in that they serve as the fundamental roadmap to guide the individual's developmental activities. In addition to constructing the IDP, each participant is paired with a mentor to assist the participant in his or her development. The program also includes both structured training and developmental assignments for the participants. The program focused on a core curriculum including emotional intelligence, diversity, mentoring, business management, political environment for national security, the Washington arena, and a Capitol Hill workshop. Successful completion of the developmental activities and goals specified in the IDP results in certification and completion of the program.

The Hay Group (Schroyer, 2002) conducted the emotional intelligence component of the development program. The EI training was included in the development program to

- facilitate participants' awareness of the importance of EI competencies in leadership positions,
- increase participants' awareness of their emotional intelligence, and
- provide opportunities for participants to build their EI competence.

The first step was to get baseline data using the Emotional Competency Inventory (ECI; Boyatzis, Goleman, & Rhee, 2000). The next step, which occurred approximately a month later, was a 2-day "Building Awareness" workshop. Two months later a 2-day "Deciding to Change" workshop took place. Approximately 3 months later all trainees participated in a 1-day "Practicing and Mastering" workshop. Finally, approximately 6 months later the 360 ECI was readministered.

The EI training program was developed with several principles in mind. There should be opportunity for assessment. This included the 360 ECI assessment, some self-reflective exercises, some interactive exercises, and opportunities to receive feedback from others. One important concept in the EI program was that various combinations of competencies can lead to success. Moreover, trainees did not have to master every competency to be successful. Candidates needed to develop both a business case and a personal case for change, focusing on their current state and their desired state. They then identified a "critical few" changes that they believed would bring about the biggest impact. Candidates distributed their training during a 12- to 14-month time frame. The training created opportunities for role playing and practicing behaviors in a safe setting. Candidates were able to try out behaviors, notice impact, and get feedback from others. Finally, one-on-one consultations and other support groups such as mentors, coaches, peers, and significant others were available to provide guidance and counsel to the trainees.

Results of the EI intervention as measured by pre-and-post 360 ECI scores are presented in Table 11.5. In the pretest, 63% of the candidates met or exceeded requirements for the EI competency model. In the post-test, 90% met or exceeded the requirements for the EI competency model. In addition, significant changes were recorded for 19 of the 20 EI competency scores. Conscientious was the only EI competency that did not show a significant change. Because of the results of the pilot, DFAS concluded that EI had substantial value for both professional and personal development. Specifically, participants in the pilot had become better change agents, were more active as team players, were more effective at building teams, and were more effective managers.

OPM'S EI INDEX FOR EMOTIONALLY INTELLIGENT ORGANIZATIONS

Early concepts of emotional intelligence focused on the individual level (see Bar-On, 1997; Goleman, 1995; Salovey & Mayer, 1990). Recently attention has been directed at the EI of teams (see Druskat & Wolff, 2001). An extension of this is conceptualizing EI as an organizational-level phenomenon. We hypothesize that the overall level of EI displayed by an organiza-

TABLE 11.5
ECI Change Results

	Pre		Post				
Competency	M	SD	M	SD	d	t	p
Self-awareness							
Emotional self-awareness	2.75	0.28	2.87	0.18	0.55	−2.80	.010
Accurate self-assessment	3.72	0.33	3.94	0.11	1.01	−3.30	.004
Self-confidence	4.43	0.46	4.70	0.31	0.69	−3.22	.005
Social awareness							
Empathy	5.16	0.73	5.58	0.40	0.75	−3.81	.001
Organizational awareness	3.79	0.30	3.92	0.12	0.60	−2.27	.040
Service orientation	4.65	0.44	4.83	0.25	0.54	−2.52	.020
Self-management							
Self-control	2.77	0.36	2.90	0.15	0.50	−2.05	.050
Trustworthiness	2.81	0.20	2.92	0.01	1.06	−2.74	.010
Conscientiousness	2.92	0.18	2.96	0.12	0.28	−1.19	.240
Adaptability	3.45	0.42	3.71	0.27	0.75	−2.84	.010
Achievement orientation	5.21	0.60	5.52	0.42	0.60	−3.43	.003
Initiative	3.61	0.39	3.78	0.24	0.55	−2.24	.040
Social skills							
Developing others	3.57	0.48	3.84	0.22	0.77	−3.46	.003
Leadership	3.52	0.48	3.84	0.20	0.97	−4.45	.001
Influence	3.32	0.56	3.61	0.35	0.63	−2.28	.040
Communication	3.60	0.43	3.81	0.21	0.65	−2.46	.020
Change catalyst	4.39	0.50	4.65	0.27	0.67	−2.86	.010
Conflict management	3.59	0.42	3.82	0.21	0.70	−3.33	.004
Building bonds	3.65	0.38	3.89	0.18	0.87	−3.35	.004
Teamwork and collaboration	4.46	0.48	4.80	0.28	0.89	−4.32	.001

tion plays a large part in its success. Most organizations do not regularly assess their own level of EI partially because of the lack of a suitable measurement instrument designed to evaluate EI at the organizational level. It is entirely possible that once such a measure is developed, it will demonstrate that those organizations high in EI are more effective in terms of such variables as customer service, employee satisfaction, and employee commitment, thus resulting in significant cost savings to the organization over time from repeat customer business and reduced turnover.

OPM researchers have developed a tool to assess an organization's EI using items from an organizational culture survey called the Organizational Assessment Survey (OAS). These items map to EI constructs. In developing the OAS, researchers used a literature review that identified 18 culture dimensions that were linked to high performance. The earliest version of the instrument contained more than 200 items. Through factor analyses and pilot testing, the number of items was reduced to 100, measuring 17 high-

TABLE 11.6
The 17 Dimensions of the Organizational Assessment Survey

1. Rewards/recognition (R&R)
2. Training/career development (T&D)
3. Innovation (INN)
4. Customer orientation (CUST)
5. Leadership and quality (LEAD)
6. Fairness and treatment of others (FAIR)
7. Communications (COM)
8. Employment involvement (INV)
9. Use of resources (RES)
10. Work environment/quality of work life (QWL)
11. Work and family/personal life (FAM)
12. Teamwork (TEAM)
13. Job security/commitment to workforce (SEC)
14. Strategic planning (PLAN)
15. Performance measures (PERF)
16. Diversity (DIV)
17. Supervision (SUP)

performance dimensions. Table 11.6 contains a listing of the 17 OAS dimensions.

EI can be broken down into two types of competencies: personal competencies and social competencies. Personal competencies determine how we manage ourselves. Self-awareness, self-regulation, and self-motivation are examples of personal competencies. Social competencies determine how we handle relationships with others. Social awareness and social skills are examples of social competencies. Development of the EI index focused on the social competencies that characterize organizational interrelationships.

Items from the OAS that related to Goleman's theoretical framework were selected to be included in an EI index by a four-stage process. This process included judgments by subject matter experts and empirical analyses using common scaling techniques. In Phase 1, 28 items were selected from the OAS that covered five of Goleman's dimensions and 17 of the 25 emotional competencies. In Phase 2, psychologists and managers reviewed and revised the original item list. This review/revision resulted in a final set of 35 items that covered all five EI dimensions and 15 of the EI competencies. The third phase involved an exploratory factor analysis using data from the OAS administrations to approximately 37,384 employees. After the factor analysis, 7 items were removed. The remaining 28 items loaded onto five factors. These results were replicated on a data set from a single agency ($N = 3,148$). The final factors represented the social competencies of EI. In the final phase, a confirmatory factor analysis (CFA) was conducted to see if the five-factor model provided a better fit than the one-factor model and to see if a seven-factor model improved the fit. The results of the CFA showed that the five-factor model was clearly superior to the one-factor model. Moreover, although the five-factor model was acceptable, the data clearly supported the superiority of the seven-factor model. Sample OAS items appearing under the factor breakouts are presented in Table 11.7 and the results of the seven-factor model are shown in Table 11.8.

Figure 11.4 summarizes the Fit indexes of the three models tested. Figure 11.5 shows a graphic depiction of the results of structural equation modeling.

TABLE 11.7
Sample Items Appearing Under the Factor Breakouts

Developing others
 Supervisors/team leaders support employee efforts to learn outside the job (e.g., membership in trade or professional organizations, coursework). (OAS 13)
Change catalyst
 Supervisors/team leaders are receptive to change. (OAS 17)
Communication
 Managers keep employees informed about the organization's conditions and operations, as well as the choices it faces (e.g., budget cuts, downsizing, reorganizations). (OAS 46)
Leadership
 Managers communicate the organization's mission, vision, and values. (OAS 29)
Employee consideration
 Managers/supervisors/team leaders work well with employees of different backgrounds. (OAS 95)
Teamwork
 A spirit of cooperation and teamwork exists. (OAS 70)
Service orientation
 Products, services, and work processes are designed to meet customer needs and expectations. (OAS 25)

Note. OAS = Organizational Assessment Survey.

TABLE 11.8
Seven-Factor Model

Factor	Alpha Coefficient	No. of Items
Developing others	.66	2
Change catalyst	.81	5
Communication	.83	4
Leadership	.75	3
Employee consideration (leveraging diversity, understanding others, developing others, and conflict management)	.77	6
Teamwork (team capabilities and collaboration and cooperation)	.81	4
Service orientation	.70	4

Fit Indexes of the Three Models Tested

Fit Index	One-Factor Model	Five-Factor Model	Seven-Factor Model
χ^2	9808.7	4608.8	2375.2
df	350	345	337
GFI	.804	.893	.947
AGFI	.773	.874	.936
CFI	.751	.879	.942
RMSEA	.089	.063	.044

FIG. 11.4. EI index. *Note.* GFI = Goodness of Fit Index; AGFI = Adjusted Goodness of Fit Index; CFI = Comparative Fit Index; RMSEA = Root Mean Square error of Approximation.

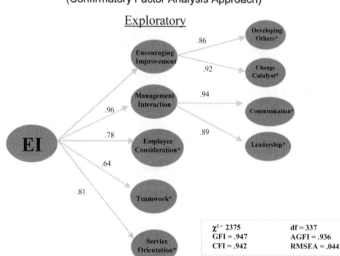

FIG. 11.5. Structural equation modeling.

RECOMMENDATIONS FOR A PRACTITIONER'S RESEARCH AGENDA

Practitioners wishing to incorporate emotional intelligence in their organizations should begin with crosswalking their competency models as exemplified in the work of the OPM psychologists and Johnson & Johnson. Wherever competency definitions in the organization overlap with EI competencies in the Goleman framework, the practitioner should ascertain the degree to which the operational definitions of the competencies are in alignment. If such alignment exits, the practitioners should begin to explore how those competencies relate to effective individual and organizational performance outcomes. Are those individuals selected for high EI viewed as leaders, not just as managers? Do their employees feel that they are cared about as people? Do their employees feel that those leaders understand their motivations? Is turnover reduced? Is productivity increased?

Many organizations are now incorporating some type of EI training in their leadership succession and development programs. For leadership succession, it may be that work samples, assessment centers and web-based assessment centers (such as that offered in Aon's Leader™) are more appropriate assessment tools for measuring EI competencies. For leadership development, OPM offers a week-long course at its Western Management Development Center on "Emotional Intelligence as a Leadership Skill." In the course, participants are introduced to how private sector companies such as Kaiser Permanente, American Express, and State Street Bank as well as the Canadian Volleyball Team are using emotional intelligence concepts to create better, more productive teams and team members. This course is linked to the emotional competencies in OPM's leadership model. Participants assess their EI competencies, analyze their relationships with others in their work environment, and create action plans to develop more cohesive relationships with team members. The prevalence of these programs, just as with the DFAS program, provides research opportunities for practitioners to institute pre and post individual and team EI measures to determine training effectiveness. Posttraining measures would ideally be given immediately following training as well as 6 months to a year later to examine impact once a participant is back on the job in a particular organizational setting.

Although the DFAS case study documented improvements in the ECI after the intervention of EI training, there were other training courses in the core curriculum (e.g., diversity, mentoring) that could have also affected the results on the post 360° assessment. Future research should attempt to identify the relative contributions of EI training and the other courses provided to the trainees in the Professional and Leadership Certification Program as well as in related management succession candidate development programs.

Now that the EI index has been developed, researchers will be able to examine the effect of an emotionally intelligent organization on a variety of organizational outcomes. For example, researchers at OPM, working with Lyle Spencer, have shown that organizational culture relates to customer satisfaction and to reduced costs in one federal agency.

The OPM psychologists also grouped the Organizational Assessment Survey Items into a number of other indexes: stress, business results, employee satisfaction, and customer service. Their follow-up research showed that the

EI Index included some items from each of the other four indexes. A future research agenda for practitioners would explore further the relations between EI at the organizational level, stress levels within the organization, business results achieved by the organization, and levels of employee and customer satisfaction in that organization. Although correlational studies are useful to postulate hypotheses among variables, causal studies should also play an important role in the practitioner's research agenda to advance our scientific knowledge of the role of EI at the individual, team, and organizational levels in creating high-performance organizations.

REFERENCES

Bar-On, R. (1997). *The Emotional Quotient Inventory (EQ-I): Technical manual.* Toronto: Multi-Health Systems.

Boyatzis, R., Goleman, D., & Hay/McBer. (1999). *Emotional Competence Inventory.*

Boyatzis, R., Goleman, D., & Rhee, K. S. (2000). Clustering competencies in emotional intelligence: Insights from the emotional competency inventory. In R. Bar-On & J. D. Parker (Eds.), *The handbook of emotional intelligence* (pp. 343–362). San Francisco: Jossey-Bass.

Buckingham, M., & Coffman, C. (1999). *First, break all the rules.* New York: Simon & Schuster.

Carless, S. (1998). Gender differences in transformational leadership: An examination of superior, leader, and subordinate perspectives. *Sex Roles, 39*(11–12), 887–902.

Cavallo, K., & Brienza, D. (2001). *Emotional competence and leadership excellence at Johnson & Johnson: The Emotional Intelligence and Leadership Study.* White Paper available online at http://www.eiconsortium.org.

Collins, J. (2001). *Good to great: Why some companies make the leap and others don't.* New York: HarperCollins.

Corts, D. B., & Gowing, M. K. (1992). *Dimensions of effective behavior: Executives, managers and supervisors.* Washington, DC: U.S. Office of Personnel Management, Personnel Resources and Development Center.

Distractions make global manager a difficult role. (2000, November 21). *Wall Street Journal,* p. A1.

Druskat, V. U., & Wolff, S. B. (2001). Group emotional intelligence and its influence on group effectiveness. In C. Cherniss & D. Goleman (Eds.), *The emotionally intelligent workplace: How to select for, measure, and improve emotional intelligence in individuals, groups and organizations* (pp. 132–155). San Francisco: Jossey-Bass.

Eagly, A. H., & Johnson, B. T. (1990). Gender and leadership style: A meta-analysis. *Psychological Bulletin, 108*(2), 233–256.

Eagly, A. H., Karau, S. J., & Makhijani, M. G. (1995). Gender and the effectiveness of leaders: A meta-analysis. *Psychological Bulletin, 117*(1), 125–145.

Eagly, A. H., Makhijani, M. G., & Klonsky, B. G. (1992). Gender and the evaluation of leaders: A meta-analysis. *Psychological Bulletin, 111*(1), 3–22.

Eyde, L. D., Gregory, D. J., Muldrow, T. W., & Mergen, P. K. (1999). *Leadership competencies for high performing organizations* (PRDC-02-99). Washington, DC: U.S. Office of Personnel Management, Personnel Resources and Development Center.

Goleman, D. (1995). *Emotional intelligence.* New York: Bantam Books.

Goleman, D. (1998, November–December). What makes a leader? *Harvard Business Review.*

Goleman, D. (1998). *Working with emotional intelligence.* New York: Bantam.

Goleman, D., Boyatzis, R., & McKee, A. (2002). *Primal leadership: Realizing the power of emotional intelligence.* Boston: Harvard Business School Press.

Gregory, D. J., & Park, R. K. (1992). *Occupational study of federal executives, managers and supervisors: An application of the Multipurpose Occupational Systems Analysis Inventory-Close-ended (MOSAIC)* (PRD-92-21). Washington, DC: U.S. Office of Personnel Management, Personnel Research and Development Center.

Hay. (1999). *What makes great leaders: Rethinking the route to effective leadership: Findings from the Fortune Magazine/Hay Group 1999 Executive Summary of Leadership Effectiveness.* 17 pages. Philadelphia: The Hay Group.

Katz, R. I. (1974, September–October). Skills of an effective administrator. *Harvard Business Review,* pp. 90–101.

Landau, J. (1995). The relationship of race and gender to managers' ratings of promotion potential. *Journal of Organizational Behavior, 16*(4), 391–400.

McCall, M. W. (1988). *The lessons of experience: How successful executives develop on the job.* New York: Lexington Books, Free Press.

McClelland, D. C. (1998). Identifying competencies with behavioral event interviews. *Psychological Science, 9*(5), 331–340.

National Academy of Public Administration. (2003). *Leadership for leaders: Senior executives and middle managers.* Vienna, VA: Management Concepts.

National Commission on Public Service. (2003). *Urgent business for America: Revitalizing the federal government for the 21st century.* Washington, DC: National Commission on the Public Service.

O'Leary, B. S., Lindholm, M. L., Whitford, R. A., & Freeman, S. E. (2002). Selecting the best and brightest: Leveraging human capital. *Human Resource Management, 41*(3), 325–340.

Osborn, R. N., & Vicars, W. M. (1976). Sex stereotypes: An artifact in Leaders Behavior and Subordinate Satisfaction Analysis? *Academy of Management Journal,* 439–449.

Ragins, B. (1991). Gender effects in subordinate evaluations of leaders: Real or artifact? *Journal of Organizational Behavior, 12*(3), 259–268.

Rodriguez, D., Patel, R., Bright, A., Gregory, D., & Gowing, M. K. (2002). Developing competency models to promote integrated human resources practices. *Human Resources Management, 41*(3), 309–324.

Rosen, R. H. (1996). *Leading people: Transforming business from the inside out.* New York: Viking Penguin.

Salovey, P., & Mayer, J. D. (1990). Emotional intelligence. *Imagination, Cognition, and Personality, 9,* 185–211.

Schmidt, F. L., & Hunter, J. E. (1998). The validity and utility of selection methods in personnel psychology: Practical and theoretical implications of 85 years of research findings. *Psychological Bulletin, 124*(2), 262–274.

Schroyer, C. J. (2002). *Developing emotional intelligence: Applications using the Emotional Competency Inventory (ECI).* Workshop presented at the annual meeting of the Society for Psychologists in Management, San Diego.

Chapter 12

Epilogue: The Agenda for Future Research

Peter Salovey
Yale University

Research on emotional intelligence has come a long way since we described a framework for considering these competencies in our first article on the topic (Salovey & Mayer, 1990). Great strides have been made even in the single decade since the utility and importance of emotional intelligence was popularized in a best-selling book (Goleman, 1995). The chapters in this volume—many written by investigators whom I proudly consider friends—suggest that the idea of an emotional intelligence has been useful to the field of organizational behavior and that outcomes relevant to business success are predicted by skills and competencies not traditionally thought to be job-related, in the technical sense, or measured by conventional tests of intelligence.

Perhaps in light of these research achievements and the popular appeal of the emotional intelligence construct, it is timely to pause and reflect on research that still needs to be carried out. In these brief comments, humbly added to the end of a wonderful and well-edited book, I would like to suggest a few (certainly not all or even most) of the questions to which we still need to turn our research attention (see also Brackett & Salovey, 2004). These comments are by no means meant as criticism of the significant scholarship represented in the chapters that preceded this one. Rather, as with any research enterprise, new findings raise new questions.

DEFINITIONAL ISSUES

At this point it is rather tedious to note that what is called emotional intelligence varies considerably from investigator to investigator (let alone from practitioner to practitioner). We have argued for many years (see Mayer,

Salovey, & Caruso, 2000, for example) that emotional intelligence should be clearly distinguished from related constructs such as more cognitively oriented intelligences (e.g., analytic, verbal), personality traits (e.g., the Big Five), social skills, and a collection of "good attributes" that only tangentially involve emotion (e.g., zeal, persistence, appreciating diversity). We also have preferred an approach that suggests that moral behavior could be an outcome of emotional intelligence but that behaving morally—being of good character—is orthogonal to emotional intelligence. That is, emotional intelligence might be necessary for moral behavior (e.g., it is difficult to imagine an individual appreciating that certain actions might hurt another person if he or she had no empathic competence), but it is not sufficient to guarantee moral behavior. A charismatic cult leader who convinces followers to part with all of their earthly possessions may be quite good at understanding and managing people's feelings but may behave in ways that many of us would consider immoral.

There is concern among many critics—a concern that I share—that a scientific construct operationalized as, roughly speaking, positive qualities of humans not measured by traditional tests of intelligence is untenable (Matthews, Zeidner, & Roberts, 2002). Now, such a definition of emotional intelligence is, indeed, a caricature, and it is unfair to paint the field with such a broad brush. Nonetheless, we stand by our suggestion that if one calls something *emotional intelligence*, it should have something to do with emotions and with intelligence. Whether these constructions are best viewed as a "true" intelligence or as sets of competencies, collections of skills, or behavior styles is an interesting but less critical issue (Mayer, Caruso, & Salovey, 1999; Mayer, Salovey, Caruso, & Sitarenios, 2001).

MEASUREMENT ISSUES

Related to concerns about conceptual definitions of emotional intelligence are concerns about operational definitions. Measures purporting to assess emotional intelligence generally have been based on either self-report, performance on ability tests, or the ratings of others in one's social or workplace environment (360 assessments). Multiple methods of measurement of the same construct should certainly be celebrated (Campbell & Fiske, 1959). This is, in fact, the only way to reduce the likelihood of spurious findings that originate from correlated measurement error in predictors and criterion variables (e.g., Green, Goldman, & Salovey, 1993).

There are problems, however. For one, the intercorrelations among measures of emotional intelligence based on these three approaches are on the low side. As but one example, Brackett and Mayer (2003) reported correlations in the .20 to .30 range between total scores on the Bar-On Emotional Quotient Inventory and the Mayer–Salovey–Caruso Emotional Intelligence Test (MSCEIT), the former a self-report inventory and the latter a performance-based ability test (Mayer, Salovey, Caruso, & Sitarenios, 2003). That individuals might not have access to accurate estimates of their skills in this area should not surprise us—thinking that one has emotional skills but, in fact, not having them at all could be a definition of low emotional intelligence itself! The difficulty, of course, is that we behave, as a field of investigators, as if measures of emotional intelligence are interchangeable, all assessing the same construct, and all with equal validity. They could be, but it doesn't look that way to me.

And this brings up a related problem: Empirically, is there anything new here? We have worked hard to demonstrate the discriminant validity of the MSCEIT, showing that its correlations are low with respect to traditional measures of intelligence (IQ) and personality (Big Five) and that it is clearly not a test of mood, self-esteem, social desirability, or other well-understood variables (e.g., Lopes, Salovey, & Straus, 2003). But other measures of emotional intelligence have not fared well along these lines. Check out, for example, the analyses reported by Brackett and Mayer (2003) focused on self-report measures of emotional intelligence. The multiple correlations between them and standard measures of personality and subjective well-being are not just high; they are alarmingly so. It will be difficult to defend against the charge that emotional intelligence is "nothing but old wine in new bottles" if our measures are substantially overlapped with pre-existing constructs.

RESEARCH DESIGN ISSUES

This problem relates to a significant challenge in research on emotional intelligence. If we are not sure that our measures of emotional intelligence are uncontaminated by other constructs—that is, if we use measures that are substantially correlated with other psychological constructs—then to demonstrate that we have anything new here, one must include measures of those constructs in one's studies and show that emotional intelligence accounts for significant variability in criterion measures over and above them. At present, it would seem advantageous to include in any study of emotional intelligence in the workplace measures of the Big Five personality dimensions, standard intelligence, social desirability, and, perhaps, alexithymia. Regression models should then include these variables along with emotional intelligence. Sometimes one doesn't have sufficient subject time or statistical power to design the study in this way—I know, I've been there too—but we should strive to organize our studies in this way and brace ourselves for criticism when we don't. I supposed it also goes without saying at this point that studies whose predictors and criterion measures are from the same source (e.g., self-report/self-report) are likely to show relations due to shared measurement error rather than, necessarily, true associations. This problem will be especially acute in cross-sectional rather than prospective studies.

THINGS WE JUST DON'T KNOW

So far, I have focused on definitional and methodological issues, but there are many substantive issues in the area of emotional intelligence deserving future research attention. I will not enumerate them here, except to focus on the one that generates the most discussion when I present my own work on emotional intelligence: culture. As workplaces become, thankfully, more diverse on many dimensions, and as we enter the era of globalization, it is certainly the case that the manner in which emotions are handled in organizations is a keystone to understanding these larger changes. Having spent a bit of time observing organizations in Japan, though not systematically, I have found that common North American workplace behaviors such as challenging the ideas of one's superiors or gloating when a rival is defeated are not universally reinforced.

To some extent, all definitions of emotional intelligence are crafted in terms of behaving, emotionally, in adaptive or functional terms, and there are cultural differences in how various behaviors would be viewed along these lines. Making small talk is valued in the Americas, being able to speak intelligently about personal topics such as politics or religion more so in Eastern Europe. Don't do business in Russia if you can't make a good toast! The recent hit movie *Lost in Translation* represents the bewilderment of Americans coping with Asian business customs for the first time. It is my sense that none of our measures of emotional intelligence are either sensitive to cultural differences—indeed, on the MSCEIT, we eliminated items that showed cultural differences in preliminary studies—nor do they measure an individual's sensitivity to cultural differences in emotional expression as a dimension of EI itself. This would be a fruitful area of future investigation.

While on this topic, let me mention a related one. We have generally found that women perform slightly better than men on the MSCEIT. It is not a large gender difference, but it is rather consistently observed. Why? Certainly, women are socially reinforced for attending to emotions of all kinds and men for suppressing feelings other than anger. But there must be more to these differences than that glib observation. Perhaps evolutionary psychologists have some thoughts on these matters. Conversely a feminist critique might also stimulate important future work.

Finally—and perhaps most important given the work that so many of the readers of this volume do every day of their lives—we need better studies of the efficacy of interventions designed to enhance the competencies involved in emotional intelligence. And I don't mean stories about the effectiveness of this or that program, or process evaluation, or documentation that such programs are enjoyed by those who participate in them. I mean the kind of controlled experiment with random assignment to a well-specified emotional intelligence intervention or to a comparison group that presents a credible alternative, with follow-up over a period of at least months, and criterion measures that include both soft and hard outcome variables. Don't get me wrong: I haven't done an experiment like this either. But this is the kind of evaluation research we will need to convince the skeptics, especially if it includes hard-headed, cost-effectiveness modeling.

COPING WITH POP PSYCHOLOGY

Let me conclude with a final, more sociological issue. This one has to do with the fact that the idea of an emotional intelligence has become part of the popular culture. Now, I enjoy the depictions of emotional intelligence in Dilbert, Zippy the Pinhead, and *New Yorker* cartoons as much as the next person. I've even tried to write about emotional intelligence for a general audience (Caruso & Salovey, 2004). That's not the problem. The difficulty is when we forget that first and foremost we are scientists and professional practitioners and that we have a responsibility to temper our claims and promises with a realism that comes from the kind of careful reading of the literature that is, quite simply, not going to be engaged in by the general public.

I suspect that in my own enthusiasm for emotional intelligence, I am occasionally guilty of overstatement or other kinds of hyperbole. But my heart sinks when I read in the popular press quotes from investigators who should know better claiming that emotional intelligence is the most important predictor of success; that it accounts for 80% or 85% or 90% of a person's performance in business, or marriage, or life in general; that it is the single determinant of all happiness and bliss; that it is entirely learned; that it is an advantage in any domain in life; or that teaching it in our schools will eliminate unwanted pregnancy, drug use, or any of a number of social ills. It is not so simple. Emotional intelligence is important, sure, but it is not a silver bullet. And when investigators make reckless claims that its "discovery" is akin to that of a cure for cancer, we invite the inevitable backlash. I don't know about you, but I want to spend the next 10 years writing up my studies of emotional intelligence rather than responding to critics.

CONCLUSION

But let's not end on such a sour note. Certainly, a harder-headed approach to emotional intelligence will serve scientists and practitioners alike quite well. We need to be able to figure out those ingredients of emotional intelligence that are truly novel, that are associated with important outcomes in the workplace, and that are teachable. And we should be critical of overly broad conceptualizations and overly optimistic claims (Daus & Ashkanasy, 2003). But we should also feel some collective pride: The contributors to this book have all, in various ways, advanced an important understanding—that when it comes to job-related success, technical skills and analytic intelligence are not enough, and we can begin to specify what else is needed. Although such a view may not be revolutionary, it does motivate important directions for future research and professional practice.

REFERENCES

Brackett, M. A., & Mayer, J. D. (2003). Convergent, discriminant, and incremental validity of competing measures of emotional intelligence. *Personality and Social Psychology Bulletin, 29,* 1147–1158.

Brackett, M. A., & Salovey, P. (2004). Measuring emotional intelligence with the Mayer–Salovey–Caruso emotional intelligence test (MSCEIT). In G. Geher (Ed.), *Measurement of emotional intelligence* (pp. 179–194). Hauppauge, NY: Nova Science.

Campbell, D. T., & Fiske, D. W. (1959). Convergent and discriminant validity by the multitrait-multimethod matrix. *Psychological Bulletin, 56,* 81–105.

Caruso, D., & Salovey, P. (2004). *The emotionally intelligent manager.* San Francisco: Jossey-Bass.

Daus, C. S., & Ashkanasy, N. M. (2003). Will the real emotional intelligence please stand up? On deconstructing the emotional intelligence "debate." *Industrial-Organizational Psychologist, 41,* 69–72.

Goleman, D. (1995). *Emotional intelligence.* New York: Bantam.

Green, D. P., Goldman, S. L., & Salovey, P. (1993). Measurement error masks bipolarity in affect ratings. *Journal of Personality and Social Psychology, 64,* 1029–1041.

Lopes, P. N., Salovey, P., & Straus, R. (2003). Emotional intelligence, personality, and the perceived quality of social relationships. *Personality and Individual Differences, 35,* 641–658.

Mathews, G., Zeidner, M., & Roberts, R. D. (2002). *Emotional intelligence: Science and myth.* Cambridge: MIT Press.

Mayer, J. D., Caruso, D. R., & Salovey, P. (1999). Emotional intelligence meets traditional standards for an intelligence. *Intelligence, 27,* 267–298.

Mayer, J. D., Salovey, P., & Caruso, D. (2000). Models of emotional intelligence. In R. J. Sternberg (Ed.), *The handbook of intelligence* (pp. 396–420). New York: Cambridge University Press.

Mayer, J. D., Salovey, P., Caruso, D. L., & Sitarenios, G. (2001). Emotional intelligence as a standard intelligence. *Emotion, 1,* 232–242.

Mayer, J. D., Salovey, P., Caruso, D. R., & Sitarenios, G. (2003). Measuring emotional intelligence with the MSCEIT V2.0. *Emotion, 3,* 97–105.

Salovey, P., & Mayer, J. D. (1990). Emotional intelligence. *Imagination, Cognition, and Personality, 9,* 185–211.

Author Index

Note: Page numbers in *italics* refer to full bibliographic citations.

Subject Index

Note: Page numbers followed by an italic *f* , *n, t* refer, respectively, to a figure, note, or table on those pages. More than one italic letter, for example *ff* or *tt,* signifies multiple figures or tables.